The New Certificate Geography Series

ADVANCED LEVEL

THE SOVIET UNION

The New Certificate Geography Series

ADVANCED LEVEL

THE SOVIET UNION

G. MELVYN HOWE, M.Sc., Ph.D.

*Professor of Geography, University of
Strathclyde, Glasgow. Formerly Reader in Geography,
University College of Wales, Aberystwyth*

MACDONALD & EVANS LTD
8 John Street London W.C.1
1968

The New Certificate Geography Series

ADVANCED LEVEL

Australasia
Africa
Latin America
North America
The United States
of America
Europe
Monsoon Asia

Other volumes in the series
are in the course of preparation

DK
17
.H6
1968

*Printed in Great Britain by Richard Clay (The Chaucer Press), Ltd.,
Bungay, Suffolk*

AUTHOR'S PREFACE

THIS study of the Soviet Union is designed to serve the needs of students preparing for the Advanced and Scholarship levels of the various General Certificate of Education examinations in geography. It may provide preliminary reading for University students and appeal to the general reader, but the requirements of Sixth Form students have been kept more especially in mind. There is no shortage of advanced books at university level—at least five such texts in English have appeared within the last five years—but there is no one text aimed specifically at bridging the gap between the Ordinary and Advanced levels. This may explain why so few students offer the Soviet Union as their region for special study in their Advanced level examination in Geography and why some examining boards exclude the Soviet Union from their syllabuses at this level. For this reason the present study is deliberately intermediate in approach, content and style. It introduces new ideas and concepts, facts and figures are as up to date as it is possible to make them, maps and diagrams have been kept simple and clear, and a lucid exposition aimed at. It is hoped that the result will satisfy both students and teachers who are searching for a readily understandable but sufficiently comprehensive text of the geography of the Soviet Union.

The book is planned on orthodox lines. First there is a survey of the general geographical framework of the country. The physical background and historical growth (based on period-pictures), resources, economy, transport, population and settlement are treated in a spatial context. Attention is drawn to some aspects of political geography and to the present political pattern. Certain new space relationships are also presented. These topics cut across regional boundaries and treat the Soviet Union as a whole.

The second, and larger part provides a regional geography of the country. Since the pattern of the human geography of the Soviet Union is, in overwhelming degree, a reflection of the nature of prevailing economic activities, economic planning has been adopted as the theme for the examination of regional differences. Eighteen principal regions are recognised and for each a uniform approach has been applied. The regional description and discussion is preceded in every case by a concise statement which summarises the main aspects of the economy of the region concerned, together with data, presented in table form, relating to the component administrative areas, populations (at the time of the last official census in 1959, or, from official estimates, for 1965) and population densities. Towns with over 150,000 inhabitants in 1964 are also listed. Generous use is made of maps to portray the economy of the regions in terms of spatial distributions of agriculture, mineral and power resources, communications and the industrial structure of towns. Most of the maps in the regional section of the book have been adapted from coloured maps which appear in ЭКОНОМИЧЕСКАЯ ГЕОГРАФИЯ (*Economic Geography of the U.S.S.R.*) edited by N. P. Nikitin, E. D. Prozorov and B. A. Tutykhin, and published in Moscow in 1966. In some instances the maps and data have been brought up to date by reference to information contained in *Soviet Geography: Review and Translation*. The latter, published by the American Geographical Society, is an invaluable journal which contains translations of articles from professional geographical journals in the Soviet Union, together with notes on production data and new developments. The simplified relief map of each region is based on the new edition of the *Times Atlas*, and insets on the same scale of parts of Britain are included for comparative purposes. Comparison is further facilitated by the frequent use of hythergraphs of selected Soviet localities alongside the hythergraph of Kew (London).

A third, brief section attempts an assessment of Soviet economic progress. Trends, outlined by A. Nove, are noted, and Soviet output of a range of commodities is compared with output in the United States, the United Kingdom and the European Economic Community (Belgium–France–Germany–Italy–Luxembourg–Netherlands) in Appendix III. The position of the Soviet Union in world production of selected commodities is also given in Appendix III. Efforts have been made to ensure the inclusion of up-to-date production data. Some may question the validity of Soviet statistical material, but it is assumed that what has been used in the book is reasonably accurate.

The English version of certain commonly used names (such as Moscow instead of Moskva) has been adopted, otherwise place names have been transliterated according to *Transliteration of Cyrillic and Greek Characters* (British Standard 2979: 1958, British Standards Institution). The second edition of M. S. Bodnarskii's *Slovar geograficheskikh nazvanii* (Dictionary of Geographical Names), Moscow, 1958 has been used as source for most of the place-names. Scales are given in imperial and metric units, temperatures in degrees Fahrenheit and degrees Centigrade, and precipitation in inches and millimetres, although conversion tables are provided in Appendix IV.

Even if he were permitted to travel widely within the country, no foreigner is capable of describing adequately the Soviet–Russian scene. For this reason frequent use is made of literary quotations from Russian sources. Sixth Form students should cultivate the habit of wider reading, but the language barrier presents serious difficulties in the case of Russian source material. For the few with some reading ability in the language, the quotations draw attention to Russian writings which can be followed up. For the others bibliographical material has been restricted to books, articles and atlases in the English language. Further references will be found in the works cited.

Thanks are due to several people. Mrs Helen Wareing introduced me to several useful books published in the Soviet Union and helped greatly by translating certain articles and map keys and searching for useful quotations. Mr A. Kiriloff and Mr F. Beardow helped with translations of selected Russian papers and suggested quotations. Miss Helen Wallis introduced me to *King George III's Topographical Collection* in the Map Room of the British Museum, Mr R. P. Duerden kindly translated the Latin text which accompanied the originals of Figs. 39 and 40, and Dr B. Davies prepared the soil profile diagrams (Figs. 29, 31, 32, 34). Photographs were provided by ФОТОХРОНИКА ТАСС (Moscow), Chief Editor of the Editorial Board of Geographical Literature of MYSL (Moscow), Soviet Weekly, Novosti Press, Camera Press, United Press International, British Museum, R. T. Smith and Thompson Organisation Ltd. Picture Service Topix. Mr R. James and Mr E. Jones generously took time to read most of the draft manuscript and offered useful comments and criticisms, though of course they are in no way responsible for opinions expressed or for any errors or omissions. Mr J. Horzelski checked my spellings of place-names and kindly provided accurate transliterations of place-names for inclusion in the Index. Mr M. Hughes, Miss M. Dawe and Mr M. G. Jones drew the final maps and diagrams from my rough compilations. I am grateful to the Associated Examining Board (A.E.B.), the Welsh Joint Education Committee (W.J.E.C.), the University of London (London), the Oxford Delegacy for Local Examinations (Oxford), the Scottish Certificate of Education Examination Board (S.L.C., S.C.E.) and the Northern Universities Joint Matriculation Board (J.M.B.) for permission to use questions taken from their past examination papers. Mr J. D. Thompson of Wm. Collins Sons (Glasgow) kindly provided the graticule (Azimuthal Equidistant Projection, centred on Moscow) used as the basis for Fig. 9. Mrs E. Horzelska has given invaluable assistance in matters of editing and kindly helped to see the book through the press. Finally I extend thanks to my wife and daughters for their patience and forbearance during the time the book was in preparation.

G. Melvyn Howe

November, 1967
  50th Anniversary of the Bolshevik Revolution★

★ Known historically as "The October Revolution" since the tsarist calendar was thirteen days behind the Gregorian calendar.

CONTENTS

Part Two

REGIONAL GEOGRAPHY

PART THREE

THE SOVIET ECONOMY

LIST OF ILLUSTRATIONS

LIST OF TABLES

xix

Part One

THE GEOGRAPHICAL FRAMEWORK

Chapter I

THE NATURE OF THE LAND

SIZE, LOCATION AND SPACE RELATIONSHIPS

THE Soviet Union is an immense country, covering approximately 8,650,000 sq. miles. It contains almost one-sixth of the land area of the world (excluding Antarctica), extending from eastern Europe across northern Asia. Africa (11·7 million sq. miles) and Anglo-America (9·5 million sq. miles) exceed it in area, but Latin America (8·0 million sq. miles) is smaller. It is over 90 times the size of the United Kingdom, nearly three times that of the United States (Fig. 2), three times the size of Antarctica, and two and a half times that of Australia. In form this vast area may be likened to a wide amphitheatre facing, and sloping, towards the Arctic Ocean. Broad plains and lowlands occupy the western and central part of the country, and an almost unbroken chain of high mountains and rugged plateaux stretches along its southern, southeastern and eastern frontiers.

For those familiar only with distances in Britain or Western Europe, it is difficult to comprehend the size of this sub-continental Euro-Asiatic land-mass. For instance, the 5000 or more miles between the Soviet Union's western frontier and the Pacific coast are roughly equivalent to the distance between London and Peking, or between Edinburgh and Cape Town. Rail journeys in the U.S.S.R. are often measured in days rather than in hours, as may be illustrated by the average train times for 1964 shown below:

Moscow to Murmansk (900 miles)	30 hours
Moscow to Leningrad (404 miles)	6–8 hours (depending on the train)
Moscow to Kiev (783 miles)	14 hours
Moscow to Baku (1580 miles)	60–65 hours
Moscow to Sverdlovsk (1129 miles)	50 hours
Moscow to Tashkent (2092 miles)	4 days
Moscow to Novosibirsk (2076 miles)	3 days
Moscow to Irkutsk (3226 miles)	6 days
Moscow to Vladivostok (5800 miles)	8 days

On the other hand, the journey by air from, say, Moscow to Khabarovsk takes only 10 hours, from Moscow to Tashkent 5 hours and from Moscow to Irkutsk 6 hours. Air travel seems, therefore, to provide the answer for fast passenger traffic within the Soviet Union.

The most northerly point of the U.S.R.R. is Rudolf Island in Franz Josef Land (82° N), though on the Soviet mainland the most northerly point is Cape Chelyuskin on the Taymyr Peninsula (78° N) (Fig. 4). More than half of the Soviet Arctic coast lies north of 70° N.

FIG. I.—The Soviet Union in its world setting.

The most southerly point of the U.S.S.R. is near Kushka (35° N) in Central Asia, where the boundaries of the Turkmen S.S.R. project to-wards Afghanistan. The fortieth parallel marks the approximate southern boundary of the western half of the Union, and the fiftieth parallel the eastern half. At most, the mainland territory of the U.S.S.R. extends through 43° of latitude (just over 3000 miles); usually it ranges between 25° and 30° of latitude (1600–2100 miles). Moscow, the capital, is at a latitude similar to those of Glasgow (Scotland) and Edmonton (Canada). Leningrad, the second largest city, lies close to the same latitudes as Lerwick

(Shetland Islands) and Anchorage (Alaska). Chita in eastern Siberia is at about the same latitude as London (*see* Fig. 2).

The longitudinal extent of the country is more than twice its maximum north–south extent. From its most westerly point near Kaliningrad on the Gulf of Danzig (20° E) to Cape Dezhneva (170° W) on the Bering Strait is about 7000 miles. A comparable distance in the western hemisphere would be from the coast of Norway westwards to western Alaska. The

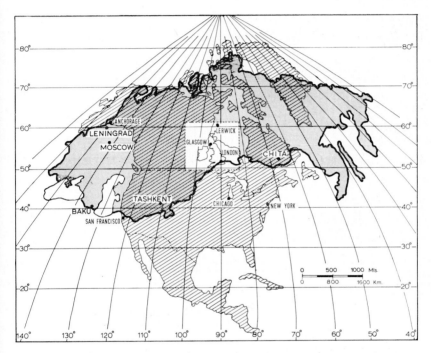

FIG. 2.—A comparison of areas and latitudes: Soviet Union—North America—British Isles.

Arctic and Pacific islands possessions apart, the Soviet Union forms a single continuous territorial block, shaped like a polygon, and is the world's greatest uninterrupted expanse of territory under one political system.

Such statements of physical extent are impressive, but what really matters is the proportion of land that is suitable for human settlement and its true economic potential. In this respect the position is not so impressive. The Soviet Union controls abundant space, but the nature of this space and its potential for human settlement vary considerably from place to place. Vast areas are unsuitable for human settlement and the bulk of the country's population inhabit only a fraction of the territory. One million square miles are desert and semi-arid steppe, 3½ million sq. miles are underlain by permanently frozen ground (Fig. 13), with all the Arctic and many Pacific shores and many of the large rivers frozen over for much of the year.

The immensity of the physical background is the primary and the most significant geographical fact about the Soviet Union. It was this vastness and the relative inaccessibility of the oceans, with corollaries of defence in

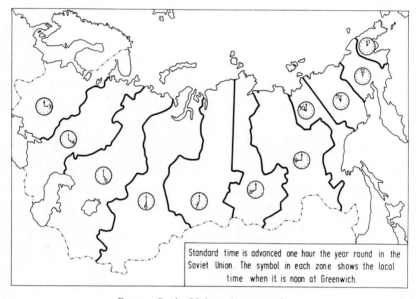

Standard time is advanced one hour the year round in the Soviet Union. The symbol in each zone shows the local time when it is noon at Greenwich.

FIG. 3.—Soviet Union: time zone chart.
[Note: British Standard Time, introduced in February 1968, is one hour in advance of G.M.T.]

depth and relative invulnerability, that provided the corner stone for the concept of the Heartland of the Old World Island propounded by the British political geographer, Sir Halford Mackinder, over half a century ago. Early in the twentieth century land power was considered to be decisive in world affairs. Mackinder's hypothesis was that the Old World Island, comprising Europe–Africa–Asia, had a sub-continental Heartland, or Pivot Area, in the region lying generally east of the Volga, in what is now Soviet territory (Fig. 5). The Heartland was considered to be strategically placed to command interior lines of communication within Eurasia, with the potential to become a power base. In Mackinder's view, the state which controlled the Heartland was in an almost unchallengeable position to attempt military and, subsequently, political mastery of the World Island, since he "who rules the World Island commands the World."

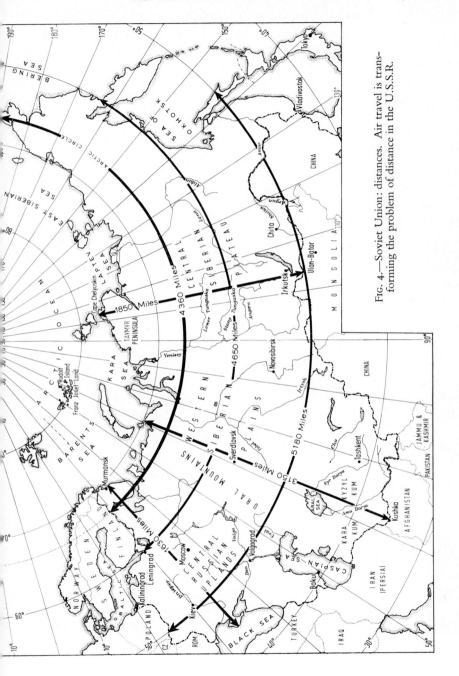

Fig. 4.—Soviet Union: distances. Air travel is transforming the problem of distance in the U.S.S.R.

The physical environment decrees that much of Mackinder's Heartland should be more aptly described as "dead heartland," particularly the deserts of the Soviet Central Asia and the cold lands of northern Siberia. Even now, in the first decade of the second half of the twentieth century, when lines of communication are improving and technical advances are leading

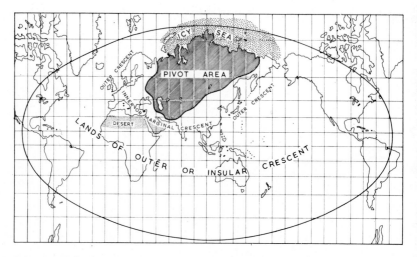

FIG. 5.—Mackinder's Heartland (1904), shown on the Mercator projection. (After J. R. Fernstrom in *Principles of Political Geography* by Weigert, Hans V. *et al.* New York, 1957.)

to the opening up of vast areas, much of this region remains undeveloped or is "developing." Yet, an exceptionally rich zone within the Heartland area, between the Volga and Lake Baykal, is developing fast, and this may well become a Heartland in its own right. The unusually rapid growth of population and manufacturing industry that has taken place in this zone suggests that in time it may become the most vital part of the Soviet Union (*see* p. 120).

RUSSIAN ISOLATION

High mountains and deserts in both the east and the south cut Russia off from the ancient civilisations of China and India. The religious barriers of Polish Catholicism prevented intercourse with Western Europe, and the partly frozen Arctic shores in the north of the country proved to be "the sealed lips of Russia." In consequence, Russia was isolated from the outside world throughout much of her history. New railways, roads and airfields tend to assist in breaking down this isolation. Regular air services link the main Soviet centres with Peking, Wuhan, Calcutta, Delhi and Bombay in the east and south; with Bucharest, Sofia, Belgrade, Budapest, Vienna, Prague, Berlin, Copenhagen, Paris, Brussels, Zürich and London in the west. The shores of the Arctic and Pacific have been made accessible to convoys and ships during a few short summer months by the use of ice-breakers following the Northern Sea Route from Vladivostok to Ark-

FIG. 6.—The relationship of the Heartland and North America, shown on the azimuthal polar projection. (After J. F. Fernstrom in *Principles of Political Geography* by Weigert, Hans V. *et al.* New York, 1957.)

hangelsk. In Eastern Europe the religious barrier has long since disappeared, and after the wholesale shift of German and Polish populations after World War II, the Soviet boundary now follows approximately the Curzon Line. Nevertheless, isolation is perpetuated by the Communist political system, which maintains an "iron curtain" as effective as any natural or religious barrier.

In terms of military strategy, however, this isolation may not be so complete. The sheer bulk of the country and adverse physical factors provided a stumbling block to Napoleon in the nineteenth century and to Hitler in the twentieth century, but later, during the era of manned bombers armed with nuclear bombs, it was the fact of the mutual proximity of the Soviet

Union and North America that loomed large (*see* Figs. 6 and 7). It was then that both the American and Soviet governments erected elaborate radar defences against bomber threats across the North Polar regions. In North America the Americans erected the Distant Early Warning (DEW) line roughly along the 70° N parallel. Long-range (intercontinental

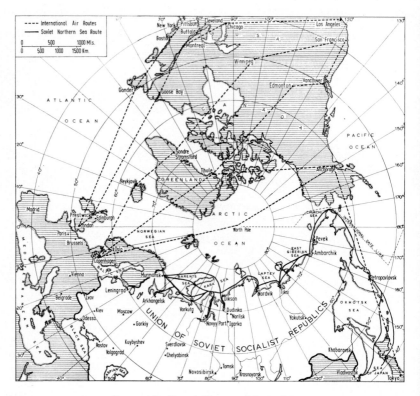

FIG. 7.—Arctic neighbours of the U.S.S.R.

ballistic) missiles and spacecraft have since superseded the manned bomber, and Ballistic Missile Early Warning Systems have been established (Fig. 8). In this respect, both polar and continental distances are of less significance. Thus, while the political isolation of the Soviet Union continues, regions in the very heart of the country are as exposed and vulnerable as those lying near the boundaries to foe armed with nuclear weapons.

The Arctic is no longer the major obstacle it was in the past. Since 1957 Scandinavian Airlines have maintained a regular and truly transpolar route from Copenhagen in Denmark to Tokyo in Japan via Anchorage (Alaska),

with alternative landings at Nord and Thule (Greenland). Other commercial airlines fly regular routes over or near the North Pole (Fig. 7).
Great Circle flying along a route passing near the north of the River
Yenisey and then across eastern Siberia is also feasible and practicable, but
is not permitted by the Soviet Government.* In 1958 the United States

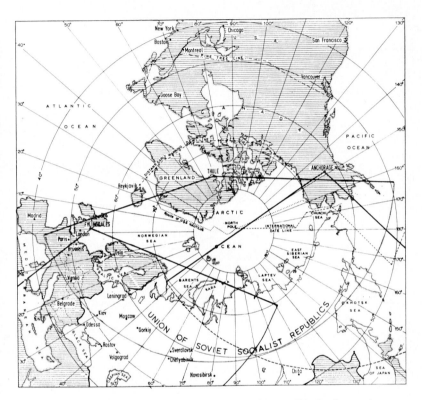

FIG. 8.—American Early Warning Systems against possible Soviet attacks.

nuclear-powered submarine *Nautilus* made a successful traverse of the
North Polar Sea from the Bering Strait to Greenland Sea (Fig. 8). On
March 17, 1959, the nuclear submarine *Skate* surfaced through the ice
precisely at the North Pole. The future may see air routes criss-crossing this
polar mediterranean, and nuclear-powered merchant submarines using it
for journeys between Europe and the Far East. That time is not yet.
The Soviet Union, with 232 million people in 1966, is surrounded by

* In January 1967 the Soviet Union and the Scandinavian countries reached agreement on reciprocal flying rights which include flights over Siberia.

33,000 miles of land and sea boundaries, most of which are on the coast-lines on the Baltic Sea, the Arctic and Pacific Oceans, the Caspian Sea and the Black Sea. About 2000 of the Soviet Union's 10,000 miles of land boundaries delimit its territory in Europe against six neighbours: Rumania,

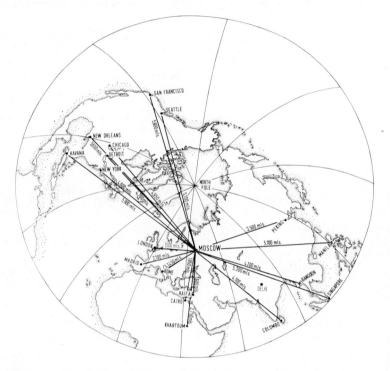

FIG. 9.—The position of Moscow in the northern hemisphere: distances in statute miles (azimuthal equidistant projection).

Hungary, Czechoslovakia, Poland, Finland and Norway. In the Middle East the Soviet Union borders on Turkey, Iran (Persia), and Afghanistan. In Asia the contact is with Pakistan and China, the Mongolian People's Republic and Korea (*see* Fig. 4).

STUDY QUESTIONS

1. Do you consider that the U.S.S.R. possesses national unity? What is the nature of the disruptive forces she has to contend with?

2. How does geography influence communications within the Soviet Union and between the Soviet Union and the rest of the world?

3. "The isolation imposed by Soviet policy, the so-called 'Iron Curtain' has only added to the country's geographical isolation." Discuss this statement.

4. Write a short essay on the strategic significance to the U.S.S.R. of (*a*) the Bosphorus–Dardanelles, (*b*) Murmansk, (*c*) Leningrad, (*d*) Vladivostok, (*e*) Bering Strait.

5. Examine the "Old World Heartland" concept of Mackinder in the light of twentieth-century technology.

6. Assess the strategic importance of the Arctic Ocean to the U.S.S.R.

7. What are the geographical essentials of a Great Power?

8. What is the geographical significance of (*a*) nuclear marine propulsion (*b*) air transport, in furthering the importance of North Polar regions?

Chapter II

STRUCTURE, DRAINAGE, GLACIATION, PERMANENTLY FROZEN GROUND, RELIEF

STRUCTURE

A PATTERN of lowland and plain, surrounded by high mountains, characterises the Russian scene, but this belies a complex geological history. The territory at present occupied by the Soviet Union comprises two very ancient continental platforms: the Russian (East European) Platform in the west, and the Siberian Platform in the east. Both platforms are composed of crystalline rocks of Pre-Cambrian age (Fig. 10) and lie at varying depths below geologically more recent deposits. These basal complexes have proved, in general, to have been resistant to the processes of folding and mountain building, and overlying deposits are in consequence only slightly disturbed. They are disposed more or less horizontally. Occasionally the ancient foundations outcrop at the surface, the larger exposures giving rise to "crystalline shields," e.g. the Podolsk–Azov Shield in the Ukraine.

Two further regions of the U.S.S.R. territory have a base of ancient folded strata: (a) the Ural–Altay–Sayan region, underlain by strata of Palaeozoic age, and (b) a vast area embracing the greater part of northeastern Siberia, eastern Trans-Baykal and the Soviet Far East (Primorye-Chukotsk), underlain by Mesozoic strata.

Together the Pre-Cambrian, Palaeozoic and Mesozoic tectonic zones form the base of the greater part of the territory of the Soviet Union. In the south they are bordered by part of the great belt of Tertiary (Alpine) folding which extends from Gibraltar and the Alps to the islands of Indonesia. Within Soviet territory this belt includes a small section of the eastern Carpathians, the Crimea, the Caucasus, the mountains of the Kopet-Dag and the Pamirs. Here volcanic activity belongs to the recent geological past, and extinct volcanoes and earth movements are common. A second mountain belt of more recent Tertiary formation borders earlier tectonic zones along the Pacific seaboard. Within the Soviet territory the belt includes the Koryak ranges, Kamchatka, Sakhalin and the Kuriles. It is composed of fold mountains in which frequent earth tremors and active volcanoes, e.g. in Kamchatka and the Kuriles, indicate that mountain-building processes are still in being.

14

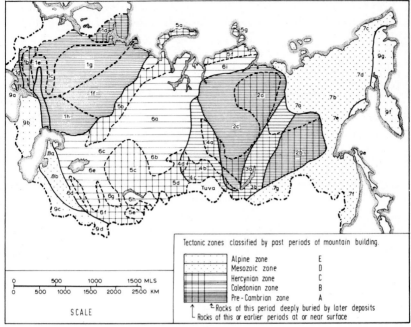

FIG. 10.—Soviet Union: tectonic zones (adapted from Plate 90 V in Vol. 1. of the *Great Soviet World Atlas*).

A. PRE-CAMBRIAN ZONE

1. *East European Platform*
   (a) Baltic Shield
   (b) Ukraine Shield
   (c) Voronezh Block
   (d) Black Sea Basin
   (e) North Ukrainian Basin
   (f) East Russian Basin
   (g) Moscow Basin
   (h) Caspian Basin

2. *Siberian Platform*
   (a) Anabar Shield
   (b) Aldan Shield
   (c) Tungus Basin

B. CALEDONIAN ZONE

3. *Eastern Section*
   (a) Pre-Baykalya
   (b) Western Trans-Baykalya

4. *Western Section*
   (a) Yenisey Range
   (b) Sayany Mountains
   (c) Minusinsk Basin
   (d) Kuznetsk Basin

C. HERCYNIAN ZONE

5. *Uplands*
   (a) Novaya Zemlya
   (b) Ural Mountains
   (c) Central Kazakhstan
   (d) Altai
   (e) Tyan-Shan
   (f) Taymyr Peninsula
   (g) Severnaya Zemlya

6. *Lowlands*
   (a) Ural–Siberian Depression
   (b) Irtysh Basin
   (c) Turgai Depression
   (d) Amu–Darya Basin
   (e) Syr–Darya Basin
   (f) Fergana Basin
   (g) Chu Basin
   (h) Balkhash Basin
   (i) Khatanga Depression

D. MESOZOIC ZONE

7. *Siberia and Maritime Country*
   (a) Verkhoyansk Range
   (b) Cherskiy Range
   (c) Anadyr Range
   (d) Kolyma Range
   (e) Dzhugdzhur Range
   (f) Sikhote-Alin
   (g) Eastern Trans-Baykalya

8. *Central Asia*
   (a) Mangyshlak Mountains
   (b) Bolshoi Balkhan Range

E. ALPINE ZONE

9. *Mountain Border*
   (a) Crimea
   (b) Caucasus
   (c) Kopet-Dag
   (d) Pamirs
   (e) Sakhalin
   (f) Kamchatka
   (g) Koryak Range

Ancient Archaean platforms lie beneath lowlands in European Russia, and beneath low but highly dissected plateau blocks in central Siberia. Where exposed at the surface, these and other areas of ancient folding (e.g. the Ural) represent vestigial remains of former greatness. They are invariably low in altitude, their roots are exposed and their relief is inverted. In contrast, in areas of Tertiary folding, denudation has had only a relatively short time in which to work, tectonic structures are conformable and landscapes youthful. Slopes are steep and mountain peaks high and jagged. Upfolds continue to form the mountain summits, and downfolds the intervening valleys.

Past periods of mountain building were of undoubted importance in the geological history of the Soviet territory. Possibly of greater significance, however, were the frequent alternations of marine transgression and regression, which occurred particularly west of the Ural in the European part of the U.S.S.R. Such advances of the sea—accompanied by the laying down of sedimentary strata—and withdrawals led to a great extent to the variety in age and character of the surface deposits over much of the U.S.S.R.

DRAINAGE

Surface waters from Soviet territory find their way into three oceans, the Arctic, Atlantic and Pacific, and into a vast area of inland drainage centring on the Aral–Caspian Basin and Lake Balkhash (Fig. 11).

TABLE I

Drainage of the U.S.S.R.

Drainage to:	Drainage area of U.S.S.R. million sq. miles	per cent
Arctic Ocean	4·4	51·0
Atlantic Ocean	1·0	11·5
Pacific Ocean	0·9	10·5
Aral–Caspian–Balkhash region of inland drainage	2·3	27·0

More than half of the country (Table I), embracing the whole of the north Russian Lowland and Siberia, from the western part of the Kola Peninsula and Karelia to the Kolyma River, drains into the Arctic Ocean. The Northern Dvina (802 miles with the Sukhona) and Pechora (1108 miles) are the chief rivers of the north Russian Lowland flowing to the Arctic. They rise in glacial morainic hills, flow gently across almost level plains through extensive forested areas, and frequently follow courses that have been altered by glacial action. The Valday glaciation (p. 20) was, geo-logically speaking, so recent here that the rivers have had insufficient time in which to develop the asymmetrical transverse profiles (high right bank, low left bank) which characterise long sections of many other Russian rivers (e.g. the Dnieper and Don in European Russia, and the Yenisey in Siberia). The rivers of north European Russia rely on melting snow as the main source of their water. Melting snow gives rise to high water in the

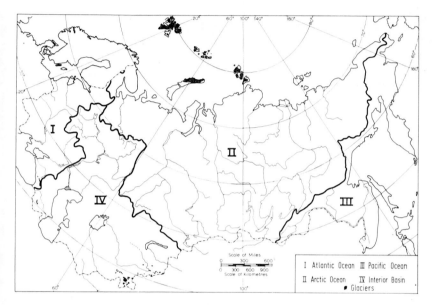

FIG. 11.—Soviet Union: major drainage basins.

spring, although extensive forests and low evaporation rates help maintain a full volume of flow in summer (Fig. 12). In this context it may be noted that by comparison rivers in Britain are rain-fed, their regimes controlled by seasonal evaporation rates, and winter flooding is not unusual.

In western Siberia, the sources of such rivers as the Ob (with Katun, 2508 miles), Irtysh (1840 miles) and Yenisey (2360 miles) are glaciers and snow-fields in the Altay, Sayans and in the mountains of pre-Baykalya. Gradients across the lowlands are very gentle and watersheds exceptionally low. River flow through the zones of steppe, forest and tundra is sluggish. Here too, snow-melt gives rise to high water in the spring. Because the thaw progresses from source to mouth, i.e. is earlier in the upper, more southerly reaches, upstream melt-water tends to overflow the river bank in the lower reaches inundating vast areas which are still frozen and underlain by permafrost, and mouths that are ice-blocked. The resulting flood-marsh and swamp harbour mosquitoes and other blood-sucking insects which make life intolerable for man and beast. Because the greater part of its catchment is underlain by permafrost, runoff in the Lena system in eastern Siberia (2644 miles) is faster than in the Ob–Irtysh system, and with rain-water supplementing snow-melt, high water occurs in the period May–June.

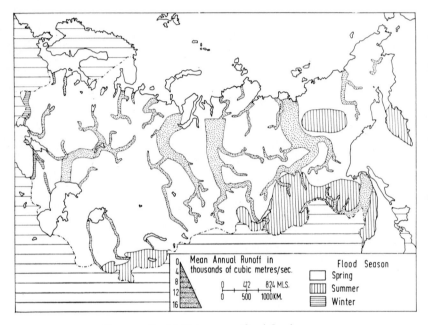

FIG. 12.—Soviet Union: runoff and flood seasons.

Just over 11% of the rivers in the Soviet Union drain into the Atlantic via the Baltic and the Black–Azov Seas. The Baltic receives the waters of the Neva (44 miles), Narva (48 miles), Western Dvina (631 miles) and Neman (550 miles); the Black–Azov Seas receive runoff waters from the Dniester (877 miles), Dnieper (1414 miles), Don (1218 miles), Kuban (582 miles), Rioni (180 miles) and Danube (1750 miles), though only the lower reaches of the Danube flow through Soviet territory. High water in these rivers generally comes in spring from the melting of a considerable snow cover, and is often accompanied by floods and waterlogging.

The Aral–Caspian–Balkhash region of inland drainage accounts for drainage from over a quarter of the U.S.S.R. The Volga (2287 miles) and its tributaries form the greatest drainage system of this region, and it is the longest river in Europe. Its source in the Valday Hills is no more than 665 ft above sea-level, and its gradient to the Caspian Sea (85 ft below sea-level), is slight throughout its length. Spring floods are usual, but during the excessive heat of the summer, evaporation so reduces runoff that shallows and sandbars are formed. To counteract this reduction in flow and at the same time improve navigation, huge barrages and multipurpose reservoirs have been constructed (e.g. at Kuybyshev and Volgograd). Unfortunately, vast open stretches of water along the Volga suffer serious loss through intense evaporation and the level of the Caspian is being appreciably reduced.

The Amu-Darya (Oxus, 1558 miles) and Syr-Darya (Iaxartes, 1773 miles) rise in the Pamirs and Tyan-Shan, and discharge into the enclosed Aral Sea, the fourth largest lake in the world (25,300 sq. miles). Fed by ground-water, glaciers and snow, these are perennial rivers which flood in the spring and summer. Flow diminishes markedly downstream, where the rivers cross the deserts (Kara-Kum, Kyzyl-Kum). The Ili (860 miles) and Chu (700 miles) centring on Lake Balkhash are similar, except that the Chu loses itself in the desert before reaching Balkhash.

Ten and a half per cent of the surface area of the Soviet Union drains to the Pacific. The basin of the Amur (formed from the confluence of the Shilka and Argun Rivers) and its tributaries account for practically 60% of these waters. Most of the feed-water of the Amur (2700 miles), the longest river of the Soviet Union, comes from the summer monsoon rains of Eastern Asia, and it is during this season that high-water stage is reached in the Amur.

The sub-freezing temperatures which persist throughout the greater part of the Soviet Union in winter cause most rivers to freeze up. In Siberia the middle and upper reaches of the Ob, Yenisey and Lena are frozen for five to six months and their lower reaches for practically eight months in the year. In European Russia, the Pechora is frozen for six and a half months, and the Northern Dvina for five and a half months. In the south and southwest the Don, Dnieper, Bug and Dniester are frozen for between three and four months. The rivers of Central Asia freeze for two to four months. The Rioni, Kura and Araks in Trans-Caucasia do not freeze. The annual freeze-up of most rivers in the Soviet Union constitutes a major obstacle to waterborne traffic.

GLACIATION

At some time during the Pleistocene period, ice sheets moved outwards from centres in Scandinavia, Northern Karelia, Novaya Zemlya, the Northern Ural, the Altay, Sayan and Pamirs and the Caucasus. Three

glacial stages have been recognised in European Russia, and a fourth earlier
stage is surmised. In order of decreasing age these are:

1. Early glacial stage.
2. Likhivin (Oka) glacial stage (Elster).
3. Dnieper–Don or Dnieper–Samara glacial stage (Saale).
4. Valday glacial stage.

The third, or Dnieper, glaciation was the most extensive in European
Russia (Fig. 13). It penetrated to the edge of both the central Russian and

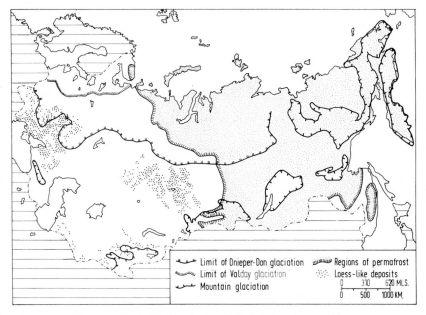

FIG. 13.—Soviet Union: limits of glaciations and permafrost.

Podolsk–Azov Uplands and thence along the foot of the Volga Upland
to the middle Ural. Great lobes extended southwards into the Dnieper and
Oka–Don Lowlands. There was a contemporary glaciation in western
Siberia, but because the climate was drier there it did not extend as far
south as the glaciation on the plains of European Russia. The ice mantle
was about 2300 ft thick in western Siberia, but over 6500 ft in European
Russia.

The fourth, or Valday, stage did not extend as far south as the previous
one, neither did it occur in western Siberia. Nevertheless it has left the
most evident traces of glaciation and accounts for many of the existing
landscape features in the areas it affected. Near the ice centres, e.g. Kola–

Karelia, the effects were mainly erosive. Surface soils were removed and rocks bared, smoothed and rounded. Innumerable irregular shallow hollows scooped out by the ice are now occupied by myriads of lakes, and long low sandy ridges (eskers) cross the region. Beyond, in the northern part of the Russian Lowland and southwards to the limit of the ice sheets, is a region of glacial deposition. Here chains of terminal moraines with broken hilly relief, gently sloping ground moraines, eskers, drumlins, boulder clay, fluvio-glacial deposits, peat bogs, marshes and lakes abound. The Lithu-anian–Belorussian–Valday Hills Ridge, a terminal moraine, is perhaps the most significant relief feature of the Russian Lowland. It also constitutes the main water divide separating north- and south-flowing drainage.

South of the terminal moraine belt of the maximum glaciation is a broad region of water-eroded relief. Here sandy and clayey plains were formed by melt-water flowing southwards from the limits of the ice sheet. South-wards again, and beyond the area of glacial cover, are extensive deposits of thick loess (Fig. 13). These mask completely the underlying relief. The loess was probably formed from fine-grained silt and sand which, having been washed southwards by melt-water accompanying the final retreat of the ice, were dried out and then transported still farther south by wind.

Remnants of shrunken Quaternary icefields and glaciers persist in the mountains of Middle Asia (Pamirs), southern Siberia (Sayans and Altay) and the Caucasus.

PERMANENTLY FROZEN GROUND

Permanently frozen ground (permafrost—*vechnaya merzlota*) underlies more than 3½ million sq. miles, or 47% of the territory of the U.S.S.R. (*see* Fig. 13). In the extreme northeast of Siberia it extends as a continuous cover, but southwards and westwards it forms islands of permanently frozen ground within areas of unfrozen ground. The thickness of the layer of permafrost varies locally. At Yakutsk it amounts to about 450 ft, while at Nordvik it is about 2000 ft. In other areas it may reach no more than a few feet. Below the lower surface of the permafrost temperatures are above freezing point.

The upper layer of the permafrost—the so-called *active layer*—thaws every summer to a varying depth, depending on latitude, vegetation cover, orientation to the sun and other factors. In peat bogs the thaw extends to a depth of about 1½ ft, in marshy areas to about 3 ft, and to about 7 ft beneath the coniferous forest. The frozen layer beneath the thaw acts as an im-pervious bed. This, together with the cool summers, means that the very meagre precipitation of northern Siberia is conserved, and the surface soil remains moist. Herbaceous vegetation, shrubs and trees with superficial root systems grow readily, but waterlogging of the soil is widespread. Black and white spruce, larch and birch (not aspen) are capable of existing where the active layer is 12 in. or more deep, though the soil must be reasonably well drained. Pines with their deep roots will flourish only in well-drained sandy soils. It is the shortness of the summer and its lack of warmth, rather than the permafrost or cold of winter, which restrict agriculture in the higher latitudes of the U.S.S.R.

The heat reserve of surface and ground-waters is often sufficient to keep large areas adjacent to watercourses, lakes, estuaries and the seas free of permafrost. It also hastens their seasonal thawing.

The summer thaw of the surface layers causes appreciable soil movement in the form of solifluction and landslides. Special so-called "active" methods of construction and engineering techniques have been devised to protect buildings, airfields, water and sewer pipes, etc. Since heated structures settle or heave if the upper layers of permafrost are thawed by conduction, many lightweight buildings are constructed on floating foundations which move as a whole, rather than in parts, should such settling or heaving take place. Substantial buildings are built on reinforced concrete piles. The piles are inserted into the permafrost layer after it has been temporarily thawed to a quagmire state by the use of superheated steam; thereafter it is allowed to refreeze. More usually, "passive" methods of construction are used. These endeavour to preserve the natural permafrost table. Sewage disposal, the piping of domestic water supplies, the protection of ground-water supplies from contamination, and even soil fertilisation, present serious difficulties in areas of permafrost.

The climatic amelioration of the early part of the present century resulted in a northward shift of the permafrost boundary and may even have reduced the thickness of the layer of frozen ground.

Opinions differ as to the origin of permafrost. Discoveries of mastodon and mammoth remains, refrigerated since the Pleistocene period, tend to support an origin during the glacial period. On the other hand, a layer of permanently frozen ground has developed in relatively recent mining dumps in the Kolyma goldfield. Seemingly both viewpoints are correct, in that some of the permafrost is of recent origin and some has been preserved since Quaternary times.

RELIEF

The broad relief regions of the Soviet Union are on such an immense scale that the same scenery tends to occur again and again over vast areas (Fig. 14). The general pattern of broad plains and lowlands, surrounded by an almost unbroken chain of high mountains, is relatively simple, yet in detail there is a surprising variety of scene. This is the result of a long and complex geological history, age-long and unremitting sub-aerial erosion, and erosion and deposition by rivers, and by ice during Quaternary times. Only a brief statement of the main relief divisions is given at this stage; details are given in the regional sections.

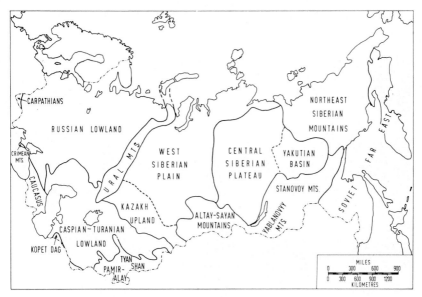

FIG. 14.—Soviet Union: major relief regions.

The *Russian Lowland* forms almost the whole of European Russia. Its general elevation is between 500 and 550 ft above sea-level, though there are parts where altitudes of over 1000 ft are attained. The Lowland rises almost imperceptibly eastwards towards the Ural, but such is the scale that the impression is that of a monotonously rolling countryside. The sedimentary rocks make up the greater part of the Lowland and are the result of alternating transgressions and regressions of the sea over the Russian Platform between Silurian and Tertiary times. They are largely undisturbed. Typically disposed in broad swelling upfolds and downfolds, these rocks tend to mask the irregularities of the foundation structures, except where the latter are exposed as the Khibiny Mountains in the Kola Peninsula in Karelia, in the Podolsk–Azov Uplands and the Donetsk Heights.

The present continental form was assumed at the beginning of the Quaternary period and followed a slight uplift of the land (or subsidence of the sea). That this occurrence was so recent geologically helps to explain the comparatively small amount of stream dissection and erosion that is evident in much of the Lowland. Quaternary glacial deposits account for many of the details of the present relief.

The *Ural* is a composite and much denuded north–south mountain system which reveals itself as a gentle swelling within the broad Russian–Western Siberian Lowland. It is a low, not a mountain, range of conventional aspect. Consequently its use to delimit Europe in the east is often rejected by geographers. In its middle and most densely populated part the

[*Fotokhronika Tass.*

FIG. 15.—The Central Ural Mountains, of low rounded relief and cut by transverse valleys, present no barrier to east–west movement. This section near Chelyabinsk has long been considered the gateway to Siberia.

Ural is neither a barrier to communications nor a climatic divide (Fig. 15).

Siberia occupies a large part of northern Asia. It extends from the eastern edge of the Ural to the mountain ranges of the Pacific watershed, and from the shores of the Arctic Ocean to the arid Kazakh Steppes and the frontiers of the Mongolian People's Republic. It falls into three distinct regions—the West Siberian Plain (or Lowland), the Central Siberian Plateau and the Northeast Siberian Mountains.

The *West Siberian Plain* lies lower than the Russian Lowland. It has been described as the perfect plain and has long been considered the world's finest example of a peneplain. It stretches 1250 miles from the Ural eastwards to the Yenisey River and is drained by the Ob, Irtysh and Yenisey.

Northward slopes are very slight and the great rivers are very sluggish, braided and tortuous. Spring high water is invariably accompanied by extensive flooding.

An abrupt change in the landscape takes place east of the Yenisey. Here the greater part of the countryside is plateau-like, extensively dissected and thickly forested. This is the *Central Siberian Plateau*. Drainage is either westwards into the Yenisey, or southwards to the Vilyuy and Lena. The trough-like valleys of the Lena and Vilyuy mark the eastern boundary of the plateau.

Beyond the Lena in northeastern Siberia the character of the land changes yet again. There is here an irregular surface of mountains, plateau blocks and rifts which are extremely difficult of access. In the northeast, mountains such as the Verkhoyansk and Kolyma Mountains, attain 10,000 ft and form a great semicircle facing the Arctic.

The Soviet Far East is that part of the U.S.S.R. which is separated from Siberia proper by the Dzhugdzhur Range and similar mountains which traverse the Pacific seaboard in a southwest to northeast direction and form a watershed for both rivers and climate. The predominant landscape is mountainous; plains are small and comparatively insignificant.

The lengthy coast fronting the Arctic and Pacific Oceans is most inhospitable. It is generally mountainous in character, and its climate, accentuated by the cold offshore Bering–Okhotsk current and by summer fogs, is most unfavourable. Kamchatka, the Kuriles and Sakhalin Island, are part of the arcuate system which runs the length of the east coast of Asia to form a section of the "fiery girdle of the Pacific."

Soviet Central Asia is essentially the *Caspian–Turanian Lowland* of the Aralo–Caspian–Balkhash Basin. It is an extensive desert area of low plateaux, eroded hills, expansive sand dunes and basins of inland drainage. The two principal rivers, the Amu-Darya (Oxus) and the Syr-Darya (Iaxartes) drain into the Aral Sea.

The mountain border encircling the Russian Lowland, Soviet Central Asia and the West Siberian Plain in the south and east is a series of Alpine-type fold mountains and associated plateaux. In the southwest the Ukrainian Carpathians reach heights of 6000 ft. In the Crimea, elevations of 5000 ft are attained. The Great Caucasus Mountains, with peaks reaching 18,500 ft and without any low passes, present a definite barrier which can be crossed only with difficulty at a few points. East of the Caspian, the Kopet-Dag attains 2900 ft in Soviet territory, but it lies mainly in Iran, where the greatest elevations are attained. The Pamir-Alay Mountains and the Tyan-Shan, with summits rising to over 20,000 ft (Mount Communism, 24,590 ft, 300 miles southeast of Samarkand), are some of the highest mountains in the Soviet Union. Between the Tyan-Shan and the Altay

Mountains lies the relatively low Dzhungarian Gate, the historic highway from China across Mongolia to the Kazakh Steppes and thence to the Volga. The Altay are followed eastwards by the Salair and Kuznetskiy Ala-Tau, the Sayans, the mountains of Tuva and those of the Pre-Baykal and Trans-Baykal regions bordering the Mongolian People's Republic and China.

PHYSICAL-GEOGRAPHICAL REGIONS

A synthesis of the physical aspects of the Soviet Union, including climate, soils and vegetation (which are dealt with in the chapters immediately following) is presented in Fig. 221 in Appendix 1. This map is based on the regional divisions published in the *Physical–Geographical Atlas of the World* (Moscow, 1964), Plates 248–9.

STUDY QUESTIONS

1. Contrast the main structural features of the European and Asiatic parts of the U.S.S.R.

2. Draw a map to show the principal rivers and the main drainage areas of the Soviet Union.

3. Map the distribution of the main *shield* lands of the U.S.S.R. Describe the origin of the landforms of any *one* of these areas.

4. Explain the distribution of the Tertiary fold mountains within the Soviet Union and describe their characteristic landform features.

5. Describe the structure and physical history of (*a*) the Russian Lowland, (*b*) the West Siberian Plain, (*c*) the Ural Mountains, (*d*) the mountain border of the Soviet Union, showing how they have influenced the present landscape.

6. To what extent does the relief of the Soviet Union reflect its underlying tectonic structure?

7. What causes the rivers of the Soviet Union to flood and at what seasons does this occur?

8. What do you understand by "river regime"? Show by reference to specific examples in the Soviet Union how river regime may influence the activities of man.

9. Discuss the origin and nature of landforms in the Soviet Union resulting from glacial erosion. Illustrate your answer by referring to specific examples.

10. Discuss the origin and nature of landforms in the Soviet Union resulting from glacial deposition. Illustrate your answer by referring to specific examples.

11. What have been the effects of the Quaternary glaciation on the present-day geography of the Soviet Union.

12. Draw a sketch-map to show the areas of *vechnaya merzlota* (permafrost). Account for the distribution shown.

13. Describe the landscape you might expect to find in *either* the Great Caucasus *or* the West Siberian Plain.

14. On a sketch-map, locate those areas of the Soviet Union which experience or are likely to experience earthquakes. Suggest reasons for the distribution shown.

Chapter III

WEATHER AND CLIMATE

VAST expanses of the Soviet territory are so positioned in the northern part of the Asiatic landmass that the amphitheatre-like arrangement of the relief features excludes warm moist tropical air masses from the lower latitudes while permitting the flow of cold air from the north. This ensures a severe continental type of climate for the greater part of the Soviet Union. The general circulation of the atmosphere in these latitudes is west to east, but since distances from the Atlantic Ocean to the Soviet Union are so great, the ameliorating influences of this ocean are limited, while those of the Pacific are severely restricted.

SEASONAL CONDITIONS

In winter in these high latitudes, outgoing terrestrial radiation exceeds incoming solar radiation, and there is a net heat loss from the land, i.e. there is a negative radiation balance (Fig. 16—January). Air temperatures are low at the surface and atmospheric pressure is high. The Siberian anti-cyclone establishes itself (Fig. 17—winter) and calm, sunny and steadily cold weather is experienced. The cold dry continental polar air masses (cP) blow out in a clockwise direction to affect most parts of the country. The northwest winter monsoon in eastern Siberia and in the Soviet Far East is part of this circulation. In the European part of the U.S.S.R. a ridge of high pressure, the "baric barrier" which extends westwards along 50° N latitude from the Siberian high, acts as an effective wind divide. To the south of the ridge bitter cold winds blow out from the anticyclone over central Asia and the Ukraine; to the north, westerlies from the Atlantic bring maritime polar air masses (mP) and their accompanying moderating influences. Such influences, not least the precipitation, extend into north European Russia and western Siberia.

The prevailing stationary winter anticyclone is accompanied by clear weather with cloud amounts nearly as low as those of tropical deserts. But the winter days are so short and nocturnal radiation is so excessive that air masses coming from the Atlantic—with a positive anomaly of 20° F (11° C) in its northeastern part—provide a greater source of heat for northern U.S.S.R. than does direct insolation, much of which is reflected

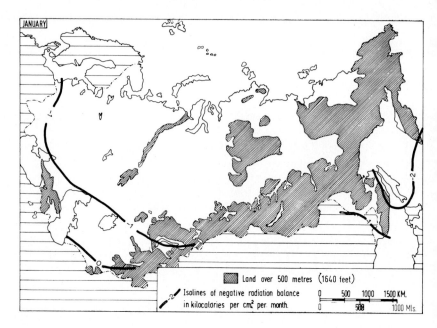

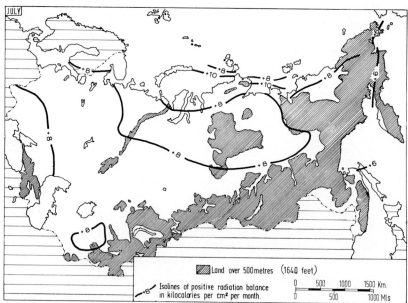

FIG. 16.—Soviet Union: radiation balance in January and July. Radiation balance is the balance of incoming solar radiation and outgoing terrestrial radiation at the surface of the earth.

from snow-covered surfaces. Consequently, winter (January) isotherms are aligned northwest–southeast in European U.S.S.R. and into Siberia as far east as 130° E (Fig. 18). Atlantic influences disappear beyond this longitude and isotherms in Siberia are more latitudinal in alignment. Until about December, Lake Baykal provides a source of heat, and isotherms are de-

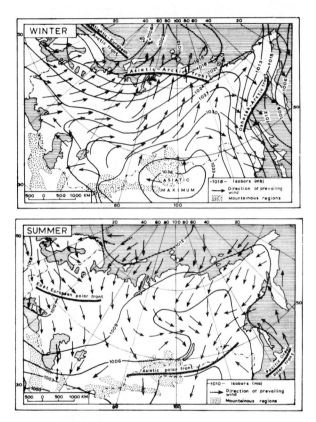

FIG. 17.—Soviet Union: average atmospheric pressure patterns and associated winds in winter and summer.

flected northwards around it. Thereafter, the frozen surface of the lake provides less heat and the effect on the orientation of the isotherms disappears.

Almost the whole of the Soviet Union has a January mean temperature below freezing point and Siberia, with the exception of the south of the Pacific coast, has a January mean below 0° F (−18° C). Winter temperatures decrease until "the pole of cold" is reached in the vicinity of Verkhoyansk-Oymyakon in northeastern Siberia, where an average January

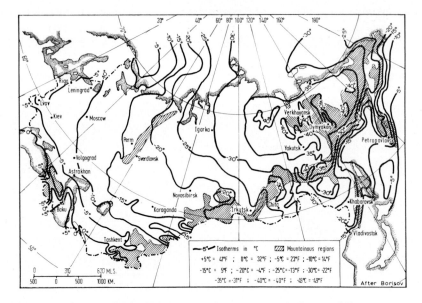

FIG. 18.—Soviet Union: mean air temperatures in January (°C).

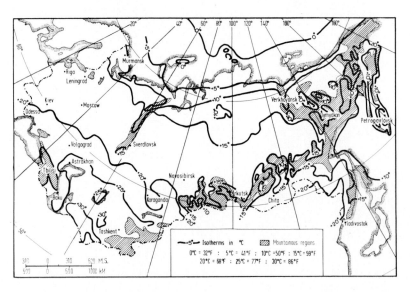

FIG. 19.—Soviet Union: mean air temperatures in July (°C).

temperature of −58° F (−50° C) is attained. The minimum recorded temperature at Verkhoyansk-Oymyakon is −94° F (−70° C). Siberian temperatures are the lowest in the world.

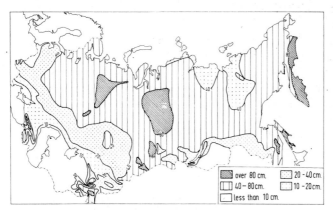

FIG. 20.—Soviet Union: depth of snow cover, showing mean maximum 10-day snow-cover thickness.

The winds blowing out from the continental anticyclone are inimical to precipitation and, in general, winter in the Soviet Union is the season of least precipitation. Nevertheless, some precipitation does occur in winter, practically all in the form of snow (Figs. 20 and 21). Within the westerly

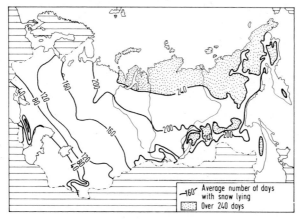

FIG. 21.—Soviet Union: average number of days a year with snow lying.

circulation north of the barometric divide (along the 50° N latitude), over the west and north of the European plain, most of the annual precipitation occurs in autumn from depressions moving westwards along the polar front. Such depressions skirt the Siberian high-pressure cell and are usually dissipated along the Arctic coast of western Siberia. Other depressions, moving along a more southerly route, by way of the Mediterranean low pressure region and the southern fringes of the Siberian high, bring maximum precipitation in winter to the south coast of the Crimea and the east coast of the Black Sea.

During the Siberian winter the air is generally bracing and calm and furs give adequate protection. There is, however, a serious climatic hazard— the *buran* or *purga* of the tundra. This is a snowstorm in which freshly fallen snow is whipped up by strong and bitterly cold winds. It is a serious danger to man and beast, dreaded throughout Siberia.

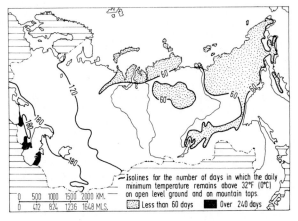

FIG. 22.—Soviet Union: average frost-free period.

The European part of the Soviet Union also experiences *burany* and sudden and violent cold spells, but the settled conditions that typify the Siberian winter are generally absent. In northern and central parts the winter cold is occasionally broken by temporary thaws (*ottepeli*) which follow invasions of moist Atlantic air. Such thaws make the ground sodden, free rivers from ice for a short time and cause disastrous floods.

In summer incoming solar radiation exceeds outgoing terrestrial radiation, and there is a net heat gain (positive radiation balance) over the territory of the U.S.S.R. (Fig. 16—July). Considerable heating of the land results, and a region of steady low barometric pressure extends from Afghanistan and northwestern India into Soviet Central Asia and the Trans-Caucasus region (Fig. 17—summer). Warm dry tropical continental air masses (cT) dominate, although the slight barometric gradients allow western oceanic influences to spread over a far wider area than in the winter. The longer hours of daylight during the summer make for temperature uniformity, and isotherms are aligned more nearly latitudinally (Fig. 19). At this season Lake Baykal is a cooling influence and in its vicinity isotherms are displaced to the south. In eastern Siberia and in the Soviet Far East under the cooling influence of the southwest monsoon isotherms turn south-wards.

Summer temperatures attain mean values in excess of 80° F (26° C) in Soviet Central Asia, but northwards there is a slow gradation to below 46° F (8° C) along the Arctic coast. It is really the length of the summer, rather than its intensity, that is of greatest significance to man (*see* Fig. 22).

The winter and summer seasons in the Soviet Union are strongly marked and differentiated, the rigours of the continental winter giving way to tropical heat within the space of a few months (*see* Table II).

TABLE II

Temperature data for selected stations in the U.S.S.R.

Station	Location	Temperature °F* Jan.	July	Mean annual temperature range ° F*
Astrakhan	Lower Volga	18·5	77·0	58·5
Barnaul	Western Siberia	0·0	67·0	67·0
Batumi	South Caucasus	41·5	73·5 (August)	32·0
Dudinka	Central Siberia	−22·0	55·0	77·0
Lenkoran	South Caucasus	36·5	75·5	39·0
Mary	Central Asia	34·0	85·0	51·0
Moscow	Central Russia	15·0	65·5	50·5
Novosibirsk	Western Siberia	−2·7	65·7	68·4
Odessa	Ukraine	25·0	72·0	47·0
Sevastopol	Crimea	36·5	75·5	39·0
Vladivostok	Far East	7·3	69·0 (August)	61·7

* For conversions to ° C see Appendix 4.

The intermediate seasons of spring and autumn are very brief. In Moscow, for instance, the mean monthly temperature rises 15° F (8° C) between April and May (comparable with the mean *annual* range in parts of western Britain), and at Verkhoyansk there is a 40° F (21·5° C) drop in the mean temperature between October and November. The suddenness of such temperature changes is no less striking than their magnitude and it further emphasises the continental character of the Russian climate. In spring—which does not usually begin before April—the *rasputitsa*, or thaw (literally "slush"), is a hazard. The snow melts and floods the streams, there is an excess of surface water, the soil is liquified and "all Russia is an epic of mud."

Low pressures over the land in summer mean indraughts of air from neighbouring areas. The Atlantic is too remote to provide any generous supply of water vapour, and the Baltic, Black and Caspian Seas are too small to make any contribution to the rainfall. The high mountain barriers in Central Asia and Siberia prevent the entry of water vapour from the Indian Ocean and restrict that from the Pacific Ocean to coastal areas. The temperature of the Arctic Ocean is too low to allow much evaporation, and few moisture-bearing winds reach the continental interior from this source. Nevertheless, late summer is the season of maximum precipitation over European Russia and Siberia, the bulk coming from thunderstorms or hailstorms in July and August, at a time when evaporation is at its greatest. Consequently, effectiveness of precipitation is considerably re-

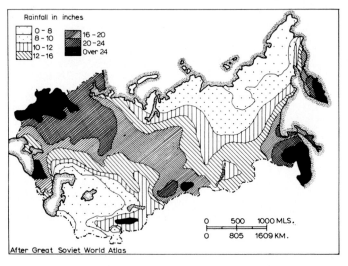

FIG. 23.—Soviet Union: average annual rainfall.

duced. The intensity and general character of the rainfall lead to crop damage, speedy runoff, and considerable soil erosion and gullying, particularly in the steppe-lands of the southern part of European U.S.S.R. Rainfall is unreliable in time and place, and in areas where the annual totals are less than 16 in. droughts are common. An additional climatic hazard for the farmer of the steppe-lands is the dry wind which blows from the Turanian area, known as the *sukhovey*. It has the effect of speeding up transpiration rates in crops, causing them to wither.

Annual precipitation throughout the greater part of the Soviet Union is scanty (Fig. 23). Aggregates are 20–24 in. (500–600 mm) in the west of the country, no more than 20 in. (500 mm) in western Siberia and 15–16 in. (380–400 mm) in eastern Siberia. Southeastern European Russia gets less than 16 in. (400 mm) per annum. Annual aggregates are below 6 in. (152 mm) in the Aralo–Caspian region. The south coast of the Crimea, with its "mediterranean" type climate, receives most of its 10–20 in. (250–500 mm) from winter depressions passing eastwards along the Mediterranean Sea, while the moist and cheerless climate of the Soviet Far East provides 25–40 in. (630–1000 mm) per annum, most of it in association with the summer monsoon. Only two areas of the Soviet Union have a generous supply of precipitation, and both are in Trans-Caucasia. These are the Kolkhida Lowland, fronting the Black Sea, and the Lenkoran Lowland alongside the Caspian Sea. Each has an annual aggregate in excess of 60 in. (1500 mm). The effectiveness of precipitation is shown in Fig. 24.

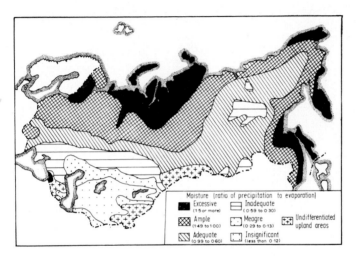

Moisture (ratio of precipitation to evaporation)

Excessive (1.5 or more)
Inadequate (0.59 to 0.30)
Ample (1.49 to 1.00)
Meagre (0.29 to 0.13)
Undifferentiated upland areas
Adequate (0.99 to 0.60)
Insignificant (less than 0.12)

Fig. 24.—Soviet Union: moisture zones.

Mountain ranges and plateaux, large inland lakes and seas, and distances of the various parts of the country from the sea, give rise to local variations, but on the whole the continental character of the climate is remarkably uniform over vast areas. It is the diurnal and seasonal rhythms of climatic phenomena which are biologically significant. In the polar regions, the 24-hour temperature rhythm is replaced by a half-year "day" and half-year "night." Radiation during this polar night shifts the coldest part of the year to February and March. Precipitation, too, shows a seasonal distribution, the maximum occurring in the summer over most of the country.

CLIMATIC REGIONS

One of the most recent attempts to regionalise the U.S.S.R. on the basis of climate is given in Plate 203 of the *Physical–Geographical Atlas of the World* (Moscow, 1964), represented here by Fig. 25. The scheme, after

Budyko, is based on indices indicative of moisture conditions, warm-season temperature conditions, and the character of the winter, as follows:

	Moisture characteristics	Dryness index	Geographical conditions
I	Excess moisture	less than 0·45	Arctic desert, tundra, wooded tundra, alpine meadow
II	Humid	0·45–1·00	Forest
III	Inadequate moisture	1·00–3·00	Wooded steppe, steppe, dry subtropics
IV	Dry	over 3·00	Desert

The dryness index is the ratio of evaporability (related to radiation balance, temperature and humidity) and precipitation.

	Thermal conditions of warm season	Sum of temperatures of earth's surface during period in which the air temperature remains above 10° C (50° F)	Geographical conditions
1	Very cold	Air temperature below 10° C the year round	Arctic desert
2	Cold	less than 1000° C	Tundra, wooded tundra
3	Moderately warm	1000°–2200° C	Coniferous forest, alpine meadow, mountain steppe and steppe of Siberia
4	Warm	2200°–4400° C	Mixed and broadleaf forest, wooded steppe, steppe, northern desert
5	Very warm	more than 4400° C	Sub-tropics, desert

The sum of the temperatures at the earth's surface is, as a rule, greater than the sum of air temperatures in the same period.

		Climatic indicators	
	Winter characteristics	Mean January Temperature in ° C	Maximum 10-day snow cover
A	Severe, little snow	below −32	less than 50 cm
B	Severe, snowy	below −32	more than 50 cm
C	Moderately severe, little snow	−13 to −32	less than 50 cm
D	Moderately severe, snowy	−13 to −32	more than 50 cm
E	Moderately mild	0 to −13	
F	Mild	above 0	

By using these criteria and their corresponding number and letter designations, the climatic conditions of each region can be designated by a combination of three quantitatively defined symbols. For example, II 4 D refers to a humid climate with warm summers and a moderately severe, snowy winter.

Reference should also be made to the physical–geographical regional divisions illustrated in Fig. 221 in Appendix 1.

1. Discuss the factors affecting the climates of the U.S.S.R.
2. Give reasons why the "cold pole" of the earth is located in northeast Siberia.
3. Describe and explain the seasonal distribution of rainfall in the U.S.S.R.
4. Describe the rainfall regimes of the "mediterranean" and "monsoon" regions of the U.S.S.R. Give reasons for the seasonal variations you mention and discuss the differences in total annual rainfall at representative stations in each region.
5. Why is the impression of Siberia as an area of deep snow fallacious?
6. Explain how and why the climates of the western coastlands of the U.S.S.R. differ from those of the eastern coastlands.
7. Write short notes to explain: otepel; purga; sukhovey.

Chapter IV

SOILS—VEGETATION PATTERNS

THE strong relationship between the distribution of natural vegetation, climate and zonal soils is evident from a study of Figs. 25, 26 and 27. The relationship between zonal soil groups and the underlying geology, however, is not always so obvious. In arid and semi-arid regions it is clearly

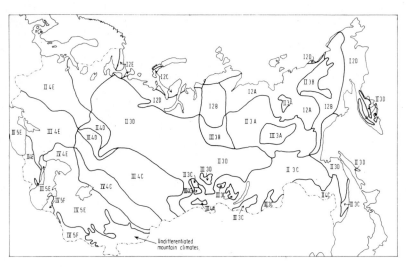

FIG. 25.—Soviet Union: climatic regions. For key, see text on p. 36.

recognisable; elsewhere it is less evident. In the north of the country morainic materials and fluvio-glacial deposits resulting from Quaternary glaciation conceal the solid rocks. Beyond the limits of the Quaternary ice, aeolian deposits (*loess*) are common. Laid down during the climatic phase that succeeded the glaciations, these silty lands originated as glacial waste which was sorted and transported by wind. In the Aral and Caspian Basins, where much of the surface has only recently become dry land, lacustrine deposits are common. Where natural soils have been cultivated and improved, they tend to be similar to one another and approximate to brown and black earths.

Although the soils–vegetation zones differ markedly from one another,

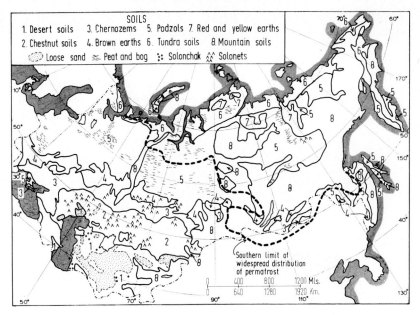

FIG. 26.—Soviet Union: soils.

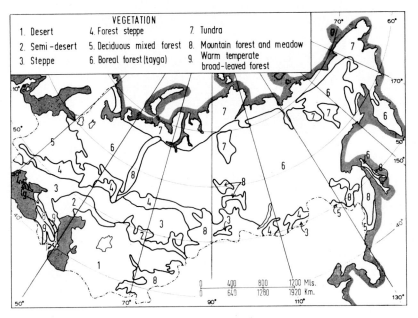

FIG. 27.—Soviet Union: natural vegetation.

especially where the natural vegetation has not been replaced by cultivation, boundaries between them are neither sharp nor straight.

DESERT

Desert occupies about $7\frac{1}{2}\%$ of the area of the Soviet Union, mainly in central Asia. It occurs between the Caspian Sea in the west and the mountain systems of Kopet-Dag–Pamir–Alay–Tyan-Shan in the south and east.

[*Myzl.*

FIG. 28.—The bare patches and poor scant vegetation of the clay flats (*takyr*) of the desert give the landscape an unfriendly appearance.

The 47° N parallel of latitude marks the approximate northern limit of desert, although isolated patches occur north of the Caspian and east of the lower Volga, in the lower Kura–Araks Basin and in the Lenkoran Lowland. A third of the desert area is composed of shifting sands, e.g. Kara-Kum, Kyzyl-Kum, Muyun-Kum. Soils are poorly developed since the role played by water and vegetation is negligible. Because of rainfall deficiency, parent rocks play a greater part in soil-forming processes here than in more humid regions.

On the plateaux of Kazakhstan towards the western margins of the desert, the soil is generally gravelly at the surface and has a very low humus content. It is the *serozem*, or grey-brown soil in which the surface horizon grades through lighter-coloured material into a layer of calcium carbonate accumulation. Gypsum also occurs in the soil profile. An intrazonal soil known as *solonchak* occurs where soluble salts brought to the surface by ground-water accumulate after evaporation.

In the piedmont plains of the southern part of the desert region, grey soils have developed on a subsoil of loess 2–3 ft below the surface. The humus content of these soils is low, but they contain appreciable amounts of carbonates and other nutrients for plant growth; where irrigation water is available, they are extremely fertile.

Natural vegetation is sparse and open, reflecting the desert conditions of the region. Two types are recognised, desert semi-shrub and desert tree-shrub. The desert semi-shrub, characterised by wormwood, saltworts and saltbush, is found in ragged clusters on clays, loams and stony desert (Fig. 28). The desert tree-shrub, comprising tree-like salt-bushes (saksuls and xerophytic shrubs), is associated with areas of somewhat greater soil moisture, such as dried-up watercourses or light sandy areas, where ground-water lies at root level.

SEMI-DESERT (ARID STEPPE)

The semi-desert, or arid steppe, is a transition stage between desert and steppe. It is found on light chestnut soils, which occupy about 5% of the Soviet territory. They occur in a compact, almost latitudinal, belt extending from the northeastern foreland of the Great Caucasus around the north of the Caspian Sea, and eastwards to the foothills of the Altay. Chestnut soils have a very low humus content and varying degrees of salinity. Patches of more alkaline soils—*solonets*—are widely distributed within the belt. Low and variable rainfall, to which the soils owe much of their character, limits their use for crop production. In consequence, dry farming and the grazing of livestock are practised. In its natural state the vegetation consists principally of drought-resisting turf grasses and herbs, such as wormwood, fescue, feathergrass and needlegrass.

STEPPE

In its natural state the steppe consists of steppe turf grasses adapted to the so-called ordinary and southern chernozem and to dark chestnut soils. Feathergrass, needlegrass and fescue are the common species, with which tall-growing herbs are associated. The vegetation grows in separate tufts or bunches, with bare ground between individual plants.

Chernozem has a deep, dark to black surface horizon, hence the term "black earth." It extends in a wide belt from the northern shores of the Black–Azov Seas and the foothills of the Caucasus eastwards to the foothills of the Altay. Spring rains and snow-melt cause a slight leaching from the surface (A) horizon, but this is balanced by surface evaporation during the hot summer. Harsh winters and late-summer droughts prevent any rapid decomposition of organic matter or heavy leaching. Thus, climatic conditions favour the accumulation of organic matter in the form of humus compounds. The resulting soils are inherently fertile. Under the layer of rich organic soil, at a depth of 3–4 ft, lies a horizon saturated with calcium carbonate (lime) (*see* Fig. 29), which imparts a crumb structure to the soil and improves its physical quality.

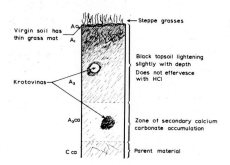

FIG. 29.—Idealised chernozem profile. (Krotovinas are the infilled holes and tracks of moles, worms and other soil fauna and are a characteristic of the Russian chernozem. They appear whitish when formed in the humic horizon and are filled with secondary calcium carbonate from below, or are dark when in the carbonate horizon and filled with humic material from above.)

Sub-types of chernozem provide the basis of four sub-zones. They are from north to south: (1) degraded chernozems; (2) normal, thick chernozems; (3) ordinary chernozem with a humus content in the soil profile lower than that in the north; (4) chernozem with a low surface humus content and a relatively thin humus horizon.

Chernozems are naturally rich soils and are widely cultivated. In some of the western parts of the Ukraine 80% or more of these soils are under the plough, and very little of the original steppe vegetation remains.

FOREST

Forest extends from the northwest of the country to the shores of the Okhotsk Sea. It covers about 30% of the entire area of the U.S.S.R. and represents about 20% of the forested area of the world. In the south it is replaced by forest steppe; this is made up of flowering herbs and frequent woodlands, with grass occupying only a subordinate position. In eastern Asia and in the northeastern Altay region lowland and mountain forests merge. North of the Arctic Circle in European Russia and in western Siberia, but north of 70°–73° N in central and eastern Siberia, the forests merge into the tundra region. Vegetation within the forest zone is varied, but two main types are usually recognised: (*a*) deciduous mixed forests, and (*b*) the boreal forest (*tayga*).

(*a*) Deciduous mixed forest occurs in the European part of the Soviet Union. It contains much oak with frequent admixtures of spruce, fir, birch and pine. There are, in addition, such other west European broad-leaved trees as ash, maple and hornbeam, together with their associated

[*Fotokhronika Tass.*

Fig. 30.—Boreal forest (*tayga*) extends as a broad belt across the middle latitudes of the Soviet Union. The forest is composed of extensive stands of a few species and is underlain by ashen-coloured podzol.

shrubs and herbs. These species are found near the eastern limit of their ranges. Much of the mixed forest has been destroyed and many of the interspersed marshes drained or dried out. Mixed forests are not found east of the Ural Mountains.

The underlying soils form a comparatively thin belt between the *cherno-zem* and *podzol* zones, and are known as brown earths or brown forest soils. Because of earthworm activity and reduced leaching they do not exhibit the distinct horizon formation of podzols, and with precipitation tending to exceed evaporation, carbonates are removed.

(*b*) The boreal forest or *tayga* has a predominance of conifers (Fig. 30). Spruce and Scots pine are the dominant trees, especially in the western part where conditions are often swampy and peat bogs widespread. In the eastern part these trees are mixed with Siberian larch, Siberian fir and Siberian pine. Permafrost underlies the Siberian tayga and much of the European forest.

The tayga develops on *podzol*, a soil with a distinctive ash-grey layer beneath a black surface of partly decomposed conifer litter (*see* Fig. 31). Podzols, which together with bog soils occupy over half the area of the Soviet Union, are heavily leached. This is the result not of heavy rainfall (precipitation throughout this zone is usually less than 20 in. (500 mm) per annum), but of the sudden release of snow-melt waters in the spring. Acidity is also high. Organic substances formed by the decomposition of forest

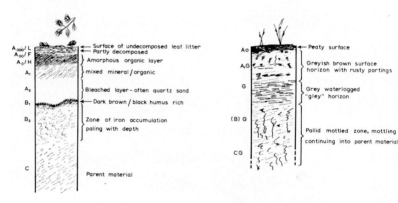

FIG. 31.—Profile of humus iron podzol.

FIG. 32.—Profile of non-calcareous, surface water, peaty gley.

waste remove lime and iron compounds and leave behind a bleached hori-zon, often composed of pure quartz sand, just beneath the acid humus layer of the A horizon. The iron compounds are washed down into the B horizon, where they often form a reddish-brown "hard pan." If there is a well-developed "pan," soils become waterlogged. During the long hard winters waterlogging slows down bacterial decomposition and gives rise to peat formation (*see* Fig. 32). Peat is more widespread in the south of the zone than in the centre and north.

The monsoon rains of the Soviet Far East ensure sufficient moisture for tree growth along the valley of the Amur River. The forest is of the warm temperate broad-leaved type and is composed of Manchurian oak with admixture of maple, ash, linden and Scots elm.

TUNDRA

Tundra occupies a belt which extends along the shores of the Arctic Ocean and inland to the northern margin of the boreal forest zone. The tundra is tree-less except for some wooded "islands" and consists of a scanty, low vegetation of moss and lichen and an area of low-growing shrubs, whinberries and cranberries (Fig. 33). Apart from the Kola Peninsula, most of the ground is permanently frozen. In consequence, the ground

[*Soviet Weekly.*

FIG. 33.—Tundra. The northern fringe of the Soviet Union consists of peat bogs, marshes, frozen soil and little vegetation.

is impervious below the few inches near the surface that thaw out during the short summer. Thus, although precipitation is slight, and summer temperatures low, waterlogging is widespread. The soils of the tundra are

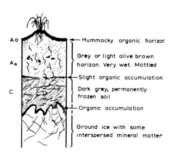

FIG. 34.—Profile of tundra soil.

A₀ — Hummocky organic horizon.

Aₐ — Grey or light olive brown horizon. Very wet. Mottled

Slight organic accumulation

C — Dark grey, permanently frozen soil

Organic accumulation

Ground ice with some interspersed mineral matter

slate-blue and of low fertility. Soil micro-organisms are inactive and organic decomposition is slow and incomplete (*see* Fig. 34). Peat bog soils are common.

C

MOUNTAIN SYSTEMS

Where slopes are not too steep for soil development, the mountain systems which skirt the Soviet Union from the Carpathians to Siberia carry a vegetation markedly different from that on the neighbouring plains. With increasing altitude and decreasing average temperatures, a zonal arrangement of vegetation occurs, not unlike that which occurs from south to north across the lowlands.

Where mountains rise out of deserts, as in Central Asia and Kazakhstan, the vegetation ranges from desert type at the base, through steppe and forest, to sub-alpine and alpine meadows near the summits. In the southern Ural the vertical zonation of vegetation ranges from broad-leaved forests in the low foothills of the western slopes, to pine/larch forest or fir/spruce tayga on the highest ridges, occasionally with a sub-alpine zone of tall meadow herbage and a few spruces.

Mountain soils are varied, but all are distinguished by shallowness and good drainage. They are very prone to erosion after the natural vegetation is disturbed. Mountain meadow and steppe soils are common in the Caucasus, Pamirs, Altay and Tyan-Shan. On the central Siberian Plateau and in the mountains of southern and northeastern Siberia the soils are mainly of the mountain forest and mountain tundra type.

TRANS-CAUCASIA AND SOUTH CRIMEA

On the Kolkhida and Lenkoran (Talysh) Lowlands, sometimes described as the "greenhouse" of the Soviet Union, and again in the southern portion of the Crimea, the "Soviet Riviera," the vegetation is different from that found elsewhere in the country. A humid sub-tropical climate provides a warm temperate broad-leaved forest of olives, laurels, junipers, vines and ferns.

Bog soils are common, but red and yellow-brown soils, leached of bases and silicates, occur in the areas of higher ground. Laterisation takes place at the surface, although waterlogging in the lower part of the soil profile often causes gleying.

Reference should also be made to the physical–geographical regional divisions illustrated in Fig. 221 in Appendix 1.

STUDY QUESTIONS

1. Assess the geographical relevance of a regional division of the Soviet Union on the basis of major zones of natural vegetation.

2. Discuss the relation between climate, soil and natural vegetation in the steppes of the U.S.S.R.

3. Discuss the relation between climate, soil and natural vegetation in the tayga of the U.S.S.R.

4. Give an account of the distribution and characteristic features of the podzol soils in the U.S.S.R. and explain the environmental factors which lead to their development.

5. What is the distribution of the chernozem soils in the U.S.S.R.? Account for their characteristic features in terms of the environments in which they develop.

6. Write short notes to explain podzol, chernozem, serozem, solonchak, solonets.

7. Write short notes to explain: tayga; tundra; steppe; desert.

8. Write an account of the physical geography of the following: (a) West Siberian Lowland; (b) Ural Mountains; (c) The Russian Lowland; (d) The Great Caucasus.

9. Divide the European part of the Soviet Union into major physical regions and give a reasoned account of one of the divisions you indicate.

10. Divide the Asiatic part of the Soviet Union into major physical regions and give a reasoned account of one of the divisions you indicate.

Chapter V

THE PEOPLING OF THE SOVIET LANDS

To relate, even sketchily, the long history of Russia from Palaeolithic times to the present day would be a formidable task and one not really relevant to this study. Instead, a series of phases, considered to be significant for a proper understanding of the life and culture of the Soviet Union of today, has been selected.

KIEV RUS

Primitive Finno-Ugrian tribes, belonging to the Ural–Altaic group of people, migrated westward from Siberia and settled in the forests of northern European Russia towards the beginning of historical time. To the south, in the marsh and mixed forest lands between the Dnieper, Western Dvina and Dniester, lived eastern Slavonic tribes (Russians). Into the open steppe-lands of the south came wave after wave of conquering nomadic peoples: Iranians, Cimmerians, Scythians, Sarmatians, Germanic Goths, Turko-Mongols and Turko-Avars. In the seventh century the Avars themselves were overrun by the Khazars, whose domination of the steppe lasted until the tenth century. The Khazars spread over the whole of the immense plains of southern Russia from the northern shores of the Black Sea and the Caspian Sea to the Ural, and to the Volga beyond Kazan. Certain eastern Slavonic tribes that had settled in the middle Dnieper, chiefly around Kiev, came under Khazar subjection. Other Slavonic people who had settled farther north, were much influenced by Scandinavians, called Varangians or Norsemen. The Varangians came to Russia from the Baltic, first as pirates and adventurers and later as traders. Following waterways and making short portages along the Neva, Lake Ladoga, the Volkhov, Lake Ilmen, the Lovat, Western Dvina and Dnieper—"the Water Road from the Varangians to the Greeks"—they made their way to Byzantium (Constantinople) where they had established trading links by the end of the eighth century.

It is believed that by the ninth century the Varangians and Slavs had organised themselves into provinces, which comprised several Slav tribes, with centres at Novgorod on the River Volkhov, and Smolensk on the Dnieper. According to Soviet historians, the Varangians were assimilated by the Slavs. The Varangians were called *Rus*★ and it was from this name that the modern word "Russia" was derived. These people settled also in Kiev—an outpost on the forest-steppe fringe near the junction of the Dnieper, Desna and Pripyat.

By the eleventh century Kiev Rus, having absorbed several petty princedoms, was taking shape as the cradle of Russia. Even Novgorod (Fig. 35)—

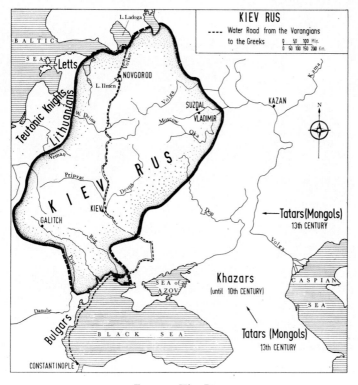

FIG. 35.—Kiev Rus.

a great trading centre and member of the Hanseatic League—accepted the leadership of Kiev.

The Dnieper–Western Dvina axis drew together the Baltic and Black Sea, and thus northern and southern Europe. This axis was the backbone and economic *raison d'être* of Kiev Rus. Kiev Rus itself provided furs, wax, honey, hides and slaves, but it was from the transit trade that she gained her real wealth and importance. Kiev, "the Mother of Russian towns," and the Kievan State absorbed many elements of civilisation through contact with

★ The term *Rus* first denoted the upper class, then the entire population and, finally, the country itself. The term "Russian State" was not officially adopted until the fifteenth or sixteenth century.

Byzantium, not the least of which were the Greek (Cyrillic) alphabet and the Greek Orthodox Christianity. Constant attacks by steppe nomads, and internecine warfare of Russian princes during the twelfth century, brought about a decline in the power of Kiev Rus. Between 1237 and 1240 Kiev was overthrown and completely laid waste by Tatars of the Golden Horde. The Mongol peoples established complete supremacy over the steppe-lands for the next two centuries.

[*K. Top. CXII. 87. British Museum.*

FIG. 36.—Plan of Moscow, 1789.

MOSCOW RUS: 15th TO 17th CENTURIES

The frequent attacks of the steppe nomads and the general instability of Kiev before its fall in 1240 gave rise to Slav migration northwards. There, in the refuge of forest and marsh, Russian princely states began to emerge from the consolidation of several smaller states. The complete suppression of these individual principalities and the creation of the new Russian State, Muscovy, in the geographically important region between Oka and Volga, was eventually attained by the ambitious and unscrupulous princes of Moscow. Here, Slav peoples from Kiev joined with the Finno-Ugrians and other Slavs who had earlier settled in the eastern forest. Isolated villages

[K. Top. CXII. 63. British Museum.

FIG. 37.—Novgorod. Eighteenth-century view of this ancient Russian trading centre.

dotted the forests and marshes and the people practised subsistence agriculture, trapping and hunting in an environment which was totally different from, and far less congenial than, that of Kiev Rus. In the long hard
winters of enforced hibernation the peasants took to handicrafts. When the
link with Byzantium was broken, Moscow became the new seat of the
Metropolitan and the centre of the Russian Orthodox (Greek) Church
(Fig. 36).

The backbone of Moscow Rus was the Volga–Northern Dvina axis, and

FIG. 38.—Kazan. Eighteenth-century view of

this remained for centuries "as closed and self-contained as the Arctic and
Caspian Sea that link its ends." To the west, beyond the borders of the
Russian homeland, the feudal monarchies of Lithuania and Poland disputed
the Baltic lands with the Teutonic (German) Knights. Following their
unsuccessful struggle with the Germans, the Lithuanians and Letts moved
eastwards into the thinly settled marshlands of Russia. In the steppe to the
southeast and south were the Mongols. The Russian homeland was thus
hemmed in on the west, south and east, and the only pioneer frontier was
in the northeast.

It was not until the reign of Ivan III (the Great), 1462–1505, that Muscovy
finally emerged supreme over all the Russian States. By 1478 Novgorod—
hitherto holding first place among the principalities, a rich and proud
commercial city with territories stretching to the north, possessed of

ancient republican liberties modelled on the Venetian type of municipal republic—was reduced to the rank of a provincial town (Fig. 37).

In 1480, following a major stalemate on a battleground to the south of Moscow, the Tatar yoke was considered to be finally lifted. Even so, different groups of Tatars maintained independent states within Russia for a long time, particularly along the Volga and in the Crimea. Kazan on the Volga was not captured until 1552 (Fig. 38), during the reign of Ivan IV (The Terrible), and Astrakhan not until 1556. The Crimea Khanate was

[*K. Top. CXII. 63. British Museum.*

Tatar centre at the great bend of the Volga.

not conquered by Russia until 1783; thus Muscovy was deprived of access to the Black Sea for some centuries to come.

During the two and a half centuries of Tatar rule (1240–1480), the Russian (Slav) people became gradually separated into three large groups: Great Russians, Ukrainians and Belorussians. The Great Russians, later to be the empire builders, had their original homeland in the mixed forest and woodland steppe. The Ukrainians (erroneously described as Little Russians, *Malorusy*) had theirs in the black earth steppe. The Belorussians (White Russians) inhabited the regions of the upper Western Dvina, upper Neman and upper Dnieper; they were the old Krivichi people, ethnologically a Lithuanian tribe who, after centuries of intermingling with neighbouring Slavs, adopted the Slavonic language and are considered a Slavonic people.

In the beginning of the sixteenth century, the Ukraine became the goal of a considerable exodus both from Poland and from Russia. Serfs who desired escape from taxes and the tyranny of landlords, refugees from the law, daring and adventurous individuals, political rebels and similar elements, escaped eastwards and southwards to the great "No Man's Land" to become farmers or to join together in semi-nomadic fugitive and adventurer Cossack groups. These Cossacks (*kazaki*, not to be confused

FIG. 39.—"Russia, Muscovy and Tartary." A sixteenth-century map taken from the *Theatrum orbis terrarum* of Abraham Ortelius (Antwerp 1570). A translation of the Latin which accompanies this map is given on pp. 55–6.

with *Kazakh*, the people of Kazakhstan in Central Asia) were generally distributed over the southern plains, but were concentrated around Kiev, the lower Don and near the present site of Zaporozhye on the Dnieper. This southward movement into the steppe, rather than a later one eastwards into Siberia, is in Russian history comparable with the westward migrations into the Great Plains of North America. The Cossacks were frontiersmen and freebooters who later became frontier guards. Polish kings used Cossacks to protect their State against incursions by the Tatars, while the Russian Tsars (shortened from Latin *Caesar*) enlisted them as border defenders and later as advance troops for the extension of Russia beyond the Ural, the Caucasus and the Caspian Sea.

By the end of the fifteenth century Muscovy was expanding eastward and northward (Fig. 39). Adventurers, traders and hunters moved in boats along the rivers and made portages through the boreal forest (tayga) and along the White Sea shores in search of furs, walrus ivory, sealskins, blubber oil, tar, pitch and other forest products which were exported by Hansa merchants from Novgorod to Western Europe. This expansion reached the estuary of the Ob by the sixteenth century. It was here that the Russian and Tatar interests were brought into collision (Fig. 40). An expedition organised by the fur-trading Strogonov family, and under the leadership of a Cossack named Yermak Timofeyevich, crossed the Ural and in 1582 conquered the town of Sibir, a Tatar stronghold on the Irtysh, near the present-day Tobolsk. Two years later Yermak was drowned in the Irtysh during a Tatar counter-offensive, and with his death, the Russians abandoned the country they called Siberia. Nevertheless, new bands of hunters and adventurers continued to move across the Ural through the sparsely populated Siberian tayga where they encountered only unorganised and ineffectual opposition from the primitive inhabitants. The movement eastwards continued roughly along the 55° N parallel, with much use being made of rivers when their direction coincided with that of the general advance.

Illuminating descriptions of the extent of the territories of the Russians and of the Tatars in the sixteenth century, and of their religions, rites and ways of life are given in Latin texts which accompany the maps "Russia, Muscovy and Tartary" (Fig. 39) and "Tartary, or the Empire of the Great Cham" (Fig. 42). Translations of the texts are as follows:

RUSSIA or the Empire of the Great Duke of Muscovy.

This map does not contain the whole of Russia, for Poland and Lithuania, which are also understood under the name of Russia, are missing. But it shows the whole of the empire of the Muscovite Duke which is bounded to the north by the Ice Sea and has for its neighbours the Tartars to the east, to the south the Turks and Poles and to the west inhabitants of Livonia and the King of Sweden. Sigismund Baro of Herberstein describes all these regions one by one, to whose writings we direct those who wish to read more of these matters. We have freely extracted from the same these few things concerning the religion, rites and way of life of the inhabitants.

As regards religion, they follow closely the rites of the Greeks. Their priests take wives. They worship images in the temples. When children are baptized, they are totally immersed in the water three times, the baptismal water being consecrated separately for each child. Although they have confession as part of the constitution, the common people look on it as necessary for princes and as appertaining to nobles. When the confession is finished, and penance according to the nature of the offence has been enjoined, they make the sign of the Cross on forehead and breast and cry with a loud voice: "O Jesus Christ, Son of God, have mercy on us." This is their communal prayer, for very few know the Lord's Prayer. They take Communion in both senses, mixing bread with wine, or the body with the blood. They give the Sacrament to boys of seven years saying that then is sin possible for man. The nobler men celebrate feast days by holding services, by eating, drinking and wearing fine clothes. The common people and slaves for the greater part work, however, saying that to feast and abstain from work is for masters. They do not believe in purgatory, but they have a service for the dead. Holy water is not sprinkled by any person other than by a priest only. They fast for seven weeks continually during Lent. They make marriage contracts and allow bigamy but scarcely consider it to be a lawful marriage. They allow divorce. Adultery is not so called unless a man takes another's wife.

The condition of women is most wretched, for they think none honourable unless she lives closed up at home and is so guarded that she can never go out. The people are cunning and deceitful and rejoice more in servitude than freedom. All confess themselves to be servants of the Prince. They rarely know peace for they are either engaged in war with the Lithuanians, Livonians and Tartars, or if they are not waging war, they are in garrisons on the rivers Tanais (Don) and Occa to keep in check the ravages of the Tartars.

They wear rectangular tunics without pleats, whose sleeves fasten tightly somewhat like the Hungarians, and short leggings, usually red, which do not reach the knees. They have sandals strengthened with iron strips. They bind their thighs but not the stomach, so that as they become young men, the more prominent their stomach becomes, they loosen the belt.

They exercise justice actively against thieves but seldom punish theft and murder by execution. They have money of silver; not circular but rectangular and some sort of oval shape.

The region abounds in excellent and most precious skins which are exported thence throughout all Europe; almost the whole area is thickly wooded.

TARTARY or the Empire of the Great Cham.

Whoever wishes to describe the Tartars, must describe many nations which are far distant from one another. Tartary is usually called today that part of the earth from the Eastern Ocean or Mangicus, which is located between the Northern Ocean and Southern Sina [China], that part of India beyond the Ganges, Sacos, Oxus (now Abiamu); the Caspian Sea, the marsh of Meotis [the sea of Azov] and almost as far as Moscow to the west; because the Tartars occupied almost all these lands and lived in those places. So that it comprises thus the Asian Sarmatia of ancient writings, and both regions of Scythia, and Serica (which perhaps is Cathay today). The name of these was first heard in Europe in the year of grace 1212.

They are divided into "hordes," a word which means in their tongue "a gathering or multitude." But as they inhabit various widely separated provinces, so neither in morals nor kind of life do they all come together.

They are men of squat stature, with broad and heavy faces, slanted and deep-set eyes. They are rough only in respect of their beard, the rest is shaven. They have strong physiques and courageous spirits.

They feed on horse-meat readily and on other animals whatever way they are

killed, except pork from which they abstain. They are most long suffering of
hunger and lack of sleep; indeed if hunger and thirst assail them when riding, they
will cut the veins of the horses they are riding on and assuage their need by drinking their blood.

And since they wander, having no fixed home, they are accustomed to direct
their journeys by the sight of stars and chiefly by the Pole star which is in their
tongue Selesnikol, that is the iron nail (according to Sigismund of Herberstein).
They do not stay long in one place, considering it unpleasant and unlucky to
remain for long in the same place. There is no system of justice among them.
They are people most greedy of plunder and without doubt extremely poor, so
that they are always striving after the goods of others. There is no use of gold and
silver among them.

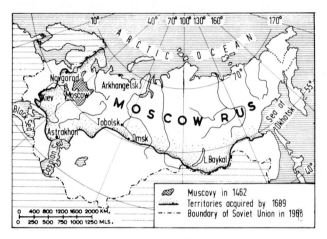

FIG. 40.—MOSCOW RUS.

The Pacific coast, some 4000 miles from Moscow, was reached in 1647,
sixty-five years after the conquest of Sibir. The area east and north of Lake
Baykal, populated by Mongol Buryats, was subjugated during the period
1641–54. By the Treaty of Nerchinsk China sanctioned in 1689 the
establishment of the Russians on the Pacific, at a time when they had not
yet reached the Black Sea (see Fig. 40). The only major addition of territory in the east after this date was the Amur basin and the coast to Vladivostok, "the Guardian of the East," which was acquired from China in
1860.

Throughout the sixteenth and seventeenth centuries the northern lands
in Russia and Siberia flourished, and trade was further stimulated by the
discovery of the White Sea route to Muscovy by the Englishman Richard
Chancellor in 1553. Three ships under the command of Sir Hugh Willoughby had set out from Gravesend, England, on May 18, 1554, ". . . to

seke the lands unknown." In August they were separated by a storm and two of them wintered in Lapland, where Willoughby and his companions perished from exposure. The *Edward Bonaventure*, commanded by Richard Chancellor, reached the North Dvina River and Chancellor proceeded to Moscow where he was received by Tsar Ivan IV, "the Terrible" (1553–84). The Tsar expressed his willingness to receive English ships and, after negotiations, to allow free market and commercial privileges to English merchants. A charter was granted and the Muscovy Company formed in 1555. This northern outlet via Arkhangelsk outflanked the Baltic trade monopolists and enabled Tudor merchants seeking furs to satisfy the luxurious tastes of the court of Elizabeth I.

ST PETERSBURG RUSSIA: 1713–1918

Up to the end of the sixteenth century the expansion of Muscovy eastwards into Asia was largely confined to the boreal forest. From the reign of Peter the Great (1689–1725), when Russia was proclaimed an Empire, the country assumed a wholly western orientation and became virtually part of Europe.★ By 1721 it had emerged as one of the great powers of Europe. At the beginning of Peter's reign Russia was shut off by hostile powers from the Black, Azov and Baltic Seas, but war with Sweden established a Russian hold on the Baltic, and in 1702 the building of St Petersburg— Russia's first "window to Europe" on the Baltic—was begun (Fig. 42). The government was moved there from Moscow in 1713 and it remained in St Petersburg† until 1918.

Under Peter's successors Russian settlement in the southern steppe was intensified. It followed in the wake of marauding Cossacks and involved for the settlers a complete change of physical environment—from forested homeland to wooded and open steppe. It was not until early in the nineteenth century that the settlers changed from stock raising to large-scale wheat farming. Russian settlement in the southern steppe was reinforced by Germans and Greeks, who gave to the region a decidedly multi-racial polyglot character.

The entire north shore of the Black Sea was eventually secured from the Turks, Prussians and Austrians by the Russo-Turkish War of 1774, after which what is now part of the Ukraine became New Russia (Novorossiysk). Bessarabia was acquired from the Turks in 1812. In the northwest the expansion was completed by the acquisition of Finland from Sweden in 1809. The boundaries of the Russian Empire now extended from their

---

★ Tsar Peter visited England in 1698. He lived at Deptford and studied shipbuilding techniques in the docks there.

† The name was changed to Petrograd in 1914, and to Leningrad in 1924.

most western possession in Poland (all of which, including Warsaw, came under the Russian throne in 1795) to the Pacific.

The expansion into the Caucasian region began with the capture of Astrakhan in 1556, when the southern part of the country was reopened after 300 years. Cossacks pushed into the Kuban and established fortifica-

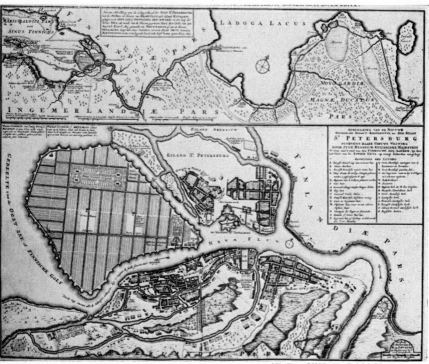

[K. Top. CXII. 69. British Museum.

FIG. 41.—Plan of St Petersburg, published by R. and I. Ottens (Amsterdam, 1745). The city was laid out to imperial standards. Streets were designed for processions and the squares made large enough to enable a regiment to march round. Domenico Trezzini, an Italian from Lugano, was the main architect of the city.

tions there, but it was not until the reign of Peter the Great that a concerted attack was made to the south. The Caspian shores, as far as Baku, were occupied in 1722–3, but the gain was shortlived for the frontier was later pushed back to the River Terek. A further advance during the latter part of the reign of Catherine II (1762–96)* reached the northern foothills, but it

* During the reign of Catherine II several English and Scottish officers were employed in the Russian Navy. Outstanding among these was Samuel Greig from Inverkeithing, Fife, who rose to the rank of Commander-in-Chief of the Russian fleet.

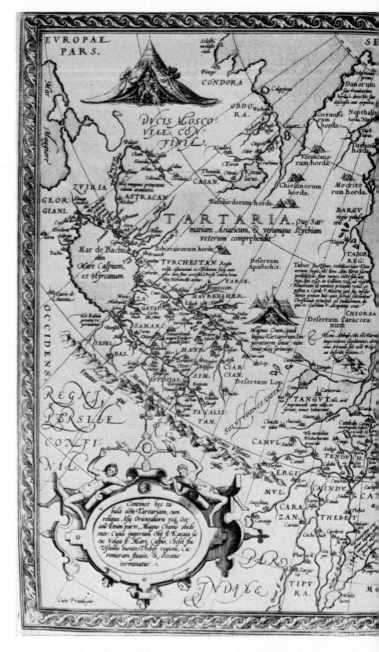

FIG. 42.—"Tartary, or the Empire of the Great Cham." A sixteenth-cen
1570). A translation of the Latin text v

taken from the *Theatrum orbis terrarum* of Abraham Ortelius (Antwerp
ompanies this map is given on pp. 56–7.

was not until the first year of the reign of Alexander I (1801–25) that the
Russians were able to cross the Caucasus to gain Tbilisi (Tiflis) and eastern
Georgia from the Persians. The conquest of Caucasus was not finally
completed until 1859 after the Turkish territory north of Batum had been
gained, and the resistance of mountain guerillas broken. It brought under
Russian control many peoples of ancient civilisation—Georgians, Armenians,
Azerbaydzhans—each distinct in language, religion and cultural traditions.
At the same time it brought Russia into contact with British influence in
Persia.

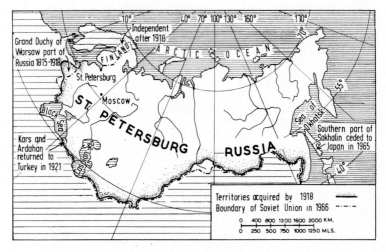

FIG. 43.—St Petersburg Russia.

Expansion into central Asia had as its primary purpose the subjugation of
the nomadic tribes that periodically foraged northwards into southwestern Siberia and the southeastern part of European Russia to harass the
Russian settlers. Cossack military pioneers from Orenburg and the southern
fringe of the Ural moved into the northern margins first, and later moved
south of the Kara-Kum and Kyzyl-Kum to overthrow the Mahommedan
centres of Tashkent (1865), Bukhara (1868), Samarkand (1868), Khiva
(1873) and Kokand (1876). Any plans that Russia might have had for
further expansion southwards had to take into account British interests in
Afghanistan. In 1907, with her prestige at a low level following the defeat
by Japan, Russia recognised these interests and has remained since within
the present boundary (Fig. 43).

SOVIET RUSSIA: 1918 TO PRESENT DAY

Russia entered World War I (1914–18) on the side of Britain and France against the Central Powers (Germany, Austro-Hungary and Turkey). She was unprepared, grossly mismanaged and lacking in good leadership. Furthermore, she was isolated from her allies except via the northern ports of Murmansk and Archangel (Arkhangelsk). Dissatisfaction among the

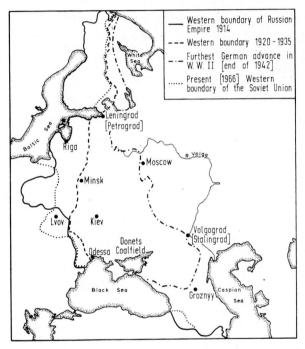

FIG. 44.—Changes in the Russian frontier since 1914.

Russian people was widespread and disorders commonplace. A revolution in March 1917* brought about the overthrow of Russian tsardom and the setting up of a provisional government composed of liberal-minded members of the middle class. A second revolution in October 1917 brought the Communists (Bolsheviks) to power, and the capital was moved back from St Petersburg to Moscow. The day after assuming power, the new Soviet Russian government proposed opening negotiations with Germany for a "just and democratic peace, without annexations or indemnities." It was

* Known historically as "The February Revolution" since the tsarist calendar was thirteen days behind the Gregorian calendar.

not until March 1918, however, that the final peace treaty was signed with
Germany at Brest-Litovsk. The price of surrender was high. Russia was
obliged to renounce control over Estonia, Latvia, Lithuania, Poland and a
major part of Belorussia. She was also obliged to cede to Turkey the districts
of Kars, Ardahan and Batumi. The independence of Finland and of the
Ukraine was recognised (Fig. 44). In consequence Russia lost about
386,000 sq. miles and some 46 million people.

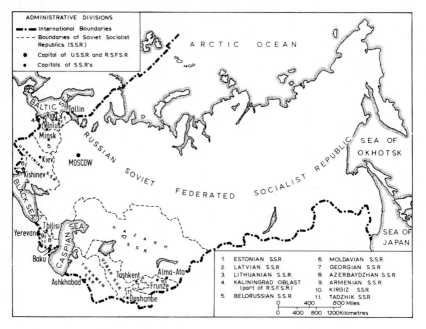

FIG. 45.—Soviet Union: administrative divisions.

Russia's allies, alarmed at her seeming defection and the unleashing of
revolutionary forces, attempted to rally anti-revolutionary ("White Russian"
as opposed to "Red Russian") opposition by landing troops and supplies at
Vladivostok, Arkhangelsk and in Persia. Their intervention won little
support, failed in its attempt to stamp out Bolshevism and the three years
of civil war that followed brought widespread destruction and untold
misery for the Russian people.

By the end of 1922 a new Russia emerged as the Union of Soviet Socialist
Republics with control over the bulk of the territories of the former
Imperial Russia. Each of the Soviet Socialist Republics is constitutionally
of equal status, although the Russian Soviet Federated Socialist Republic
(R.S.F.S.R.), extending from the Baltic to the Pacific, is by far the largest

in area and population. The R.S.F.S.R., together with the Ukrainian and the Belorussian Soviet Socialist Republics, were the founder members of the federated U.S.S.R. It was some years before the borderlands were organised into Soviet Socialist Republics on the basis of their national cultures and admitted as full members of the U.S.S.R. Turkmen and Uzbek were admitted in 1925, Tadzhik in 1929, Kirgiz, Kazakh, Georgia, Azerbaydzhan and Armenia in 1936 (Fig. 45).

FIG. 46.—Territorial readjustments in western Europe after World War II.

Within each of the Republics there are administrative units of lower status enjoying varying degrees of self government, viz. *Oblasts* (provinces), *Kray* (territories), Autonomous Soviet Socialist Republics (A.S.S.R.), Autonomous Oblasts (A.O.) and National *Okrugs* (districts, N.O.).

All the territories lost by Russia as a result of World War I, except for Finland and part of Poland, were regained by the U.S.S.R. at the end of World War II (Fig. 46). Other territories, which had never been part of Russia, were also acquired at this time, e.g. the Trans-Carpathian Ukraine (formerly the Ruthenian area of Czechoslovakia) and Oblast Kaliningrad (formerly the northern half of East Prussia). Pieces of territory near

Leningrad and in the far north were taken over from Finland. The Baltic States of Estonia, Latvia and Lithuania were reincorporated into the Soviet Union during the early part of the war. Bukovina and Bessarabia were taken from Rumania and made into an enlarged Moldavian S.S.R., with a portion added to western Ukraine. Eastern Poland became part of either the Ukraine or Belorussia. In the Far East, southern Sakhalin and the Kurile Islands were regained from Japan.

TABLE III

U.S.S.R.: Constituent Republics, 1965

Republic	Capital	Area (sq. miles)	Population (millions) Estimated January 1 1965
R.S.F.S.R.	Moscow	6,592,443	125·8
Ukraine	Kiev	232,618	45·1
Kazakhstan	Alma-Ata	1,063,242	11·9
Uzbekistan	Tashkent	157,336	10·1
Belorussia	Minsk	80,154	8·5
Georgia	Tbilisi	29,488	4·5
Azerbaydzhan	Baku	33,089	4·5
Moldavia	Kishinev	13,050	3·3
Lithuania	Vilnius	25,174	2·9
Kirgizia	Frunze	76,023	2·6
Tadzhikistan	Dushanbe	55,058	2·5
Latvia	Riga	24,903	2·2
Armenia	Yerevan	11,506	2·1
Turkmenistan	Ashkhabad	187,181	1·9
Estonia	Tallin	17,413	1·3
U.S.S.R.	Moscow	8,598,678	229·198*

* Estimated population at January 1, 1966, was 232 millions.

RUSSIAN SOCIETY

Early Russians lived in small communities (clans), and society was organised on a tribal basis, practising a primitive form of communism. Property ownership as it is generally understood was non-existent. With the growth of Russia as a nation-state under a bureaucratic and autocratic government, the peasants found themselves increasingly tied to the estates of the tsars and nobles under conditions which were far from idyllic. Peasants were not permitted to leave the estates of their landlords, nor to move to those of other landlords. Legal serfdom prevailed. Those serfs who escaped the authority of the landowners, the Church or the State, and lived as freebooters in the southern steppe-lands, were known as Cossacks. It was not until 1861, during the reign of Alexander II, that the serfs were finally emancipated and their position eased. Liberated peasants were organised in village communities governed by elected elders. These were the village communes or *mir*. The peasants in the villages cultivated their lands on a co-operative and communistic basis, all fields being held in common. Land, and fishing and grazing rights, were continually re-allocated according to the strength and needs of different families. Individual peasants thus lacked permanence or continuity of ownership of land that belonged to the village community. In 1913, of the 910 million acres classed as agricultural land, 380 million acres were grouped in large estates belonging to the royal family, the nobles, and the Church; the remaining 530 million acres were divided up into over 20 million peasant holdings averaging a little over 25 acres apiece. Among the peasant holdings were to be found those of a class of more substantial and wealthier peasants known as *kulaki*. These *kulaki* had taken advantage of new legislation introduced after the first Russian Revolution of 1905 which allowed peasants to leave the village community and consolidate their strips into independent farms. They developed their holdings as capitalist farms and employed their poorer neighbours for hire under conditions no less burdensome than those on the estates of the landowners.

The Revolution of 1917, which installed the Bolshevik government, proceeded to set up a socialist state of factory workers and agricultural peasants, based on Marxist–Leninist ideology. All land was declared national property and the big private estates of the tsars, the Church and the nobles were expropriated. Some expropriated land was allocated to peasants, later to demobilised soldiers and settlers from towns. On the industrial and commercial side, all the large industrial enterprises such as banks, means of transport and foreign trade, were nationalised. Unfortunately, there were too few people with the necessary technical and managerial skill to take over efficiently, and a period of painful adjustment to the new order followed. The country was beset by civil war, food requisitioning, food shortage, social tensions and a multitude of problems—all attended by immeasurable human suffering. It was not until 1928, after a compromise was reached between nationalised and private economy under the New Economic Policy (1921–8), that production in most branches of the economy was back to, or a little above, the 1913 level.

Since 1928 the economic life has been determined by Five-Year Plans which involve advance planning in all branches of the economic and cultural life of the country. Under the first Five-Year Plan, begun formally in 1928, stress was laid on the development of heavy industry, particularly in outlying areas rich in natural resources and inhabited by national minorities. The second Five-Year Plan (1933–7) was aimed at strengthening the defensive capacity of the Soviet Union, and about half of the total investment in new heavy industrial constructions was allocated to areas beyond the Ural. Some stress was given to increasing the output and improving the quality of consumer goods under this Plan, but targets were not achieved. The third Five-Year Plan, to run from 1938–42, was cut short in June 1941 when Germany attacked the U.S.S.R. Under the Plan, stress was to be laid on war industries. Industrial output had been increasing appreciably in the Ural, the Volga, Siberia and Central Asian areas, but following the German invasion the whole of the national economy was switched to the war effort. The Supreme Soviet adopted a fourth Five-Year Plan in 1946, a fifth in 1951 (containing measures to stimulate the development of agriculture, improve the output of consumer goods and expand internal trade), and a sixth in 1956 (demanding priority for further development of heavy industry and an increase in agricultural production). In consequence of changes made in planning methods (e.g. collective farms were given greater authority over planning their own output, and industrial establishments in various basic industries were turned over from Union to Republic control), the sixth Five-Year Plan was abandoned and a Seven-Year Plan for 1959–65 adopted. This Plan has now been completed. The target was an 80% increase in industrial output and a 70% increase in gross agricultural output. Special attention was to be devoted to the mechanisation of agriculture and easing the arduousness of industrial labour, to automation, to new technological processes and to housing. As regards rail transport, there were plans for increasing to 85% the use of diesel or electric traction; 79% of the total rail traffic was carried by electric and diesel stock in 1964.

STUDY QUESTIONS

1. "Since the very beginning of Russian history waterways have played an important part in the economic life of the country and in the Middle Ages they were of international importance for the whole of European trade" (S. P. Turin). Discuss this statement.

2. Examine the reasons why the early principalities of Moscow and Novgorod grew up within the forest belt.

3. Examine the factors which helped Russian exploration and settlement in what is now the Asiatic part of the U.S.S.R.

4. "The country was like a garden without a gate." Examine this end-of-seventeenth-century description of Russia.

5. Comment on the contribution of the Slavic groups to the territorial expansion of the Russian state.

6. Summarise the achievements of Chancellor and Willoughby in the search for a Northeast Passage from Britain to the Far East.

7. What in your opinion have been the most important factors influencing the position of the western frontier of the Soviet Union?

8. Distinguish between "Russia" and the "Soviet Union."

9. "The Soviet Union is really an 'empire' similar to the British Commonwealth." Critically examine this statement.

10. To what extent can the Soviet Five-Year Plans be looked upon as practical exercises in the planned utilisation of geographical resources?

11. Write short notes to explain: (*a*) Soviet Socialist Republic; (*b*) Oblast; (*c*) Kray; (*d*) Autonomous Soviet Socialist Republic; (*e*) Autonomous Oblast; (*f*) National Okrug.

Chapter VI

AGRICULTURE AND FORESTRY

AGRICULTURE

No more than 20% of the land area of the Soviet Union is in agricultural use. In the remainder, agriculture is severely restricted by a harsh physical environment. The agricultural heartland is broadly confined within a triangle, its apex near Novokuznetsk, and its two sides bounded by lines drawn therefrom to Leningrad and Odessa. Within this triangle are found the mixed forest soils in the north, followed southwards by the black earths and chestnut soils. The mixed forest soils extend as a wedge from European Russia to near Perm in the Ural, and beyond as a narrow belt as far as the Ob. In this area maritime (i.e. Atlantic) influences upon the climate are evident in the slightly increased precipitation. This land was originally forested with a mixture of deciduous and coniferous trees, but early inhabitants were able to maintain themselves by agriculture in the clearings. With increased settlement clearings were extended by cutting and burning. The somewhat longer frost-free period in this zone compared with the shorter one in the boreal forest (tayga) to the north, allowed deciduous trees to grow here. Their heavier leaf fall increased the supply of humus to the surface layer of the soil, and the consequent richer undergrowth, consisting mainly of perennial grasses, encouraged the rearing of farm animals. This mixed forest zone played an important part in the history of the country, for it was here that the early Slavs, fleeing from the Asiatic invaders of the steppes, found shelter (*see* Chapter V). Under the influence of a settled agricultural life the Slavs and Finno-Ugrians were welded into groups which later coalesced to form the first Russian state. All suitable land has long been cultivated and the hardier cereals grown. Flax and hemp have long provided fibres for industrial use, and the potato is a widely grown crop. Hay, alfalfa (lucerne) and other forage crops do well and support dairying and stock raising.

South of the mixed-forest soils the black earths (chernozem) tend to coincide with the so-called "tillable steppes." The higher humus content of the upper layers of the chernozems (3–6%), compared with that of the podzols to the north, accounts for the greater agricultural productivity reached in these lands. The steppes extend from the Ukraine into western Siberia and have produced grain for many centuries seemingly without any great loss of fertility. The main handicaps to their utilisation are largely climatic. Recurrent droughts give rise to serious crop failures. In summer the dry soils are particularly liable to wind erosion, and heavy rain showers give rise to gullying and the loss of precious topsoil. Large-scale mechanised agriculture tends to accentuate these difficulties. The diversification of crops, construction of tree belts for wind-breaks, and utilisation of the waters of the Volga, Don, Dnieper and Dniester for irrigation assist in counteracting the effects of these hazards.

Chestnut and brown soils extend from the Crimea Steppes across the Volga delta and through northern Kazakhstan to the extreme south of western Siberia. They are the result of extreme temperatures, low rainfall and high summer evaporation, and show tendencies towards salinity. Chestnut soils are very fertile when supplied with enough water, but their irrigation has to be carefully controlled. A rise in the water table is liable to produce alkalinity at, or near, the surface and leads to the formation of *solonchak* and *solonets* (*see* p. 41).

The agricultural heartland so defined has a cool continental semi-arid climate, somewhat similar to that of the spring wheat region of the Prairie provinces of Canada, or the Dakotas of the United States of America. In the north, mixed farming is the rule. Root crops, oats, rye and wheat are widely grown, together with flax on the better clay soils, and potatoes on the sandy soils. A great deal of woodland remains, but there are some good pasture lands. Market gardening (truck farming) and dairying, related to the market rather than to favourable conditions of climate and soil, are found around most towns.

Some 75–80% of the brown forest soils and the degraded chernozems to the south are cultivated. The bulk of the land is sown to cereals; winter wheat leads in the west, spring wheat in Siberia. Sugar beet is an important crop in the west and exceeds other crops in value per unit area. Much of the land is given over to pastures (in rotation with crops) and cattle are raised for meat and dairy produce. Pigs and poultry are additional enterprises.

On the steppe-lands to the south in the zone of the true black earths and chestnut soils, cereal cultivation (particularly winter wheat) is the main agricultural enterprise. Sunflowers and other industrial crops, dairying, beef, poultry and sheep raising are important additional activities. On the northwestern humid margins of the steppe-lands, as much as 60% of the land is arable. The proportion of land under the plough is far less in the drier east and south. Crop yields in the south, where the unreliable character of the meagre precipitation tends to make the harvest somewhat precarious, are lower than they are farther north. For this reason irrigation has been introduced in certain areas, particularly along the Dnieper and lower Don.

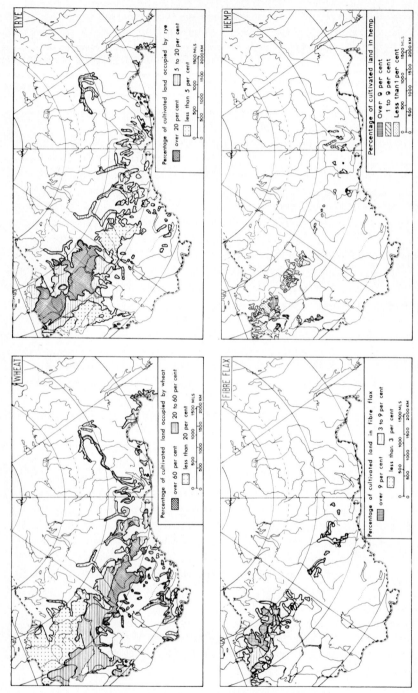

Figs. 47–50.—Soviet Union: distribution of wheat-, rye-, fibre flax-, and hemp-growing areas

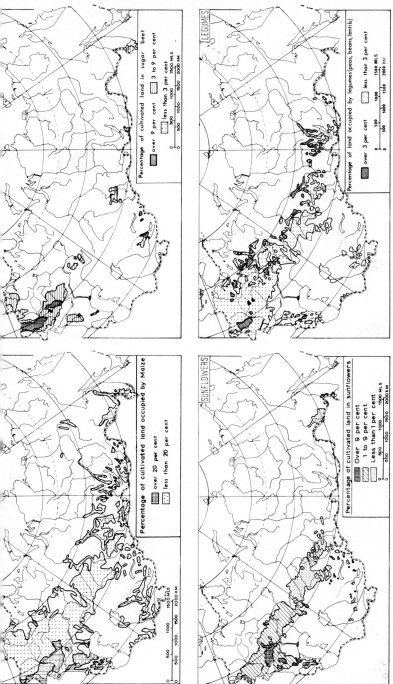

FIGS. 51–4.—Soviet Union: distribution of maize-, sugar beet-, sunflower-, and legume-growing areas.

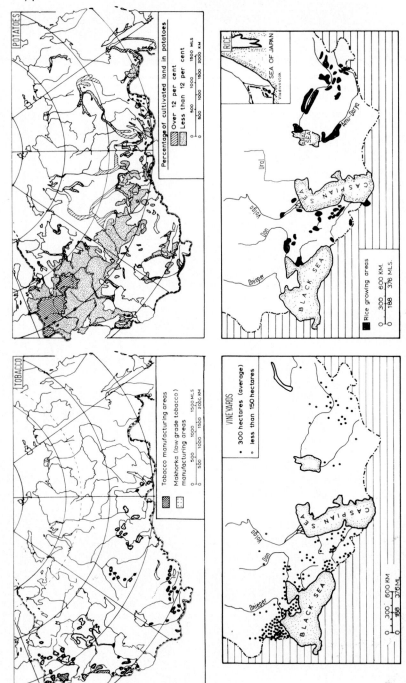

FIGS. 5-8.—Soviet Union: distribution of tobacco-growing and potato-growing areas; distribution of vineyards and of rice-growing areas.

The agricultural heartland tapers off in Siberia, where the growing season is shorter, precipitation is less and climatic conditions generally are more extreme. Here spring wheat constitutes the main crop, and dairying, raising of beef cattle and sheep are ancillary activities.

The areas devoted to the individual crops and to livestock are shown in Figs. 47–62.

The agricultural heartland is bordered on the north and northeast by immense expanses which are forest-covered, underlain by permanently frozen ground, or generally too cool for regular agriculture. The high latitudes virtually ensure a high proportion of boreal forest and tundra. In fact $5\frac{1}{2}$ million sq. miles, or some two-thirds of the U.S.S.R. are so covered.

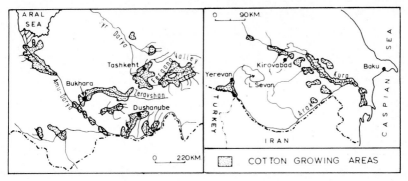

Fig. 59.—Soviet Union: distribution of cotton-growing areas.

Agricultural activities in the tundra regions are limited to reindeer herding, and, in the occasional clearings in the tayga, to cattle raising, and to growing potatoes, cabbages and some cereals. The middle Lena valley is a favoured area. Here, with chernozem-like soils, a short hot summer, and permafrost helping to conserve the limited rainfall, cattle are raised and some millets, oats and rye cultivated.

Any northward expansion of the agricultural frontier has to meet very unfavourable conditions. Summers are short, cloudy and cool although the unusually long days at that time permit increased photosynthesis in crops and vegetation (Fig. 63); the frost-free period is brief, little more than 160 days at Leningrad, 130 at Moscow and 95 days at Irkutsk (Fig. 22); and precipitation decreases sharply eastwards, away from the Baltic (Fig. 23). The podzols of the northern latitudes are deficient in soluble plant foods, low in colloids, poor in structure and are acidic. They require heavy manuring and liming if they are to sustain agriculture, but even where this is possible yields are so low that the cost of the treatment seems unjustified. Only the surface layers of the permafrost thaw during the short summer and the frozen subsoil impedes drainage and cultivation. There are vast acres

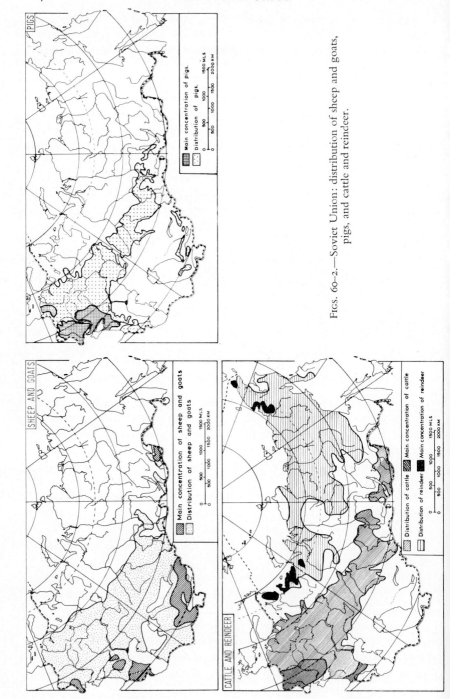

Figs. 60–2.—Soviet Union: distribution of sheep and goats, pigs, and cattle and reindeer.

of badly drained land near Leningrad and Moscow and huge expanses of bog in the Western Siberian Plain.

The thermal regime of the lands to the south and east of the agricultural heartland of the U.S.S.R. is favourable for agriculture, but here again expansion of agricultural land is restricted. Precipitation is slight and high rates of evaporation reduce its effectiveness. Because of the variability of the rainfall both in amount and in distribution, only occasional years have sufficient moisture for crops in such areas as the middle and lower Volga lands (Povolzhye), and complete crop failure is commonplace.

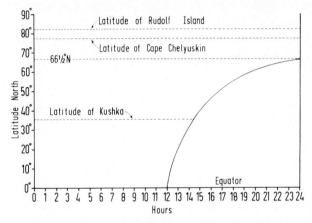

FIG. 63.—Length of day and night at various latitudes on June 21st and December 21st.

In the Aral–Caspian Basin precipitation is totally inadequate for crops and there are a million square miles of desert and semi-arid steppe. Lack of precipitation is now being compensated by artificial irrigation in large areas of Soviet Central Asia.

The dreaded *sukhovey*, the dry, hot desiccating southeast or southerly wind which blows in the steppe, can destroy within a single day a promising crop, the result of a year's adequate rainfall. Plants wilt under its influence because their roots are unable to supply sufficient moisture to compensate for the high transpiration rates resulting from the blasts of hot air and the accompanying low relative humidities.

The important crop areas outside the agricultural heartland are regions of intensive cultivation in the limited warm-temperate and sub-tropical parts of the country. In Trans-Carpathia and Moldavia conditions are suitable for the growing of vines. Moldavia, once an area of subsistence agriculture, now has one-third of all Soviet vineyards. The southern coastlands of Crimea and the lower slopes of the Great Caucasus are suitable for apples, pears, plums, peaches, apricots, figs, grapes and tobacco.

D

The Kolkhida and Lenkoran Lowlands of Trans-Caucasia are the only areas of the Soviet Union which combine high temperatures and heavy rainfall. The main crops here are tea, citrus fruits, tung oil, tobacco, vegetables and maize.

There are limited areas of highly productive farmland within the desert and semi-deserts of Soviet Central Asia. These are the irrigated lands which lie in the piedmont zone where mountains and desert meet, within mountain valleys (e.g. Fergana Valley) or in long narrow tongues along the main river courses through the desert. Specialisation tends to be in high-grade cotton. Alfalfa (lucerne), grown in rotation with cotton, provides the basis for livestock raising. Mulberry trees, fruit trees, vines, rice, sugar beet, hemp, tobacco and soft fruit are also grown. Crop specialisation in local areas is a common feature of irrigated lands.

The basic agricultural regions of the U.S.S.R. are shown in Fig. 64. They are based on particular crop and livestock combinations, as follows:

1. Hunting and reindeer herding.
2. Reindeer herding and scattered agriculture.
3. Dairying of the North.
4. Animal husbandry and arable agriculture of Yakutia.
5. Flax, potatoes and dairying.
6. Dairying and potatoes.
7. Dairying and pigs (with fodder crops).
8. Sugar beet, grains, dairying, beef and pigs.
9. Grains, potatoes, hemp, dairying, beef and pigs.
10. Grains, oil crops, dairying, and beef.
11. Grains, dairying, beef and sheep.
12. Dairying, beef and grains.
13. Grains, dairying and beef.
14. Sheep raising of the desert and semi-desert pastures (and some cattle raising in the semi-deserts).
15. Mountain livestock of the Caucasus, with dairying, beef and sheep.
16. Mountain livestock of Central Asia, with sheep, beef and dairying.
17. Mountain livestock of the Altai, with sheep, beef and dairying.
18. Fruit, vines and tobacco.
19. Sub-tropical perennial crops.
20. Cotton.
21. Southern intensive crops and grains, with beef, dairying and sheep.
22. Grains and animal husbandry of Southern Siberia and Far East.
23. Animal husbandry of Southern Siberia and the Far East.
24. Grains, rice, soya bean and animal husbandry of the Far East.
25. Suburban market gardening and dairying.
26. Agricultural areas separated by vast areas of forest and other non-agricultural land.

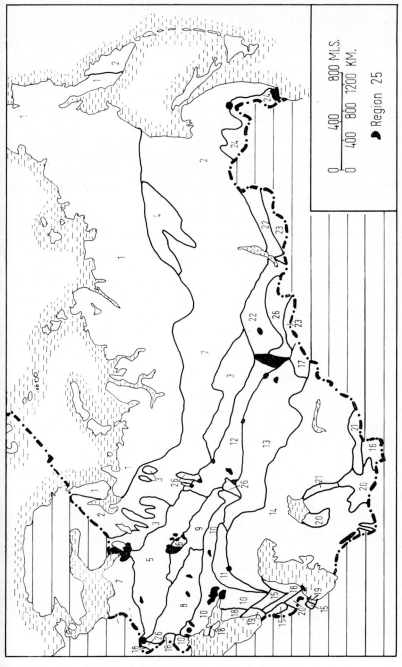

FIG. 64.—Soviet Union: agricultural regions. (ЭКОНОМИЧЕСКАЯ ГЕОГРАФИЯ Moscow, 1966.)
See text for explanation.

ORGANISATION OF AGRICULTURE

Before the first World War, Russia was a classic example of a country with an overpopulated countryside. Agriculture supported over 85% of the population, the bulk of whom were illiterate poverty-stricken peasants. It was organised at a low level of efficiency, and what export there was (e.g. wheat through Odessa) was based on underconsumption within the country itself rather than on an internal surplus. Some 42% of the total agricultural land belonged either to the tsar, to the Church or to the 30,000 or so country squires. Only 58% belonged to the peasants. Of this amount, 23% belonged to 3·4 million rich peasants (*kulaki*). The remainder belonged to 18·6 million poor (*biednyaki*) and medium-placed (*serednyaki*) peasants. There were about 11 million landless agricultural workers (*batraki*).

The Bolsheviks "socialised" all the land of the country and since 1929 agriculture has been organised on the basis of giant collective farms (*kolkhozy—kollektivnoe khozyaistvo*), and state farms (*sovkhozy—sovietskoe khozyaistvo*). Individual peasant holdings no longer exist, except for some personal plots of between half and one and a quarter acres. The idea of collectivisation was obnoxious to the peasants when it was first introduced under Stalin. It was opposed in many ways with great ingenuity, but the two forms of property, the collective farm (*kolkhoz*) and state farm (*sovkhoz*) are now firmly established and are used as instruments of Communist economic and social policy.

The *kolkhoz* is a co-operative undertaking set up by the peasants themselves. The chairman of the *kolkhoz* is theoretically elected by its members, but the local Communist organisation usually influences the election of the successful candidate. Except for the land, which is state-owned and loaned rent-free to the peasants for their perpetual use, the means of production on the *kolkhoz* and the outbuildings belong to its members rather than to society as a whole. Members have full charge of their property which is disposed of by the highest managerial meeting. This meeting decides annually how much of the farm's output is to be sold to the State, how much is to be distributed among its members, and how much is to be left for the productive and other needs of the collective farm itself. This latter share is known as the common, or indivisible fund. Payment is based on the socialist principle: "from each according to his abilities, to each according to his work." The economy of the collective farm is based on the output of the communal land which is the main source of property for the members of the collective. Because of the joint ownership, each *kolkhoznik* receives a share of the total income, in both money and kind, in proportion to the amount and quality of work performed. The actual value of the share depends upon two factors: the total income of the collective farm, and the extent to which the individual farmer participates in the common work. The basic measure for remuneration is the so-called "work-day unit."

Although obliged to participate in common work, each *kolkhoznik* is entitled to a small personal plot of land, the size of which is determined by decision of the general membership meeting. The private plot can be used to keep some productive livestock and grow subsidiary crops to provide extras for the family, or else for personal recreation. There were 37,600 *kolkhozy* in the Soviet Union in 1965 and their cultivated area was 114 million hectares. Some were essentially mixed farms, others specialised in particular crops, e.g. sugar beet in the Ukraine, cotton in Uzbek. Every effort is made to avoid the dangers of monoculture.

Sovkhozy (state farms) are organised on lines similar to those of manufacturing industry, and workers are paid in accordance with existing rules governing pay and skill. Such farms are used for experimental work and are aimed at raising agricultural standards. Some specialise in plant breeding, others in livestock breeding. Many have been located in areas not previously cultivated such as the virgin and long-fallow lands of Siberia and Kazakhstan (*see* p. 287). There were 10,075 *sovkhozy* in the Soviet Union in 1965 with a total cultivated area of 86·7 million hectares. In comparison with *kolkhozy*, they play a secondary role in Soviet agriculture.

FORESTRY

Timber is one of the great natural resources of the Soviet Union. *Lesa S.S.S.R.* (Moscow, 1961) credits the U.S.S.R. with 832 million hectares of timber-covered land. This is divided between 300 million hectares of inaccessible forest and 532 million hectares of accessible, economically exploitable forests, a distinction between total forest area and immediate exploitation which should be borne in mind.

On the basis of area, the Soviet Union may be justified in claiming more than a quarter (27%) of all the world's forests, rather less than one quarter (24%) of the total timber reserves, and over half (54%) of the coniferous reserves. The reserves of conifers represent the world's largest remaining source of softwoods.

The forests are unevenly distributed (Fig. 65). The European part of the country, with 80% of the population, has less than a quarter of all the Soviet forests. In the Asiatic part the situation is reversed. Yet, even in the European U.S.S.R. the densely populated and industrially developed central and southern regions either lack forests completely or have a great deficiency of them. It is the northern and eastern parts which have the surplus. Increasingly longer and uneconomic hauls of timber are becoming necessary in order to supply the deficient regions.

Most of the timber destined for the domestic market is carried by rail, for only the Volga River and its tributaries and to some extent the Dnieper River, which originate in wooded regions and flow southwards, offer cheap water transportation. Rivers which traverse the northern forested regions—the Onega, Northern Dvina, Mezen, Pechora, Ob, Yenisey and Lena—flow north to the Arctic. Timber is floated down them and as-

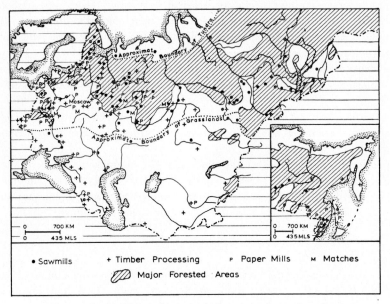

• Sawmills   + Timber Processing   P Paper Mills   M Matches
⬛ Major Forested Areas

FIG. 65.—Soviet Union: forestry, timber processing and products.

sembled at sawmill centres (e.g. Igarka) near the river mouths. From such centres, it is shipped out along the Northern Sea Route or towed upstream (southwards) to Krasnoyarsk, Novosibirsk, Barnaul and other industrial centres.

The main timber-producing regions are (Fig. 66):

1. *North and Northwest European U.S.S.R.*, where pine and spruce are the main species. At one time this region was geared to exports abroad via Arkhangelsk, Mezen, etc., but increasing amounts of timber are now despatched along the White Sea–Baltic canal to sawmills and pulp and paper mills around the shores of Lake Ladoga in Karelia.

2. *West European U.S.S.R.* with broad-leaved and pine forests in the Baltic Republics, oak and pine in Belorussia, and pine, fir, beech and oak in the Carpathians. The region has suffered from overcutting and war-devastation during World War II, but is favourably located for transport facilities and markets.

3. *The Central Industrial Region* has coniferous and mixed forests. It occupies an intermediate position between the mainly timber-producing parts (upper and central Volga) and the mainly timber-consuming parts (the oblasts of Moscow, Kaluga, Orel and Tula). The region enjoys good rail and water transport facilities and has a third of the wood-processing plant of the U.S.S.R.

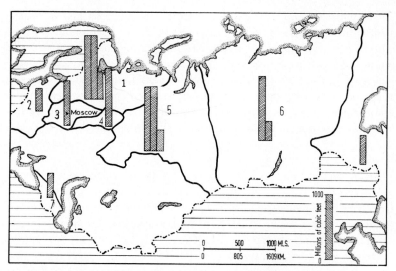

FIG. 66.—Soviet Union: regional cuttings of commercial lumber, 1960.

1. North and Northwest European U.S.S.R.; 2. West European U.S.S.R.; 3. Central Industrial Region; 4. Ural; 5. West Siberia; 6. Eastern Siberia and Soviet Far East; 7. Caucasus.

4. *The Ural*, where spruce and pine are the main species. Large quantities of timber are either floated down the Kama and other large tributaries via the Volga system to south European U.S.S.R., or else transported westwards by rail.

5. *West Siberia* has vast supplies of larch, fir and Siberian "cedar" (pine). The latter is of high quality and particularly suitable for veneers, furniture, packing boxes, pencils, structural timber and other industrial uses.

6. *Eastern Siberia and the Soviet Far East* have larch, pine, spruce, fir and broad-leaved forests, as well as birch, maple, aspen, basswood, walnut, oak, elm and ash. At present only conifers are cut for timber.

7. In the *Caucasus* forests are restricted to the foothills and slopes of the Great Caucasus. Oak, beech and fir are the main species with admixtures of ash, maple, hornbeam and birch. The forests are highly productive, but logging is difficult.

Prolonged overcutting, destruction during World War II, and the need to bring in timber from ever-increasing distances, have led to a progressive shift of sawmills, cellulose. and paper plants and other wood-using industries from the southern, western and central regions of European U.S.S.R. to northeast European U.S.S.R., to the Ural and to Siberia. Something like three-quarters of the total annual cut is now concentrated in these regions.

Not without good reason is wood called "the universal raw material." Besides fuel (nearly half of the timber cut in the Soviet Union is for fuel wood), it is used for wood pulp (producing cellophane, rayon, artificial wools and many plastics), paper, card and associated products, sawn planks, structural timber (joists, rafters), prefabricated houses, railway sleepers, telegraph poles, turpentine, resin and other wood chemicals, veneer, plywood, furniture, door panels, packing boxes and a host of other purposes. Trees also provide valuable shelter-belts, as in the Kamyshin–Volgograd and Belgorod–Don areas and along 1200 km (750 miles) of railway in the Povolzhye.

An attempt to counteract the "mining" of the forest was made under the sixth Five-Year Plan (1956–60) when 3·9 million hectares of replacement trees were planted. The Seven-Year Plan (1959–65) provided for afforestation over a further area of 262 million hectares and the planting of 11 million hectares of trees.

Despite vast resources, the Soviet Union is unable to satisfy more than 80% of her timber needs. Demand continues to increase, but serious transport and labour problems have yet to be resolved.

STUDY QUESTIONS

1. Write an essay on the "agricultural heartland" of the U.S.S.R.

2. Examine the areas outside the agricultural heartland which are important for agriculture.

3. Discuss the distribution and importance of any *one* of the following in the agriculture of the U.S.S.R.: (*a*) sugar beet; (*b*) sunflowers; (*c*) cereals; (*d*) potatoes; (*e*) fibre; (*f*) dairying; (*g*) beef cattle.

4. Describe the features of traditional Russian and contemporary Soviet agrarian systems.

5. Write short notes to explain the following: (*a*) Kolkhoz; (*b*) Sovkhoz; (*c*) Five-Year Plan; (*d*) Kombinat.

6. Describe the distribution of the softwood forests in the Soviet Union in their geographical context. Discuss their exploitation and use in affecting the economic geography of the Soviet Union.

Chapter VII

FUEL, POWER AND MINERAL RESOURCES

IT is in its mineral resources that the great natural endowments of the Soviet Union appear most conspicuous. Resources of coal, petroleum, natural gas and iron ore are large, and there are abundant reserves of most of the important non-ferrous minerals with the possible exceptions of nickel, tin and wolfram.

COAL

The country's natural endowment is probably richest in coal. The Soviet Union claims to have 58% of the world's reserves. The most productive coalfields are the Donets (Donbass), Kuznetsk (Kuzbass), Ural, Moscow, Karaganda and eastern Siberian. Total production (in million metric tons and including anthracite and lignite) was 513 in 1960; 517 in 1962; 532 in 1963; 578 in 1965, and the 1966 plan figure was 598. The intention is to raise the annual output to 1200 million tons by 1980.

The earliest field to be developed was the Donbass in the steppes of eastern Ukraine and the adjoining parts of the R.S.F.S.R. (Fig. 67). The northern limit of the coalfield is marked by the Northern Donets River, from which it derives its name, and through the centre of the field runs the Donets Ridge, rising to 1200 ft. The exploited coalfield covers nearly 9000 sq. miles, but proved deposits extend west along the middle Dnieper to Polesye. This "Greater Donbass" covers more than 23,000 sq. miles, but in the mid-1960s the western extension was exploited only locally and on a small scale.

The vast reserves of the Donbass include much coal of high quality. Of the proved reserves 32% are anthracite or sub-anthracite, 21% are coking coals, and 47% bituminous or sub-bituminous. The coal is of Carboniferous age, preserved in a deep trench within the underlying crystalline foundation of the Russian Platform. The seams vary in thickness but rarely exceed 5 ft; the average is just under 3 ft. Faulting is considerable along both the northern and southwestern margins. Production in the early 1960s averaged about 185 million tons, or approximately 36% of the national total. Planned production for 1965 was 258 million tons. Donbass coal is the basis for large-scale heavy industry in the Ukraine.

The second largest producer is the Kuznetsk Basin (Kuzbass), over 2000 miles east of the Donbass. The coal seams extend from near Anzhero-Sudzhensk to 40 miles south of the town of Kuznetsk and westwards to the Ob River, and cover an area of about 5000 sq. miles. The quality of the coal is high and there is a considerable proportion of good coking types. Seams vary in thickness from as little as $2\frac{1}{2}$ ft to as much as 100 ft; the commonest seam thickness is about 7 ft. Production in 1960 was 84 million tons, or approximately 17% of the national output. Planned production for 1965 was 118 million tons. Long hauls are involved in transporting

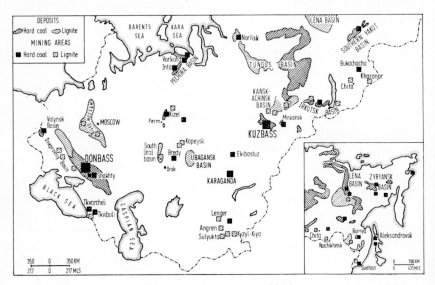

FIG. 67.—Soviet Union: coalfields.

Kuzbass coal to consumers in the Ural and Central Industrial Regions (*see* Fig. 71). Industrialisation within the Kuzbass itself began with the construction of a big metallurgical plant at Novokuznetsk (formerly Stalinsk) in 1932. Since then ever-increasing amounts of coal are being used locally, and the industry works on iron ores from deposits at Abakan brought in by the South-Siberian Railway.

Third in importance after the Donbass and Kuzbass are the Ural fields, which lie on both the eastern and western slopes of the Ural Mountains. The combined production of these fields was 62 million tons in 1960 (12% of national output). Planned production for 1965 was 67 million tons. The Kizel coals are the best, but they are not of coking quality. The other deposits in the Ural are low-quality coals or lignite, those within Oblast Chelyabinsk being the most important. The coals are suitable for generating electricity, but the lack of coal of coking quality is a serious handicap for the metallurgical plants of the Ural. These rely on Kuzbass coal which has to be transported over a thousand miles, and Karaganda coal brought 600 miles from Kazakhstan.

The lignite of the Moscow Basin has long provided fuel for electricity stations and for heating purposes. It is not of coking quality and cannot be used in metallurgical industries. In spite of its low grade, demand is such that the Moscow Basin now ranks fourth coal producer in the U.S.S.R. Production was 43 million tons in 1960. Scheduled production for 1965 was 41 million tons. This reduction in planned production follows the increased availability of piped natural gas from the Volga–Ural area, the Ukraine and Azerbaydzhan. Natural gas, a cheaper fuel than coal, is being increasingly put to more use.

The Karaganda field, within the arid steppe of Kazakhstan, has been described as the third coal base in the Union. Its coals are of coking quality, but because of their high ash content (over 20%) they have to be mixed with superior Kuzbass coals before they are used in the blast furnaces in the Ural and Middle Asia Regions. Production was 26 million tons in 1960. Planned production for 1965 was 57 million, an increase from 5 to 8% of the national production.

The Pechora Basin, in the northeast of European Russia, is a newly developed field of outstanding importance, where production commenced only in the 1930s, becoming significant after World War II when the railway from Kotlas to Vorkuta was constructed. In 1955 production was 14 million tons; in 1960, 16 million tons; planned production for 1965 was 22 million tons. Exploitation of this field, lying as it does within the Arctic Circle and subject to harsh climatic conditions, requires the overcoming of many technical problems, but the good quality of the coal recovered (it is all bituminous) makes the working of the field a justifiable and economic proposition. Most of the coal is exported to northwest European Russia; the remainder is conveyed up the Ob and Irtysh Rivers to Siberia.

Apart from the Kuzbass there are many scattered coalfields in Siberia and the Far East. They include the Cheremkhovo–Irkutsk fields and the big lignite deposits of the Kansk–Achinsk and the Minusinsk Basins, the main local sources of power for the development of industry. Some 60% of the country's coal reserves lie within the Tunguska and the Lena Basins of northern Siberia, a location so distant from the markets in southern Siberia or European Russia that transportation costs are prohibitive. It seems unlikely that they will be intensively utilised in the foreseeable future. Mining at Norilsk is undertaken for local copper and nickel smelting. In the Buryat A.S.S.R. and in Oblast Chita deposits of brown coal are used to power local industry and for locomotives on parts of the Trans-Siberian

Railway. Scattered coalfields in the Maritime Provinces and on Sakhalin Island contain good coals, but at present these are used only for local heating and power generation, and for shipping.

Supplies of coal in Middle Asia are limited and of poor quality. A number of small deposits occur in the Fergana Basin and the surrounding mountains. They are worked for local needs, but have to be supplemented by coal from the Kuzbass or Karaganda fields.

The mining of coal has mounted rapidly since World War II, production having been increased, since 1950, by practically 100% up to 1960, and by 150% up to 1965. Coal, however, constitutes a diminishing proportion of the total energy consumption as the use of cleaner and more convenient fuels (petroleum and natural gas) increases.

PETROLEUM

At the turn of the century the Baku field in the Caucasus was the largest single oil-producing area in the world and was the mainstay of Russian oil industry up to the Second World War. Though oil was first obtained from the naphtha area to the northwest of Groznyy, the real start of the Russian petroleum industry came in 1873 with the sinking of wells to the north of Baku. There are many wells at Baku, but most are on the Apsheron Peninsula to the north, or else in the waters of the Caspian. Other fields of moderate size occur at Groznyy and Maykop. Pipelines run from the fields of the Caucasus foothills to the Black Sea at Tuapse and Poti, and from Baku to Batumi (Fig. 68). Other pipelines link the fields with the Caspian at Makhachkala, whence oil is transported by tanker to the Volga.

In 1953 Caucasus production was surpassed by that of the so-called "Second Baku" fields. These lie between the middle Volga and the Ural and were first opened in 1929. There are five major groups of oilfields: (1) the Perm area, with Krasnokamsk as the largest centre; (2) along the Volga near Kuybyshev, with Syzran as its centre; (3) the Tuymazy area, with its new and rich field at Shapovo and new town of Oktyabrskiy; (4) Buguruslan in Oblast Orenburg; (5) the Belaya Valley around Ishimbay and Sterlitamak. Refining is carried out at a number of centres in each field, notably at Krasnokamsk, Ufa, Sterlitamak and Syzran, although refining capacity has been insufficient to cope with crude oil production. Much of the crude petroleum has to be transported to distant refineries at Groznyy and Makhachkala, where refinery capacity now outstrips the slackened pace of local petroleum production. Pipelines link the Volga–Ural fields with European Russia, and extend east to Irkutsk. The 3400-mile Comecon Line, known as the "Druzhba" or "Friendship" pipeline, links Kuybyshev on the Volga with east European countries (Poland, East Germany, Czecho-

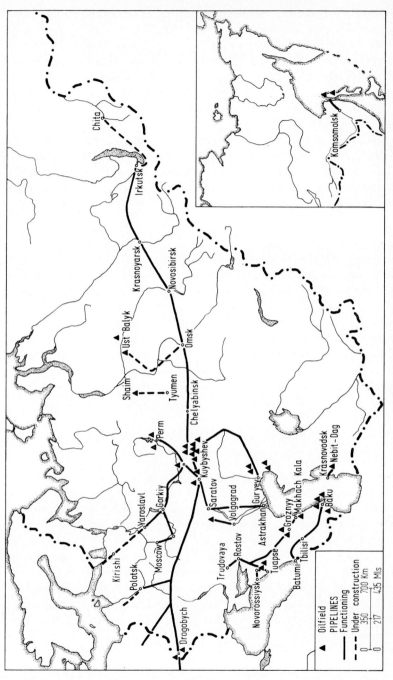

Fig. 68.—Soviet Union: oilfields and oil pipelines.

slovakia and Hungary), and there are extensions of this line to the Baltic ports of Klaypeda and Ventspils.

Minor oil-producing areas in western Ukraine (Brody), Turkmen (Nebit-Dag), Uzbekistan (Fergana), Kazakhstan (Emba) and Sakhalin Island maintain small, though constant, percentages of the country's total oil production.

In 1963 the Soviet Union was responsible for 16% of the world total petroleum output (206 million metric tons) and was the second major world producer after the United States of America. Of that amount well over 70% came from the "Second Baku" fields which, despite their inferior quality compared with the Caucasus oil, have a strategic location between the industrial regions of the Ukraine and the Ural. Soviet production of oil was 224 million metric tons in 1964, and 243 million metric tons in 1965.

NATURAL GAS

Closely related to petroleum is the natural gas industry. Gas from the oil wells was formerly allowed to burn off, but since 1955 it has been stored and distributed by a network of pipelines. The main sources of this primary fuel are at present in the North Caucasus (Stavropol, Krasnodar), Trans-Caucasia (Baku), Ukraine (Dashava and Shebelinka), in the Povolzhye (Saratov) and Soviet Central Asia (Bukhara and Fergana) (Fig. 69). The development of fields depends greatly on the construction of pipelines to the consuming areas. A massive increase both in the network of gas pipelines and the production of natural gas is planned. Production was 90 billion cu. m. in 1963 and the planned figure for 1965 was 128 billion cu. m.

ELECTRICITY

The bulk of the electricity produced in the Soviet Union comes from thermal stations which use cheap coal, natural gas or fuel oil (Fig. 70). No more than one-fifth comes from hydro-electricity generating stations. Most of the hydro-electricity stations are in Siberia and Soviet Central Asia where, though the hydro-electric potential is great, it is unlikely to be fully developed because of its remoteness from centres of population. Great rivers, such as the Dnieper (Kakhovka, Dneproges, Dneprodzerzhinsk, Kremenchug, Komev and Kiev—total capacity 3½ million kw) and the Volga (Kuybyshev and Volgograd, each with a capacity of 2½ million kw) in European Russia, and the Yenisey (Krasnoyarsk), Angara (Irkutsk, Bratsk), Ob (Novosibirsk) and Irtysh (Bukhtarma) in Siberia have been harnessed for hydro-electric purposes. The buttress dam at Bratsk on the Angara has created one of the world's largest reservoirs with a capacity of 170,000 million cu. m. This in turn provides energy for one of the world's

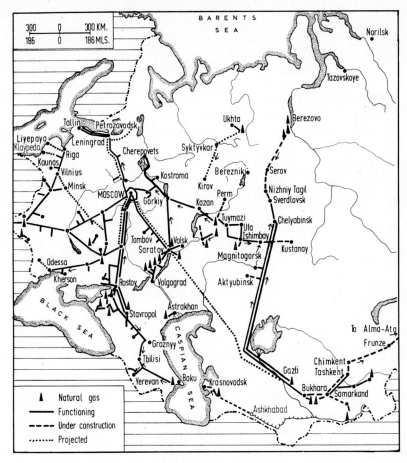

FIG. 69.—Soviet Union: natural gas fields and gas pipelines.

largest hydro-electricity stations with a capacity in excess of $4\frac{1}{2}$ million kw. A capacity of $4\frac{1}{2}$ million kw has been reported for the Irkutsk station and 6 million kw for that at Krasnoyarsk. Navigation, irrigation and recreational facilities are often important adjuncts of the electrical function. Soviet production of electricity was 459 billion kw-hours in 1964 and 507 billion kw-hours in 1965.

FERROUS METALS

In addition to her adequate resources of mineral fuels, the Soviet Union appears to be as fortunately endowed with iron ore. Soviet scientists claim that the country has 41% of the world's iron ore. Some of the largest

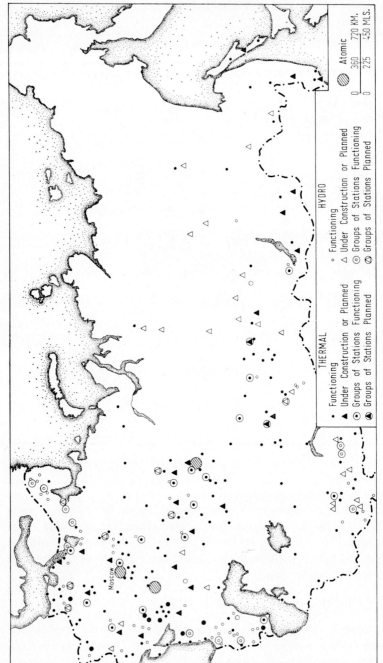

Fig. 70.—Soviet Union: electricity generating stations.

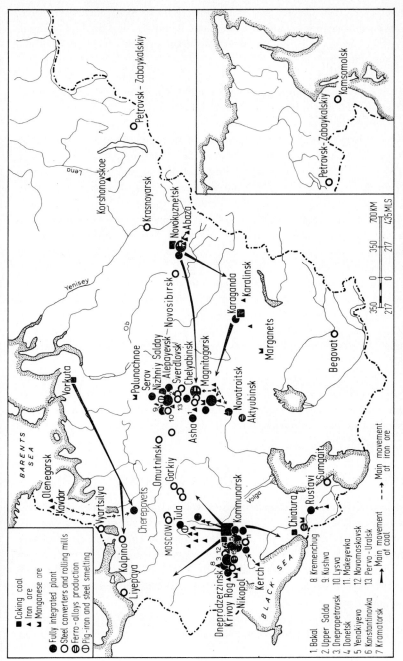

FIG. 71.—Soviet Union: distribution of ferrous metallurgy industry.

reserves of iron ore are in the Ukraine (Krivoy Rog), Crimea (Kerch), central European Russia (Kursk Magnetic Anomaly) and the Ural (Magnitogorsk, Tagil, Bakal) with other important deposits in Kazakhstan and Siberia (Fig. 71).

By far the largest production—about 60% of the total Soviet production of iron ore (146 million tons in 1964 and 153 million tons in 1965) comes from the deposits in European Russia, though only about 44% of the proved and probable reserves are located there. Some of the best ores are in Krivoy Rog (53–64% iron). Much of this is mined by open-cast methods, but increasing amounts are won from deep workings reached by shafts. The greater part of the iron-smelting industry of the country is supplied from this one field. The ore from the Kerch Peninsula is low in iron (37–40%) and high in phosphorus. The Kursk Magnetic Anomaly is largely magnetite quartzite (25–45% iron), but certain rich ores contain 53–57% iron. Production from Kursk is expected to increase now that improved large-scale shaft-mining techniques have been evolved to exploit these deep-seated reserves.

Production from the Ural amounts to about 35% of the national total. About half of the output was from near Magnitogorsk (metallic content 50–54%), the remainder from poorer-quality ores at Bakal and in the Kachkanar groups. Other iron-ore deposits of significance are in Kazakhstan (Turgay field and Atasuskiy field), in Siberia (Temir-Tau, Gornaya Shoriya, Bratsk) and in Trans-Caucasia (Dagestan).

Manganese and chromium are abundantly available minerals in the Soviet Union, which is the world's largest producer of both. There are adequate resources of nickel, titanium and vanadium, but not of cobalt, molybdenum and tungsten, three alloying metals used in the production of high-speed steels.

NON-FERROUS METALS

Deposits of ores of non-ferrous metals are large. According to Soviet sources, the U.S.S.R. now has more known reserves of copper than any other country in the world. Kazakhstan is richly endowed. Kounradskiy, Dzhezkazgan and a deposit near Leninogorsk being the chief producers. Copper deposits are also found in the Ural, Middle Asia, in the Kola Peninsula and in the lower Yenisey Valley. Estimated output in 1962 was 634,900 tons.

Lead and zinc are in good supply in the Kazakh Republic, in the northern Caucasus, and in the Maritime Provinces of the Far East. About a third of the nickel reserves are in the Monchegorsk–Pechenga region of the Kola Peninsula.

The Soviet Union appears to be well endowed with all other minerals. So little is known of the detail of the geology of vast areas of the country that there may well be large resources yet to be discovered. On present evidence it would seem that, in an emergency, there are very few naturally occurring minerals for which the Soviet Union would be dependent on outside sources.

STUDY QUESTIONS

1. On an outline map show the distribution of the major coal reserves of the U.S.S.R. Discuss their exploitation.

2. Analyse the location of mineral oil refining in the U.S.S.R.

3. Write a short essay on *either* hydro electricity in the Soviet Union *or* natural gas in the Soviet Union.

4. On an outline map show the distribution of the major iron-ore reserves of the U.S.S.R. Discuss their exploitation.

5. Give a geographical account of the production and utilisation of non-ferrous metals in the U.S.S.R.

6. On an outline map show the distribution of the major gold reserves of the U.S.S.R. Discuss their exploitation.

Chapter VIII

THE GEOGRAPHICAL DISTRIBUTION OF MANUFACTURING INDUSTRY

GROWTH OF MANUFACTURE

UNTIL the Communist Revolution in 1917, Moscow and St Petersburg (Petrograd, Leningrad) were the foci of economic life. Large-scale manufacturing industry, as distinct from handicrafts, was confined to European Russia and the Ukraine, while the outlying dependencies served simply as sources of raw materials and markets for manufactured goods. Fifty years later the map of manufacturing concentrations (Fig. 72) shows that industry

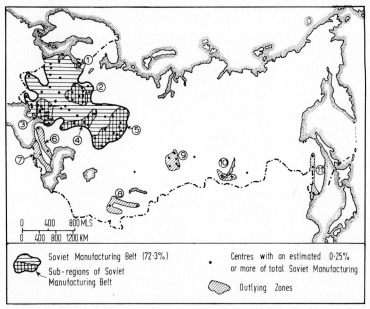

FIG. 72.—Soviet Union: areas of manufacturing concentrations. (All percentages are of total U.S.S.R. production.)

1. Leningrad sub-region, 4·9%; 2. Moscow–Gorkiy sub-region, 18·1%; 3. Eastern Ukraine sub-region, 14%; 4. Middle Volga sub-region, 5·0%; 5. Ural sub-region, 11·75%; 6. North Caucasus Zone, 2·1%; 7. Trans-Caucasus Zone, 4·0%; 8. Central Asia Zone, 2·65%; 9. Kuznetsk Basin–Novosibirsk Zone, 4·05%; 10. Lake Baykal Zone, 1·35%; 11. Far East Zone, 1·85%.

(Based on Lonsdale and Thompson, 1960.)

96

has expanded south into the Caucasus, southeast into Soviet Central Asia and east into Siberia. This trend, initiated by the second Five-Year Plan in 1932 and maintained by successive Five-Year Plans, was hastened by World War II and sustained by the Cold War.

MANUFACTURING CENTRES

The Soviet Union is now the world's second largest industrial country after the United States of America. The map of Soviet manufacturing industry (after Lonsdale and Thompson) shows a major belt with several sub-regions extending from the Baltic and the Ukraine eastwards to the Ural (Fig. 72). This belt contains 72·3% of the total U.S.S.R. production.

SUB-REGIONS

The sub-regions are as follows (the figures in brackets refer to their percentage contribution to the national production).

Moscow–Gorkiy (18·1%)

This sub-region is devoted especially to the fabrication of complex and precision machines and instruments. Machinery, machine tools, motors, ball-bearings, motor vehicles, railway equipment and aircraft are other metal products. These are followed by textiles and clothing, chemicals, foodstuffs and printing. The sub-region relies heavily on raw materials brought long distances from other parts of the country.

Eastern Ukraine (14%)

This includes the Donbass, Dnieper Bend, Krivoy Rog and Zhdanov districts. Production is related mainly to iron and steel, heavy chemicals and heavy engineering.

Ural (11·75%)

This region is characterised by the production of heavy iron and steel. There are also engineering, heavy chemicals and wood-using industries.

Middle Volga (5%)

Industry in this "Volga Bend" region is closely related to such available resources as petroleum, natural gas, timber, potash, common salt and electricity. Petro-chemical industries, such as synthetic rubber and man-made fibres, fertilisers and alcohol, together with paper-making, heavy chemicals and engineering, are major enterprises.

Leningrad (4·9%)

Manufacturing industries here are very similar to those in the Moscow region in that they rely largely on imported raw materials. The wide range of products includes machinery and transport equipment, chemicals, textiles, printing and consumer goods.

In addition to these sub-regions there are several large towns with agglomerations of industry, which lie within the main manufacturing belt but do not form part of any sub-region. Each is responsible for a 0·25%, or more, of total manufacture. The towns include Kiev, Lvov, Riga, Tallin, Kaunas, Vilnius, Kaliningrad, Vitebsk, Kursk, Tula, Voronezh, Tambov, Penza and Izhevsk.

OTHER ZONES

Six important manufacturing zones are located outside the main belt. In order of decreasing importance, with percentage contribution to national total in brackets, they are:

Kuznetsk Basin–Novosibirsk (4·05%) in southern central Siberia, specialising in heavy metallurgy, machinery, engineering and chemicals.

Trans-Caucasia (4%) where the major resource is petroleum, but where there are in addition supplies of coal, iron ore, ferro-alloy, and non-ferrous metals and non-metallic minerals. Oil refining, petro-chemicals, iron, steel, engineering, textile and food processing are the main enterprises.

Soviet Central Asia (2·65%) where chemicals, engineering and textiles are the main products of manufacturing industry.

North Caucasus (2·1%) where the industries have features similar to those of Trans-Caucasia in that petroleum is the major resource. Petro-chemicals, grain and animal products, and concrete are the main manufactured products.

The *Far East* (1·85%) zone comprises the Amur–Ussuri region with manufacturing confined largely to Vladivostok, Khabarovsk and Komsomolsk. Products include the by-products of wood, iron and steel, marine engineering and shipbuilding, oil refining and food (fish and crab) processing.

The *Lake Baykal* (1·35%) zone, embracing Cheremkhovo-Irkutsk, specialises in heavy chemicals and engineered articles.

Omsk, Karaganda, Krasnoyarsk and Chita each contribute 0·25%, or more, of total Soviet manufacturing, but are not within any of the above zones.

STUDY QUESTIONS

1. Illustrate some of the ways in which coal has influenced the location of Soviet industry.

2. Illustrate some of the ways in which hydro-electric power has influenced the location of Soviet industry.

3. Illustrate some of the ways in which oil has influenced the location of Soviet industry.

4. Show how the distribution of the steel industry in the Soviet Union is related to access to its raw materials, or to its markets, or to both.

5. To what extent is steel production a reliable index of industrial strength?

6. Examine the distribution of heavy engineering industries in the U.S.S.R.

7. Examine the distribution of light industries in the Soviet Union and assess their importance in the economy of the country.

Chapter IX

TRANSPORT

For the economic development and integration of an area so vast as the Soviet Union the importance of an adequate transport system is obvious. In the U.S.S.R., however, several physical phenomena—persistent ice on waterways during the winter, sandstorms, snowstorms (*purga*), permafrost and thaw (*rasputitsa*)—create major difficulties and make special precautions necessary.

By far the largest proportion of freight (83% by ton-miles) is moved by rail (in Britain, by contrast, 80% of the freight is moved by road). The railway is the basic and almost universal form of transport in the Soviet Union and is an all-purpose land carrier—it handles passengers (57% in 1964) and freight* throughout the year in every direction. The vast and generally flat terrain of much of the country has greatly facilitated the laying of the permanent way. Water transport on river and lake is important for certain kinds of bulk cargoes, but winter ice imposes an annual standstill. No more than 12% of the country's freight is moved by water. The rigours of the climate along the northern and eastern coasts reduce maritime transport to two to three months a year. Road transport, though speedy and flexible for short hauls, is relatively unimportant and accounts for little more than 4% of freight. Few motor roads exist, so that road haulage concentrates mainly on the carriage of goods within towns and cities. Inter-city road freight transport is developing, but certainly not to the same extent as, say, in the United States of America, where the excellence of the road system and the flexibility of the "truck" have combined to make road transportation a serious rival of the railway for many long-distance hauls. Pipelines for the transport of petroleum and natural gas, and transmission lines for electricity, are becoming increasingly important.

RAILWAYS

The railway system of the U.S.S.R., with 80,810 miles (129,300 km) of mainly broad-gauge (5 ft 0 in.) lines in 1965, is the second largest national network in the world. At the time of the Revolution in 1917 the route

---

* Coal and coke (25%); sand, stone, cement (20%); timber (6–7%); ores (6–7%); oil and petroleum products (6–7%); ferrous metals (5%); grain and flour (5%—seasonal July–October): see J. N. Westwood, *Soviet Railways Today*, Ian Allan Ltd., London (1963).

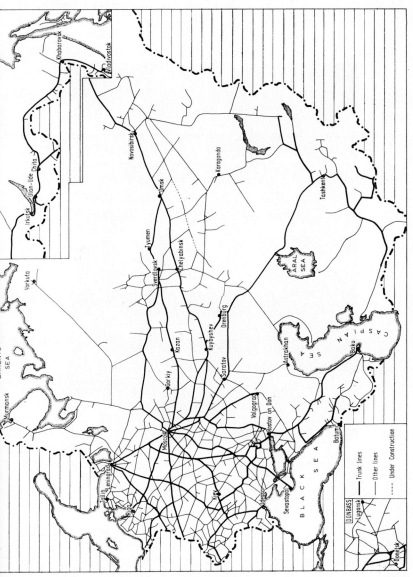

Fig. 73.—Soviet Union: railways.

length was 43,800 miles (70,000 km). Most of the lines are in the European part of the U.S.S.R. (Fig. 73). Eleven radiate from Moscow, the focus of the system. East of the Volga there is no real network, and most of the railways are isolated single-track trunk lines, with a small number of feeders, extending into Siberia, the Far East, Central Asia and Trans-

[*Fotokhronika Tass.*

Fig. 74.—Freight trains on the Trans-Siberian Railway near Irkutsk. The chief eastbound commodity on this section of the electrified line is oil, and the most important item moving westwards is coal.

Caucasia, reaching out to productive agricultural areas and mining areas, and providing inter-regional links.

Trunk lines such as those which now link Moscow and Leningrad, Moscow and Gorkiy, Leningrad and Warsaw, Moscow and Sevastopol, and Moscow and Rostov, were completed in the second half of the nineteenth century. Local and shorter branch lines within the Donbass and the Ukraine generally were also laid in the same period. The main emphasis at that time was on lines to bring coal and metals from the Donbass to the Moscow region, and grain to the Baltic and Black Sea ports. Eastward in the Ural, the line linking the metallurgical centres of Sverdlovsk and Perm was not joined to the Russian network until 1896. The longitudinal Sverdlovsk–Orsk line, skirting the eastern Ural, was laid much later.

The *Trans-Caspian* was the first railway to be built in what is now Asiatic U.S.S.R., running from Krasnovodsk to Samarkand (1888) and thence to Tashkent (1899). It was not linked with the main system until the *Trans-Aral* trunk line (the "cotton line") from Tashkent to Orenburg

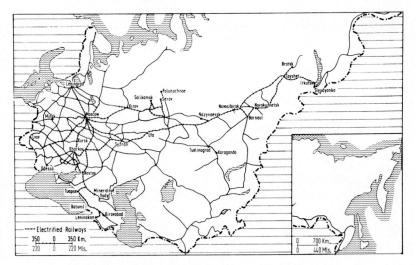

FIG. 75.—Soviet Union: electrified sections of the railways network.

(formerly Chkalov) was completed in 1905. The *Trans-Siberian* is a true transcontinental line which links the European and Asiatic parts of the Soviet Union. It is the longest railway in the world (Moscow to Vladivostok: 5787 miles) and probably the most important. Not completed until 1916, when the Chita–Khabarovsk section was opened to traffic, it has been instrumental in opening up the vast resources of Siberia and in spreading Great Russian influences eastward. The 3400-mile section Moscow–Irkutsk is now electrified (Figs. 74 and 75). The *South-Siberian* line runs from Magnitogorsk in the Ural to Prokopyevsk and Novokuznetsk in the Kuzbass via Tselinograd (formerly Akmolinsk) and Pavlodar, and helps to relieve the heavily worked section of the Trans-Siberian line between Chelyabinsk and Novosibirsk (Fig. 76). This line has been further extended via Abakan to Tayshet on the Trans-Siberian Railway. The *Turk–Sib* line, completed in 1930, links Tashkent and Alma-Ata with Novosibirsk on the

Trans-Siberian Railway. The lines from Leningrad to Murmansk, and from Kazan to Sverdlovsk, were among the first major railway constructions undertaken by the Soviets. Another line from Petropavlovsk to Karaganda and beyond to Lake Balkhash has proved to be of immeasurable importance, as has the Vorkuta–Kotlas–Konosha line which links the Pechora coalfield to the Moscow–Arkhangelsk trunk line.

Apart from the Konosha–Vorkuta, the Moscow–Arkhangelsk and the Leningrad–Murmansk lines, there is virtually no railway development north of 60° N. There is a light railway from Norilsk to Dudinka, otherwise the vast areas east of the Ural and north of the Trans-Siberian line are

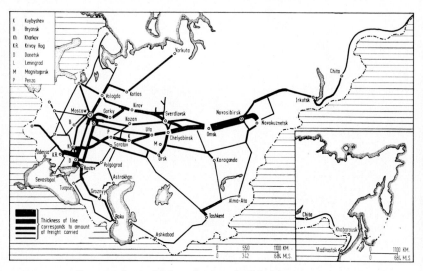

FIG. 76.—Soviet Union: density of rail freight movements.

without railways. The projected North-Siberian Railway, planned before World War II to pass around the north of Lake Baykal and to link Tayshet on the Trans-Siberian with Sovetskaya Gavan on the Pacific coast (Sea of Japan), has not been completed. A western section now extends from Tayshet through Bratsk to Ust Kut; in the east, Sovetskaya Gavan is linked with Komsomolsk and Khabarovsk.

While the general features of much of the country are an advantage in railway construction, many difficulties exist in railway working and maintenance. In areas of permafrost the instability of the ground, in association with the expansion of underground waters on freezing, and solifluction in surface layers on thawing, causes damage to railway lines, cuttings, embankments, bridges and other structures. Concrete and gravel are used to consolidate surfaces. In the same areas water for locomotives—being in short supply—has often to be obtained from deep wells that penetrate the permafrost. Bridging some of the wide rivers also requires specialised engineering, as does the laying of track in the swampy areas of western Siberia or the mountainous areas of eastern Siberia and the Caucasus. Shelter belts consisting of one or more lines of trees or bushes are planted as protection against drifting snow. In parts of central Asia there is the hazard of drifting sand, and where railway lines are in danger of being buried by this, grasses and bushes are planted alongside the lines in belts several hundred yards wide.

WATERWAYS

Despite the fact that the Soviet Union has the world's greatest system of waterways, its use is severely restricted by several factors, mostly related to climatic conditions. The winter cold causes a freeze-up of most rivers for long periods each year. At Kiev on the Dnieper, at Rostov on the Don and at Astrakhan on the Volga, the freeze-up and consequent closure last for three months. Northwards and eastwards the freeze-up lasts longer: more than six months on the Pechora and over seven months in the lower reaches of the Yenisey and Lena in Siberia.

Another drawback to using the river systems is the south–north direction of flow of the majority of rivers which, in Siberia especially, does not accord with the latitudinal movement of people and freight. Furthermore, rivers flowing northwards discharge into a sea which is frozen for nine months, or longer, every year. Spring floods caused by melt-water and decreased volume in the dry months are additional disadvantages. On the other hand, because of the flatness of much of the countryside, gradients are slight, currents slow and rates of discharge relatively small. The flatness of the terrain has also fostered the cutting of canals to link important rivers, e.g. the Volga–Baltic, Moscow–Volga and Volga–Don Canals. The Volga–Baltic (the reconstructed and modernised eighteenth-century Mariinsk Canal system) links the Rybinsk Reservoir with Beloye Lake and Lake Onega, where connections are made westwards to the Gulf of Finland, and northwards to the White Sea. The Moscow–Volga Canal links the Moscow and Volga Rivers—a distance of 80 miles. The Volga–Don Canal (63 miles), was opened in 1952, joining the lower Volga with the Don and thence with the Sea of Azov. Moscow has since then been an inland "port of five seas" (Fig. 77).

The Volga has been an artery of communication for centuries and is the key to the Soviet inland waterway system (Fig. 78). Aided by a series of dams, which impound the Volga waters for hundreds of miles upstream, navigation for steamers during the ice-free period is ensured upstream as far as Kalinin and downstream to Astrakhan. The Dnieper is the second most important river for water transport. The barrage (Dneproges) at Zaporozhye impounds a reservoir some 56 miles long which has drowned the cascade of rapids formerly interrupting navigation at this point. The Kakhovka Reservoir below the Zaporozhye Dam and completed in 1956,

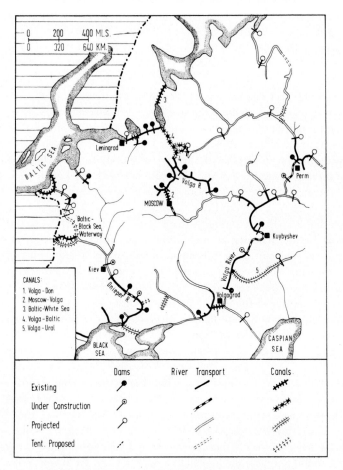

FIG. 77.—Navigable waterways in European U.S.S.R.

is even larger (124 miles) and facilitates navigation in the lower reaches of the river. Nevertheless, the final entry of the Dnieper into the Black Sea remains a long shallow estuary. The Northern Dvina is much used for the floating of timber.

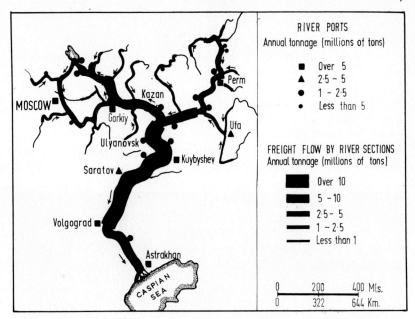

FIG. 78.—Volga River system: ports and freight density. (*Source:* Taaffe and Kingsbury, *Atlas of Soviet Affairs.*)

The great Siberian rivers, the Irtysh, the Ob and the Yenisey, would be navigable almost throughout their entire courses, but their development is restricted since the ice-free period is so short (Fig. 79).

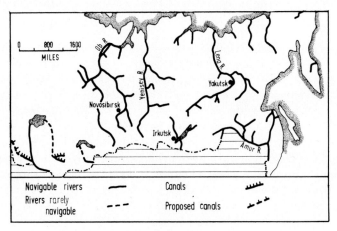

FIG. 79.—Navigable sections of rivers in Asiatic U.S.S.R.

SEAS

Like many of the rivers, the surrounding seas are affected adversely by ice. Ports on the Sea of Okhotsk are closed for over six and a half months. Farther south, Nikolayevsk-na-Amure and Sovetskaya Gavan on the Pacific are closed for considerable periods, although Vladivostok, frozen over for three to four months, is kept open by ice-breaker (*see* Fig. 220). Nearby Nakhodka remains ice-free for a longer period than Vladivostok. Most Arctic Ocean ports are closed for over eight months, some ice persisting throughout the year. Ports in the White Sea have ice for over five

[*Soviet Weekly*.

FIG. 80.—Convoy of ships on the Northern Sea Route, accompanied by ice-breakers and spotter helicopter.

months and are kept open only with difficulty. Murmansk on the Barents Sea benefits from the ameliorating influence of the North Atlantic Drift (*see* Fig. 128), and is open for navigation all the year round. The Northern Sea Route between Arkhangelsk and Vladivostok is kept open for two to three months during the summer only at great cost. Ice-breakers are essential, and aircraft are used for ice observation (Fig. 80). Ports along the route—Tiksi (Lena), Dikson (Yenisey), Salekhard (Ob), Naryan-Mar (Pechora) are located near the river mouths for the transhipment of cargoes between ocean-going vessels and river boats. The maintenance of this route must be for prestige or strategic reasons, for it handles less than 10% of the maritime traffic of the U.S.S.R.

The principal ports in the east Baltic and the Gulf of Finland are kept open by ice-breaker, but others are closed for periods of up to four months. Ice also occurs along the north coasts of the Black Sea and the Sea of Azov, but the main ports can be kept open by ice-breakers.

ROADS

Road haulage is responsible for no more than 4–5% of the ton-miles of freight in the U.S.S.R. The adverse effects of snow, frost, drifting sand, earthquake and flood make road maintenance and expansion of the system both costly and difficult and, though the road network is now ten times longer than before the Revolution, it still amounts only to 160,000 miles of hard-surface roads. The total length of "motor roads" was 220,000 miles in 1964.

The main trunk roads, such as those radiating from Moscow to Leningrad, Minsk, Simferopol, Tbilisi, Orsk, Arkhangelsk and Ulan-Ude, are generally asphalt or grit-covered (concrete suffers adversely from frost). Apart from these there are few paved roads away from the larger towns, and transport is often difficult in winter and early spring.

In the Great Caucasus, mountain roads such as the Georgian, Osetian and Sukhumi Military Highways are justly famous. In eastern Siberia, Yakutsk is connected by three roads to the coast at Magadan (Kolyma Highway), Okhotsk and Ayan; and to Never on the Trans-Siberian Railway (Aldan Highway). In the permafrost zones, current transport policy favours roads against railways, since they are cheaper both to build and to maintain. The lofty mountainous country of Tadzhikistan in Central Asia is served by the Pamir Highway linking Dushanbe (formerly Stalinabad) and Kashgar in Sinkiang, while the traditional caravan route through the Dzhungarian Pass is now followed by a road from Alma-Ata to Urumchi. The capital of the Mongolian People's Republic, Ulan Bator, is linked to the Trans-Siberian Railway at three points—at Novosibirsk by the Chuya Highway, at Achinsk by the Usa Highway and at Ulan-Ude. The route Ulan-Ude to Ulan Bator is followed by both road and rail and is continued into China (Peking).

The main function of road transport in the U.S.S.R. is to cater for local needs, primarily in retail trade, agriculture and construction, but also for deliveries to and from railway and river terminals. There is very little long-distance traffic.

AIR

The main purpose of air transport is the carriage of passengers (42 million in 1965) and mail, and the rapid delivery of high-value freight. Supplies for remote mining camps and Arctic stations are also carried by air. Regular services connect the principal towns within the Union as well as with those

E

of many European and Asiatic countries. Moscow is the centre from which
the majority of the services radiate (Fig. 81). Turbo-jet and turbo-prop
aircraft carry over two-thirds of all passenger air traffic in the U.S.S.R.

Auxiliary uses of aircraft, for which light piston-engined planes are used,
include surveying, ice reconnaissance, weather observation, crop spraying,
ambulance service and forest patrols.

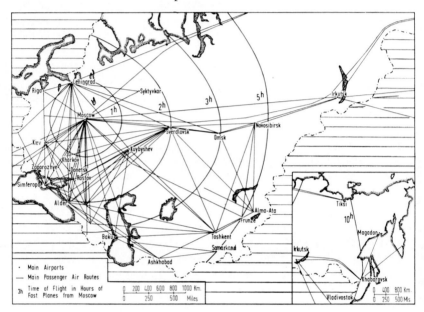

FIG. 81.—Soviet Union: main passenger air routes.

PIPELINES

Much Soviet oil and natural gas is conveyed by pipeline, and a comprehensive network of trunk pipelines is under construction. Pipeline
transport of oil and gas is cheaper than rail transport, since the flow is
continuous and there is no return of "empties." The decision taken in 1958
to concentrate henceforth upon oil and gas for the nation's energy needs
(oil and gas will supply two-thirds of the national energy needs by the
early 1970s) will inevitably lead to the laying down of more pipelines.
Pipelines have so far been laid from the Baku and Groznyy districts to the
Caspian and Black Sea ports, from the Caucasus to the Donbass, and from
the Volga–Ural region to the Moscow region and to Irkutsk in Siberia (see
Fig. 68). The two gas pipelines from the Bukhara district in Middle Asia
to Chelyabinsk and Sverdlovsk are of great importance in supplying fuel
to the Ural Region (Fig. 69).

1. How does geography influence communications within the Soviet Union, and between the Soviet Union and the rest of the world?

2. Describe the railway pattern of the Soviet Union. What natural difficulties does railway construction have to contend with in the U.S.S.R.?

3. Write short notes on: (*a*) the Trans-Siberian Railway; (*b*) Turk–Sib Railway; (*c*) Trans-Caspian Railway; (*d*) Central Siberian Railway; (*e*) South Siberian Railway.

4. Give an account of the principal internal waterway communications of the Soviet Union and show their relation to physical conditions and economic development.

5. Comment on the advantages and disadvantages of the development of a wide system of canals in the Soviet Union.

6. Assess the importance to the U.S.S.R. of the following canals: (*a*) Volga–Baltic; (*b*) Volga–Don; (*c*) Moscow–Volga.

7. Assess the importance of railways in the integration of economic and political life in Soviet Asia.

8. Assess the importance of aircraft in the integration of economic and political life in the U.S.S.R.

9. Assess the growing importance of oil and gas pipelines in the general transportation system of the U.S.S.R.

Chapter X

POPULATION AND SETTLEMENT

POPULATION

SOME 232 million people (1966 estimate) inhabit the 8·6 million sq. miles of Soviet territory. This population is the third largest of any world state after China and India. Nevertheless, the total is small in relation to the vast area over which it is spread. Very large areas are unoccupied, and the overall density is no more than 25 persons per square mile. This compares with an overall density of approximately 560 persons per square mile in the United Kingdom, 350 in India, 150 in China and 52 in the United States.

Despite the high degree of national autonomy within the country, the Soviet Union is ruled by Great Russians who make up about 52% of the total population. Together with the Ukrainians (18%), Belorussians (3·5%), and small numbers of Czechs, Slovaks, Bulgars and Rumanians, they make up more than three-quarters of the total population (Table IV). They are

TABLE IV

Most numerous nationalities in the U.S.S.R. at the 1959 Census
(in millions)

Russians . . . . . 114·1	Moldavians . . . . 2·2
Ukrainians . . . . 37·3	Germans. . . . . 1·6
Belorussians . . . . 7·0	Chuvashes . . . . 1·5
Uzbeks . . . . . 6·0	Latvians . . . . . 1·4
Tatars . . . . . 5·0	Tadzhiks. . . . . 1·4
Kazakhs . . . . . 3·6	Poles . . . . . 1·4
Azerbaydzhanians . . . 2·9	Mordovians . . . . 1·3
Armenians . . . 2·8	Turkmenians . . . . 1·0
Georgians . . . . 2·7	Bashkirs . . . . . 0·9
Lithuanians . . . . 2·3	Estonians. . . . . 0·9
Jews . . . . . 2·3	Kirgiz . . . . . 0·9

of Slav origin and are traditionally Orthodox in religion. They form a homogeneous body in much of the Russian Lowland and in Siberia, and predominate in most cities and the new farming areas of Soviet Central Asia and Kazakhstan.

After the Slavs the Turkic peoples are the most numerous and important. The Turkic group (Uzbeks, Turkmen, Kirgiz, Kazakhs, Tatars, etc.) is most continuous in the Central Asian Republics and forms about

11·5% of the total. In so far as there are any cultural links, other than those of history and language which bind the Turkic peoples, they are those of Islam. Except for the Yakuts in the Lena Valley, a northeastern spread of the Turkic element now intermingled considerably with people of Slavonic blood and Orthodox religion, the Turkic peoples are all Moslem. The so-called Caucasians comprise about 3% of the total population. They include the Japhetic peoples of Georgia and Armenia, and other groups living in the mountain valleys.

The Finno-Ugrian groups of northern Russia have been increasingly pushed outward by Slavonic settlement. Finns are to be found mainly in the north and west, and also in a belt of Finnish settlement in Asiatic Russia. Their territories lie north of the main Slavonic belt and extend to the Yenisey, but there has been much intermingling with the incoming Slav population. Apart from the Finns of Karelia and the Estonians along the Baltic, the Finno-Ugrian nationalities number no more than 2% of the total.

About 2·3 million Jews, 1·4 million Poles and 1·6 million Germans are scattered throughout various parts of the Soviet Union. The 1·4 million Latvians and 2·3 million Lithuanians belong to the so-called Slavonic–Baltic group of peoples. They are closely related to the Slavs, but display some features of other Baltic peoples. Germans, Latvians, Estonians and Finns are mainly Lutheran in religion; the Lithuanians and Poles are Roman Catholic.

In the southwestern part of the country, the Moldavians are of Rumanian stock. The Tadzhiks of Central Asia are related to the Iranians (Persians). Some Mongol and Palaeo-Asiatic groups exist in Siberia and in the Soviet Far East; the Buryats form the largest Mongol group.

The Slav peoples occupy the economic core of the country; other groups are distributed largely peripherally. A growing proportion of Great Russians and Ukrainians are finding their way to those parts of the Caucasus, Central Asia and south Siberia, where economic development is taking place. As time goes on, an ever-increasing proportion of the Soviet population will become mixed ethnographically; and since the process of mixing is irreversible, the future existence of non-Slav groups as meaningful cultural entities must inevitably be limited.

The bulk of the population of the Soviet Union is contained in an area bounded by Leningrad–Sverdlovsk–Magnitogorsk–Rostov–Baku–Batumi and Odessa (Fig. 82). Two-thirds of the population live south of 60° N and west of the Volga. Within this region there is considerable variation of density, ranging from moderate settlement (25–30 persons per square mile) to closer settlement (50–125 persons per square mile). In the black earth and wooded steppe country of the Ukraine, the countryside is closely settled,

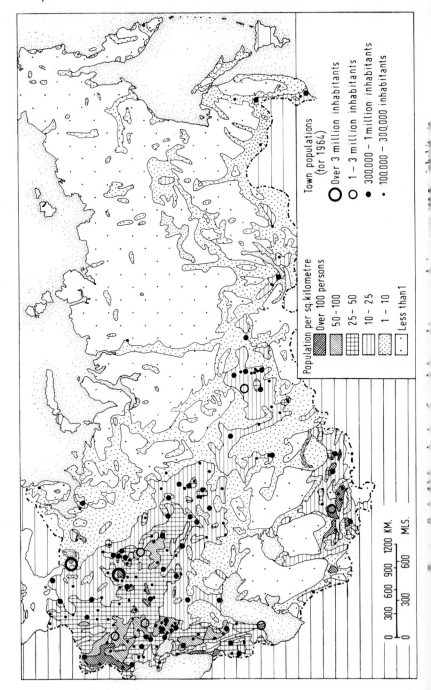

Town populations (for 1964)
○ Over 3 million inhabitants
○ 1 – 3 million inhabitants
● 300,000 – 1 million inhabitants
· 100,000 – 300,000 inhabitants

Population per sq.kilometre
Over 100 persons
50 – 100
25 – 50
10 – 25
1 – 10
Less than 1

0   300 600 900 1200 KM.
0   300   600 MLS.

and population densities are in excess of 125 persons per square mile. This is an area that has many towns.

Outside the main area of population, and amid the empty vastness of Siberia there are outliers of moderate settlement (in the Kuzbass, around Omsk and around Irkutsk), and in the irrigated areas of central Asia.

The distribution of the population reflects the distribution of extractive and manufacturing industry and of cultivated land. The latter reflects decreasing amounts of effective moisture to the south and east towards the Caspian and Aral desert areas, and short cool summers and a widening zone of permanently frozen subsoil, towards the north and east. In Siberia the zone of habitable land is reduced to a narrow corridor along the southern fringe by the Trans-Siberian Railway.

Where serfdom prevailed, between the sixteenth to nineteenth centuries, movement and colonisation were severely restricted. With the emancipation of the serfs in 1861 there was a great movement of people, many, indeed, leaving the country altogether. Between 1891 and 1900 over half a million Russian subjects (mainly Jews and Poles) emigrated to the United States of America, many to escape political oppression. Others emigrated within Russia and Siberia—those, for example, who moved out of the more thickly populated areas of west and southwest Ukraine to colonise the unsettled and sparsely populated areas to the south and southeast.

Movement of population involving regional redistribution appears to have been a continuous process both from area to area, and from countryside to town. Movement has been directed to the Ural, Siberia and the Far Eastern territories. Much of it was officially encouraged; no small amount was made under compulsion. Under the tsars, a policy of exile was used as a means of colonising the empty spaces of Siberia. Political convicts and ordinary criminals were sent to Siberia in much the same way as Britain sent convicts to her colonies during the eighteenth and nineteenth centuries. The Soviet administration has also sent political prisoners and criminals to Siberia. Peasants (*kulaki*) who resisted collectivisation in the early 1930s were deported to Siberia, as were intelligentsia from Polish, Estonian, Latvian, Lithuanian, Ukrainian and Rumanian territories annexed by the Soviet Union during and after World War II. Mass deportations were not uncommon, and forced labour was employed in road making, timber felling, peat cutting, building, mining, etc. Large camps for housing these workers (estimated at between 4 and 6 million) have existed in such areas as the Kazakh Desert and the extreme north (e.g. Vorkuta), where climatic conditions are considered to be too difficult for normal voluntary labour (Fig. 83).

Planned resettlement associated with industrial and agricultural developments has led to considerable movement of people into Soviet Asia. In the case of the Virgin and Idle Lands Project, which started in earnest in 1954, there was voluntary recruitment of new settlers. Grants were offered to cover the cost of removal, journeys were assisted, and wage and other incentives were provided to attract manpower to the new territories.

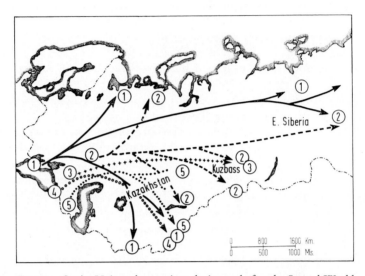

FIG. 83.—Soviet Union: deportations during and after the Second World War. Arrows indicate origins and reported areas of exile of the following nationalities:

1. Crimean Tatars; 2. Volga Germans; 3. Kalmyk; 4. Karachai–Balkas; 5. Checken-Ingush. (*Source:* Taaffe and Kingsbury, *Atlas of Soviet Affairs.*)

Members of the Communist Party were sometimes obliged to take up residence in new surroundings as a political duty.

The German occupation of much of the European part of the U.S.S.R. during World War II, and the consequent evacuation of industrial enterprises to the east; the acceleration of industrialisation in the U.S.S.R. as a whole; the need to increase the exploitation of the enormous coal reserves,

TABLE V

Population of the U.S.S.R., Siberia and the Far East at the 1939 and 1959 Censuses (in thousands)

	1939	1959	Increase	Percentage increase
U.S.S.R.	170,467	208,827	38,360	22·0
Siberia and the Far East . . .	16,576	21,738	5,162	31·2
West Siberia (excl. Oblast Kurgan) .	8,910	11,252	2,342	26·3
East Siberia (excl. A.O. Tuva) .	5,328	6,788	1,460	27·4
Far East (excl. Oblast Sakhalin) .	2,338	3,698	1,360	58·2

water power, ore deposits and timber resources of the east when those of the west could no longer meet industrial demands; the cultivation of the virgin lands and defence considerations—all have contributed to a recent easterly displacement of the population of the Soviet Union (Table V).

Much of the increase in Siberia and the east is due rather to the influx of Great Russians and Ukrainians than to natural increase of existing popula-

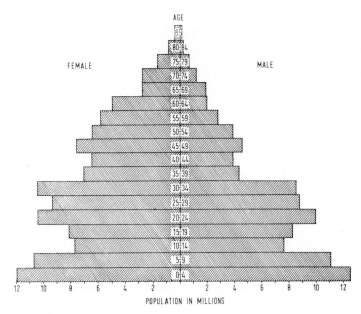

FIG. 84.—Soviet Union: Age/sex distribution of population, 1959. (Official census.)

tions. The population of Siberia and the Soviet Far East together is little more than 10% of the whole country, and large areas are still virtually uninhabited, a fact that should not go unnoticed in relation to China's large and crowded population.

Because of several boundary changes, early population statistics for Russia and the Soviet Union are not strictly comparable, but the following figures (related to the contemporary boundaries for the years shown) provide an indication of population growth:

1724— 20·0 million	1946—175·0 million
1897—126·9 million	1956—202·2 million
1921—106·0 million	1959—208·8 million
1939—170·6 million	1963—223·1 million
	1966 (est.)—232·0 million

Excessive losses during the last 50 years—estimated to be as much as 80 million people (one and a half times the population of the United Kingdom in 1961)—give a decided age and sex imbalance to the population of the Soviet Union (Fig. 84). Fatalities, and the consequent deficit of live births, resulting from two world wars, revolution, civil war, enforced collectivisation of agriculture, the dissolution of family life by voluntary or compulsory migration within the country, have all contributed to a large deficit of young people (particularly those between the ages of ten and nineteen years). There are also far more women than men, particularly in the middle-aged group. Up to 1965 the labour force of the country was sadly depleted and heavily strained by the deficit of young people. Inducements have been provided to increase the size of families. Mothers of five or more children are awarded medals—e.g. Motherhood Medal (Second Class) for five children, and Motherhood Medal (First Class) for six children. Women with ten children receive the order of Mother Heroine with a scroll from the Praesidium of the Supreme Soviet of the U.S.S.R. Years of normal fertility since World War II are now (in 1967) providing satisfactory recruitment for the future labour force. In 1959, women over 32 years outnumbered men by practically 21 million. A very high proportion of these women were widows. This female surplus accounts for the large number of women in the Soviet labour force employed in such industries as lumbering, construction, agriculture, and mining, in addition to the professions (e.g. medicine), and jobs (e.g. in offices) that are more usually associated with male workers.

The *United Nations Demographic Yearbook 1965* quotes the following statistics for the Soviet Union:

Birth rate (per 1000 of population)	Death rate (per 1000 of population)	Population increase (percentage)
31·4 (1940)	18·3 (1940)	
26·4 (1950–4)	7·2 (1961)	1·6 (1958–64)
25·3 (1955–9)	7·5 (1962)	
22·4 (1960–4)	7·2 (1963)	1·5 (1960–4)
18·4 (1965)	6·9 (1964)	
	7·3 (1965)	

The steep decline in the birth rate since 1960 is very marked and is considered to be the consequence of rising standards of living and increasing urbanisation. Unless the downward trend can be reversed, long-range economic development plans may be damaged by manpower shortages. The death rate is exceptionally low. This is not so much a reflection of the longevity of the population, or the improvement of health conditions, but rather of the fact that those who, under normal circumstances, would now be reaching the end of their expectation of life, have already died as a result of one or other of the several calamities that have beset their generation during the last half century. The average life span in the U.S.S.R., which was 32 years in 1897–8, and 44 years in the period 1926–9, had lengthened to 67 years by 1955–6. In 1962–3 the expectation of life at birth was 65 years for men and 73 years for women.

SETTLEMENT

URBAN DEVELOPMENT

In 1926 the country was predominantly agricultural, with rather less than 18% (one in five of the population) living in towns. There has been considerable industrial development since that time, with the result that the urban proportion of the population has risen from 33% in 1939 to over 50% in 1965 (*see* Table VI). One person in two in the Soviet Union now

TABLE VI

U.S.S.R. urban and rural populations, 1926 to 1965

	Population in millions			Percentage of total	
	Urban	Rural	Total	Urban	Rural
1926	26·3	120·7	147·0	18	82
1939 (pre-war boundaries) .	56·1	114·5	170·6	33	67
1939 (post-war boundaries) .	60·4	130·3	190·7	32	68
1959	100·0	108·8	208·8	48	52
1963 (January 1) . . .	115·1	108·0	223·1	52	48
1964 (January 1) . . .	118·6	107·7	226·3	52	48
1965 (January 1) . . .	121·5	107·5	229·2	53	47

Source: Statistical Yearbooks of the Central Statistical Administration (*Narodnoye Khozyaystvo S.S.R.*), Moscow, 1964 and 1965.

lives in a town. In the United Kingdom four persons out of five (80% in 1961), and three persons out of five in the United States (63% in 1960) live in towns. Part of the increase in urban dwellers in the U.S.S.R. may be accounted for by natural population growth in the towns themselves. For the most part (about 60%), however, it is due to movement from the countryside to the towns, where increasing and intensive industrialisation provides a powerful magnet for peasants whose labour has become redundant through the mechanisation of agriculture.

The process of urbanisation has been more rapid in mining and manufacturing regions than in predominantly agricultural areas; the most spectacular growth of cities has been in the coalfields and in the areas of heavy industry. In 1939, when the Soviet Union had 170·6 million inhabitants and 56 million urban dwellers, there were 90 towns with populations over 100,000. In 1959, when the population had risen to 208·8 million inhabitants, of whom 99·8 million were urban dwellers, there were

147 towns with over 100,000 inhabitants. Over half of the urban population lived in these largest towns. The most notable feature of the urban development in the U.S.S.R. in the 20-year period 1939–59, was the remarkable increase of population in towns in an extensive zone running from the middle Volga into Siberia as far east as Krasnoyarsk. In this zone, which includes the "Second Baku," the Ural, Kuzbass and Karaganda, almost all the towns increased their populations by 50% or more, but there were several centres, including a number of the larger ones, which doubled their populations. The latest available population figures (January 1, 1965, estimated) for the same towns show continued increases (Table VII).

TABLE VII

Population changes of cities in the zone middle Volga-central south Siberia, 1939–65 (thousands)

	1939	1959	1959 as percentage of 1939	1965 (January 1 —est.)	1965 as percentage of 1959
Kuybyshev . . .	390	806	206	948	118
Kazan	398	647	162	762	118
Saratov	372	581	156	683	117
Perm	306	629	205	764	122
Ufa	258	547	212	665	122
Nizhniy Tagil . .	160	339	212	370	109
Sverdlovsk . . .	423	779	184	919	118
Orsk	66	176	265	210	119
Chelyabinsk . .	273	689	252	805	117
Magnitogorsk . .	146	311	213	348	112
Petropavlovsk . .	92	131	143	158	121
Omsk	289	581	201	721	124
Novosibirsk . .	404	886	219	1029	116
Novokuznetsk . .	166	377	228	475	126
Barnaul . . .	148	305	216	382	125
Karaganda . . .	156	397	255	482	121
Krasnoyarsk . .	190	412	215	541	131

Isolated centres which lie outside this zone of greatest urban development and which grew rapidly in the 25-year period 1939–64 include (the percentage increase between 1939 and 1964 is shown in brackets) Minsk, the capital of Belorussia (300%), and Kishinev, the capital of Moldavia (250%). The capitals of most of the central Asian Republics also show remarkable increases: Dushanbe (385%) in Tadzhikistan, Samarkand (172%) in Uzbekistan, Frunze (390%) in Kirgizia and Alma-Ata (280%) in Kazakhstan. In the Far East, Komsomolsk (286%) and Khabarovsk (198%) on the Amur show the most significant percentage increases.

Of the eight "million-cities" in the U.S.S.R. on January 1, 1965 (three in 1959), Moscow (Moskva) with a population of 6,443,000 showed a 40%

increase over its 1939 total; Leningrad showed an increase of 8% to 3,641,000 (although there was a decrease of 3% between 1939 and 1959), and Kiev an increase of 60% to 1,348,000. Baku, Tashkent, Gorkiy, Kharkov and Novosibirsk attained a million inhabitants after the 1959 census (*see* Fig. 85). Their populations (January 1, 1965) and percentage population increases (1939–65), the latter in brackets, are as follows:

Baku	1,147,000	(48%)
Tashkent	1,106,000	(100%)
Gorkiy	1,085,000	(59%)
Kharkov	1,070,000	(28%)
Novosibirsk	1,029,000	(155%)

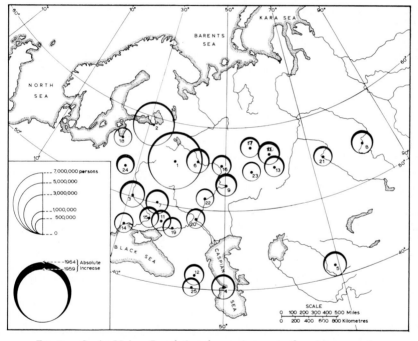

Fig. 85.—Soviet Union: Population changes in twenty-five cities, 1959–64.

1. Moscow; 2. Leningrad; 3. Kiev; 4. Baku; 5. Tashkent; 6. Gorkiy; 7. Kharkov; 8. Novosibirsk; 9. Kuybyshev; 10. Sverdlovsk; 11. Donetsk; 12. Tbilisi; 13. Chelyabinsk; 14. Odessa; 15. Dnepropetrovsk; 16. Kazan; 17. Perm; 18. Riga; 19. Rostov; 20. Volgograd; 21. Omsk; 22. Saratov; 23. Ufa; 24. Minsk; 25. Yerevan.

SETTLEMENT PATTERNS

The pattern of the old Russian towns reflected something of the long struggle against invaders. It was concentric, with streets radiating from the centre, the *Kreml* (Kremlin or fort), which was built originally of timber but later of stone. Another typical feature of Russian towns was the collection of low, wooden houses on the outskirts, of the same type as the peasant *izba* or hut. The smaller towns were distinguished by a single, broad main street, which in spring and autumn was a sea of mud (*rasputitsa*). A few of the cities in the west, notably Kiev, obtained the Magdeburg rights (a civic constitution) under Polish rule, and in some towns traces of western influence still remain. The influence of Byzantium was, however, far stronger throughout European Russia, and evidence of this may be found in all the older towns. Painted minarets, domed mosques and tombs in Samarkand and Bukhara belie the influence of Allah and his prophet Mahomet in Central Asia. In Trans-Caucasia, monasteries and churches with spires and bells, and cathedrals at Mtskhet and Echmiadzin bear witness to Christianity. For all these subtle regional influences, every Soviet town and city from the Baltic to the Pacific, and from Central Asia to the suburbs of Leningrad, now bears the stamp of uniformity of pattern in the shape of stiff, regimented blocks of flats. The only relief is provided by some public buildings, which have been built with an abundance of Greek columns, gables and apexes, according to the Soviet idea of classical design.

STUDY QUESTIONS

1. Examine the ethnic structure of the population of the U.S.S.R.

2. Describe and account for the distribution of the Slav element in the population of the U.S.S.R.

3. Describe and account for the distribution of the Turkic element in the population of the U.S.S.R.

4. Examine the major changes which have taken place in the distribution of population in the U.S.S.R. during the last 50 years.

5. Comment on the distribution of urban and rural populations in the Soviet Union.

6. Examine the progress of urbanisation in the Soviet Union during the last 30 years.

7. Discuss the distribution of cities with over one million inhabitants within the Soviet Union.

PART TWO

REGIONAL GEOGRAPHY

Chapter XI

REGIONAL DIVISIONS OF THE SOVIET UNION

> I love my country, but with a strange love,
> My reason will not conquer it!
> But I love—I know not why—
> The cold silence of its steppes,
> The swaying of its boundless forests,
> Its rivers which, in flood, are like the seas.
>
> M. Yu. Lermontov, in My Country.

NATURAL, POLITICAL AND ECONOMIC DIVISIONS

CONTRASTS within the Soviet Union are legion. There are mountains and plains, tundras and forests, swamps and deserts, steppes and oases. One finds such extremes as Mount Communism in Tadzhikistan, 24,600 ft high and the Caspian Sea with its shores 400 ft below sea-level, the cool, humid climate of the low rolling country around Moscow, the sub-tropical environment of Baku, the true desert of Turkmenistan, the monsoon-like conditions of the territories in the Far East, the extreme cold of northeast Siberia, and the "cold pole" near Verkhoyansk and Oymyakon. Tropical rain forest is the only major vegetation zone not found within the boundaries of the Soviet Union.

Russian geographers, following L. S. Berg, distinguish ten main natural regions: tundra, tayga, mixed forest, forest steppe, steppe, semi-desert, desert, sub-tropical areas, mountainous areas and broad-leaved forest. Such divisions are sometimes used for regional description within the framework of each of the main, traditional divisions of the former Russian Empire, viz. Russia, Siberia, Far East, Central Asia and Caucasia. Since these traditional divisions are obsolete and contrary to the spirit of Soviet policy, it would be illogical to perpetuate them.

The component states of the Soviet federation are based on the Marxist national-territory principle. Such political recognition of nationality groups tends to stabilise internal boundaries, while economic determination of the boundaries in such a rapidly developing country calls for almost constant change. Yet the political divisions in the European part of the U.S.S.R. appear much the same today as they did when they were first formed by the government of Catherine the Great in the latter part of the eighteenth century.

The present fifteen Soviet Socialist Republics ("Union Republics") may be classified into three groups, representing three significant elements in Russian history.

1. The Russian Soviet Federated Socialist Republic (R.S.F.S.R.), with about three-quarters of the territory of the country and about 125 million people, equates broadly with the Muscovy core of the Russian states and the Muscovite Empire.

2. The Soviet Socialist Republics of Georgia, Azerbaydzhan, Armenia (Trans-Caucasia) and of Turkmenistan, Uzbekistan, Tadzhikstan, Kirgizia and Kazakhstan (Middle Asia) constitute a southern group which represents the southern expansion of Russia into the steppe and desert lands. This movement began in the seventeenth century with the conquest of nomadic peoples and involved the Russians in a new way of life.

3. The Ukraine and Belorussian Soviet Socialist Republics, the new Republics of the Baltic (Estonia, Lithuania and Latvia) and Moldavia constitute a western group along the European frontier. This group represents the westward orientation of Russia which began with Peter the Great and which continued after World War II with the advance of the frontier westward from Leningrad and into Finland, the material westward shift of the country of Poland to the Oder–Neisse line, and the recovery of the Baltic States and East Prussia early in the War.

Cutting across administrative divisions are the systems of economic regions which involve the grouping of political regions. Between the 1920s and 1957, economic planning and production were based on fifteen economic regions. In June 1957, 105 new economic regions were created as "the further perfection of the organisation of administration in industry and building" (*Pravda*, April–June 1957). The new units, called "Economic Administrative Regions of the U.S.S.R.," corresponded generally to political regions and bore little relation to economic phenomena. The traditional *oblast* was held inviolate and each was included in its entirety in one or another region. Early in 1961 details of yet another scheme were released under which the Soviet Union, with the exception of Belorussia and Moldavia, was divided into seventeen economic regions.

CONCLUSION

To understand the complexities of the geography of the Soviet Union, it is necessary to consider it in regions; yet ideas of man–land relationships, or syntheses of the physical, historical and social geography of areas, normally adopted by western geographers for purposes of regionalisation, cannot readily be applied since the pattern of human geography in the U.S.S.R. is, to a high degree, a reflection of the prevailing planned economic activity. In this book, therefore, the 1961 economic regions have been adopted as the framework for the examination of regional differences. However, because

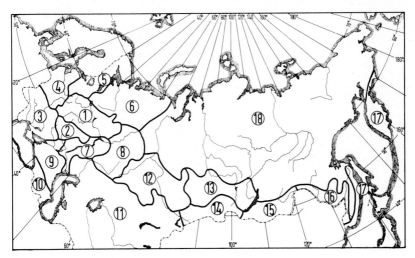

Fig. 86.—Soviet Union: regional divisions.

1. Central Industrial Region
2. Central Chernozem Region
3. Ukraine and Moldavia
4. West Region
5. Northwest Region
6. North Region
7. Middle and Lower Volga–Lower Don Region
8. Ural Region
9. North Caucasus Region
10. Trans-Caucasus Region
11. Middle Asia
12. Southwest Siberia
13. Central South Siberia
14. Southern Borderland
15. Trans-Baykalya
16. Amur Region
17. Pacific Region
18. North Siberia

these regions sometimes involve the association of widely dissimilar economic districts (in keeping with the peculiar Soviet insistence on, and understanding of, "complex" and "specialised" economies),★ certain modifications suggested by Taskin have been adopted for some Asian parts of the U.S.S.R. (Fig. 86).

★ The term "complex" implies units using the same materials, related industries, those which most profitably combine with each other, etc. Coal and chemical industries; coal, metallurgical and machine-building industries; sugar-beet growing and sugar factories; fodder grasses and dairy farming; large populated areas and market gardening, etc., would come into this category. Coal mining and cotton growing; non-ferrous metallurgy and the paper industry, machine building and the fishing industry would not be considered as economic complexes. "Specialised" in this case

1. Indicate the methods which you would use to establish a regional subdivision of the Soviet Union and justify your result.

2. Examine the geographical basis of the present administrative divisions of the U.S.S.R.

3. Examine the geographical basis of the economic planning regions of the U.S.S.R.

4. The limits of Europe and Asia defined in textbooks and by various authorities are arbitrary and different. Examine the practical difficulties involved in defining the limits of Europe and Asia within the U.S.S.R. for study purposes.

5. "Mountains divide, rivers unite." Discuss and illustrate this statement in the context of the Soviet Union.

---

must be understood not as a single branch of the economy but as a number of inter-related branches of the economy (i.e. complex). Complexity is related to the fact that in each economic region it is considered essential to have heavy industrial undertakings as the leading branch of the national economy. This cult of heavy industry does not admit of the possibility of the existence of an economic region based on say forestry, fishing or hunting—so typical of the northern areas of the U.S.S.R. For further discussion of these aspects see J. P. Cole and F. C. German: *A Geography of the U.S.S.R. The Background to a planned Economy*, London, 1961, pp. 19–37.

Chapter XII

CENTRAL INDUSTRIAL REGION

THIS region, transitional with respect to climate, soils, drainage, vegetation, and agriculture, has as its core the metropolis Moscow—the political, administrative, economic and cultural centre of the Soviet Union—together with major concentrations of specialised manufacturing industries of All-Union status. It occupies an area approximately three times that of the United Kingdom, and extends to Rybinsk Reservoir in the north, beyond Smolensk in the west, to the southern boundaries of the oblasts of Bryansk, Tula and Ryazan in the south, to the Volga near

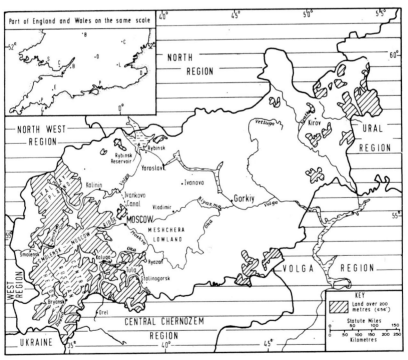

FIG. 87.—Central Industrial Region.

Kazan in the east and to the eastern boundary of Oblast Kirov in the north-east (Fig. 87).

Area . . . 280,300 sq. miles
Population . . (1959) 32,994,000

Administrative unit	Area sq. miles	Population in thousands 1959	Density persons per sq. mile	Percentage urban
Oblast Kalinin	32,600	1,802	55	44
Oblast Smolensk . . .	19,300	1,140	59	32
Oblast Kaluga	11,500	936	81	37
Oblast Bryansk . . .	13,500	1,547	114	35
Oblast Tula	9,900	1,912	192	61
Oblast Moscow . . .	18,100	10,938	604	78
Oblast Yaroslavl . . .	14,000	1,395	98	58
Oblast Vladimir . . .	11,200	1,402	124	57
Oblast Ryazan	15,300	1,444	93	30
Oblast Gorkiy	28,700	3,590	127	52
Oblast Ivanovo . . .	9,300	1,306	140	66
Oblast Kostroma . . .	23,300	919	39	39
Oblast Kirov	47,400	1,919	41	37
Mariyskaya A.S.S.R.. . .	9,000	647	73	28
Chuvashskaya A.S.S.R. . .	7,100	1,098	156	24

Towns with over 150,000 inhabitants in 1964

	Population in thousands		Percentage increase
	1959	1964	1959–64
Moscow . . .	6,040	6,443	6·8
Gorkiy	942	1,085	15·1
Yaroslavl . . .	407	478	17·5
Ivanovo . . .	335	389	16·1
Tula	316	366	16·0
Kalinin . . .	261	306	17·1
Kirov	252	296	17·5
Ryazan . . .	214	287	34·1
Bryansk . . .	207	267	29·0
Rybinsk . . .	182	208	14·4
Kostroma . . .	172	202	17·5
Vladimir . . .	154	196	27·3
Smolensk . . .	147	183	24·6
Kaluga . . .	134	169	26·0

PHYSICAL ASPECTS

RELIEF

Although the region occupies part of Russian Lowland (the so-called Great Russian or East European Plain), relief tends to be varied, with general elevations between 500 and 550 ft, and occasional parts over 1000 ft; the term "plain" is therefore somewhat inappropriate. Rather is the region one of monotonously rolling lowland. It rests on a relatively stable geological foundation of Pre-Cambrian crystalline rocks—the Russian Platform (p. 14).

The region bears the evidence of Quaternary glaciation in fluvio-glacial drifts, drumlins and erratic boulders. Morainic hills, such as the Smolensk–Moscow Ridge, are interspersed with depressions occupied by lakes. Peat bogs and marshes are commonplace, and the sources and upper reaches of streams tend to be diffuse. The line of terminal moraines extending from Lithuania and Belorussia (Belorusskaya Gryada) and terminating in the Valday Hills (maximum height 1053 ft) in the northwest of the region constitutes the main water divide between drainage to north and south.

The more southerly parts of the region contain immense stretches of sand, which are succeeded southwards by loess and weathered chernozem. The latter are better drained and drier than the soils to the north. Streams tend to have clearly marked sources, while their courses are usually distinguished by pronounced and high right banks and low left banks, liable to flooding during spring high water.

DRAINAGE

Practically the whole of the Central Industrial Region is drained by the Volga and its tributaries. This river rises amid swamps and marshes in the Valday Hills near Lake Seliger and flows eastwards in a circuitous and gently graded course, eventually to leave the region near Kazan. The south and west are drained by the Oka and its Klyazma and Moskva tributaries, the northeast by the Vetluga and Vyatka, and the west by the Dnieper and Desna. The economic usefulness of these rivers is seriously curtailed because they are frozen over for about six months each winter. Despite this the Volga, the largest river in Europe, is the most important waterway system of the U.S.S.R. It receives most of its water from melting snows in spring, when sizeable floods are likely, though since the 1930s these spring floods have been controlled by reservoirs. By such control surplus water held back in the spring is used to maintain the level of the river during summer and autumn, at which periods shoals and shallows formerly interfered with river navigation. A dam near Ivankovo has impounded the Volga Reservoir which raises the level on the upstream side to beyond Kalinin. Downstream from Ivankovo come first the Uglich Reservoir, then the Rybinsk Reservoir, formed by two dams, one on the Volga and the other on its tributary, the Sheksna. These reservoirs provide water for the Moscow Canal and Moscow River, giving Moscow a deep-water route for navigation to the Volga River. A dam at Gorodets, 35 miles upstream from Gorkiy, forms the Gorkiy Sea. On the middle Volga, beyond the limits of the Central Industrial Region, other multipurpose

reservoirs have been constructed—e.g. at Kuybyshev and farther
downstream near Volgograd (p. 214). At Volgograd the Volga–Don
Canal provides an outlet from the Volga to the Sea of Azov and Black
Sea, and thence to open sea. As a result of these constructions and of older
canal systems and lakes, Moscow is provided with links to the Baltic,
White, Caspian, Azov and Black Seas, and has come to be called the "Port
of the Five Seas" (Fig. 77).

CLIMATE

The climate of the region is of the cold continental type with humid
winters. Compared with the climate of Britain, winters generally are
colder and summers only slightly warmer; rainfall aggregates are less and
the annual distribution is different (Fig. 88).

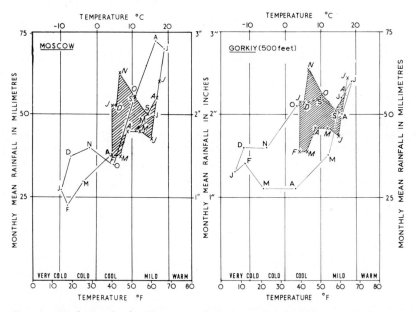

FIG. 88.—Hythergraphs for Moscow and Gorkiy. The shaded hythergraphs with
x symbols in this and all other similar illustrations are for Kew, England, and are
added for comparative purposes.

In summer there are usually no more than five months with mean
temperatures over 50° F (10° C). In winter three to five months have mean
temperatures below freezing level (32° F, 0° C). In the west the temperature
range is about 50° F (10° C), but it increases in the east to 70° F (21° C).
Precipitation is everywhere slight, the humid western parts receiving no
more than about 28 in. (712 mm), the drier southeastern margins less than

16 in. (400 mm). Maximum precipitation occurs during summer at a time when rainfall effectiveness is appreciably reduced through evaporation. Much of the winter precipitation comes in the form of snow, which lies for five to six months at depths of 1–1½ ft. Atlantic influences penetrate into western parts of the region, and winters here tend to be overcast and raw. In the east however, away from the maritime influences and nearer the Siberian anticyclone, winters tend to be crisp and bright and the cold is intensified. The climate in the east of the region is not unlike that of the south of Canada east of the Rockies.

NATURAL VEGETATION AND SOILS

The transitional nature of the region is further reflected in the natural vegetation and soils. Both occur in roughly parallel zones aligned west–east. In the north the region is still essentially forested, with conifers (tayga) predominating. Between the Volga and the Oka the conifers have ad-

[*Fotokhronika Tass.*

Fig. 89.—Woodlands of graceful silver birch trees are characteristic of the countryside near Moscow. Birch is a deciduous tree of the tayga, in which other species are mostly conifers.

mixtures of birch, oak, maple and ash (Fig. 89). Podzols, overlain by glacial deposits in the north and by immense stretches of sand in the south, underlie both the coniferous and the mixed forest zones. South of the Oka there is a zone of predominantly broad-leaved forest, containing limes and poplars.

This thins out to woodland steppe farther south. This zone of broad-leaved forest coincides roughly with brown forest soils which grade into leached black earths farther south (p. 43).

THE ECONOMY

AGRICULTURE AND FORESTRY

The Central Industrial Region has never been a leading agricultural area. The short, cool, growing season, the low annual rainfall (of which the effectiveness diminishes towards the southeast), and the generally infertile soils, combine to produce an unfavourable physical environment. Mixed farming, embracing such crops as rye, oats, wheat, potatoes, flax and cabbages, is customary. Sheep, pigs and cattle are frequently kept. Near the towns there is considerable market gardening and dairying. Where forest persists north of the Volga, rather less than a quarter of the area is sown to crops. Paper, pulp and other forest industries are common. South of the Oka the range of crops widens to include maize, sugar beet, hemp, tobacco and deciduous fruits (Fig. 90).

MANUFACTURING

Manufacturing industry in the region is the result more of tradition and geographical inertia than of favourable location in relation to supplies of power and raw materials. The courts of the tsars, and the presence of the nobility in Moscow, encouraged early artisan industries which relied on raw materials brought in from other regions. Today the market afforded by the largest concentration of people in the U.S.S.R., the presence of a large and skilled labour force, an industrial tradition, and government planning combine to maintain a modern industrial complex which, like the earlier industries, continues to look far afield for its raw materials and sources of power.

Lignite in the Moscow coal basin, peat (the Soviet Union has about 60% of the world's peat resources), some iron ore near Tula, and scattered deposits of phosphate, and such agricultural products as flax, hemp and potatoes are the only raw materials available within the Central Industrial Region for manufacturing industry (Figs. 90–91). The lignite and peat are used to generate electricity, and there are plans to exploit further the Kursk iron ore reserves in the northwest of the Central Chernozem Region, but neither the electricity nor the readily available iron ore is sufficient to meet local demand. Coal, iron ore, pig iron, steel, petroleum and a wide range of minerals, metals and raw materials have to be imported from other parts of the country. A substantial amount of electricity, generated at

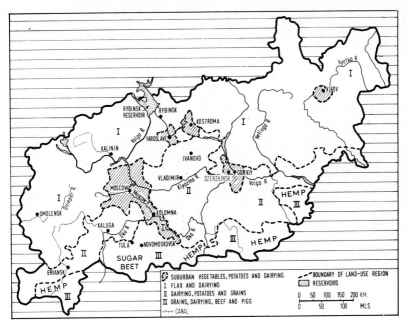

FIG. 90.—Central Industrial Region: agricultural land-use regions.

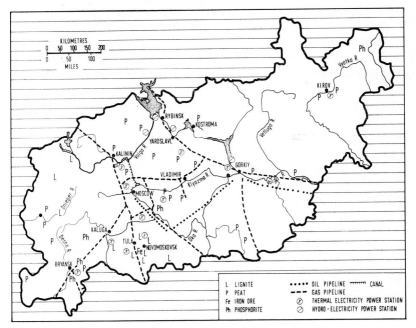

FIG. 91.—Central Industrial Region: mineral and power resources.

barrages on the Volga and elsewhere, is imported via grids; and natural gas, a basic fuel for both industry and electricity production, is piped from the north Caucasus (mostly from Stavropol), from western Ukraine (mainly from Dashava), and from the Volga–Ural area (mainly Saratov). In addition oil is piped from the Middle Volga Region.

The old-established textile industry of the region was originally based on local wool, flax and hemp. The wool was a by-product of sheep rearing for meat production, while flax and hemp were fibre crops suited to the relatively wet and cool climate and poor podzolic soils of the area. Additional supplies of wool are now brought into the region from middle Asia and the Ukraine, flax and hemp from the Baltic Republics and Belorussia, and raw cotton from Middle Asia and Trans-Caucasia. The woollen industry of the U.S.S.R. continues to be located in the Moscow area at such centres as Kuntsevo, Pavlovskiy, Zagorsk and Posad, although there are some mills in the Ukraine (Kiev, Kharkov), in the Northwest Region (Leningrad) and in Middle Asia (Alma-Ata, Frunze). Cotton mills in the oblasts of Ivanovo (Ivanovo, Shuya, Kineshma), Vladimir (Vladimir, Kovrov), Moscow (Moscow, Orekhovo-Zuyevo, Noginsk) and Yaroslavl are responsible for 80% of the cotton textiles of the U.S.S.R. Kostroma and Yaroslavl are the main producers of linen goods.

The iron, steel and metal-working industries at Tula utilise local ores for foundry work and for making cast steel. Elsewhere in the region the metallurgical industry, which first worked up iron ore found in the marshes between Kaluga and Gorkiy, relies on steel brought in from Krivoy Rog in the Ukraine and from the Ural, iron ores from Kursk in the Central Chernozem Region, and also on converted scrap metal. Around Moscow itself there are steel converters and rolling mills which serve engineering works. These in their turn produce general machinery, motor vehicles, railway equipment, aircraft, machine tools, precision instruments and ball bearings. Similar metallurgical complexes occur at such places as Elektrostal, Vyksa, Kulebaki and Gorkiy. At Gorkiy ferrous materials are produced for shipbuilding, aircraft, motor vehicles and electrical goods; at Kolomna, for railway locomotives; at Yaroslavl, for rail and marine engines and motor cars; at Kalinin, for railway rolling stock and electrical engineering; at Vladimir, for farm machinery and metal products; at Ivanovo, for general machinery, and at Bryansk, for mechanical and electrical engineering, farm machinery and railway equipment (Fig. 92).

The rapidly expanding chemical industry of the Soviet Union is well represented in the Central Industrial Region. Moscow has a wide range of light chemical and pharmaceutical plants: Yaroslavl, Tambov, Voronezh and Yefremov produce synthetic rubber; Voskresensk and Novomoskovsk, sulphuric acid; Shchelkovo, Orekhovo-Zuyevo and Klin, synthetic fibres;

Lyubertsy, Klin and Vladimir, plastics; and Dzerzhinsk–Gorkiy, fertilisers, caustic soda and synthetic fibres.

Woodworking and paper industries are also important, as are the service and food-processing industries serving the large urban markets. There is hardly a town in the Central Industrial Region which does not engage in

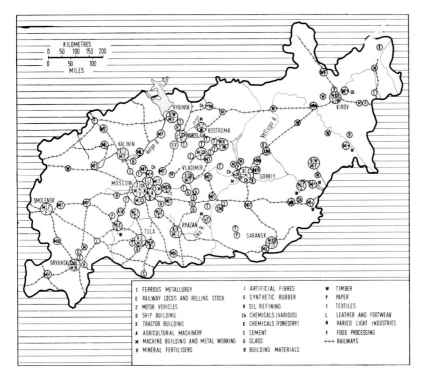

FIG. 92.—Central Industrial Region: railways and industrial structure of towns. NOTE that in this and in all other similar illustrations the town circles are relative only and are not in strict proportion to their populations.

manufacturing of some kind. This is not to say that the industrial landscape is in any way as close-textured as that found in parts of England. The distance from Manchester to Bolton or from Birmingham to Wolverhampton is a mere 12 miles; but the distance separating Moscow and Kalinin or Moscow and Vladimir is of the order of 100–110 miles (cf. London to Bristol or London to Birmingham). Rather is the region a series of industrial nodes, e.g. Moscow and its satellite towns, Gorkiy and its satellites, Ivanovo–Kineshma–Kostroma, Tula–Novomoskovsk, etc., separated by extensive rural areas.

POPULATION AND CITIES

It was in the area that has become the Central Industrial Region, mainly between the Volga and the Oka, that the rebirth of Rus (Muscovy) took place after the Mongol invasions. Slavic people entered the area in spite of its originally wooded nature and unproductive soil. Today over 33 million people, mainly Great Russians, live in the region, but in no more than five of the oblasts—Moscow, Ivanovo, Yaroslavl, Vladimir and Gorkiy— do the urban populations exceed 50% of the total. The remaining eight oblasts and three A.S.S.R.s are mainly rural. Nevertheless, the wealth of the whole region lies not in its farms but in its cities, and of these Moscow is by far the largest and most important.

MOSCOW (6,443,000)

Kiev Rus near the transition zone of forest and steppe, and long exposed to the inroads of Mongol Tatars from the east, finally fell to Batu, the nephew of Jenghiz Khan, in the thirteenth century. The unity of Kiev Rus collapsed and the embryo state moved far to the north to the safety of the forest and marsh. Here the centres of influence were Novgorod and Moscow. Novgorod was a trading post, controlling routes to the Baltic and White Seas, and a member of the Hanseatic League; Moscow, a frontier post situated well to the east, became the rallying point where forces for the final breaking and pushing back of the Tatars were mustered, while Novgorod's fortunes gradually waned with the decline of the Hanseatic League.

Twice during the thirteenth, and once in the fourteenth century, Moscow was burned and plundered by the Tatars, but by the second half of the fifteenth century, having annexed the majority of the surrounding principalities, the Grand Duchy of Moscow became the focus for the unification of a Russian state. Ivan III made Moscow the capital and himself "Tsar of all the Russias."

In the sixteenth century the growth of Moscow was interrupted by fires and further Tatar invasion, but the presence there of state administration represented by the tsar's court, the boyars *duma* (council), the assembly of the *zemstvo* (an advisory organ drawn from elected representatives), the residence of the Russian metropolitan (the "third Rome" after the fall of Constantinople in 1453), and the concentration of businesses and workshops, assured the city of a premier position in the life of the Russian realm. Moscow proved to be the cradle of the Russian people and the springboard for the conquest of enormous territories. Its political functions were eclipsed for some 200 years when the capital was transferred to St Petersburg in 1712, but it continued to play a leading role in the cultural and artistic life of the country and has remained its major commercial and industrial city. The government returned to Moscow after the Revolution of 1917. Today, besides being a symbol of the nation's past, Moscow is the largest city of the Union and plays the leading role in the political, administrative, economic, artistic, literary and intellectual life of the country.

In 1156 Yuri Dolgoruki, Prince of Suzdal, built a wooden *kremlin* (citadel) at Moscow on the site of an earlier settlement, and around this, near an easy crossing of the Moskva River, the township grew. The site was on the outer convex bank of a north-swinging meander of the Moskva River, and between two small streams—the Neglinka and the Yauza—which joined the main river at this point (Fig. 36). The water barriers were ineffectual defence lines, as was the surrounding flat and dismal countryside. Rather was the site a refuge in the backwoods between the Oka and upper Volga, well away from the Tatars. Even so, it held a commanding position in a central part of the Russian Lowland near the hub of the great river systems of European Russia. By means of short portages Moscow has links with the Dvina, Dnieper, Volkhov and Narva, in addition to its direct connection via the Oka and Volga to distant ports on the Caspian Sea and beyond.

With Moscow's increasing importance, the area occupied by the city has grown and its appearance changed. It now covers nearly 128 sq. miles (330 sq. km). In the absence of pronounced physical obstacles the city retains its original radial-ring plan of streets (Fig. 93) and presents a striking summary of the life of old and modern Russia. There still remain in the suburbs some wooden houses reminiscent of the peasant *izba* of the villages, standing alongside large blocks of flats built since World War II (Fig. 94), and, nearer the centre, town residences with pillared porticos which belonged to the former aristocracy. There are factories producing motor vehicles and machine tools, medieval Orthodox churches with the oriental splendour of gilded and painted domes, and sports stadia; there are narrow irregular lanes and recently widened 16-lane thoroughfares. And there is the Kremlin.

The Kremlin contains within its red-brick battlements three cathedrals, the tsar's palace and palaces of the former nobility, a museum and an imposing clocktower (Fig. 95). This architectural ensemble was joined in 1961 by the Palace of Congresses, a graceful structure of glass and steel, in which are held meetings of the Supreme Soviet. In front of the Kremlin lies the vast space of Red Square, witness of many major events in Russian history. Across the Square to the east is the city's largest store (GUM or State Department Store) and towards the river to the south from Red Square stand conspicuously the brightly painted baroque onion-domed spires of St Basil's Cathedral (Fig. 96).

To provide Moscow with a navigable waterway the Moscow Canal was completed in 1937. It joins the Moscow River in Moscow with the Volga, 80 miles to the north, through a system of eight locks. A dam constructed with a hydro-electric power plant of 30,000-kw capacity on the Volga near Ivankovo (in the neighbourhood of Dubna) raises the water level on the river upstream as far as 45 miles above the city of Kalinin to form the

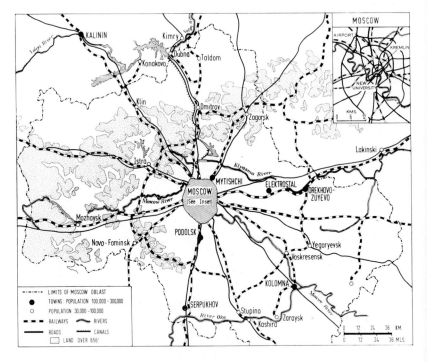

FIG. 93.—Position of Moscow.

Volga Reservoir. One-third of the water collected in the reservoir is used to feed the Moscow Canal, the remainder to feed the Uglich Reservoir a little way downstream. As has been noted, Moscow, 400 miles from the nearest sea, is yet accessible to five seas. Self-propelled barges, with a total load capacity of about 22,000 tons, reach the city during the seven-months ice-free period. River traffic, however, is slow and is economical only for the transport of such bulky low-cost goods as lumber, coal and grain.

In the mid-nineteenth century, Moscow became the focus of the railways of European Russia. Eleven trunk railways now connect the city with all parts of the U.S.S.R. The terminal stations are linked by an outer ring railway and an inner underground railway (the Metro). Each of the 70 stations of the Moscow Metro Railway has a distinctive architectural design of its own.

Moscow is not yet plagued by the congestion of motor traffic that characterises London, Paris, Rome or New York, although the public omnibus and underground transport facilities are well used by com-

[R. T. Smith.

FIG. 94.—Old and new in Moscow. Moscow is replacing old wooden houses by modern high rectangular blocks of flats.

muters. Nevertheless the development of motor transport aggravated the problem presented by narrow streets. This has been overcome by the straightening and widening of main thoroughfares, such as Gorkiy Street and Sadovaya Ulitsa, to as much as 100-ft width. In this process whole buildings have been moved bodily, either backwards or about face.

The raising of the level of the Moscow River after the completion of the

F

Moscow–Volga Canal necessitated the construction of eleven new bridges and the lining of the river with grand embankments. These now provide some of the chief thoroughfares of the city.

The use of aircraft introduced another element into the geography of Moscow's transport. The original civil airport at Vnukovo, 17 miles southwest of the city centre has proved to be inadequate and a new international airport, Sheremetyevo, capable of handling 1500 passengers an hour, has been laid out in the southeast at the same distance from the city. Yet another airport, one of the world's biggest, at Domodedovo, 20 miles to the southeast, has been in operation since March 1964.

Despite the distances involved, the ease of rail transport over the generally flat expanses of the Union has encouraged the setting up of a wide range of industries in Moscow, which is now the country's largest industrial producing centre, and heavy industries take pride of place. Metallurgy and the textile industries together account for approximately 45% of the gross production in these categories. Consumer goods industries are becoming increasingly important. Enterprises such as the Likhachev Car Plant, Sergei Ordzhonikidze plant, the Red Proletariat plant, Frezer and Kalibr (instrument-making) plant, the Hammer and Sickle (Serp i Molot) plant, Stan-

[*Mysl.*

FIG. 95.—The Moscow Kremlin viewed from Kropotkinskaya embankment.

Camera Press.

FIG. 96.—The heart of Moscow at night. The Red Square (Krasnaya Ploshchad, meaning "bright square") is on the left. The star-topped clock tower on the right is the Spasskaya Tower of the Kremlin and Lenin's tomb is in the foreground. The polygonal pyramid surrounded by cupolas is the Cathedral of St Basil (1555), built to commemorate the subjugation of the Khanate of Kazan.

kolit plant and the "Dynamo" plant produce a wide range of industrial products and supply electrical fitments, machine tools and precision instruments. There are also enterprises producing pharmaceutical and heavy chemicals, synthetic rubber, footwear, silk, wool, synthetic fibres and other products, which take advantage of the presence of abundant skilled labour and a great market of 7 million people in the capital and over 33 million in the Central Industrial Region as a whole. The Moscow area alone is responsible for approximately 16% of the total industrial output of the U.S.S.R.

OTHER CITIES AND TOWNS

Gorkiy (1,085,000), previously Nizhni-Novgorod, lies 240 miles east-northeast of Moscow, a distance equivalent to that between London and Middlesbrough or London and Falmouth. Gorkiy owed its earlier importance to a favourable position at the confluence of the navigable Volga and Oka Rivers and "backed" by the flourishing Moscow Region (Fig. 97).

[*Fotokhronika Tass.*

FIG. 97.—Gorkiy, at the confluence of the Volga and Oka Rivers. The city was once called Nizhni Novgorod and its Fair has been famous for centuries.

Local forests provided timber for shipbuilding, supplying, as early as the sixteenth century, a yearly "caravan" of boats which carried products from the Moscow Region to the Caspian, and returned laden with the products of the south and east. Shipbuilding is still carried on at Gorkiy, as are trading activities that originated in the exchange and barter of an early trade fair located here.

Other local industries produce motor vehicles (the Molotov plant is reputed to be the largest in Europe), aircraft, engineering (ships, submarines, railway rolling stock, locomotives and tanks—all made at an industrial suburb, Sormovo) and textiles, and include oil refining and petrochemicals, flour milling and confectionery making (Fig. 92). The city, sixth in size in the Soviet Union, is linked by rail with Moscow, Kotlas, Perm and Sverdlovsk, and via a branch line with Arzamas on the Trans-Siberian Railway.

Yaroslavl (478,000) on the right bank of the Volga at its confluence with the Kotorosl River, lies some 160 miles north-northeast of Moscow. Founded in 1024 it was an important town in the Rostov–Suzdal Principality, but was annexed by Moscow early in the fifteenth century. During the next two centuries it was a sizeable trading post on the White Sea–Volga–Near East route, but with the establishment and rapid rise of St Petersburg on the Baltic in the eighteenth century its industries and trade suffered a temporary decline. Today, however, Yaroslavl is a major industrial centre and river port at the point where the main railway line north from Moscow to Arkhangelsk crosses the Volga. Among its manufactures are motor-vehicle tyres made from synthetic rubber, textiles, motor vehicles, locomotives and ships.

Ivanovo (389,000) is, after Moscow, the largest centre of the textile industry in the Soviet Union. Its first mill, built in 1751, used imported cotton but is now supplied from Middle Asia. Other industries of this "Manchester of the Soviet Union" include textile machinery and chemicals. Situated about 150 miles northeast of Moscow, Ivanovo was a centre of strikes and revolutionary movements from the end of the nineteenth century, and in the early twentieth century it was an important stronghold of the Bolsheviks.

Tula (366,000) is the most important of the industrial centres of the region south of Moscow. It is situated on the Upa, tributary of the Oka River, 120 miles south of the capital near the junction of the mixed forest zone and the steppe. Founded as a frontier fortress against the Tatars, it later grew as a metal-working centre specialising in armaments and samovars. Nowadays the emphasis is on arms, machine tools, sewing machines, agricultural and general machinery, tanning, flour milling and sugar refining.

Kalinin (306,000), formerly Tver, is situated on the main Moscow–Leningrad Railway at its crossing of the navigable Volga. In the thirteenth century it became capital of the important and independent principality of Tver and for a time rivalled Moscow, but fell to that principality in the fifteenth century. Its chief industries include textiles (cotton and flax), engineering (railway rolling stock, textile machinery), radios and electrical equipment.

Kirov (296,000) (formerly Vyatka and, before 1780, Khlynov), is capital of the predominantly rural oblast of the same name. Founded in 1181 as a colony of Novgorod, it later became capital of a medieval principality. Sacked by Tatars in the fourteenth and fifteenth centuries it eventually came under the rule of the Principality of Moscow (1489). A flourishing trading centre on the road to Siberia during the seventeenth and eighteenth centuries, Kirov now functions as an important railway junction and industrial centre. The city has rail links with Arkhangelsk (via Kotlas), Leningrad (via Vologda), Moscow (via Gorkiy 480 miles), and with the Ural region (via Perm and Sverdlovsk). Its industries and products include machine tools, rolling stock, agricultural implements, leather and shoes, fur processing and woodworking. Kirov is also a regional cultural centre with research and technical institutes.

Ryazan (287,000), on the right bank of the Oka River, 120 miles southeast of Moscow, has experienced a remarkable increase of population in recent years (34% between 1959 and 1964). It is a flourishing industrial town within a generally agricultural area and has factories for agricultural machinery, flour milling, fruit canning, distilling, woodworking, shoe making, clothing and electric light bulbs. The main railway from Moscow to Kuybyshev passes through the city.

Bryansk (267,000), 215 miles southwest of Moscow and at the head of navigation of the Desna River is, with nearby *Bezhitsa* (82,000), an important industrial centre. It has the largest railway engineering works in the Soviet Union (conveniently sited at the junction of several routes), iron and steel works (in the northern suburb of Maltevsk), sawmills, flour mills, distilleries and cement works. In World War II the town was held by the German army for practically two years (October 1941–September 1943).

Rybinsk (208,000) is a port on the Volga at the southern terminal of the Volga–Baltic waterway (Mariinskiy Canal System). It lies at the southeast end of the Rybinsk Reservoir and functions as a trading and transhipment centre for timber, oil, grains, building materials and fish. Local industries include sawn timber, matches, linen, aircraft engines, ships and agricultural machinery.

Kostroma (202,000), on the left bank of the Volga 200 miles northeast of Moscow, is an old wood-working and linen centre with, in addition, footwear, engineering (mechanical excavators), flour, flax-seed oil and shipbuilding industries.

Vladimir (196,000) is among the oldest of Russian towns. Founded in 1150, it was capital of the Grand Principality of Vladimir until it fell to

Muscovy in the fourteenth century. It lies on the main Moscow–Gorkiy Railway, but was comparatively insignificant until the 1930s when textile, chemical, machine-tool, precision instruments and farm engineering industries were established there.

Smolensk (183,000) is another very old Russian city, dating from the ninth century. Favourably located on the Dnieper on the so-called "Water Road from the Varangians to the Greeks," it became an important trade and distribution centre. In modern times it manufactures linen (it has one of the largest linen mills in the Soviet Union), textile machinery, electrical goods and clothing. Other activities include flour milling, distilling, brewing and wood-working. In 1812 it lay on the route of Napoleon's armies advancing on Moscow, and in 1941 before the eastward advance of Hitler's armies, and it was razed to the ground on both occasions.

Kaluga (169,000) is a machine-building centre and railway junction on the Oka, 90 miles southwest of Moscow. Railway rolling stock, electrical, telephone and telegraph equipment, matches, glass and leather are among its varied products.

STUDY QUESTIONS

1. Suggest a division of the Central Industrial region into geographical regions. Discuss the bearing of physical factors upon economic activities in any *two* of the regions recognised.

2. Give a reasoned account of the transitional character of the physical environment of the Central Industrial Region.

3. "The Muscovite region is the real heart of Russia, not only through its geographical position but also owing to its exceptional density of population and its commercial, industrial and administrative activity" (Jorre). Expand this statement.

4. "It may be that the time is not far distant when the capital of the U.S.S.R. will not only be connected with all the seas in the European part of the country, but will also become a great trading centre and port." Comment on the extent to which this 1944 prediction of S. P. Turin has been realised.

5. Examine the site, location and functions of the following towns: Ivanovo; Yaroslavl; Tula; Gorkiy; Kalinin; Kirov; Ryazan.

6. Examine the influence of the industrial concentration on the pattern of agriculture in the Central Region.

7. Analyse the extent to which the Central Industrial Region is deficient in raw materials and food.

8. Write a geographical essay on "Moscow—the Metropolis."

Chapter XIII

CENTRAL CHERNOZEM REGION

 The Central Chernozem Region is sometimes included as part of the Central Industrial Region but its more southerly location, its generally rural character and dominantly agricultural economy justify its separate treatment. It comprises the oblasts of Orel, Kursk, Belgorod, Voronezh, Lipetsk, Tambov, Penza and the Mordovskaya A.S.S.R., and abuts on the Middle and Lower Volga (Povolzhye)–Lower Don Region in the east, the Ukraine–Moldavian Region in the west and the Central Industrial Region in the north (Fig. 98). It is a rich agricultural region, devoted to the cultivation of cereals (especially wheat), sugar beet, sunflowers and maize, and also to dairying and stock raising.

Area . . . 101,000 sq. miles
Population (1959). 11,197,000

Administrative unit	Area sq. miles	Population in thousands 1959	Density persons per sq. mile	Percentage urban
Oblast Orel	9,500	926	96	24
Oblast Kursk	11,500	1,481	130	20
Oblast Belgorod . . .	10,500	1,227	117	18
Oblast Voronezh . . .	20,200	2,363	117	35
Oblast Lipetsk	9,300	1,144	122	30
Oblast Tambov . . .	13,200	1,547	117	26
Oblast Penza	16,700	1,510	91	33
Mordovskaya A.S.S.R. . .	10,100	999	98	18

Towns with over 150,000 inhabitants in 1964

	Population in thousands		Percentage increase
	1959	1964	1959–64
Voronezh . . .	448	576	28·7
Penza	255	315	23·5
Kursk	205	245	19·5
Lipetsk. . . .	157	226	43·9
Tambov . . .	172	203	18·0
Orel	150	197	31·3

148

PHYSICAL ASPECTS

RELIEF

The western section of the region extends over a part of the central Russian Uplands; the central section is part of the flat upper Don Plain (sometimes called the Tambov Plain), and the east encroaches on the Volga Heights (Fig. 98). The central Russian Uplands represent a broad upwarp of the Russian Lowland, which slopes gently westwards to the valley of the Dnieper and more abruptly eastwards to the valley of the Don.

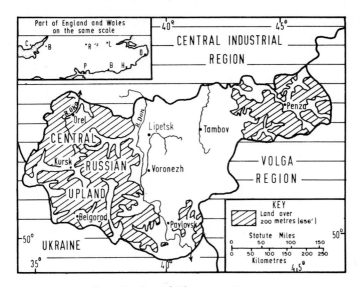

FIG. 98.—Central Chernozem Region.

Summits between 850 and 950 ft are severely dissected by a considerable number of recent and currently developing gullies, some reaching as much as 500 ft below the general surface level. The gullies and ravines are the result of deforestation, the ploughing of slopes and overgrazing, aggravated by the shower nature of the precipitation. South of Orel the uplands were not glaciated and are entirely loess-covered.

The Don or Tambov Plain is a flat, alluvial area filling the broad (150 miles) depression between the eastern slopes of the central Russian Uplands and the Volga Heights. During Pleistocene times it was occupied by a lobe of the ice sheet which extended as far south as Pavlovsk. Broad river terraces covered with loess-like sandy hills are the principal landscape forms. The watershed between the Don and the north-flowing Oka and its tributaries is an insignificant feature.

The portion of the Volga Heights that lies within this region is well dissected in several directions and presents only a few low ridges with gentle
slopes.

DRAINAGE

Most of the Central Chernozem Region is drained southwards by the
Don and its tributaries. Part of the Tambov Plains drains northwards via
the Tsna to the Oka while the west of the central Russian Uplands drains to
the Dnieper. Like the Volga to the east and the Dnieper to the west, the
Don has a high, steep right bank, frequently 200–300 ft above the river, and
a low flat left bank which is flooded in spring.

CLIMATE AND NATURAL VEGETATION

Tambov is at virtually the same latitude as London, but if its climate is
taken as representative of the region, its summers are somewhat hotter
(warmest month 68° F (20° C)) and its winters much colder (coldest month
13° F (−10·6° C)) than those of London (Fig. 99). Compared with those

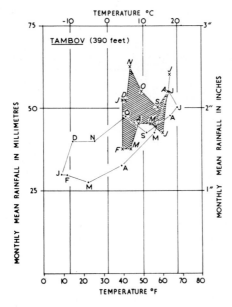

FIG. 99.—Hythergraph
for Tambov.

of the Central Industrial Region, conditions are also drier, annual precipitation aggregates ranging from 20 in. in the northwest to less than 16 in.
in the southeast (Tambov: 19·1 in. = 485 mm); maxima come in late
spring. With decreasing aggregates comes increasing variability, aggravated further by high evaporation losses during the summer, and also by

the desiccating effect of occasional dry, hot southeast or south winds (*sukhovey*). Summer precipitation is less effective than winter precipitation (although the amounts are similar in the two seasons) in maintaining the flow of streams and the soil moisture reserves. Winter precipitation comes mainly in the form of snow, which lies for up to four months at a mean depth of 1–1½ ft. The insulating effect of this shallow snow cover is important, for the soil remains warm enough to allow winter-sown seeds to start germinating quite early in the spring.

The greater part of the region lies in the forest steppe (*leso-stepye*) zone, underlain by thick, though somewhat leached, chernozem soils. The true steppe with chernozems comes in southeast of Voronezh. Though large forested areas still occur, much forest has been removed and the land turned to agricultural use; the steppe areas are all under cultivation.

THE ECONOMY

AGRICULTURE

Nowadays well over half the region is farmed, with a wide range of crops. It is transitional between the Central Industrial Region, with its small-scale grain, flax and potato-growing, and the extensive grain and sunflower culture of the Ukraine. Crops include wheat, sugar beet, maize, hemp, sunflowers, oats, millet, barley, rye, tobacco, fruits, together with fodder crops for the sheep, pigs and cattle that are kept practically everywhere. Market gardening and dairying form the chief agricultural occupations around all the large towns (Fig. 100).

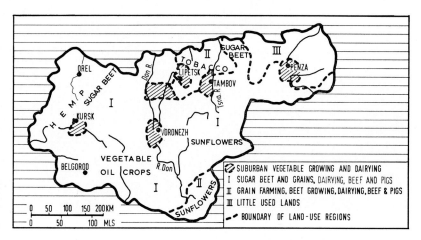

FIG. 100.—Central Chernozem Region: agricultural land-use regions.

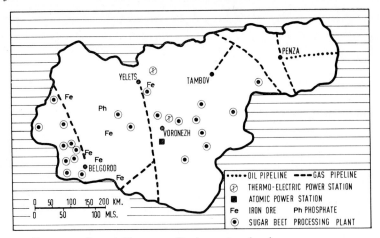

FIG. 101.—Central Chernozem Region: mineral and power resources.

INDUSTRIAL ACTIVITIES

Agriculture-based industries, such as food and sugar processing, and alcohol production from grain and potatoes, rely on local raw materials; for heavy industry the only local source of any importance is the Kursk Magnetic Anomaly (Figs. 101 and 102), which is one of the principal sources of iron ore in the Soviet Union. Rich bodies of iron ore of more

[*Fotokhronika Tass.*

FIG. 102.—Opencast mining of iron ore at the Kursk Magnetic Anomaly. This is one of the principal sources of iron ore in the Soviet Union.

than 50% metallic content lie in pockets interbedded with ferruginous quartzites. So far, because of the wide extent of the deposits, only the high-grade ore has been worked and the quartzites have been treated as a spoil. However, much of the quartzite is comparatively rich in iron—it may, in fact, contain over 40% iron—and it is planned to use this material also. At the Mikhailovka works, 50 miles northwest of Kursk (in 1967 in their eighth year of production), extraction is by opencast methods and the resources here have been proved to have a potential of some 500 million tons of rich ore and 9500 million tons of quartzite with over 40% iron. These figures apply to a depth of 600–1000 ft only; the quartzites extend to unknown depths and represent an almost inexhaustible supply of iron ore.

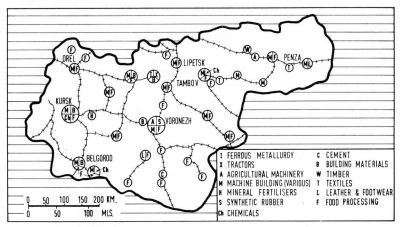

Fig. 103.—Central Chernozem Region: railways and industrial structure of towns.

Kursk ore is used in the modern integrated steel plant at Lipetsk, which relies on good-quality coking coal imported from the Donbass, even though this involves a very long and costly haul. It also supplies the metallurgical industries of the Central Industrial Region and of the Ukraine.

Manufacturing industry within the Central Chernozem Region is at present limited, but with the increasing availability of piped natural gas from both the Ukraine and the northern Caucasus and the existence of a nuclear power station (420 Mw) 30–40 miles south of Voronezh, it seems likely that industrial developments will occur. There is a potential source of labour among the large rural population, and an intermediate location on a good transport system, orientated mainly north to south and converging on the Central Industrial Region in the north and the Ukraine in the south, is an additional advantage for industrial development. The high-grade cement from Oblast Belgorod, based on local supplies of chalk, is already of importance throughout the Union (Fig. 103).

POPULATION AND CITIES

For a long time the area that is now the Central Chernozem Region was a frontier land peopled by Don Cossacks, semi-nomadic groups of horsemen who had escaped southwards from the oppression of Russian princes (see p. 54). The frontier zone was moved southwards to the lower Don and Black Sea Steppe and the lands to the north became settled and cultivated. Since the eighteenth century the whole of the region has been a productive agricultural area supporting a dense rural population. It is unfortunate that past farming practices have led to widespread gullying and erosion, resulting in the loss of acres of precious soil every year, and considerable effort is now being expended to check this "rape of the earth."

The population in the forested area in the north lives mainly in log huts (izba), but in the steppe areas of the south adobe-filled frame huts (khata) are the usual habitations. Cities are comparatively small and widely spaced and are, in the main, administrative centres of the respective provinces or districts (oblasts).

Voronezh (576,000), chief town of the Central Chernozem Region, is an important industrial centre which has experienced a remarkable increase of population in recent years (29% between 1959 and 1964). It was first established as a Khazar town and later became a Russian fort (sixteenth century) against the Tatars. Voronezh now functions as a collecting and processing centre for agricultural products and produces synthetic rubber, locomotives and railway rolling stock, aircraft and agricultural and earth-moving machinery.

Penza (315,000), founded as a military centre on the River Sura in the seventeenth century, now serves as administrative and economic centre of Oblast Penza. It has varied engineering, food- and wood-processing industries.

Kursk (245,000), first founded in the ninth century, was completely destroyed during the Tatar invasion of the thirteenth century and remained in ruins until the sixteenth century, when it was rebuilt as a military outpost of the Moscow domain. Agriculture-orientated industries such as sugar, alcohol and synthetic rubber manufacture are supported by agricultural machinery, machine building and allied industries, developed in association with the exploitation of the extensive local deposits of iron ore.

Lipetsk (226,000), is a market town (trading mainly in cattle) with a leather industry and flour mills, to which a large integrated iron and steel plant and machine-building (tractors, farm machinery) works have been added. Its metallurgical activities seem destined to dominate in the future, and there has been a pronounced population increase in recent years (44% between 1959 and 1964).

Tambov (203,000), originally a fortified outpost against Tatar raids and later a staging post on the Moscow–Astrakhan route, has long been a market town for grains and other agricultural produce. Its industries are agriculture-orientated and include flour milling and general food processing (sugar, fruit), chemicals (potato alcohol), synthetic rubbers and tractors.

Orel (197,000) is a market town near the transition between the steppe and wooded steppe where the main Moscow–Kharkov railway line crosses the Oka River. It markets grain and livestock, and manufactures linen and textile machinery. Its population increased by 31% between 1959 and 1964.

STUDY QUESTIONS

1. Describe the main features of the geography of the Central Chernozem Region.

2. Write a short description of the agricultural activities of the Central Chernozem Region.

3. Discuss the problem of soil erosion in the Central Chernozem Region and outline the steps which are taken to reduce it.

4. "Perhaps the most significant development for the Soviet ferrous industry has been the initiation of large-scale exploitation of the 'Kursk Magnetic Anomaly' (K. M. A.)" (Hooson). Examine this statement with particular reference to the location of these iron ore deposits.

5. Examine the site, location and functions of the following towns: Voronezh; Tambov; Kursk; Penza; Lipetsk.

Chapter XIV

UKRAINE–MOLDAVIA

THE Ukraine S.S.R. and the Republic of Moldavia (created after World War II) together have an area five times that of England, but their combined populations are much the same as that of England, just over 44 millions. Ukraine–Moldavia is a leading arable agricultural region, a principal industrial centre with extractive and engineering industries, and one of the most closely settled areas in the Soviet Union. It is situated in the southwest of the country and abuts on Rumania, Hungary, Czechoslovakia and Poland (Fig. 104). Within the U.S.S.R. Ukraine–Moldavia ranks second in importance to the Russian S.S.R.

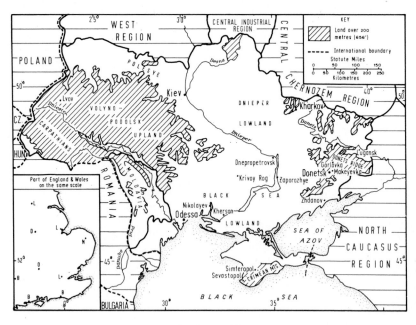

FIG. 104.—Ukraine–Moldavia Region.

Area   .   .   .   .   245,200 sq. miles
Population (1959)   .   .   44,773,000

Administrative unit	Area sq. miles	Population in thousands 1959	Density persons per sq. mile	Percentage urban
Ukraine S.S.R.				
Oblast Lugansk . . .	10,300	2,457	238	79
Oblast Donetsk . . .	10,200	4,265	417	86
Oblast Zaporozhye . .	10,400	1,466	140	57
Oblast Dnepropetrovsk . .	12,400	2,708	220	70
Oblast Kharkov . . .	12,200	2,517	207	62
Oblast Poltava . . .	11,200	1,630	145	30
Oblast Sumy . . .	9,400	1,512	161	32
Oblast Chernigov . . .	12,200	1,553	127	22
Oblast Kiev . . .	11,100	2,821	254	55
Oblast Cherkassy . . .	8,100	1,504	184	23
Oblast Kirovograd . .	9,200	1,218	132	31
Oblast Vinnitsa . . .	10,300	2,141	207	17
Oblast Zhitomir . . .	11,500	1,603	140	26
Oblast Khmelnitskiy . .	8,100	1,609	200	19
Oblast Rovno . . .	7,800	927	119	17
Oblast Volynsk (Lutsk) . .	7,700	890	114	24
Oblast Lvov	4,700	1,268	272	46
Oblast Ternopol . . .	5,400	1,088	202	16
Oblast Drogobych . .	3,700	847	228	28
Oblast Zakarpatsk . .	4,900	923	186	28
Oblast Stanislav . . .	5,400	1,098	204	23
Oblast Chernovtsy . .	3,100	776	251	26
Oblast Odessa . . .	12,800	2,028	158	47
Oblast Nikolayev . . .	9,600	1,015	106	39
Oblast Kherson . . .	10,500	827	78	40
Oblast Crimea . . .	9,900	1,202	122	64
Moldavskaya S.S.R. . . .	13,100	2,880	220	22

Towns with over 150,000 inhabitants in 1964

	Population in thousands		Percentage increase
	1959	1964	1959–64
Kiev	1,104	1,348	22·0
Kharkov . . .	934	1,070	14·6
Donetsk . . .	699	809	15·8
Dnepropetrovsk . .	660	774	17·1
Odessa . . .	667	735	10·1
Zaporozhye . .	435	550	26·6
Lvov	411	496	20·8
Krivoy Rog . . .	388	488	25·9
Makeyevka . . .	358	399	11·4
Zhdanov . . .	284	361	27·0
Gorlovka . . .	293	337	15·0
Lugansk . . .	275	330	20·0
Kishinev . . .	216	282	30·6
Nikolayev . . .	226	280	23·9

Towns with over 150,000 inhabitants in 1964—Contd.

	Population in thousands		Percentage increase
	1959	*1964*	*1959–64*
Dneprodzerzhinsk . .	194	218	12·3
Simferopol . . .	186	213	14·5
Kherson . . .	158	210	33·0
Sevastopol . . .	148	192	30·0
Chernovtsy . . .	146	172	18·0
Poltava . . .	143	170	19·0
Kirovograd . . .	128	153	19·6

PHYSICAL ASPECTS

RELIEF AND DRAINAGE

The small arc of the Carpathian Mountains that lies within the region is one of the lower sections of those ranges, where the highest peaks are less than 7000 ft (e.g. Mount Goverla, 6752 ft; Mount Petros, 6627 ft). Slopes are generally heavily forested, with beech on the lower slopes, and pine and fir above.

Along the foot of the Carpathians to the northeast flow the Prut and Dniester Rivers, which embrace between them the portion of the Podolian Upland that is now the Moldavian Republic.

> "Here the azure skies shine long,
> Here the reign of cruel storms is brief."
> *A. S. Pushkin*

Between the Dniester and Dnieper Rivers is the Volyno-Podolian Upland, an asymmetrical plateau, 600–1000 ft high, higher in the west and sloping gradually downwards to the east (Fig. 104). It is composed of Tertiary deposits and loess, and is much dissected by ravines. Along the river valleys there are occasional outcrops of crystalline rocks which belong to the basal Podolian–Azov (Ukraine) Crystalline Shield.

Beyond the bounding escarpment of the Volyno-Podolian Upland in the north lies the Polesye Lowland, an extensive area of oak–pine forest and swamp (the Pripet Marshes). Only the southern third of Polesye lies within the region (the remainder lies in southern Belorussia). The broad flat Polesye with its sluggish winding rivers constitutes the northwestern part of the Dnieper Lowland which, in its turn, merges eastwards into the central Russian Uplands. In Pleistocene times, during the third (Dnieper–Don) glacial stage, a lobe of the ice sheet occupied the Dnieper Lowland (cf. the Don Valley to the east), causing the formation of depressions and warping of the land surface. With the eventual retreat of the ice the low-lands were left extensively covered with sands and clays, with swamps and a poorly developed drainage system. These conditions continue to prevail in Polesye, but on the lower Dnieper the lowland, which extends east of the river for more than a hundred miles, has dried out long ago.

The distinctive steep and high bluffs of the right bank of the Dnieper and the low terraces of its left bank are well displayed near Kiev (Fig. 105). At Zaporozhye the Dnieper cuts through the ancient crystalline rocks of the Podolian–Azov Shield in a 40-mile long stretch of rapids. At one time the

[*Fotokhronika Tass.*

FIG. 105.—The Dnieper River at Kiev, viewed from the high west bluff towards the low sandy left bank.

rapids presented a serious hazard to shipping and interfered with Dnieper navigation, but in 1932 following the completion of the Dneproges Dam, they were submerged beneath a deep reservoir.

The Donets Ridge (Azov Heights) is a deeply dissected upland, rising to heights of over 1000 ft. It is a shield structure and represents an eastward extension of the Volyno-Podolian Upland beyond the Dnieper. Along the Black Sea from the northwestern shores of the Sea of Azov westwards to the mouth of the Danube is a strip of flat coastal plain, 50 to 100 miles wide, known as the Black Sea Lowland. This loess-covered region is itself almost perfectly flat, but in places reaches the coast in cliffs up to 100 feet high.

Three-quarters of the Crimea peninsula are occupied by a gently rolling northern plain, the remainder is by a southern rim of mountains—the Krymskiye Gory (Crimean Range)—reaching to over 5000 ft, and declining eastwards to the Peninsula of Kerch. The 4-miles wide isthmus of Perekop links Crimea with the mainland.

CLIMATE, NATURAL VEGETATION AND SOILS

In the Ukraine–Moldavia Region the climate is dominated by anti-cyclonic circulations, the Asiatic anticyclone during the winter and the Azores anticyclone in the summer. Characteristically there is a continental climate with rapid changes in the temperature element between winter and summer. Spring is everywhere a brief and fleeting season; autumn is rather more protracted (Fig. 106).

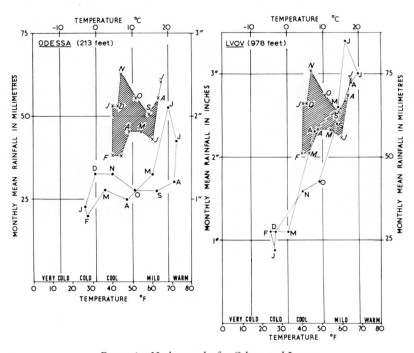

Fig. 106.—Hythergraphs for Odessa and Lvov.

January mean temperatures range from 28° F (−2·2° C) in the south-west (note the ameliorating influence of the Black Sea in winter) to 18° F (−7·8° C) in the northeast. July temperatures range from 68° F (20° C) in the northwest to 74° F (23·3° C) in the southeast. At this time

"the huge steppe sun shines evenly everywhere,
without blinking, without losing itself among the trees."

M. Prishvin

Annual precipitation aggregates exceed 40 in. (1016 mm) in the higher parts of the Carpathians, but are only 25–30 in. (635–762 mm) on the Volyno-Podolian Upland, less than 20 in. (508 mm) in the southeast and 8–16 in. (203–406 mm) along the Black Sea coast. Rainfall variability is such that in individual years aggregates may be anything between 70% and 125% of the mean annual values. Maximum precipitation occurs in the summer half of the year (particularly in the first half of the summer). It takes the form of heavy rainstorms and gives rise to erosion of the soil and the formation of ravines. On the other hand, relative humidity in summer is low—about 40% at noon in July and August; evaporation rates are high. Droughts, often to the accompaniment of desiccating *sukhovey* from the east, are quite common. To some extent ley farming (*travopolye*) and irrigation in association with multipurpose dams (e.g. at Zaporozhye, Kakhovka, Kremenchug and Dneprodzerzhinsk on the Dnieper) help to supplement the limited precipitation of the growing season, but the dreaded *sukhovey*, which is especially frequent in May and August, can cause fruit blossoms to wither, vegetation to suffer irreparable damage and the loss of an otherwise promising harvest. The pernicious effects of these hot, dry winds may be judged from the fact that, during the autumn of 1903, the *sukhovey* brought about the recession, through evaporation, of several square miles of the Sea of Azov for a period of five days. Winter precipitation is only slight and takes the form of snow, lying from 40 to 80 days. As in the Central Chernozem Region the slight snow cover (12–16 in. 30–40 cm) is important in so far as it insulates the soil, which in consequence remains sufficiently warm to permit the early germination of seeds sown in the late autumn.

Chekhov's description of the Ukraine Steppe is evocative of the summer drought and the wide fields of this area:

> "In the meantime before the eyes of the travellers spread the wide, boundless plain, crossed by a chain of hills . . . reaped rye, tall grass, spurge, wild hemp,—all turned brown by the heat, reddish and half-dead, now washed by the dew and caressed by the sun, was coming to life, ready to flower again. . . . But a short time passed, the dew evaporated, the air became still, and the cheated steppe again acquired its sad July appearance. The grass wilted, life was stilled. . . . And now on a hill a lonely poplar appeared. . . . Beyond the poplar, like a bright yellow carpet, from the top of the hill to the edge of the road, stretch fields of wheat. . . . But now the wheat has flashed by. Again the scorched plain stretches on, burnt hills, hot sky, and a kite again hovers over the earth."

The zones of natural vegetation and soil types merge imperceptibly into one another from northwest to southeast. The extensive forests of oak and pine in Polesye stand on podzol and bog soils; to the southeast, in the region of the forest-steppe and steppe, there is a change to deep fertile chernozems and chestnut soils, both of which are loess-covered. In only a few comparatively small areas does grass remain in the steppe-lands; such areas are protected nature reserves.

THE ECONOMY

AGRICULTURE

The flat steppe-lands of the east and the rolling and dissected Volyno-Podolian Upland of the west have long been ploughed and given over to vast acres of cereals—wheat, barley and maize—and to such industrial crops as sunflowers, sugar beet, flax and potatoes. Arable farming predominates and wheat is the chief crop.

Crop combinations change from northwest to southeast in relation to soil type and climate (Fig. 107). In the northwest on the "islands" of dry land

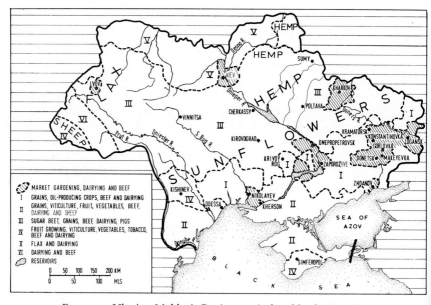

Fig. 107.—Ukraine–Moldavia Region: agricultural land-use regions.

among the marshes of Polesye, and in the lower valley of the Desna, flax growing and dairy farming are the main enterprises. Southwards wheat, barley, millet. buckwheat, rye, flax, potatoes and sugar beet seem to play an equal share in a general type of farming. In the central zone the concentration is on cash crops in which the extensive cultivation of sugar beets and wheat predominates. Wheat and sugar beet cover vast expanses of monotonous landscape and are produced in ever-increasing quantities, even though conditions tend to be rather dry for high yields of sugar beet. This is one of the most productive areas in the world for wheat and has long been known as the "Granary of Russia." The sugar beet provides sugar for domestic use and also a valuable cattle feed. Southwards, sunflowers form part of the crop combination. The oil extracted from their seeds is not only edible but is also used in the woollen industry and in the manufacture of fine paints and soaps. Potatoes provide food for both humans and livestock, as well as industrial alcohol, starch and vodka.

[*Fotokhronika Tass.*

FIG. 108.—Harvesting sunflowers in Moldavia. Sunflowers are grown for their seeds which are pressed to extract vegetable oil or mixed with maize and peas for cattle fodder.

Heavy thundery rains and strong winds are climatic hazards of the agricultural areas. Shelter belts to break the force of the winds, strip cultivation to reduce the extent of areas of exposed soil, contour ploughing to stop the downslope movement of soil, and brushwood dams to trap soils in gulleys are a few of the steps taken to attempt to reduce their ravages.

Lucerne (alfalfa), maize and fodder grasses support large herds of cattle. Around all towns both suburban market gardening and dairying are carried on. In Moldavia grain and livestock raising are all-important, but viticulture and the growing of fruits (apples, pears, cherries, plums), nuts, vegetables and tobacco are typically associated with the area. Along the foothills of the Carpathians crops are varied and include rye, wheat, maize, sugar beet, flax, hemp, tobacco and sunflowers (Fig. 108). Potatoes and other vegetables are grown in quantity and orchards abound. Large numbers of cattle, both dairy and beef breeds, are grazed on the Carpathian slopes.

RESOURCES AND INDUSTRY

Agriculture-based industries such as flour milling, sugar refining and meat packing are represented in the majority of the cities and towns of the Ukraine–Moldavia Region, but more especially in the western part (Fig. 109). However, none of these is as important as the activities associated with the heavy industry of the Donbass in southeast Ukraine. Here are to be found the oldest centre of coal production and the largest ferrous metal-

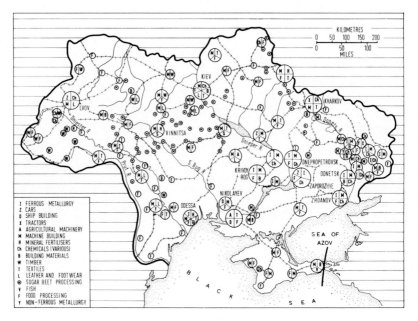

FIG. 109.—Ukraine–Moldavia Region: railways and industrial structure of towns.

lurgical region of the Soviet Union. Unlike the industries of the Central Industrial Region, which have to rely almost exclusively on imported raw materials, those of the Donbass are based on ample and varied local supplies.

The Donets Ridge contains the Donbass with its range of coals, including good coking coal (*see* p. 85). The relative importance of the Donbass in the U.S.S.R. has declined as output from newer fields, such as those in central south Siberia (Kuzbass), Kazakhstan (Karaganda), Ural (Kizel and Chelyabinsk-Kopeysk) and the Pechora Basin (Vorkuta), has grown, but Donbass still produces more than half of the Union's coking coal and about 35% of total coal production (*see* Fig. 110).

The presence of coking coals was an important factor in the early growth of metallurgy in this area. At Krivoy Rog, about 200 miles from the Donbass on the west side of the Dnieper River (cf. the distance between London and Middlesbrough), is located the Union's largest single source of haematite ore, with a metallic content of between 54 and 64% (*see* p. 94). "Enriched" ores are carried by rail to large integrated iron and steel plants in the Donbass, and for the return journey wagons are loaded with coke for use in the iron and steel industry located at Krivoy Rog. The Kerch

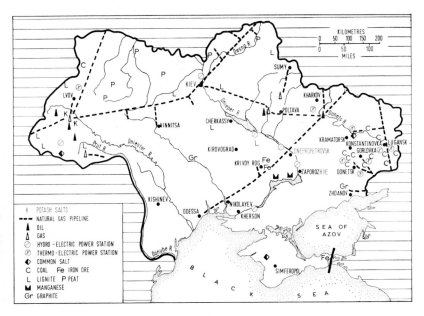

FIG. 110.—Ukraine–Moldavia Region: mineral and power resources.

Peninsula provides a second source of iron ore, but its quality is not as high as that from Krivoy Rog. Nevertheless, its transport across the Sea of Azov is cheap, and a large integrated metallurgical plant has been built at the important port of Zhdanov. The Kursk Magnetic Anomaly in the Central Chernozem Region (p. 152) provides a further source of iron ore.

At Marganets and Nikopol on the Dnieper, and lying between the Donbass and Krivoy Rog, is one of the world's major deposits of manganese (used in the production of special hard steels). A wide variety of other minerals used in the metallurgical and chemical industries is available in the Ukraine, such as bauxite, mercury, salt, fireclay and limestone. The building of several dams on the Dnieper has added an abundant supply of hydroelectricity to the resources of the region, and natural gas from the eastern

Donbass is playing an important role in metallurgy. Indeed, few great industrial areas are as well endowed with locally available raw materials or power resources as is the Ukraine (Fig. 110).

The geographical distribution of these resources has led to three major concentrations of heavy industry: (1) Donets Basin; (2) Dnieper Bend; (3) Coast of Sea of Azov (Fig. 111).

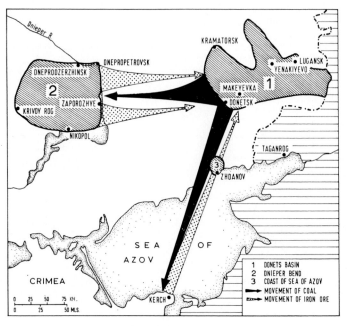

FIG. 111.—Ukraine–Moldavia Region: major concentrations of heavy industry.

Donets Basin (Donbass)

Within the 180-mile long Donets coalfield are to be found major producers of coal, pig iron, steel, chemicals and gases. Donetsk (formerly Stalino) on the western side of the coalfield is the main city. Originally known as Hughesovka (Yuzovka), it took its name from a Welshman, John Hughes, who, as head of the New Russia Metallurgical Company, founded the first ironworks here in 1869. One-time mechanic at the Cyfarthfa Iron Works in Merthyr Tydfil in South Wales, and later manager of his own iron works at Newport, Hughes had been invited by Tsar Alexander III to help to develop the Russian iron and steel industry. He took several of his countryfolk with him to found what is now the oldest steel metallurgical town in the Donbass. Donetsk is a city of mine shafts, blast furnaces, steelworks, rolling mills, engineering works, chemical plant—and supports a population of 809,000 people.

"The Yuzovka I knew no longer exists. Today there is a prosperous industrial city in its place. In those days (before the Revolution) it was a slummy settlement ringed with wooden hovels and clay huts. . . . A startling crimson flame danced above the blast furnaces. Greasy soot dripped from the sky. Nothing in Yuzovka was white. Whatever had started out as white was a blotchy, yellowish grey,— shirts, sheets, pillowcases, curtains, dogs, horses, cats. It rarely rained in Yuzovka and hot, dry winds swept the streets, stirring up the piles of dust, soot and chicken feathers into clouds. . . ."

K. *Paustovsky*, from his *Autobiography*.

Other centres such as Makeyevka, Yenakiyevo, Konstantinovka, Kramatorsk and Lugansk have collieries and large integrated iron and steelworks and associated coke-chemical plants. Apart from Lugansk (formerly Voroshilovgrad), these centres are situated on the western side of the coalfield nearest to the Krivoy Rog ores.

Dnieper Bend

This area is located between the towns of Zaporozhye, Dnepropetrovsk and Krivoy Rog and its metallurgical industry is based on coal transported from the Donbass, iron ore from Krivoy Rog, manganese from Nikopol and bauxite from the Ural. Machine-building and chemical industries are also located there. Industrial growth has received a further stimulus from newly available supplies of electricity from hydro-electric generating stations at Zaporozhye (Dneproges) and elsewhere along the Dnieper. The main centres are Dnepropetrovsk, Zaporozhye, Krivoy Rog and Dnepro-dzerzhinsk.

Coast of Sea of Azov

As would be expected, iron and steelworks have been built where Kerch iron ore is unloaded for transit to the inland steelworks of the Donets basin. This is at Zhdanov (cf. the Llanwern, Dowlais–Cardiff, and Port Talbot–Margam works in South Wales) where the huge Azovstal works are but a part of the great industrial complex which includes general machinery and shipbuilding industries. The port of Zhdanov exports coal and metallurgical products. Taganrog, another port on the shores of the Azov Sea east of Zhdanov, also has some ferrous metallurgical industry. Both ports are icebound for two and a half months in the year.

Other Industrial Centres

Outside the three industrial areas Kharkov is the most important industrial centre. It has a complex of machine-building and mechanical industries. Kiev, the administrative and intellectual capital of the Ukraine S.S.R., is also an important transport centre and has light industries: the seaport of Odessa, kept open most years by ice-breakers, has light engineering, chemical and textile industries; Kherson, a major port for handling oil and grain, is also a textile-manufacturing centre.

At Borislav and Drogobych, in the foothills of the Carpathians, is a small but valuable oilfield. Production is not great but it is useful on account of its location, since its existence dispenses with the need to haul oil 1200–1400 miles to western Ukraine from the oilfields of the Volga–Ural or from the Caucasus.

A rich source of natural gas occurs at Dashava in western Ukraine. The gas is sent to Leningrad via Pinsk and Minsk (700 miles) and to Moscow via Kiev (700 miles). Further supplies of natural gas occur in northeastern Ukraine, at Shebelinka, Sumy and Poltava.

TRANSPORT AND COMMUNICATIONS

The road and rail communications of the Ukraine–Moldavia Region are the densest and most highly developed in the Soviet Union. An arterial road via Zaporozhye and Kharkov links Sevastopol in the Crimea with Moscow, a distance of 800 miles. There are also several other lesser roads, but it is on rail transport that the region depends most heavily. The railway system is particularly dense in the Donets coalfield (Fig. 73). The Dnieper river (1425 miles long) is a major inland waterway for the region and, like the Volga to the east, it is being transformed by the construction of huge impounding dams. The dams are constructed primarily for electric power generation, but the reservoirs facilitate navigation. The reservoir at Novaya Kakhovka provides irrigation water for the Black Sea Steppe. When projects at Kiev and Kanev are completed and added to those already in existence near Zaporozhye, Novaya Kakhovka and Kremenchug, the lower Dnieper will become a chain of lakes, and Kiev itself will be a port open to ocean-going vessels for the duration of its ice-free period of 265 days in the year. There are reports of a plan to link the Dnieper and the Neman Rivers by ship canal—a scheme that would make Kiev an inland port similar to Moscow.

POPULATION AND CITIES

Practically 45 million people (21% of the total Soviet population) live in the Ukraine–Moldavia Region. Densities in the countryside are between 60 and 250 inhabitants per square mile, but in parts of western Ukraine (upper Dniester Valley and the Volyno-Podolian Upland), the Dnieper Lowlands and the Donbass they exceed 250 persons per square mile. With the exceptions of certain oases in Middle Asia, these rural densities are higher than anywhere else in the Soviet Union. Rural settlement, which was at one time dispersed, now takes the form of single compact villages belonging to huge *kolkhozy*. The houses are generally constructed of prefabricated wood sections and the settlements are usually strung along routeways ("street villages"), near a watercourse, or in a gulley where water is available.

[*Fotokhronika Tass.*

FIG. 112.—Kiev, capital of Ukraine S.S.R.

Kiev (1,348,000), situated on the high western bank of the Dnieper 300 ft above the level of the river and just a few miles below its confluence with the Desna, is the administrative, commercial and cultural capital of the Ukraine S.S.R. (Fig. 112). The city was capital of Russia long before Moscow and has been described as the "Mother of Russian towns." It is an important focus of rail, river and road routes. Local industries (both in Kiev and in the industrial suburb of Darnitsa on the low east bank of the river) rely on raw materials and fuels brought in from other parts of the country. Manufactures include machinery of several kinds, chemicals, commercial vehicles, motor cycles, river craft, aircraft, leather and foot-wear, and general food products (Fig. 109). One of the "million" cities of the Soviet Union, Kiev increased its population by over one-fifth be-tween 1959 and 1964.

Kharkov (1,070,000) was founded in the seventeenth century as a military outpost on the southern frontier of Muscovy, but its importance dates from the nineteenth century with the rise of the Donbass as an industrial base. Kharkov functions as the gateway from Moscow to the Donets Basin and is a focal point for eight rail routes. Industrialisation has proceeded rapidly, but the city and its industries were severely damaged during World War II. Replanned and rebuilt by 1956, it is now the largest single industrial centre in the Ukraine–Moldavia Region, with engineering works producing locomotives, tractors, aircraft, turbines, electrical and mining equipment, machine tools, agricultural machinery, motor cycles and bicycles. Though a "million" city, it is growing more slowly than Kiev and its population increase in the five-year period 1959–64 was only 15%. It now ranks seventh in size in the Soviet Union.

Seventy miles southwest of Kharkov is *Poltava* (170,000). As the seventh-century centre of the Ukrainian Cossacks, it is of historical interest. Now it is a commercial town with textile, food and engineering industries.

Within the Donbass there is a hierarchy of towns, at the peak of which stands *Donetsk* (809,000), surrounded by several satellite suburbs. It is the principal economic, administrative, cultural and industrial centre of the Donets basin, with coal mining, iron and steel, metal working, machinery and chemicals as the main industries. *Makeyevka* (399,000), *Gorlovka* (337,000), *Lugansk* (330,000), *Kramatorsk* (135,000) and *Konstantinovka* (99,000) are all industrial cities with individual specialisations. In addition to their coal mining and heavy industry they produce machinery, transport equipment and chemicals. Lesser manufacturing centres include Volno-vakha, Ilovaysk and Yasinovataya which have in addition important trans-port functions, linking places that produce raw materials with those producing semi-finished goods and with cities producing finished articles. In the urban hierarchy of the Donets basin there follow such exclusively iron and steel producing centres as Khartsyzsk, Kommunarsk and Yenakiyevo, chemical centres such as Rubezhnoye and Lisichansk, and other centres of the coal industry such as Krasnyy Luch.

Dnepropetrovsk (774,000) is the chief centre of the heavy industry area of the Dnieper Bend. It stands on the high right bank of the Dnieper River almost opposite the confluence with the Samara. The town was founded in the latter part of the eighteenth century when, under Catherine the Great, Russian territories were being extended to the west bank of the Dnieper, but it was not until the construction of railway links with the Donbass, Moscow and Odessa that industrialisation commenced and its population increased. It has developed steel industries (on the basis of Krivoy Rog iron ore, Donbass coal, Nikopol manganese, and hydro-electric power from Dneproges), heavy engineering (locomotives, rolling stock, bridge girders, mining machinery) vehicle tyres and chemical industries. *Zaporozhye* (550,000), founded as a fortress against the Crimean Tatars in 1770, is now a major industrial centre well known for its alloy steel (based on cheap Dneproges electricity, local pig iron and alloys), rolled steel, engineering and chemicals. The local abundance of hydro-electricity was decisive in the siting of a plant at Zaporozhye to smelt clayey bauxite from north of Serov in the Ural. *Krivoy Rog* (488,000) is, like Zaporozhye, a rapidly expanding steel and engineering centre. The populations of both cities increased by over 25% in the period 1959–64. The near-by reserves of high-quality iron ore provide the basis not only for the local iron mining and steel-making and engineering industries but also for the well-developed metallurgical industries of the Donbass. *Dneprodzerzhinsk* (218,000), on the Dnieper, about 20 miles upstream of Dnepropetrovsk, is in many respects a suburb of the latter. It produces high-grade steels, chemicals, railway rolling stock and cement, using hydro-electricity generated near by; the city also has river port functions. Ninety miles west of Dneprodzerzhinsk and just within the Volyno-Podolian Upland, is *Kirovograd* (153,000). It has agricultural machinery and food industries. *Odessa* (735,000), picturesquely situated on terraced hills 20 miles northeast of the mouth of the Dniester river, is one of the chief ports of the Soviet Union (Fig. 113). The present town was founded in the fourteenth century by the Tatars, but during the course of its history it has undergone several vicissitudes at the hands of Lithuanians, Poles, Turks, Germans and revolutionaries, and suffered also from the effects of famine and diseases. The port exports grain, timber and sugar; imports are mainly petroleum, coal, iron and cotton. Agricultural implements, cranes, lathes, transport equipment, grain elevators are manufactured and motor vehicles assembled in its industrial suburbs. Caucasus oil is refined here, and there is much processing of flour, sugar and hides. Odessa is a major cultural centre with a cosmopolitan population which increased by about 70,000 in the five-year period 1959–64. Farther east at the mouth of the River Bug, is *Nikolayev* (280,000), founded as a shipbuilding and naval base at the end of the eighteenth century. Many ocean-going vessels of the Soviet Union are built here, and there are also agricultural engineering works, food and light industries. *Kherson* (210,000) was established about the same time as Nikolayev and for the same purpose. The port, on the Dnieper, 15 miles from the river mouth, exports grains and manganese and imports oil from the Caucasus. In addition to shipbuilding it also has agricultural machinery, textile and food industries. The population of Kherson increased by a third between 1959 and 1964. *Lvov* (496,000) (Polish *Lwow*, German *Lemberg*) was a centre of Polish culture and Roman Catholicism until 1939 when, with the two southeastern provinces of Poland (Volhynia and Galicia), it became part of western Ukraine. It was a medieval city at the focus of routes from Volhynia and Podolia and along the Dniester River. Its industries include food processing, textiles, electrical equipment and motor vehicles.

[*Fotokhronika Tass.*

FIG. 113.—Odessa harbour viewed from the seashore boulevard. Odessa, on the Black Sea, is one of the chief ports of the Soviet Union.

Kishinev (282,000) is capital of the Moldavian Republic, the former Rumanian province of Bessarabia, between the Rivers Prut and Dniester. In addition to its administrative and cultural functions it possesses varied light industries concerned with food and wine, leather and tobacco processing. *Chernovtsy* (172,000), on the Prut within the Carpathian foothills, is an ancient town of Kiev Rus. It has experienced Polish, Austro-Hungarian, and Rumanian rule, but was taken over by the U.S.S.R. from Rumania in 1947. It has textile, food and light engineering industries.

Crimea, linked to the Ukraine by the narrow Perekop Isthmus, has been part of the Ukraine–Moldavian Region since 1954. It is, nevertheless, distinctive and in certain respects unique. Wheat and sunflowers are grown on the mineral-rich steppe soils of the northern two-thirds of the peninsula, but drought conditions associated with a semi-arid climate make agriculture hazardous. The narrow strip of coast south of Krymskiye Gory

(Crimean Mountains) and between Yalta and Alushta is protected from cold northerly winds and has a Mediterranean-type climate. Enjoying mild damp winters (when the rest of the Union is frozen up) and long, warm, dry summers, this section of the Black Sea coast is a popular resort area. Of the several towns here, each with its quota of hotels and sanatoria (holiday homes), Yalta is the largest, and probably the best known, through the world attention it achieved in 1945, when Churchill (U.K.), Roosevelt (U.S.A.) and Stalin (U.S.S.R.) held a conference there to discuss Allied policy. *Simferopol* (213,000) on the northern slopes of Krymskiye Gory is an important administrative and transport centre. *Sevastopol* (192,000), standing on the southwest tip of the peninsula near the site of the ancient Greek colony *Chersonesus*, is the chief Soviet naval base on the Black Sea. It is famous in British history as the scene of the siege by the Anglo-French armies during the Crimean War (1854–56). The battlefields of Balaclava and Inkerman are near by. *Kerch* (114,000) on the extreme eastern end of the peninsula is a port and centre of an iron-mining and metallurgical district. It occupies the site of the ancient Greek town of *Panticapaeum*.

STUDY QUESTIONS

1. Suggest a division of Ukraine–Moldavia into geographical regions. Discuss the bearing of physical factors upon economic activities in any *two* of the regions recognised.

2. Write a short description of the agricultural activities of the Ukraine and Moldavia.

3. Analyse and discuss the industrial development of the Donets coalfield.

4. Discuss the evolution of the iron and steel industry in the Ukraine.

5. Assess the importance of the Donbass–Dnieper complex in the industrial economy of the U.S.S.R.

6. With reference to the U.S.S.R., discuss the modification of mid-latitude grasslands by man.

7. Give a geographical account of vine cultivation and wine production in Moldavia.

8. Give a geographical account of the utilisation of *either* the River Dnieper, *or* the River Dniester.

9. Account for the large amount of arable farming and large agricultural population in the Ukraine.

10. Estimate the importance of climate in the agricultural geography of the Ukraine.

11. Make a geographical comparison of *either* Kiev and Kharkov *or* Donetsk and Krivoy Rog.

12. Examine the site, location and functions of the following towns: Lvov; Odessa; Zaporozhye; Zhdanov; Nikolayev; Dnepropetrovsk; Simferopol.

13. Make a comparative study of the Black Sea ports.

14. Write a geographical essay on the tourist industry of the Crimea.

15. In what areas of the Ukraine has gullying become acute and why? Give an account of the ways by which gullying is being controlled.

G

Chapter XV

WEST REGION

This Region, which is generally agricultural in economy but has an expanding industrial zone along the Baltic coast, embraces the three Baltic Republics of Lithuania, Latvia and Estonia, the republic of Belorussia (White Russia) and Oblast Kaliningrad. It stretches westwards to the Baltic Sea and the international boundary with Poland, eastwards to the boundaries of the Central Industrial Region and the Northwest Region, southward to the northern boundary of the Ukraine–Moldavia

FIG. 114.—West Region.

Region, and northwards to the Gulf of Finland (Fig. 114). Invasions by Tatars, Teutonic Knights, Swedes, Poles, French and Germans have given the region a chequered history. Furthermore, it has suffered considerable deportations and mass movements of population. Lithuania, Latvia and Estonia were three fully independent countries in 1940, before being annexed by the U.S.S.R. The western half of Belorussia was formerly part of Poland. Oblast Kaliningrad (an outlying part of the R.S.F.S.R.) represents the northern half of the former German province of East Prussia; the German town of Königsberg was renamed Kaliningrad.

Area . . . . 154,000 sq. miles
Population (1959) . . 14,673,000

Administrative unit	Area sq. miles	Population in thousands 1959	Density persons per sq. mile	Percentage urban
Estonian S.S.R. . .	17,000	1,196 (1,273)*	67	56
Latvian S.S.R. . .	25,000	2,094 (2,241)*	85	56
Lithuanian S.S.R. .	26,000	2,713 (2,949)*	109	39
Belorussian S.S.R. .	80,000	8,060 (8,533)*	101	31
Oblast Kaliningrad .	6,000	610	104	64

Towns with over 150,000 inhabitants in 1964

	Population in thousands 1959	1964	Percentage increase 1959–64
Minsk	509	717 (707)*	41·0
Riga	580	658 (657)*	13·5
Tallin	282	330 (328)*	17·0
Vilnius . . .	236	298 (293)*	26·2
Kaunas. . . .	214	269	25·8
Kaliningrad . . .	204	253	24·0
Gomel	168	216	28·5
Vitebsk . . .	148	187	26·2
Mogilev . . .	122	156	28·0

* January 1, 1965 (est.).

PHYSICAL ASPECTS

RELIEF

Physically the West Region consists of lowland and occasional low hills, with much evidence of post-Pleistocene glacial deposition. The sandy moraines extending from north of Brest through Minsk, make up the Belorussian Hills (their continuation eastwards is the Smolensk–Moscow Ridge). They represent the southern limit of the Valday glacial stage and constitute the main Baltic End Moraine. These hills, 70–80 miles wide and 600–1000 ft high, barely modify the general flatness of the region but form an important divide between north-flowing (Baltic) and south-flowing (Black Sea) rivers. They also provide a "dry" route between Poland and the Soviet Union for road and rail. Along this route Napoleon's army

[*Mysl.*

FIG. 115.—Polesye, "land of forest clearing," along the Pripyat River, in Belorussia
This is an area of swamp and extensive forests of pine, oak, willow and alder.

moved in 1812 and Hitler's army in 1941. The area to the north of the hills is a classic example of morainic deposition—an undulating glacial plain (the Neman and Polotsk Lowlands) with festoons of low morainic hills, smoothly rounded drumlins, thousands of lake-filled basins, swamps and erratic boulders. The plain itself terminates in many miles of low, sandy coast on the Baltic, and in cliffs (the "Glint") on the Gulf of Finland.

South of the Belorussian Hills lie extensive areas of glacial outwash sands. Along the upper Dnieper and Berezina there are cultivated lowlands, but within the broad shallow trough of the Pripyat River lies the swampy region of Polesye (Fig. 115).

"... Polesye has remained in my memory as a sad and mysterious country."

K. Paustovsky

Into the trough of Polesye there drained melt-water from the Pleistocene ice sheet, and with it great quantities of deposits of sands and clays, which in such a flat area have poorly developed drainage. This has led to the formation of very extensive swamps—the Pripet Marshes—through which the streams wind sluggishly. Polesye forms the northwest section of the Dnieper Lowland (*see* p. 158).

CLIMATE, NATURAL VEGETATION AND SOILS

By Russian standards, winters in the region are mild. Average January temperatures vary from 26° to 30° F (−3° to −1° C) in the Baltic coastlands to 17° to 18° F (−8·5° to −7·5° C) inland (Fig. 116). Occasional invasions

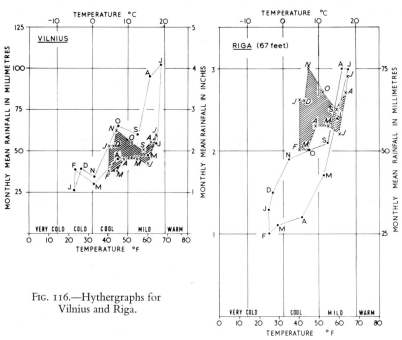

FIG. 116.—Hythergraphs for Vilnius and Riga.

of milder, moister air from the Atlantic during this season cause temporary thaws (*ottepeli*). Summers are cool, the average July temperature ranging from 58° to 60° F (14·5° to 15·5° C) in the north to 66° F (19° C) in the south. Average annual precipitation is 20–26 in. (500–660 mm) with a slight summer (May–September) maximum. Winter precipitation comes in the form of snow, which lies for about four months, but depths are generally less than 1 ft.

The soils developed on both the glacial clays and the sands tend to be podzolised and are of varying degrees of fertility. Boulder clays and sediments deposited in ice-dammed lakes are reasonably fertile and well cultivated, but the sandy areas are invariably wooded with pine, spruce, oak and maple. Areas of swamp and bog are large, and increase in area and frequency towards the south. In Polesye, where swamp and bog are dominant, there are extensive forests of oak and pine.

THE ECONOMY

AGRICULTURE AND FORESTRY

Agriculture is limited to small scattered fields within the forest, swamp and morainic hills. Main crops are rye, oats, barley, wheat, flax, potatoes, beet and also fodder (grass and clover) for cattle (Fig. 117). This is the

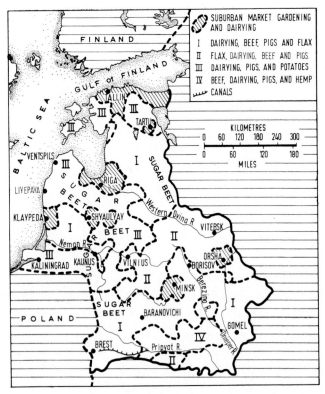

FIG. 117.—West Region: agricultural land-use regions.

chief flax-growing region of the U.S.S.R. The crop is grown in a six-year rotation with fodder crops. Flax-processing mills and linen mills are located in a number of towns such as Yelgava, Pyarnu, Vitebsk and Orsha, but the greater part is sent to linen mills in the Yaroslavl and Kostroma districts east of Moscow. Cattle are raised for both beef and milk, and latterly there has been an appreciable increase in the number of pigs and sheep. All parts except the coastal zones are important for dairy produce, particularly for milk and butter. Such activities as flour milling, milk processing, butter and margarine manufacture, meat packing, fruit and vegetable canning and general food processing are widely distributed. Much of the produce is sent to other parts of the Soviet Union, in particular to the Leningrad district.

Widespread forests—they occupy well over a quarter of the total area of the region—have given rise to an important timber industry. Gomel and Bobruysk are especially important for sawn timber, wood veneers, pulp, paper, furniture, matches and prefabricated houses.

FISHING INDUSTRY

Unlike most other parts of the Soviet Union, the three Baltic Republics have sea coasts, which are, moreover, less hampered by ice than those near the head of the Gulf of Finland. Leningrad is ice-bound for four or five months from December onwards, but the average duration of the winter freeze at Baltiysk, the outport of Kaliningrad, is only four weeks. With the help of ice-breakers Baltiysk, Klaypeda, Liyepaya, Tallin and Ventspils are kept open to shipping throughout the winter, but Riga, at the southern tip of the Gulf of Riga, is ice-bound from the end of December until the middle of April.

People in the West Region are more bound to the sea than those of other parts of the U.S.S.R.—many gain their livelihood from fishing and from service in the merchant navy. Trawler fleets from the Baltic ports operate within the Baltic itself, in the North Sea, and in the Atlantic Ocean (around Iceland, Newfoundland, Labrador and Greenland) and land catches of herring, cod and other species. Flatfish, pilchards, sprats and eels are taken in local waters. Smoking, drying, freezing and general fish processing take place at the Baltic ports prior to long-distance distribution to consumers in the interior of the Union.

TRADING AND INDUSTRIAL ACTIVITIES

The Baltic Republics are transit lands for goods from interior regions such as the central Belorussian and the Volga lands. Traditionally they are orientated to foreign trade. Their ports are the best means of access to the North Atlantic, and for decades before the Revolution of 1917 they played a leading role in Russia's foreign trade. This necessitated good communications with the Russian interior, and the railway network linking the ports with inland cities is impressive (Fig. 118). The volume of trade with the non-Communist world has decreased (all trade with countries outside the U.S.S.R. is arranged by the central authorities), but that with Soviet satellite countries continues to grow. Riga, Tallin, Klaypeda and Baltiysk are busy, well-equipped ports; Pyarnu, Ventspils and Liyepaya are smaller, with a more local trade, but they function also as service ports for navy and air forces stationed on the Baltic.

The region lacks coal, but shale-oil deposits in the northeast of the Estonian S.S.R. are important both locally and farther afield (Fig. 119). Heavy oil and gas distillation takes place at Kokhtla Yarve, and the gas is conveyed by pipeline westwards to Tallin and eastwards to Leningrad. Power generation is supplemented by local peat and wood, and by water at a station on the Narva River. There are no metal ores, and raw material for industry is not plentiful. Potash found near Starobin in south central Belorussia supplies a mineral fertiliser industry, and there is limestone for a rapidly expanding cement industry. Manufacturing industries tend to specialise in products that combine the application of skill with relatively small quantities of raw material brought in from other parts of the Union. Many of the Baltic ports are producers of machinery (for food processing, textiles and precision equipment), electrical and electronic equipment, machine tools, electric rail cars, diesel engines, optics and furniture, and despite the absence of local sources of raw material and local markets, there is significant production of chemical products such as dyestuffs, rubber goods and fertilisers, together with textile and leather goods. Industries directly related to the sea, such as shipbuilding (merchant and naval), equipment used in shipping, and fish processing are also found in these ports (Fig. 118). As a group, the Baltic coast ports constitute a developing industrial area which is more the result of their maritime position, tradition of foreign trade, and government planning than of the availability of supplies of energy and raw materials.

POPULATION AND CITIES

The West Region supports about 14·7 million people. In Estonia, Latvia and in Oblast Kaliningrad the town populations are large and well above the national average of 54%. Everywhere else in the region the population is essentially rural. In the main, the countryfolk live in dispersed wooden farmsteads, but with the gradual introduction of collective farms (*kolkhozy*) more and more are living in compact villages. The region as a whole, and particularly the Baltic States following their annexation in 1940,

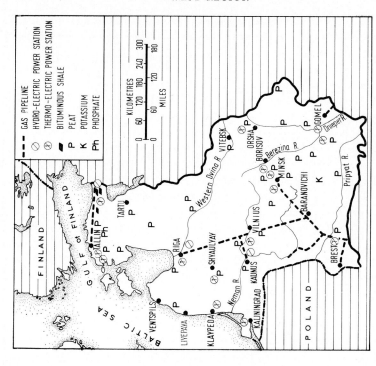

FIG. 119.—West Region: mineral and power resources.

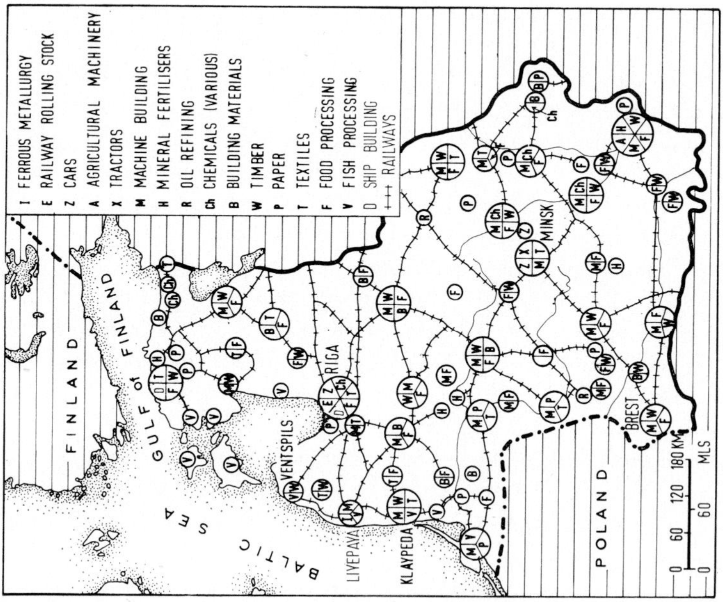

FIG. 118.—West Region: railways and industrial structure of towns.

have experienced sizeable deportations of people and suffered from mass emigration. At present most of the main towns contain a large Russian element of new settlers.

Minsk (717,000), located near the western boundary of the Soviet Union, is the largest city of the West Region. It has had a stormy history and changed more than once from Russian to Tatar, Polish, Swedish or Lithuanian control. It was situated on Napoleon's invasion route and was occupied by the Germans from 1941–4. By the end of World War II the city was in ruins, but has since been rebuilt. Minsk is the capital of the Belorussian S.S.R. and is important as a commercial and industrial city manufacturing, among other things, heavy lorries, tractors, commercial vehicles, machine tools, radios, textiles and leather goods (Fig. 118).

Riga (658,000), capital of the Latvian S.S.R. is the major outlet for western U.S.S.R. It is situated at the southern extremity of the Gulf of Riga 8 miles above the mouth of the Western Dvina, and connected by inland canals with the basins of the Dnieper and Volga. The city was once an important member of the Hanseatic League and has a long tradition of foreign trade. Exports include flax, timber, wooden goods and dairy produce; imports include sugar, industrial equipment, coal, fertilisers and raw materials for local industries. Riga engages in shipbuilding, engineering and the manufacture of chemicals and is a major rail centre and airport handling traffic with Scandinavia and Western Europe. It also has the famous Rigas Yurmala seaside resort area. Unlike most other peoples of the U.S.S.R. the majority of those living in Riga are Lutherans by religion.

Tallin (330,000), on the Gulf of Finland, is the capital of the Estonian S.S.R. and a large seaport. Like Riga it was a member of the Hanseatic League and it continues to have important trading functions. Exports from its large port include timber, paper and cement; imports include cotton and coal; local manufacturing industries embrace textiles, paper making, cement, timber products, engineering and shipbuilding.

Vilnius (298,000), capital of the Lithuanian S.S.R., was centre of a very much larger historic Lithuania which, shortly after the destruction of Kiev Rus (p. 48), extended from the Baltic Sea to the Ukraine. The present city bears the imprint of Polish, Jewish, Russian, German and Lithuanian cultures, although its population is now largely Lithuanian and Russian. It is an important inland railway junction with some industry, devoted mainly to agricultural machinery and electrical goods.

Kaunus (269,000), like Vilnius, has had a chequered history. It was founded in the eleventh century at the confluence of the Neris and Neman Rivers, since when it has suffered several attacks and occupations by Teutonic Knights, Poles, Russians and Germans. It is now second town of the Lithuanian Republic but with only limited cultural and industrial functions.

Kaliningrad (253,000), and the oblast of that name, were ceded to the Soviet Union by the Potsdam agreement at the end of World War II. The oblast represents the northern half of the former German province of East Prussia and the town the German Königsberg. Both form an outlying part of the R.S.F.S.R. in which the German population has been replaced by Russians. Kaliningrad and its outport Baltiysk together form an important ice-free port and naval base. This most recent Russian "Window on the West" combines shipbuilding, engineering, chemicals and woodworking with important commercial functions.

Gomel (216,000), now largely restored after almost complete destruction during World War II, is a regional centre in southeastern Belorussia. It has agricultural machinery, timber and fertiliser industries.

Vitebsk (187,000) on the Western Dvina, is yet another town in the West Region which was severely damaged during World War II. Its slow recovery from the degradation of 1944 is based on timber, linen, food and engineering industries.

Mogilev (156,000), on the Dnieper, was important during Kiev Rus times when the river was a recognised highway. Now its limited commercial functions are supported by some engineering, chemical and food industries.

STUDY QUESTIONS

1. Suggest a division of the West Region into geographical regions. Discuss the bearing of physical factors upon economic activities in any *two* of the regions recognised.

2. Make a geographical study of the river systems of the West Region. Illustrate your answer with a sketch-map.

3. Assess the potential in the West Region for dairying and the arising of beef cattle, pigs and poultry.

4. Examine the post-war development of light manufacturing in the Baltic Republics.

5. Compare Riga and Kaliningrad as ports.

6. Examine the site, location and functions of the following towns: Kaunas; Vilnius; Tallin; Minsk.

Chapter XVI

NORTHWEST REGION

THE Leningrad area, with its wide range of industries of national and international importance, is the focal point of this otherwise poor and predominantly rural region (Fig. 120).

Area . . . . 198,600 sq. miles
Population (1959) . . 7,471,000

Administrative unit	Area sq. miles	Population in thousands 1959	Density persons per sq. mile	Percentage urban
Oblast Leningrad . . .	33,000	4,561	137	86
Oblast Novogorod . . .	21,000	740	34	38
Oblast Pskov	21,000	954	44	27
Oblast Murmansk . . .	56,600	567	10	92
Karelskaya A.S.S.R. . . .	67,000	649★	10	63

★ 696,000 on January 1, 1965 (est.).

Towns with over 150,000 inhabitants in 1964

	Population in thousands		Percentage increase
	1959	1964	1959–64
Leningrad . . .	3,321	3,641	9·8
Murmansk . . .	222	272	22·6
Petrozavodsk . .	136	157	15·5

PHYSICAL ASPECTS

STRUCTURE AND RELIEF

The physical landscape is everywhere dominated by the effects of the Pleistocene glaciations. North of a line from Leningrad to Lake Ladoga to Lake Onega, Pre-Cambrian granites, schists and gneisses, which belonged to the structural core of the country (the Fenno-Scandian Shield) and were already peneplaned, were subjected to a succession of glacial advances and retreats. Bare rock surfaces, ice-scoured basins, whale-backed drumlins and sinuous eskers bear witness to glacial action. Everywhere there are lakes, big and small, named and unnamed, and a labyrinth of rivers and waterways (Fig. 121). The plateau-like Khibiny Mountains, 2000–4000 ft high

Fig. 120.—Northwest Region.

in the Kola Peninsula are an exception in a monotonously rolling landscape of lakes and swamps where heights above 1500 ft are rarely attained.

Where the southern edge of the Archaean Fenno-Scandian Shield abuts upon limestones and clays of Cambrian and Silurian age, a zone of differential erosion is marked by a prominent escarpment, which runs south of Leningrad and westwards to near the Estonian coast, where it is known as the

"Glint." The broad depression at the base of the escarpment is occupied by lakes, of which the largest are Ladoga and Onega, covering 7000 and 3800 sq. miles respectively.

To the south the countryside is one of low plateaux and marshy lowlands (Volkhov-Lovat), strewn with such glacial depositional forms as moraines and eskers and with sandy deposits and irregular heaps of detritus. The Valday Hills in the extreme southeast of the region constitute a prominent morainic ridge rising to over 700 feet.

[*Mysl.*

FIG. 121.—Karelian scene. One of the scores of lakes that stud the hard rock shield country of Karelia.

DRAINAGE AND WATERWAYS

Drainage systems have been disturbed by glaciation and seem to have little obvious pattern. Rivers are immature and there are frequent rapids and waterfalls which afford potential for hydro-electricity production. The Gulf of Finland is linked with the Volga system via a series of canals and rivers. The waterway follows the Neva from Leningrad, then skirts the southern shores of Lake Ladoga to the River Svir, thence via Lake Onega, the Vytegra and Kovsha Rivers to the River Sheksna which joins the Volga at Rybinsk Reservoir. The number of locks on this, the old Mariinsk

Canal System, has been reduced from 38 to 7, and the whole waterway completely renovated and renamed the Volga–Baltic Canal, which is capable of handling ships with loads up to 2700 tons. Another waterway link via the Sheksna River, Lake Kubenskoye and the Sukhona joins the Northern Dvina River. Ocean-going vessels can travel from the Gulf of Finland to the White Sea along the White Sea–Baltic Canal, but the route is reported to be little used. The Volkhov, flowing to Lake Ilmen and thence to Lake Ladoga once formed part of the historical "White Road" from the Baltic and Gulf of Finland to the Black Sea and Byzantium. The hydro-electricity generating station on this river is the largest of six supplying power to Leningrad.

CLIMATE

In contrast to most other parts of the Soviet Union, the climate of this region is characterised by a relatively high frequency of maritime air. Winters are long, cold and raw. Winter temperatures range from 18° to

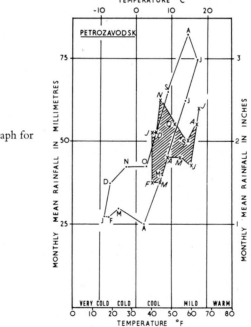

FIG. 122.—Hythergraph for Petrozavodsk.

20° F (−8° to −7·5° C) near the head of the Gulf of Finland and along the north coast of the Kola Peninsula, to about 10° F (−12° C) in the east of the region (Fig. 122). Skies are frequently overcast and there is much fog. Occasional invasions of milder moister air from the Atlantic cause temporary thaws (*ottepeli*). Summer days are long and cool, with mean temperatures during the period April–October from 40° to 50° F (4° to 10° C) but in July average mean temperatures range from near 60° F (15·6° C) in the south to 50° F (10° C) in the north. Precipitation aggregates range from about 25 in. (635 mm) on the Baltic Coast to less than 16 in. (400 mm) along the White Sea. Maxima occur during the period July–September. Winter snow lies for about four months in the southwest and more than six months in the north, although depths rarely exceed 12 in. (30 cm).

"On clear frosty nights is seen (from the Khibin mountains) a bright and beautiful aurora borealis. The whole sky blazes with multicoloured ribbons and shafts of light which continually change form and irridesce with endless hues."

G. D. Rikhter, 1946

NATURAL VEGETATION AND SOILS

The northern shores of the Kola Peninsula in the extreme north of the region lie within the tundra. Southwards the tundra merges into a poor, thin boreal forest although the tayga is well represented in Karelia. The area south of Novgorod and west of Leningrad lies within the mixed forest zone. About half the region is covered by forest. Everywhere the soils are infertile podzols which become extremely thin and poor within the tundra.

THE ECONOMY

AGRICULTURE

Agriculture, which reaches its economic northern limits within the Northwest Region, is everywhere restricted by the harsh environment and the widespread forest cover. Modest amounts of barley, oats, rye, wheat, flax, potatoes, cabbages and hay are grown and there is a small amount of dairying and rearing of cattle and horses. Near Leningrad glacial clays have been drained and utilised for market gardening to provide fresh vegetables for the second largest city in the Soviet Union (Fig. 123).

FISHING

In the Barents and White Seas a continuation of the warm North Atlantic Drift meets the cold waters of the Arctic, and there is a rich plankton (minute algae, protozoa, rotifers, crustacea, molluscs, etc.) which provide food for fish. Oblast Murmansk and Karelia are important for their fishing industry. Cod, herring and sea perch are caught, and landed at the ice-free ports of Murmansk and Port Vladimir. Here fish is canned and processed, and there are ancillary activities of glue making, cod-liver oil extraction and the making of fish meal. Kandalaksha, Kem and Belomorsk are important fishing centres on the White Sea.

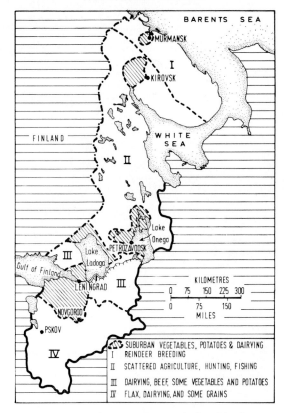

FIG. 123.—Northwest Region: agricultural land-use regions.

FOREST INDUSTRIES

Karelia and Oblast Leningrad are part of the traditional home of the Russian timber industry. Sawmills abound and pulp, paper, plywood, furniture, prefabricated houses, cellulose, matches and laminates are produced at centres along the Murmansk–Leningrad Railway (e.g. Petrozavodsk), around Lake Onega (e.g. Kondopoga) and Lake Ladoga (e.g. Petrokrepost, Lakhdenpokhya and Olonets), at Leningrad and Murmansk. Timber is exported from Belomorsk, Murmansk and Leningrad (Fig. 124).

MINING INDUSTRY

Increasing attention is now being given to the exploitation of the mineral wealth of the region. In the Khibiny Mountains of the Kola Peninsula there are exceptionally large reserves of apatite (phosphate rock), which form the basis of a phosphate fertiliser industry both locally in Kirovsk and

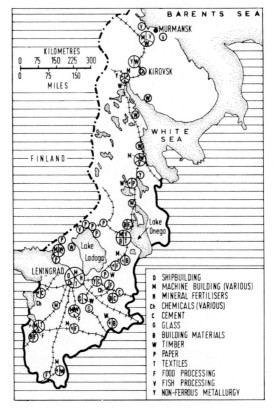

FIG. 124.—Northwest Region: railways and
industrial structure of towns.

in Leningrad 500 miles away. The Kola Peninsula also contains important
deposits of nickel and cobalt (at Nikel and Monchegorsk), copper, iron ore
(at Olenegorsk and Monchegorsk), nepheline (at Kirovsk) and mica which
have given rise to large-scale mining, refining and chemical enterprises in
Kirovsk and Kandalaksha. In Karelia there are scattered low-grade deposits
of iron ore and several non-metallic minerals (Fig. 125).

POWER RESOURCES

Coal and petroleum are not found in the region and recourse is made to
peat and lignite, and in the case of the Red October and the Dubrovsk
electricity-generating stations in Leningrad, to shale-oil gas from Kokhtla
Yarve in the Estonian S.S.R. On the other hand, there is an abundant
supply of hydro-electricity, particularly from stations on the Volkhov,
Svir and in the far north, on the Tuloma. The Kola Peninsula has the most

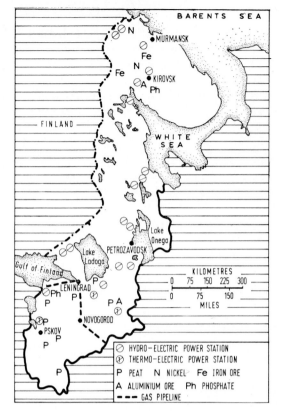

FIG. 125.—Northwest Region: mineral and power
resources.

northerly electric grid transmission system in the world, supplying Leningrad, where it supplements thermal electricity based on coal supplies drawn
from as far afield as the Vorkuta field and the Donbass. The presence of
hydro-electricity generating stations in places gives rise to small industrial
nuclei. Kandalaksha and Nivastroy in the Kola Peninsula have aluminium
smelters using hydro-electricity generated on the Niva River. The Volkhov
station provides power for aluminium smelters which utilise bauxite
mined at Boksitogorsk, 60 miles to the southeast, and nepheline mined in
the vicinity of Kirovsk in the Kola Peninsula, 330 miles to the north.

MANUFACTURING INDUSTRY

Manufacturing industry in the Northwest Region is centred mainly on
Leningrad which was the first Russian city to feel the impact of the Industrial Revolution (Fig. 126). The Elektrosila works is one of the biggest

producers of electrical equipment in the world and absorbs nearly half of the entire labour force of the city. The remainder are largely employed in the Lenin Plant for machine tools, in the Red Triumph rubber works (the biggest in Europe), in chemicals (providing half of the Russian output of fertilisers, plastics, paints and synthetic rubber), textiles, food processing, ship building, light industries (clothing, footwear, porcelain) and printing. Leningrad is also the largest centre for book production in the Soviet

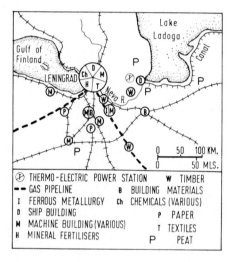

Fig. 126.—Leningrad industrial area.

℗ THERMO-ELECTRIC POWER STATION W TIMBER
━ ━ GAS PIPELINE B BUILDING MATERIALS
I FERROUS METALLURGY Ch CHEMICALS (VARIOUS)
D SHIP BUILDING P PAPER
M MACHINE BUILDING (VARIOUS) T TEXTILES
H MINERAL FERTILISERS P PEAT

Union. The bulk of the goods is manufactured from raw materials imported into the city either from abroad or from within the Union, e.g. timber from Karelia, apatite from Kola.

Metal products from iron and steel works at Cherepovets on the shore of the Rybinsk Reservoir, and derived from Kola Peninsula iron ore, are sent to Leningrad for fabrication.

Apart from Leningrad there are only small manufacturing centres. Flax, sawmilling, food processing and leather industries are located at Novgorod, Pskov and Velikiye-Luki. Petrozavodsk has been a ferrous metallurgical centre since pre-Revolutionary times.

TRANSPORT AND COMMUNICATIONS

The movement of raw materials from source to processing and manufacturing centres, and thence to consuming centres or export points, presupposes an adequate transportation system. The routes on which the exploitation of the Kola Peninsula and Finno-Karelia depend are the Baltic–White Sea Canal and the Leningrad–Murmansk Railway. The former, completed in 1933, enables merchant ships to ply between the Baltic and

White Seas with bulk freights such as timber, apatite and granite. The 900-mile long Leningrad–Murmansk railway line, the first major piece of railway construction under the Soviets, not only aids the exploitation of Kola–Karelia, but also enables Murmansk to function as the outport for Leningrad during the winter (Fig. 124). Leningrad is the main railway focus. The 404-mile line to Moscow, the first important railway to be built in Russia, and one of the straightest in the world, was completed in 1842. It is electrified throughout and the Leningrad–Moscow journey can be made in as little as 5 hr. 20 min. (1965 timetable). The important Volga–Baltic Canal has been noted above.

[*Fotokhronika Tass.*

FIG. 127.—Leningrad: view of the Neva embankment. Memorial to Peter the Great in the foreground; the University is on the far side of the river and the eighteenth-century Cathedral and the Peter and Paul (Petropavlovskaya) Fortress lies beyond the bridge.

POPULATION AND CITIES

The Leningrad–Novgorod Region has long been a meeting-place for Russians of Slavonic speech, Scandinavians of Teutonic speech and Karelians of Finnish speech. It is also transitional between the land-based cultures of the interior and the sea-based cultures of the Baltic S.S.R.s. In the Middle

Ages both Novgorod and Pskov were flourishing centres on the "Water Road" when Moscow was comparatively isolated and unimportant. However, both were eclipsed when, after the acquisition of the Neva area from the Swedes, St Petersburg (Leningrad) was founded at the beginning of the eighteenth century.

Now over 60% of the 7½ million people of the Northwest Region live in Oblast Leningrad. Rural populations are sparse and vast areas in the Kola Peninsula and in Karelia are uninhabited. In the northern areas there is a mixed population of Russians and Karelo-Finns, the latter speaking their own non-Russian languages. The Russians were attracted by the excellence of the fisheries and mineral deposits.

Leningrad (3,641,000) is sited on a marshy swamp within three distributaries of the Neva River and between the Gulf of Finland and Lake Ladoga. The city is laid out to generous standards with long wide streets like the Nevsky Prospect and boulevards, huge squares and spacious parks, interwoven by canals (Fig. 127). Such buildings as the Winter Palace of the tsars (now the Hermitage, home of one of the finest art collections in the world), St Isaac's Cathedral, and the Admiralty, which stand in striking contrast to mammoth, modern blocks of flats and sports stadia (e.g. Kirov Stadium) built during the Soviet regime. The blocks of flats are essentially utilitarian and contribute to the solution of an appalling shortage of houses precipitated by the widespread damage inflicted by the Germans during a two-and-a-half-year siege in World War II.

> "I love you, Peter's creation,
> I love your severe, graceful appearance,
> the Neva's majestic current,
> the granite of her banks,
> the tracery of your cast-iron railings,
> the transparent twilight, the moonless gleam
> of your still nights,
> when I write and read in my room without a lamp,
> and the huge sleeping buildings in the deserted streets
> are clearly seen, the Admiralty spire is bright,
> and one dawn hastens to succeed another, not letting
> the night's darkness rise to the golden heavens
> and leaving a bare half-hour for the night.
> I love the still air and the frost of your severe winter,
> the sleighs racing on the banks of the wide Neva. . . ."★
>
> *A. S. Pushkin*

★ This prose translation of *The Bronze Horseman* is taken from the Penguin book of Russian verse.

Besides its important industrial functions, Leningrad's admirable position ensures a continuing role as an important point of contact with Western Europe. Although ice-bound for four to five months, it is the chief port of the U.S.S.R., and handles up to 700 ships a year. It is also a focal point for road and rail from the Baltic Republics, Poland, the Ukraine, Moscow, the Ural, Vorkuta, Arkhangelsk and Murmansk. Leningrad's two and a half

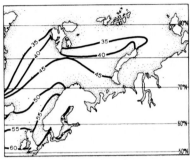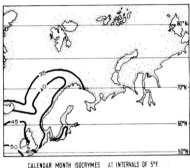

CALENDAR MONTH ISOTHERES (Not normal isotherms) AT INTERVALS OF 5°F.   CALENDAR MONTH ISOCRYMES AT INTERVALS OF 5°F.

FIG. 128.—Surface sea-water temperature conditions affecting the Northwest Region: Calendar month isotheres and isocrymes.

NOTE. The two charts are based on "Maximum and minimum monthly sea surface temperatures charted from the World Atlas of Sea Surface Temperatures" by Louis W. Hutchins and Margaret Scharff. (*Sears Foundation Journal of Marine Research*, Vol. VI, No. 3, December 15, 1947.)

Individual isotherms were plotted for each month and all twelve plottings super-imposed on one chart. The whole area occupied at any time during the year by a particular mean temperature was thus delimited. On drawing the envelope around the area, the equatorial boundary provides the "isocryme" which is the isotherm for the temperature in question at the time of greatest cooling, irrespective of the month in which this occurs. In the same way the poleward boundary provides the "isothere" or isotherm or maximum warming.

The designations "Calendar Month Isotheres" and "Calendar Month Isocrymes" are appropriate, since nominal calendar months are the basis of all calculations rather than the warmest and coldest thirty-day periods. It should be emphasised that the two charts give monthly means; absolute maximum and minimum temperatures of any locality could be several degrees more extreme.

centuries' history has been turbulent; of several memorable events the massacre of 1905, when strikers from the Putilov works (now the vast Kirov metal foundries) were fired on, "The February Revolution" of 1917 and the Bolshevik Revolution of 1917 were outstanding. Leningrad has been an intellectual and cultural centre since its foundation. The great national academies were moved to Moscow when Leningrad ceased to be capital but the city continues to house several institutes, schools, libraries and museums.

Murmansk (272,000) is the world's largest polar city. At 69° N its latitude is comparable with those of Jan Mayen Island, central Greenland, Baffin Island and the north coast of Alaska. Warm waters from the North Atlantic Drift pass round the north of Norway and keep the port ice-free the year round (Fig. 128). For this reason Murmansk has proved an important "backdoor" from Russia to the West, summer and winter alike.

FIG. 129.—Novgorod: Part of the walls and towers of the Kremlin of this ninth-century town, with the Volkhov river in the background.

Never was this function more amply demonstrated than during World War II, when the port was used to receive vital supplies from allies of the Soviet Union. Murmansk is sited at the head of a long fiord, the only one on the north coast of the Kola Peninsula, and is the terminus of the railway from Leningrad. It is the principal Soviet fishing port of the western Arctic, and an important naval base with well-equipped shipbuilding and repair yards.

Petrozavodsk (157,000) on Lake Onega represents a concentration of industrial population engaged in ferrous metallurgy and the lumber industry. Founded by Peter the Great in the early eighteenth century, it manufactures iron and steel goods, including tractors for the lumber industry, and is the centre of the timber industry with important saw mills.

[*Fotokhronika Tass.*

In ancient Rus, *Novgorod* (89,000) on the Volkhov, was an important commercial entrepôt and intellectual centre (Fig. 129). *Pskov* (108,000) on the Velikaya and *Velikiye Luki* (75,000) on the Lovat, were trading centres and "suburbs" of Novgorod. The former greatness of the three towns has been completely eclipsed by Leningrad and today they are no more than local market towns. *Vyborg* (Viipuri, 63,000) an old Finno-Karelian town acquired from Finland in 1944 is a timber-exporting centre. It has lost much of its hinterland and been superseded by Kotka (in Finland) as outlet for the Lake Saimaa forest region.

STUDY QUESTIONS

1. Suggest a division of the Northwest Region into geographical regions. Discuss the bearing of physical factors upon economic activities in any *two* of the regions recognised.

2. Describe, with the aid of a sketch-map, the scenery and characteristic occupations of the regions passed through in the course of a rail journey from Leningrad to Murmansk.

3. Examine the position of Leningrad in relation to the national and regional market.

4. Why was Leningrad described as "a window on the west"? Is this description still valid?

5. Compare the geography of the present and former capitals, Moscow, Leningrad and Kiev.

6. Assess the importance of Murmansk seaport to the Soviet Union.

7. Examine the mineral resources of the Kola Peninsula and their exploitation.

Chapter XVII

NORTH REGION

THIS vast, sparsely populated forest region is more than three and a half times the size of the British Isles, and stretches from the White Sea and Lake Onega to the northern Ural, a distance of some 700 miles (Fig. 130).

Area	.	.	.	444,900 sq. miles
Population (1959)	.	.	3,389,000

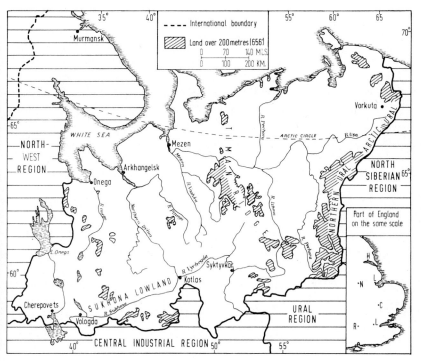

FIG. 130.—North Region.

Administrative unit	Area sq. miles	Population in thousands 1959	Density persons per sq. mile	Percentage urban
Oblast Vologda . . .	56,900	1,307	23	35
Oblast Arkhangelsk . . .	229,000	1,278	5	53
Komi A.S.S.R. . . .	159,000	804*	5	59

* Est. 950,000 on January 1, 1965.

Towns with over 150,000 inhabitants in 1964

	Population in thousands		Percentage increase
	1959	1964	1959–64
Arkhangelsk . .	256	303	18·2
Vologda . . .	139	159	14·3
Cherepovets . . .	92	152	65·1

PHYSICAL ASPECTS

RELIEF AND DRAINAGE

This is a region of low and monotonous relief that owes its character in large measure to glacial deposition rather than to any pre-Pleistocene processes. Except in the worn-down Palaeozoic Timan Ridge, stretching from Cheshskaya Bay to the source of the Vychegda River, and in the Ural–Pay-Khoy Range in the extreme east, the countryside is mainly below 600 ft. Minor relief features, invariably moraines, eskers or fluvio-glacial material, are largely concealed by the ubiquitous boreal forest. The two headwaters of the Northern Dvina, the Vychegda and Sukhona, occupy an ancient glacial valley formed by the damming of northbound drainage by the edge of the Pleistocene ice sheet. A long low ridge—which appears to be a terminal moraine—running along the southern boundary of the region, is the main water parting between rivers draining northwards to the Arctic and those draining southwards to the Caspian.

Drainage in the region is largely northwards to the Arctic, by the Northern Dvina and Mezen systems in the western section and the Pechora system in the eastern part. As few railways have been built, the rivers and their tributaries provide the chief means of communication. Unfortunately, their usefulness is curtailed by the long period during which they are frozen, six months each year in the southwest and over eight months in the north-east. Since the ice-free period is shorter in the upper, more southerly courses of the rivers, interior navigation commences long before the river mouths are open for navigation.

CLIMATE, NATURAL VEGETATION AND SOILS

Continentality is the distinguishing characteristic of the climate. Winters are prolonged and severe and accompanied by a heavy snowfall. Summers last no more than three to four months, they are only moderately warm and are broken by recurrent indraughts of polar continental air and associated cold spells. Spring has a sudden onset, and like autumn is a fleeting season (Fig. 131). The northern part of the region tends to be generally cloudy,

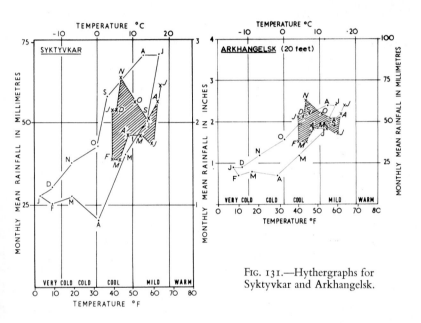

FIG. 131.—Hythergraphs for Syktyvkar and Arkhangelsk.

especially in the summer; it is prone to autumnal and winter gales and these give rise to snow blizzards. Winter cold increases in severity from southwest to northeast with January mean temperatures ranging from 14° F to —7° F (—10° to —22° C); summer warmth falls off latitudinally (July mean temperatures range from 65° F (18° C) in the south to 45° to 50° F (7° to 10° C) in the north. Except in the Ural where aggregates of over 30 in. (760 mm) are received, precipitation is slight and no more than 16–20 in. (400–500 mm). Though maxima occur in the period July–August, in association with thunderstorms, winter precipitation gives rise to appreciable snow cover (depths in excess of 2 ft in the east and centre of the region) which lasts five and a half months in the south and over eight months in the north. Snow melt in the spring takes place over a period of four to five weeks, although individual days of maximum melting can produce as much as 0·2 in.-layer of water, conditions that are conducive to flooding. Floods, low rates of evaporation and, in the north, permafrost (there is a layer of frozen subsoil $3\frac{1}{2}$–$6\frac{1}{4}$ ft below the surface in the delta of the Pechora), together give rise to waterlogging and vast expanses of swamp and bog.

Most of the region is covered with tayga, the boreal forest of conifers, pine and spruce, and deciduous birch underlain by infertile and water-logged podzols, and frequently in permafrost conditions. North of the River Mezen, and along the Arctic shores there is tundra—mosses, lichens, a few stunted shrubs. In some sheltered spots, there are small copses of Arctic birch and similar dwarf species. The whole of the tundra is under-lain by permafrost.

THE ECONOMY

AGRICULTURE

The growing season for crops is short and cool—there are no more than 90 days with temperatures in excess of 50° F (10° C). Agriculture is restricted, and limited to such crops as rye, oats, hemp, peas, cabbages and potatoes, grown on small patches of cleared land, usually along the southern margins of the tayga (particularly around Vologda). Animal husbandry comprises cattle and pig rearing. The livestock spend most of the year in-doors, though some use is made of riverside meadows in the summer. Reindeer herding and fishing are also carried on (Fig. 132).

FORESTRY AND WOOD-USING INDUSTRIES

Up to a century ago the only commercial products of the forests that cover over two-thirds of the catchment areas of the Northern Dvina and Pechora were furs (sable, marten, fox, hare, squirrel) and to a lesser degree, salt (e.g. at Solvychegodsk); the forest was dotted with small fur-trading posts. Within the last 100 years, however, the timber industry has been developed and temporary camps, housing lumberjacks, are to be found everywhere. Exploitation has taken place mainly within the tayga of the Northern Dvina Plain; the forested portions of the Mezen and Pechora Basins being rather inaccessible, the timber industry is less well developed there. High-quality timber, cut during the winter from stands along the Dvina and its tributaries, is floated downstream on the spring thaw to saw-mills at Arkhangelsk at the mouth of the river. Here it is sawn into planks, pit props, railway sleepers and telegraph poles, pulped for paper making and used for wood chemicals and turpentine. Wood is also the main domestic fuel and building material of the region.

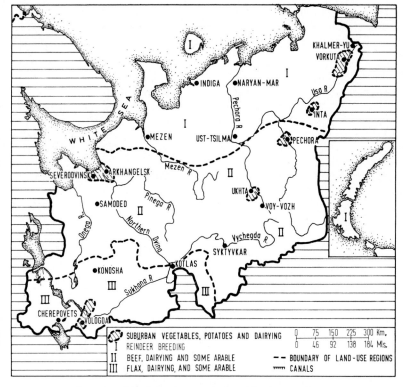

FIG. 132.—North Region: agricultural land-use regions.

Arkhangelsk is the largest sawmilling centre of the Soviet Union, and Severodvinsk, across the Dvina from Arkhangelsk, is its main timber-exporting port. Other centres of the timber industry are Onega, Mezen, Vologda, Kotlas, Syktyvkar, and several other places along the Vologda–Arkhangelsk and Vologda–Vorkuta Railways.

MINERAL RESOURCES

Coal was discovered along the western flank of the Ural Mountains and within the upper Pechora Basin during the 1930s but full-scale development did not commence until 1942, after a railway line had been laid between Kotlas and Vorkuta (Fig. 133), at a time during World War II when the Donets coalfield of the Ukraine had been overrun by the Germans. The coals are bituminous and some are of coking quality. Reserves are considered to be greater than those of the Donbass and their quality is as high. However, the fact that they lie deep beneath lacustrine and marine sediments, in a region of extremely rigorous climate and permafrost, presents serious technical difficulties for their exploitation. The main mining centres are Vorkuta and Pechora; Inta, Gornyatskiy, Khalmer-Yu and Oktyabrskiy are subsidiary centres. Some of the coal is sent to Labytnangi, for Arctic shipping, or into Siberia along the Ob and Irtysh Rivers, but the bulk is

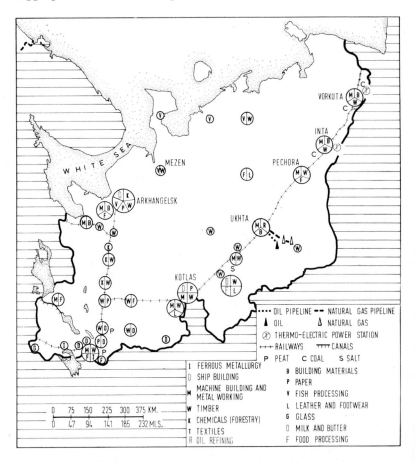

FIG. 133.—North Region: mineral and power resources, railways and industrial structure of towns.

sent by rail to cities in north European U.S.S.R. and to the Cherepovets iron and steel plant over 1000 miles away on the north shore of Rybinsk Reservoir.

Oil-bearing strata are being tapped near Ukhta and Voy-Vozh in the valley of the Izhma (Fig. 133). Some of the oil is refined at Ukhta, though it is thought that the bulk is railed to refineries at Kazan, Gorkiy and

Yaroslavl. Natural gas, not associated with petroleum, occurs near Voy-Vozh and Dzhebol. This is transported to Perm (Ural Region).

Though the coal of the Pechora Basin probably meets the requirements of the whole of the Northwest and North Regions, and the oil and gas resources the requirements of the North Region, there are no resources of minerals for manufacturing. Apart from the timber industry, small engineering works and some barge-building yards at Arkhangelsk (Northern Dvina), Kotlas (Sukhona) and Syktyvkar (Vychegda), manufacturing industry proper is absent.

TRANSPORT AND COMMUNICATIONS

Rivers have long provided the routes through the North Region. Richard Chancellor's discovery of the White Sea in the sixteenth century opened up an important water route to Moscow via the Northern Dvina, the Sukhona and Vologda rivers, and inaugurated a flourishing trade between England and Russia through the Muscovy Company. This route was eclipsed when the Baltic outlet via St Petersburg (Leningrad) was opened in the eighteenth century, but it attained a new importance with the rising demand for timber. The Northern Dvina River system now provides a most valuable means of transporting timber from the otherwise inaccessible tayga to the coast.

There was no rail link between Arkhangelsk, Vologda and Moscow until 1897, and the remainder of the North was without roads or railways until the Second World War. To meet the special needs of wartime economy, at a time when the Germans had overrun the Donbass and advanced to the outskirts of Leningrad, a railway was built from Kotlas to Vorkuta to bring coal to the industrial areas of the Central Industrial Region and another was constructed from Belomorsk to Obozerskaya, thereby bringing Murmansk traffic on to the Arkhangelsk line. The few roads that exist are generally unmetalled or poorly surfaced, and are usually impassable in winter and spring. They carry little or no long-distance traffic.

POPULATION AND SETTLEMENT

Despite the vast size of the North Region the population is less than $3\frac{1}{2}$ million. This scanty population consists largely of Nentsy (an intrusive Mongoloid people) in the tundra areas, and Komi (a Finno-Ugrian group) in the tayga. There are, however, large numbers of Russians living among them, and the Russian culture and way of life have been largely adopted. In Oblast Arkhangelsk and the Komi A.S.S.R. over half the population lives in towns; densities are no more than five persons per square mile.

H

Only in Oblast Vologda in the south, where the tayga begins to give way to mixed forest and where agriculture has been important for a long time, do densities rise to 20–25 persons per square mile.

Arkhangelsk (303,000), at the mouth of the Northern Dvina, is the leading city. Besides its port functions, which date from the end of the sixteenth

FIG. 134.—Arkhangelsk: loading timber at the port.

century, it has fishing, timber, shipbuilding, textile (jute sacks) and engineering industries. It is claimed that the port, and that of nearby *Severodvinsk* (113,000) can be kept open by ice-breakers throughout the severest winters, although the shipping season normally lasts from mid-May to the end of November only (Fig. 134). Arkhangelsk is the terminus of the railway from Moscow via Vologda–Konosha–Obozerskaya.

Vologda (159,000), founded in 1147, has a fine nodal position at the head of navigation of the Northern Dvina system of waterways and at the crossing point of the Moscow–Arkhangelsk Railway with that of the Leningrad–

Perm line. It now functions as an important collecting centre for dairy products and agricultural commodities such as oats, hemp, flax and linseed.

Cherepovets (152,000), at the northern end of Rybinsk Reservoir, is an important metallurgical centre providing steel for the engineering industries in the Leningrad–Moscow–Gorkiy areas. *Syktyvkar* (94,000), an old settle-

[*Fotokhronika Tass.*

ment on the Vychegda River, is the administrative centre of the Komi Autonomous Republic. It has timber, ship-repairing, food, leather and shoe-making industries.

STUDY QUESTIONS

1. Describe the main features of the physical geography of the North Region.

2. Examine the forest and mineral resources of the North Region and the problems associated with their exploitation.

3. Examine the importance of the North Dvina River as a route and as a waterway.

4. Assess the importance of the Barents Sea ports to the fishing industry of the U.S.S.R.

5. Discuss the main features of the geography of Arkhangelsk.

6. Comment on the location of large-scale ferrous metallurgy at Cherepovets in terms of energy and iron ore supplies and of markets.

Chapter XVIII

MIDDLE AND LOWER VOLGA–LOWER DON REGION

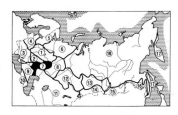

THIS region comprises the lands along the Volga from near Kazan to the Caspian Sea that are known as the Povolzhye, together with that part of the valley of the lower Don that lies within Oblast Volgograd (Fig. 135). Administratively it embraces the Tatar A.S.S.R. and the oblasts of Ulyanovsk, Kuybyshev, Saratov, Volgograd and Astrakhan.

This basically agricultural region has very important oil and natural gas resources and developing petro-chemical and engineering industries.

Area . . . . 161,000 sq. miles
Population (1959) . . 10,940,000

Administrative unit	Area sq. miles	Population in thousands 1959	Density persons per sq. mile	Percentage urban
Tatarskaya A.S.S.R. . . .	26,000	2,847	109	42
Oblast Ulyanovsk . . .	14,000	1,118	78	36
Oblast Kuybyshev . . .	21,000	2,257	109	62
Oblast Saratov	39,000	2,167	57	54
Oblast Volgograd . . .	44,000	1,849	41	54
Oblast Astrakhan . . .	17,000	702	41	52

Towns with over 150,000 inhabitants in 1964

	Population in thousands		Percentage increase
	1959	1964	1959–64
Kuybyshev . . .	806	948	17·7
Kazan	647	762	17·8
Volgograd . . .	592	700	18·1
Saratov . . .	581	683	17·5
Astrakhan . . .	296	342	15·7
Ulyanovsk . . .	206	265	28·7
Syzran	149	165	10·8

209

PHYSICAL ASPECTS

RELIEF

Near Kazan the Volga flows through broad swampy lowlands, but southwards from here to Volgograd its valley is dominated on its west side by high, cliff-like slopes; its left bank gives on to a plain of low relief. The western side of the valley is formed by the east-facing slopes of the asymmetrical Volga Heights which, rising gently eastwards from the Don

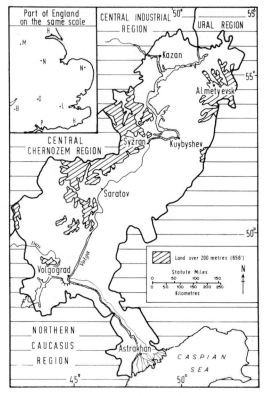

FIG. 135.—Middle and Lower Volga–Lower Don Region.

valley to heights of 500–600 ft and occasionally to over 1000 ft (as in the Zhiguli Hills within the Samara bend of the Volga near Kuybyshev), drop suddenly to the Volga. For the most part the Heights are unglaciated, but sub-aerial erosion of sandstones, clays and chalk under semi-arid conditions has produced many deep ravines and gorges. This dissection is particularly evident along the slopes facing the Volga where the Sura, Syzran and other tributaries have cut back deeply into the Heights. (The Yergeni Hills, included later in the North Caucasus Region, are a lower, southerly extension of the Volga Heights, forming a divide between the Volga and the Don.) At Volgograd, however, the Volga turns suddenly away from its bounding ridge in a pronounced bend to the southeast, to debouch into the Caspian Sea some 300 miles to the southeast.

The lowland on the eastern side of the Volga is broken only by the western fringe of the Belebei Upland which lies within the region northeast of Kuybyshev. This eastern side of the valley is generally featureless and marshy, and an alluvial plain stretches eastwards to the Turanian Lowland.

Southeast of Volgograd the course of the Volga runs parallel with that of its main distributary, the Akhtuba, in an open floodplain which contains innumerable abandoned courses and cut-off lakes, terminating in a broad, marshy reed-covered delta on the Caspian Sea. The Caspian Sea was in the past much larger and extended over these lower reaches of the Volga.

CLIMATE

The regional climate is essentially continental. Occasional occluded Atlantic depressions, passing near the northern limit of the region, reduce the extremes of temperature there, but January mean temperatures are

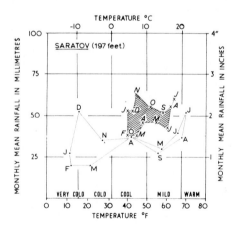

FIG. 136.—Hythergraph for Saratov.

everywhere below freezing level, e.g. Kazan 7° F (−14° C); Saratov 11° F (−12° C); Astrakhan 19° F (−7° C) (Fig. 136). In July conditions are hot, temperatures ranging from 68° F (20° C) in the north to over 77° F (25° C) in the south. During the period mid-April to September the scorching *sukhovey* frequently blows. Rainfall is everywhere scanty and irregular in distribution. Conditions become progressively drier towards the south-east, where semi-desert is reached. The north receives an aggregate of about 17 in. (430 mm) and the south less than 9 in. (230 mm). Maxima occur in the summer half of the year, mainly in the form of heavy showers. Losses through evaporation and rapid runoff are severe, and during settled anticyclonic weather droughts are commonplace. A winter snow cover of 1½–2 ft, lasting for about four months, is typical of the north; it rarely exceeds 1 ft in the south and lasts no more than a month.

NATURAL VEGETATION AND SOILS

Because conditions on the high, west side of the Volga are cooler and more humid than on the low eastern side, there is a difference in the natural vegetation. The tayga in the extreme north of the region gives way south-wards to deciduous mixed forest which extends farther south on the Volga Heights than in the Trans-Volga (Zavolzhye) area. On the east side, natural steppe and chernozem begin to appear just south of Kuybyshev, but on the west woodland and wooded steppe, overlying brown earths, continue south to near Saratov. Similarly, the change from steppe to semi-desert occurs near latitude 51° N on the east side of the Volga, nearer 48° N on the west. Saline soils (*solonets*) are frequently associated with chestnut soils in the lower reaches of the Volga.

Throughout the region ploughing has led to the breakdown of the soil structure and loss of friability, with consequent extensive soil erosion and gullying. Since drought is a constant threat (according to Borisov one in every three or four years during the past 70 years has been a drought year), agriculture has formidable problems, and every effort has to be made to alleviate the adverse effects of the droughts that are inevitable in the continental climate of the region. Ley farming (*travopolye*) as practised here offers one method of improving soil structure and conserving soil moisture; it involves a regular alternation on the same land of a number of years under grass–legume mixtures and a number of years of arable cropping. The roots of grasses and legumes and manure from grazing stock build up the organic matter of the soil, improve its cohesion and increase its moisture-holding capacity. The planting of large shelter belts of deciduous trees, often hundreds of miles long, and irrigation offer other means of counteracting the effects of drought.

THE ECONOMY

AGRICULTURE

Despite the climatic hazards and the dangers of crop failure, the Lower Volga–Lower Don Region is a leading producing area of spring wheat, winter rye, oats, flax, hemp, oil seeds (especially sunflower seed) and maize.

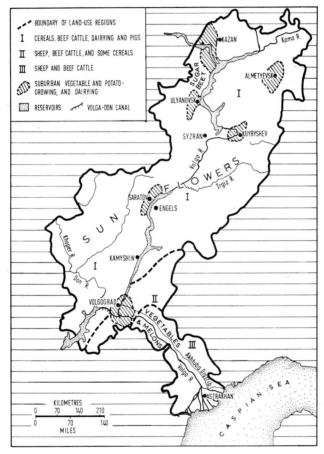

FIG. 137.—Middle and Lower Volga–Lower Don Region: agricultural land-use regions.

Beef cattle, pigs, sheep, horses and poultry are raised and dairying is common near the towns (Fig. 137). In the areas of more mixed farming in the north and west, potatoes and sugar beet are important. Semi-tropical fruits, rice, melons and vegetables are grown in the floodplain of the lower Volga

Valley below Volgograd; peaches, apricots and vines thrive along the drier margins. In the semi-desert beyond the Volga–Akhtuba Valley sheep are raised for meat and wool on an extensive system; there is barely enough vegetation for grazing so seasonal movement between pastures is necessary.

Agriculturally based industries include flour milling, meat canning, cheese and butter making, soap manufacture, candles, leather and felt boots, and cotton spinning.

FUEL AND MINERAL RESOURCES

Until the early 1930s the lands along the middle and lower Volga and along the lower Don seemed destined to remain essentially agricultural. The Volga functioned as an important and historic highway, but the extent of its power potential and the resources of the neighbouring lands were not appreciated. Since then the river has been harnessed for hydro-electric power generation and for irrigation water, and the great riches of oil and natural gas of the Volga–Ural field ("Second Baku") are being fully exploited. The region as a whole has undergone a very rapid growth of industry, trade and settlement.

This late industrial revolution of the region followed the construction under "The Great Volga Scheme" of a series of multipurpose barrages throughout the course of the river. These dams were intended for hydro-electricity generation and for water conservation for several purposes—irrigation, the control of seasonal differences in water level and of soil erosion, and navigation aids. There are in the Central Industrial Region three relatively small stations at Ivankovo, Uglich and Scherbakov (now Rybinsk) and one larger one, Gorodets, at Gorkiy, but those in the Volga–Don Region at Kuybyshev (2500 Mw) and Volgograd (2500 Mw) are among the most powerful hydro-electric stations in the world. Together with three more projected stations—near Cheboksary (Central Industrial Region), near Balakovo and near Astrakhan—they will make the valley of the Volga outstandingly important in hydro-electricity production. Some of the power is used locally, but most is sent westwards to central Russia, and to Moscow in particular.

The reservoirs formed by the dams on the Volga cover several hundreds of square miles and have transformed large areas through the inundation of valuable alluvial land. Some settlements (e.g. Stavropol, some hundred miles above Kuybyshev) have had to be resited. Such vast water surfaces are naturally subject to high evaporation rates during the summer and the Volga system loses tremendous volumes of water thereby. In consequence the water level of the Caspian Sea is being lowered and there have been adverse effects on the fishing industry, the shipping facilities and the Kara–Bogaz–Gol sodium sulphate industry. To offset the water losses, a grandiose scheme—the Pechora–Vychegda Diversion Project—has been evolved, to divert northern waters into the Volga.

Although the Volga–Ural oilfields had been known for several decades, serious prospecting began only during the 1930s, and large-scale development took place after World War II. Well over 60% of the Union's output of oil now comes from this field. Though discontinuous, the Volga–Ural oilfields extend over an area as large as the British Isles and are credited with 80% of the Union's oil reserves. The field is exploited in an area north and east of Volgograd, through Saratov, Syzran, Kuybyshev and Almetyevsk to Ufa and Perm (the last two being in the Ural Region). Drilling is concentrated in relatively few areas, e.g. Almetyevsk, Shugurovo, Syzran, Volgograd (and Oktyabrskiy and Perm in the Ural Region), but the bulk of the field's production comes from an area within 150–200 miles of Almetyevsk; indeed, this represents the greatest part of the Union's total production. Production from the margins of the field is relatively limited (Fig. 138). Refineries are located at Kazan, Kuybyshev, Syzran, Saratov and Volgograd, and there are pipeline links with consuming areas—the Ural, Siberian towns as far east as Irkutsk, and westwards, central European Russia, East Germany, Poland, Hungary, Czechoslovakia—and to an oil-loading terminal at Ventspils in the Latvian S.S.R.

Natural gas is exploited west of the Volga at such centres as Yelshanka (linked with Saratov and Moscow), Kotovo (linked with Kamyshin) and Frolovo (linked with Volgograd).

The region has no coal resources. Common salt (Lake Baskunchak), phosphate (Oblast Ulyanovsk) and sulphur (Oblast Kuybyshev) are important resources for the fishing and fertiliser industries.

MANUFACTURING

The location of this region's resources of hydro-electricity, petroleum and natural gas in relation to the Union's other industrial regions and the distribution of population is of great economic value to the U.S.S.R. as a whole. It is also a factor that attracts industries into the region. Oil and gas serve as raw materials within the region for a wide range of petro-chemical industries producing synthetic fibres, synthetic rubber, plastics, fertilisers, ethylene and alcohol, while the abundant supplies of electricity are important to the location of engineering industries. The resulting complex includes industries engaged in the manufacture of oil-drilling equipment, electrical equipment, marine engines and boilers, ball-bearings and agricultural machinery (Fig. 139) and localised chiefly in Kuybyshev, Kazan, Ulyanovsk, Syzran, Saratov and Volgograd. This is the modern industrial development that has become predominant over the region's more traditional agriculture-based manufacturing and engineering.

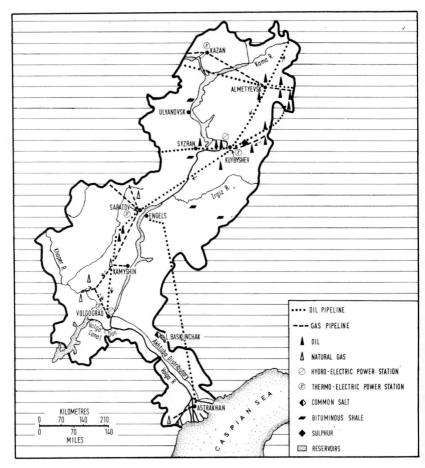

FIG. 138.—Middle and Lower Volga–Lower Don Region: mineral and power resources.

TRANSPORT AND COMMUNICATIONS

The Volga is an economic link both within the Povolzhye and with other regions of the U.S.S.R.; it is estimated that the Volga system carries nearly 50% of the inland water transport tonnage of the entire Union (Fig. 78). Its sphere was extended westward after the completion of the Volga–Don Ship Canal south of Volgograd (Fig. 140) in 1952, giving free access to the Sea of Azov and the Black Sea.

The highly irregular regime of the Volga, with flood levels in April and May followed by low-water levels during the summer, has been much modified by the barrage constructions along its course; the chain of deep

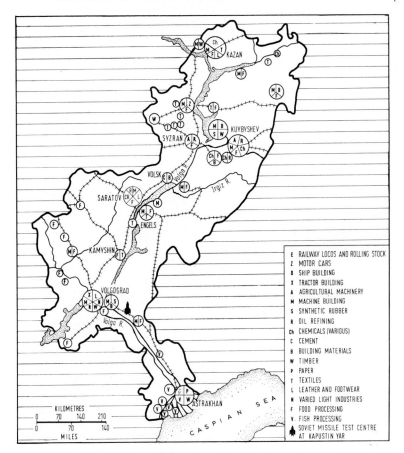

FIG. 139.—Middle and Lower Volga–Lower Don Region: railways and industrial structure of towns.

lakes and the locks that now exist greatly aid navigation. Despite the fact that the river is frozen over for several months during the winter, its huge carrying capacity for bulk cargoes makes it a vital part of the Soviet transportation system. At the mouths of the Volga distributaries, sandbars and the falling water level of the Caspian Sea make it necessary to trans-ship cargoes from Caspian steamers to shallow-draught Volga river-steamers at "12-Foot Roads," an artificial island port in the Caspian Sea, 125 miles from Astrakhan.

Downstream traffic on the Volga system is mainly in timber—as rafts (Fig. 141) or as deck cargo—and oil (for the under-utilised Caspian re-fineries); upstream traffic is mainly in coal, pig iron, wheat, salt, sulphur-free Caspian oil, oil products and building materials.

Formerly north–south communication through the region was virtually brought to a halt when the river was frozen or at low-water level. A railway now runs parallel to the river along the right bank, from near Kazan to Volgograd, and thence along the left bank to Astrakhan. Railway traffic is less affected by seasonal changes than is waterway traffic, but this

[*Mysl.*

FIG. 140.—Near the entrance to the Volga–Don Canal.

advantage is offset by rail costs, which are more expensive per ton-mile than those for water traffic.

Not all transport movement through the region is longitudinal; the former frontier-like character of the Povolzhye has largely been dispelled by the construction of railways running across the region from east to west, and the regional character is now more of a transit zone, with five main trunk lines crossing the Volga (Fig. 139). Freight traffic densities on these lines are very high, especially between Kuybyshev and Syzran (*see* Fig. 76), with a general preponderance of westbound traffic, particularly of oil, iron, steel and coal, towards Moscow and the Central Industrial Region. The most important commodity exported by rail from the region itself is oil, of which large amounts are sent eastwards to Siberia (approximately half the region's oil production is exported by rail). Pipeline oil transport is more economical and is being increasingly used.

[*Fotokhronika Tass.*

FIG. 141.—Timber floating down the Volga near the city of Kuyby-shev. The logs are fastened together in giant rafts which are pulled by a tug. The wooden cabin on the raft is for the crew.

POPULATION AND CITIES

The lands along the Volga were the meeting place of Tatar and Muscovite cultures. Bulgars who had settled near the Kama–Volga confluence in the ninth to twelfth centuries succumbed to Mongol-Tatars of the Golden Horde in the thirteenth century. These Tatars copied the culture and settled

way of life of the Bulgars and established a breakaway Khanate centred on
Kazan. In 1552 that city fell to Ivan the Terrible and the way was opened
for a rapid Russian advance down the Volga to Astrakhan. Ulyanovsk
(formerly Simbirsk), Kuybyshev (Samara), Saratov and Volgograd
(Tsaritsyn) were founded during the sixteenth and seventeenth centuries
purely as military establishments. Russian colonisation proceeded slowly

FIG. 142.—Kuybyshev: view of the Volga embankment, backed by the houses
of Pristanskaya Street.

and full Russian political control over the Volga lands was not achieved
until the end of the eighteenth century when, under Catherine the Great,
links between the middle Volga Tatars and the Tatars of Crimea and Constantinople were severed. At this time, colonists from central Europe and
from Germany in particular (Catherine was herself German) were settled
on the right bank of the Volga. The Tatars of Crimea and members of the
Volga German community were dispersed throughout the Soviet Union
during World War II and have not been allowed to return.

The large number of Russians who have moved into the Volga–Don Region (and particularly into the large cities) during recent phases of economic development have greatly diversified the ethnic variety of the region. Intermarriage between Russian and non-Russian groups has diluted the individuality of the latter, who are being increasingly assimilated into the Russian way of life.

[*Fotokhronika Tass.*

Though it is practically twice the size of the United Kingdom the Volga–Don Region has an overall population density which is only one-eighth that of the United Kingdom (67 per square miles compared with 577). In Oblast Kuybyshev and the Tatar A.S.S.R. there are approximately 110 persons per square mile, but in the former almost two-thirds of the population are urban, whereas in the latter less than 43% live in towns. Oblast Ulyanovsk is largely rural, but over half the populations of the oblasts of Astrakhan, Volgograd and Saratov live in towns. In fact, between 1939 and 1959, the urban population of the region as a whole grew more quickly than that of any other region in the European part of the U.S.S.R.

Kuybyshev (948,000), temporary capital of the Soviet Union during the second World War, is the most important city of the region. Situated on the left bank of the Volga at the most easterly point of the river loop to the east, at its confluence with the Samara, the city holds a strategic and focal

FIG. 143.—Saratov. The bridge which spans the Volga at Saratov is claimed to be the longest in Europe.

position (Fig. 142). Functioning first as a defence outpost, then as a trading point for the exchange of goods brought overland from the east and via the Volga from north and south, it later acquired industries based on agriculture, such as food processing and flour milling (Fig. 139). It is a fully developed industrial and commercial centre and the undoubted hub of the middle Volga, with important rail links to Siberia and the Soviet Far East via Ufa and Chelyabinsk, to Middle Asia via Orenburg and to European U.S.S.R. via Syzran, a nearby giant hydro-electricity generating station, oil refineries, petro-chemical industries, engineering of many kinds, food processing and woodworking. It is significant that Kuybyshev doubled its population between 1939 and 1959 and is now one of the eight largest cities of the Soviet Union.

Kazan (762,000), an old Tatar trading and administrative centre, is now the capital of the Tatar A.S.S.R. First situated on a small left-bank tributary (Kazanka) of the Volga, it now stands by the "Kuybyshev Sea," the waters dammed by the barrage at Kuybyshev. Kazan has excellent communications, in the Volga waterway and the trunk rail link with Moscow

[*Fotokhronika Tass.*

and Sverdlovsk. It is a centre for oil refining, the Tatar A.S.S.R. being the Union's main oil-producing area. To early-established manufacturing industries of soap, candles, woollens, leather and fur have been added petro-chemicals and engineering, the latter diverse enough to include the making of farm machinery, typewriters, calculating machines and computers. The Kazan *Kremlin* is claimed to rival that in Moscow in its splendour and picturesqueness.

Volgograd (700,000), known as Tsaritsyn until 1925 and Stalingrad between then and 1961, is sited on the high right bank of the Volga near the great river bend to the southeast. This point is only 45 miles distant from the Don. The early fortress town established here in 1589 grew as a major transhipment point for goods portaged between the two rivers. Scene of a major engagement in 1918 during the civil war, and again in World War II when bitter fighting between Russian and German troops reduced it to rubble, the city has been completely rebuilt and repopulated. Its importance has been enhanced since the opening of the Volga–Don Canal in 1952 and the completion of a giant barrage and hydro-electricity station near by in 1960. The industrial functions of Volgograd include heavy metallurgy, engineering (especially tractors), shipbuilding, oil refining, petro-chemicals, sawmilling and timber working, together with food products, leather goods and footwear. Year-round navigation is prevented by ice, which forms here early in December and does not break up until the first week in April, but there are direct rail links with Moscow, Saratov, Astrakhan and the Donbass. Though it is an important southern gateway to the Volga region, Volgograd lacks strong functional connection with the middle reaches of the river, and it is becoming increasingly related to the steel-producing areas of the Ukraine.

Saratov (683,000) was founded in 1590 on the left bank of the Volga, but was moved to its present site on the right bank in the seventeenth century. Situated at the lowest bridging point of the Volga (Fig. 143), it is an important rail junction. Traditional distributing functions (for grain, timber, salt, tobacco, fish, tallow and skins) and industries such as flour milling and tobacco manufacturing are now supplemented by oil refining and petro-chemicals. The city both draws on Caucasus oil (brought by pipeline from Astrakhan) and local crude oils. Engineering includes agricultural machinery, aircraft and ball-bearings. One of the Union's greatest reserves of natural gas resources lies just north of the city. Opposite Saratov on the left bank stands *Engels* (116,000), former capital of the Volga Germans (who were expelled from the area in 1942).

Astrakhan (342,000) stands on an island in the delta of the Volga, on the left bank of the main distributary and 45 miles from the Caspian Sea. It is an important river port, with a dredged channel to the sea, and despite the need for transhipment of cargoes (noted above) transport movements continue to be focused on the city. World-renowned sturgeon fisheries are centred here; *vobla* (Caspian roach), salmon, whitefish and herring are also caught, though the fishing industry has been adversely affected by the falling water level of the Caspian caused by the upstream use and control of the Volga waters. The river at Astrakhan is frozen over from about the third week in December until the second week in March, but railways across the semi-desert areas that surround the northern Caspian maintain all-season links northwards to Volgograd and southwards to Kizlyar and the Caucasus.

Ulyanovsk (265,000) and *Syzran* (165,000) mark important rail crossings of the Volga. They are river ports as well as industrial centres in a generally agricultural area.

It is salutary to remember that the distances that separate the cities of Astrakhan, Volgograd, Saratov and Kuybyshev are of the order of 200 miles, somewhat greater than the distance between London and Plymouth or London and Middlesbrough.

STUDY QUESTIONS

1. Suggest a division of the Middle and Lower Volga (Povolzhye)–Lower Don region into geographical regions. Discuss the bearing of physical factors upon economic activities in any *two* of the regions recognised.

2. In what ways and for what reasons has the Volga River been controlled?

3. Examine some of the problems hindering agricultural expansion in the Povolzhye.

4. Write an account of the geography of the floodplain of the River Volga between Volgograd and Astrakhan.

5. Analyse the factors which favour or hinder the growth of manufacturing industries in the Povolzhye.

6. Examine the contribution of the Middle Volga Region to the energy supplies of the U.S.S.R.

7. Discuss, with particular reference to the River Volga, the significance of river régimes in the human and economic geography of the U.S.S.R.

8. Examine the site, location and function of the following towns: Saratov; Kuybyshev; Volgograd; Kazan; Astrakhan.

9. Account for the ethnic variety of the population of the Volga–Don region.

10. Attempt an assessment of the economic function of the Volga–Don region in its relation to the distribution of population and the great industrial concentrations of the U.S.S.R.

Chapter XIX

THE URAL REGION

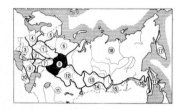 THE Ural Region does not cover the whole of the Ural Mountains, but only their southern part—the Central and Southern Ural, with their foothills—along with parts of the adjoining West Siberian Lowland on the east and the Belaya-Kama Lowlands on the west (Fig. 144). Administratively it covers the oblasts of Perm, Sverdlovsk, Chelyabinsk and Orenburg and the autonomous republics of Bashir and Udmurt. Because of its rich resources of iron, gold and asbestos and its strong economic links with the region, the northwestern part of Oblast Kustanay (Kazakhstan) is also included.

Area . . . . 299,000 sq. miles
Population (1959) . . 16,620,000

Administrative unit	Area sq. miles	Population in thousands 1959	Density persons per sq. mile	Percentage urban
Udmurt A.S.S.R. . . .	16,000	1,333	83	44
Oblast Perm	63,000	2,998	47	59
Oblast Sverdlovsk . . .	75,000	4,048	54	76
Oblast Chelyabinsk . . .	34,000	2,982	88	76
Bashkir A.S.S.R. . . .	56,000	3,335	60	38
Oblast Orenburg . . .	48,000	1,831	39	45
Oblast Kustanay (part) . .	7,000★	90★	13★	30★

★est.

Towns with over 150,000 inhabitants in 1964

	Population in thousands		Percentage increase
	1959	1964	1959–64
Sverdlovsk . . .	779	919	18·0
Chelyabinsk . . .	689	805	17·0
Perm	629	764	21·6
Ufa	547	665	21·5
Nizhniy Tagil . .	339	370	9·1
Izhevsk . . .	285	351	23·0

226

Towns with over 150,000 inhabitants in 1964—Contd.

	Population in thousands		Percentage increase
	1959	*1964*	*1959–64*
Magnitogorsk . .	311	348	12·0
Orenburg . . .	267	306	14·8
Orsk	176	210	19·4
Kurgan . . .	146	198	35·7
Zlatoust . . .	161	175	8·9
Kopeysk . . .	161	168	4·3
Kamensk-Uralskiy. .	141	158	12·0

FIG. 144.—Ural Region.

PHYSICAL ASPECTS

RELIEF AND DRAINAGE

The boundless Russian–West Siberian Lowland is interrupted by a meridional intrusion of ridges extending some 1400 miles from the Arctic to the Mugodzhary Mountains. These are the Ural Mountains, which are not particularly high—often not over 3000 ft—though they have long been considered a boundary between the European and the Asiatic territories of the Soviet Union.* The mountains lie on the western edge of a broad belt of Palaeozoic folding of which the greater part is buried beneath the Tertiary deposits of western Siberia. Folding, along a longitudinal axis, was asymmetrical and slopes are steep on the east and gentle on the west. The water divide is towards the eastern side.

Four parts of the Ural are recognised: The *Polar Ural* and the *Northern Ural* (which form the boundary between the North Region and the North Siberian Region) run southwards from near the head of Kara Bay to latitude 61° N. They form a distinct range 15–20 miles wide, with summits above 3000 ft. Occasionally the main range is flanked on the west by two or three other ranges. Between 61° N and 64° N the summits assume a gently rounded appearance and several broad flat, marshy transverse valleys cross the mountains.

The *Central Ural*, from latitude 61° N to 55° N, is lower in altitude than the ranges to the north. Broad swellings, 1000–2000 ft high, are cut by a multitude of transverse valleys, gorges and enclosed basins and the whole range is not more than 50 miles wide. It cannot be described as "mountainous," for it is no barrier to east–west movement and has been used as the main gateway to Siberia for centuries. The branches of the Trans-Siberian Railway that pass this way have gentle gradients and there are no high passes to be negotiated; for instance, that between Perm and Sverdlovsk never rises above 1200 ft.

The *Southern Ural*, between 55° N and 51° N, broadens to about 100 miles and is composed of several parallel ranges. The most easterly of these which is the watershed, rarely exceeds 2500 ft in height; those to the west have occasional summits over 5000 ft. Southwards the Ural assumes the character of a dissected plateau 1000–1500 ft high, terminated in the south by the great westward bend of the Ural river. South of this (in the Middle

---

* For theoretical-academic purposes the Moscow section of the All-Union Geographical Society recommended in 1958 that the border between Europe and Asia should be drawn along the eastern flank of the Ural, the Mugodzhary Mountains, the Emba river, the north shore of the Caspian, the Kuma-Manych depression and the south coast of the Sea of Azov to the Kerch Straits. The Sea of Azov belongs to Europe, as do the Ural; the Caucasus lie wholly in Asia. Such a conventional division is not recognised in the organisation of Soviet life or in the facts of Soviet geography.

Asia Region) the Mugodzhary Mountains form the natural termination of the Ural; these are two gently sloping ridges 800–1200 ft high, which grade beneath the Kazakh Steppe south of latitude 40° N.

The most extensive of the Pleistocene glacial stages, the Dnieper–Don, did not reach the Central and Southern Ural, and the present relief, the vestigial remains of a once mighty mountain system, is the result of the age-long processes of sub-aerial erosion and the depositional activity of rivers.

On the western flanks of the Ural drainage is by way of the Kama, Belaya and Ufa Rivers into the Volga and thence to the Caspian Sea. Drainage of the eastern Ural is into the Arctic Sea, through the Rivers Tobol, Miass, Nitsa, Tura and Tavda which join the Ob. The Ural River takes the waters of the Southern Ural to the Caspian Sea.

CLIMATE AND NATURAL VEGETATION

The climate of the Ural Region is continental and severe, but with a considerable range of regional and local variations, caused by the diversity and complexity of the relief, the wide range of latitude covered by the Region and the contrasts in the aspects of its several parts. Winters are everywhere cold; the January mean temperature at Perm is 2° F (−17° C) and at Zlatoust 4° F (−16° C) (Fig. 145). Sub-freezing temperatures per-

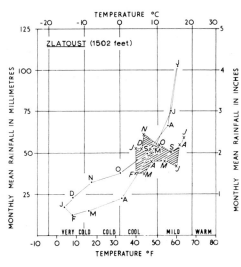

FIG. 145.—Hythergraph for Zlatoust.

sist for over five months. Winter conditions in the Southern Ural are as cold as in the Pechora area, some 600 miles farther north. Snow 2 ft or more deep lasts for five to seven months. Summers are mild to warm with temperatures ranging from 60° F (16° C) in the north to 68° F (20° C) in the south. The July mean temperature at Perm is 64° F (18° C) and at

Zlatoust 61° F (16° C). Winds often bring intense heat and thick dust to the south of the region during this season. Annual precipitation is 24–28 in. (610–710 mm), though it may attain 30 in. (760 mm) in the northeast and fall to less than 10 in. (255 mm) in the southeast. Aggregates on the western slopes of the mountains exceed those on the east by 4–6 in. (100–150 mm). Thus the mountains have contrasts of climate, but they do not constitute a sharp climatic divide.

Spring and autumn are brief transitional seasons lasting no more than four to six weeks. During these seasons the north tends to be cloudy, but in the south clear weather generally results in frequent temperature inversions, which are reflected in inverted zonation of vegetation.

The Central Ural carries a coniferous forest (tayga) of the spruce–fir type with admixtures of birch, aspen and pine. Soils are podzolic. In the Southern Ural the forest gradually gives way to wooded steppe (with outliers of deciduous forest), thence to open steppe, overlying chernozem. In this area the normal vertical zonation of vegetation may be reversed (in response to temperature/humidity inversions), with pine–birch concentrated in the foothill valleys, oak forests on the lower slopes and lime, maple and elm on the higher slopes—the trees requiring higher temperatures growing at the higher altitudes.

THE ECONOMY

FORESTRY

Despite exploitation by an early charcoal-smelting iron industry, 70% of the Ural Region remains forest-covered and a most valuable source of timber, providing about 20% of the total timber output of the Soviet Union. Novaya Lyalya, Krasnokamsk, Krasnovishersk and Berezniki are well-known centres for paper, pulp and cellulose manufactures. Krasnokamsk, Nizhniy Tagil, Zlatoust and Chernikovsk are important for sawmills. Much of the timber exported is floated along the Kama to the Volga, for distribution downstream.

AGRICULTURE

The extent of arable agriculture is limited by the forest cover and by the generally adverse physical environment. In the vicinity of large towns, such as Perm, Sverdlovsk and Chelyabinsk, market gardening and dairying are the main activities, related to urban markets rather than to favourable conditions of soil and climate. In some favoured areas in the north and along the southern fringes of the forest, fodder crops, grains (barley, oats, rye and wheat, in a north–south sequence), flax and pasture occupy most of

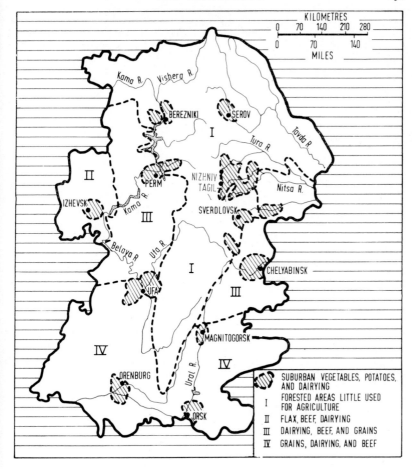

FIG. 146.—Ural Region: agricultural land-use regions.

the available arable land (Fig. 146). The steppe-lands of the Southern Ural lie within the area of the "Virgin and Long Idle Lands Project," which was ploughed up in 1954–5 by workers on large *sovkhozy* and planted to spring wheat. The initial wheat monoculture in this southern region is being gradually replaced by a more mixed form of agriculture, introducing other crops, such as maize and sunflowers, and the raising of cattle and sheep.

MINERAL RESOURCES AND MANUFACTURING INDUSTRIES

The role of agriculture in the economy of the Region is secondary to mining and industry. The Ural Region is exceptionally well endowed with

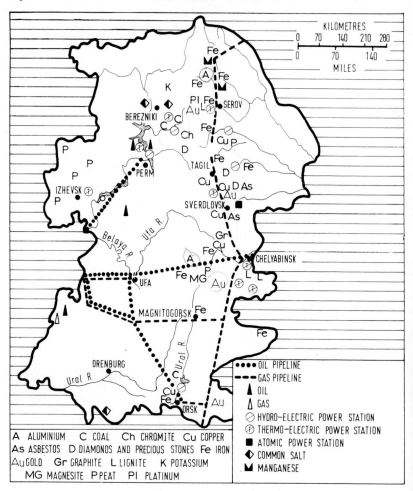

FIG. 147.—Ural Region: mineral and power resources.

metals and minerals (Fig. 147) which supply the raw materials for ferrous and non-ferrous metallurgy, engineering, machinery, machine tools, chemicals and a range of allied industries. Iron, copper, bauxite, manganese, nickel, cobalt, tungsten, chrome, titanium, vanadium, gold, potash and precious stones are all found in the Ural, more particularly on the eastern slopes. The discovery of petroleum on the western slopes (Volga–Ural field) led to the development of what is now the premier oil-producing region in the Union.

Iron ore

The manufacture of pig iron, using local resources of ore, water power and charcoal, was started in the Ural by the Strogonov family in the seventeenth century. In the eighteenth century the Demidov family continued the industry, which remained small-scale, with low productivity until after the first World War. Iron remains the basic industrial metal in the region and several new and more productive deposits are now being worked. Major centres of iron ore mining are Magnitogorsk (Magnitnaya Gora), Khalilovo, Nizhniy Tagil (Vysokaya, Lebyazhka), Blagodat, Bakal and Kachkanar. The high-grade magnetite (40–70% iron content) of Magnitnaya Gora in the valley of the upper Ural river is worked by opencast methods, but this source, at the present rate of mining, seems likely to be exhausted within the next generation. The reserves now being worked in the vicinity of Nizhniy Tagil may similarly be reaching exhaustion. Because of this, the reserves of haematite, magnetite and limonite in Oblast Kustanay (Rudny mines) astride the Tobol valley, 200 miles east of Magnitogorsk, are being increasingly developed to supplement supplies to that city. The low-grade but very large deposits at Kachkanar are earmarked for use in the northern part of the region.

Coal

The coal which occurs on both the western and the eastern slopes of the Ural mountains are of qualities unsuited for use in the metallurgical industry. The Kizel field produces low-quality coal (used in thermal electricity generating stations) and lignite; the latter can be used as blast furnace fuel after mixing with better-grade coals from the Kuzbass (to reduce sulphur content). South of Chelyabinsk lies the important Korkino-Kopeysk lignite–peat field, producing fuel for thermal electricity stations. There is also a small deposit of good-quality coal at Dombarovskiy near Orsk, in the extreme south of the region. Other scattered deposits of low-grade coal occur, but the region lacks good-quality coking coal, a deficiency that is a hindrance to the full exploitation of the rich mineral wealth, particularly the iron ore, of the region. Suitable coal is imported from Karaganda and the Kuzbass to make up the deficiency.

In 1930 Stalin said: "Our industry, like our national economy, relies in the main on our coal and metallurgical base in the Ukraine. Our task is this, that while continuing to develop this base in every possible way for the future, we must at the same time begin to create a second coal and metallurgical base. This must be the Ural–Kuznetsk Combine, the combination of Kuznetsk coking coal with the ores of the Ural." In the period up to the beginning of the second World War this second coal and metallurgical base was created, involving two-way traffic—coking coal in one direction and iron ore in the other, to support iron- and steel-producing centres 1200 miles apart. Since then the pattern of fuel supplies has changed: Karaganda and Ekibastuz in Kazakhstan now provide coking coal for the Ural. Despite the shorter haul involved in this traffic (about 800 miles), the greater quantity of coal is still imported to the Ural from Kuzbass.

Oil and gas

Oil from the Kama and Belaya Valleys (part of the Volga–Ural field) is conveyed by pipeline to Perm, Ufa, Ishimbay and Orsk. Oil refining and the petro-chemical industry now lead in the economy of the western Ural, with Perm as the most important centre.

Natural gas is imported from the Volga–Ural Region and from the Gazli–Kagan area in the Middle Asian desert near Bukhara. Gas, a cheap fuel for power production, may well, through its availability to the Ural, affect the quantity of coke needed by the iron- and steel-producing plants.

Iron and steel production

Raw materials being immediately available or readily imported into the region, the Ural is now outstanding as one of the U.S.S.R.s two great concentrations of iron, steel and rolled steel production. The Ural and the Ukraine together produce 84% of the Union's pig iron and 76% of its crude steel. A northern production area, centred on Nizhniy, Tagil, Sverdlovsk and Serov (the last two are 200 miles apart), is supplied with coal from the Kuznetsk Basin and the Kizel field; it may eventually be supplied from the Pechora Basin. For iron ore it increasingly relies on the Kachkanar field. A hundred and thirty miles to the south, centred on Chelyabinsk, Zlatoust, Magnitogorsk and Orsk-Novotroitsk (Chelyabinsk to Orsk is over 300 miles) a southern production area is becoming increasingly reliant on Karaganda-Ekibastuz coal and Turgay iron ore; this area has the prospect of receiving increasing natural gas supplies from west of the Ural and from Middle Asia.

Heavy engineering is closely integrated with steel production. Nizhniy Tagil specialises in railway rolling stock; Sverdlovsk produces mining machinery, steel-rolling equipment, machine tools, railway wagons and coaches and electrical equipment. Chelyabinsk-Kopeysk, besides having huge tractor works, also supply agricultural machinery, bulldozers, earth scrapers, oil-drilling equipment and electrical goods. Miass produces lorries and Zlatoust high-grade stainless steels.

Non-ferrous metals

Bauxite, copper, lead, zinc and platinum are especially plentiful in the Ural. Bauxite, found generally widespread but in particularly large deposits near Krasnoturinsk, is converted into alumina and aluminium there and at Kamensk-Uralskiy; it is also exported to Zaporozhye in the Ukraine and to Yerevan and Sumgait in Trans-Caucasia. There are copper deposits in Oblasts Chelyabinsk, Sverdlovsk and Orenburg and in Bashkir A.S.S.R.; and there are important copper smelters at Kyshtym and Karabash (40 and 50 miles northwest of Chelyabinsk respectively) and at Gay (20 miles northwest of Orsk). The lead and zinc foundries at Chelyabinsk are supplied from nearby resources. Lead and zinc are also obtained in economically valuable quantities from silver and copper ores in the Ural. Platinum is mined in Uralets and Kosya.

Other minerals

The largest deposit of high-grade asbestos in the Soviet Union is found at Asbest on the eastern slopes of the Ural, 40 miles northeast of Sverdlovsk. Commercial gold mining began in the Ural over a century and a half ago and there are rich deposits of diamonds and other precious and semi-precious stones. Jewel cutting and polishing are crafts traditionally associated with Sverdlovsk; emeralds are particularly important.

Some of the world's largest deposits of salts lie in the Ural Region. In the upper Kama Valley, north of Perm, Solikamsk and Berezniki have huge deposits of potassium and magnesium salts and of sodium chloride. These are the basis of one of the largest centres of heavy chemicals production in the Soviet Union, with enterprises devoted to the production of potash, soda, sulphuric acid, synthetic ammonia and mineral fertilisers. Chemical salts are exploited also in the Southern Ural at Iletsk. Coal from the Kizel field is used for by-product chemicals at Gubakha, and similar by-products are derived from the Karaganda and Kuzbass coals used in the coke ovens of metallurgical centres such as Chelyabinsk, Sverdlovsk and Magnitogorsk.

TRANSPORT AND COMMUNICATIONS

Although five west–east trunk lines traverse the Region, the several industrial areas of the Ural Region have, as yet, no completely integrated railway intercommunicating system. The Trans-Siberian Railway between Chelyabinsk and the Kuznetsk Basin, and its offshoot from Sverdlovsk to Omsk, have some of the highest freight densities in the U.S.S.R. (Fig. 76). There is, however, a marked imbalance on these sections, westerly traffic (coal, grain and timber) being greatly in excess of easterly traffic (iron ore and petroleum). This imbalance applies also to the South Siberian line between the Kuzbass and Magnitogorsk via Tselinograd (Akmolinsk) and to the Karaganda–Magnitogorsk line. Both are heavily used in the westward direction, for coal freight and, increasingly for iron ore from Kustanay (Turgay valley). The longitudinal line Orsk–Kartaly–Troitsk–Chelyabinsk–Sverdlovsk–Nizhniy Tagil–Serov carries mainly iron ore, coal and oil. There is a large westward rail movement of primary products for fabrication in other parts of the Union, especially of iron and steel (*see* Fig. 148).

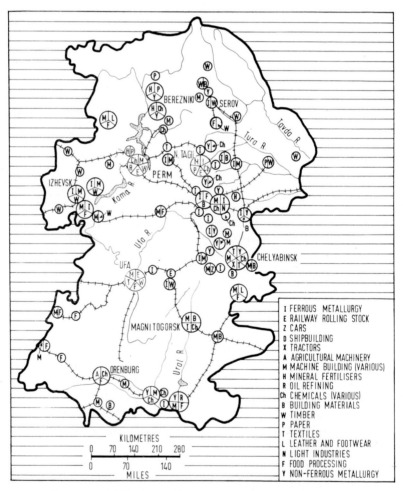

FIG. 148.—Ural Region: railways and industrial structure of towns.

Although considerable quantities of oil are still conveyed by rail, and by river tanker down the Kama River to the Volga, these means of transport are slowly being superseded by pipelines. Petroleum from the Volga–Ural field is distributed by pipeline to Ural towns and thence eastward by the same means to Omsk, Novosibirsk, Krasnoyarsk and Irkutsk.

Water transport remains the chief method of moving the timber exported from or moved within the Region.

POPULATION AND CITIES

Although it is three times greater in area, the Ural Region has a population (16½ millions) only one-third that of the United Kingdom. Two-thirds of the population live in towns; the forested countryside is only sparsely populated.

In recent decades the tempo of industrialisation throughout almost the whole of the Ural Region has been such that urban populations have more than doubled. There are now 17 cities each with over 100,000 inhabitants. The increase is due more to net migration into the region than to local rural depopulation, for the size of the rural populations has remained fairly constant. Places where populations have doubled since 1939 are Sverdlovsk, Chelyabinsk, Zlatoust, Berezniki and Serov. Others have experienced even greater increases: Miass (now 117,000) has increased by three times; Krasnoturinsk (62,000) by six times; Korkino (88,000) by over seven times; Novotroitsk (78,000) has a population 26 times larger than that of 1939.

Ethnically the people are overwhelmingly Russian, though there are sizeable concentrations of non-Slavic speaking groups. In particular there are the Udmurt and Komi-Permyak (north of the Kama River) who speak Finnic languages, and the Bashkirs (east and west of the Belaya River) who speak Turkic languages. These non-Slavs are being increasingly assimilated into the Russian way of life as more and more Russians migrate to the Region, especially in the developing oilfields of the Bashkir A.S.S.R. Administrative boundaries based on ethnic differences are rapidly losing validity in the Ural Region.

The main concentrations of population are at Sverdlovsk, Chelyabinsk and Magnitogorsk on the eastern slopes of the Ural, and at Perm and Ufa on the west. There are moreover scores of workers' settlements and clusters of population associated with mines and oil wells.

Sverdlovsk (919,000) was founded when copper mining started near by in

I

1721, when the town was called Ekaterinburg in honour of Catherine I, wife of Tsar Peter the Great. Located within the tayga in the eastern foothills of the low Central Ural, Sverdlovsk has since developed as an important route focus and industrial centre. Railway lines converge on the city from seven directions. Its industries include the manufacture of iron and steel, engineering, woodworking and chemical and copper enterprises (Fig. 148). The city is regional capital of the northern part of the Ural Region. Its population increased by 80% between 1939 and 1959, and by another 18% between 1959 and 1964; it is now probably near one million, which would make it one of the eleven or twelve million-cities of the Soviet Union.

Chelyabinsk (805,000) is capital of the southern part of the region. Like Sverdlovsk it is an important route focus and industrial centre. As the starting-point in 1891 of the Trans-Siberian Railway, it has long been considered the gateway to Siberia. It has extensive ferrous and non-ferrous metal-working industries, chemicals and food processing. Its population increased by 150% between 1939 and 1959 and by a further 17% between 1959 and 1964. As in Sverdlovsk, the total population may now be one million.

Perm (764,000), situated on the Kama River below its confluence with the Chusovaya (which river provides an important route through the Ural to Sverdlovsk), is the focus of the upper Kama industrial area. It has chemical, fertiliser and pulp-making industries based on local salt and timber supplies and engineering works which utilise steel processed in the eastern Ural. Perm developed early as an oil-refining centre on the Volga–Ural field and is now the chief centre for refining and petro-chemicals; nowadays local production of oil has to be supplemented by imported oil and natural gas. A possible increase in hydro-electricity generation at a station sited just upstream from Perm could arise from the projected Pechora–Kama diversion scheme (see p. 215). The present population, over twice that of 1939, increased by 21·6% in the period 1959–64.

Ufa (665,000), on the navigable Belaya, tributary of the Volga near its confluence with the Ufa River, is an important river port, focus of railways from Chelyabinsk, Ulyanovsk and Kuybyshev, and of pipelines from the Volga–Ural oilfield. The town has a refinery, expanding petro-chemical industries, engineering works specialising in oilfield equipment, paper mills and flour mills.

Nizhniy Tagil (370,000), in a valley on the eastern side of the Ural a few miles from the point where the Tagil River debouches on to the west Siberian Lowland, is a metallurgical centre with one of the largest integrated iron and steelworks in the Soviet Union. Ural ores and local and imported coals provide the basis for the industry, with which are associated coal by-products, industrial chemicals and engineering (largely railway rolling stock construction). Local forest supply lumber and raw materials for paper, pulp and cellulose industries.

Izhevsk (351,000) is capital and economic and cultural centre of the Udmurt A.S.S.R. It possesses steel sheet mills and metal-working industries and has an old-established firearms factory.

There are two other cities with populations of over a quarter of a million. *Magnitogorsk* (348,000) on the banks of the Ural River and within the steppe-lands is a major metallurgical centre. It relies on ores from Magnitnaya Gora and from Turgay, and on coking coal from Karaganda. The city was founded in 1931, but boasted a population of 146,000 in 1939 and 311,000 in 1959. *Orenburg* (Chkalov) (306,000), was founded in 1737 as a Russian fortress against Kazakh nomads. The railway from Kuybyshev to Tashkent crosses the Ural River at its site. It is now an agricultural centre with food processing and engineering industries, specialising in agricultural machinery.

Although a smaller centre, Orsk–Novotroitsk, in the steppe country of the extreme south of the region calls for special mention. This complex has grown phenomenally during the past few decades and the combined population now numbers over a quarter of a million. *Orsk* (210,000) is a meat-packing and oil-refining centre, and *Novotroitsk* (78,000) is a nearby new metallurgical centre. There are plentiful supplies of iron, copper, chromite, nickel and titanium in reasonably close proximity to the complex; coal of coking quality is available from nearby Dombarovskiy and, by importing, from Karaganda; oil can be brought in from Guryev (Emba field) or from Ishimbay and Ufa (Volga–Ural field). On the basis of the ready availability of these raw materials there have developed at Orsk–Novotroitsk integrated alloy steelworks specialising in high-quality chrome and nickel alloy steels, engineering (farm machinery and rolling stock) and oil refining and chemical industries. By reason of its general natural endowments and favourable geographical location, the continued expansion of this complex and of surrounding towns seems to be assured.

1. To what extent does the Ural form a major physical divide in the U.S.S.R.?

2. Make an examination of the metallic and non-metallic mineral resources of the Ural Region.

3. Discuss the ways in which the Ural Mountains have (*a*) helped, and (*b*) hindered, the economic development of the Soviet Union.

4. Analyse the factors which favour and hinder the growth of manufacturing industries in the Ural Region.

5. Write a geographical essay on Trans-Ural routes.

6. Attempt a comparison of the mineral resources of the Ukraine with those of the Ural Region.

7. Examine the site, location and functions of the following towns: Sverdlovsk; Chelyabinsk; Perm; Nizhniy Tagil; Magnitogorsk.

8. Critically examine the energy reserves and energy needs of the Ural Region.

9. How do you account for the fact that much of the population of the Ural Region is concentrated in large urban centres?

Chapter XX

NORTH CAUCASUS REGION

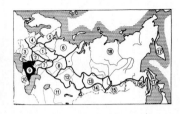

THE North Caucasus Region extends from the Great Caucasus mountains in the south to the lower Don in the north and from the Caspian Sea in the east to the Sea of Azov and the Black Sea in the west (Fig. 149). The region is twice the size of the United Kingdom, but has only a fifth of its population. It is predominantly agricultural in the Caucasus foreland and industrial in the lower Don–Donets area.

Area . . . . 166,700 sq. miles
Population (1959) . . 11,834,000

Administrative unit	Area sq. miles	Population in thousands 1959	Density persons per sq. mile	Percentage urban
Oblast Rostov	38,900	3,314	85	57
Oblast Krasnodar . . .	32,300	3,766	117	39
Oblast Stavropol . . .	31,100	1,866	60	30
Kabardino-Balkarskaya A.S.S.R..	4,800	420	88	38
Severo-Osetinskaya A.S.S.R. .	3,100	449	145	53
Checheno-Ingushskaya A.S.S.R. .	7,500	771	96	41
Dagestan A.S.S.R. . . .	19,400	1,063	54	30
Kalmyk A. O. . . .	29,600	185	6	21

Towns with over 150,000 inhabitants in 1964

	Population in thousands		Percentage increase
	1959	1964	1959–64
Rostov-on-Don . .	600	720	20·0
Krasnodar . . .	313	385	23·0
Groznyy . . .	242	314	29·8
Taganrog . . .	202	234	15·9
Ordzhonikidze . .	164	208	27·0
Shakhty . . .	196	207	5·6
Sochi	127	179	41·0
Stavropol . . .	141	165	17·1
Makhachkala . .	119	152	27·6

241

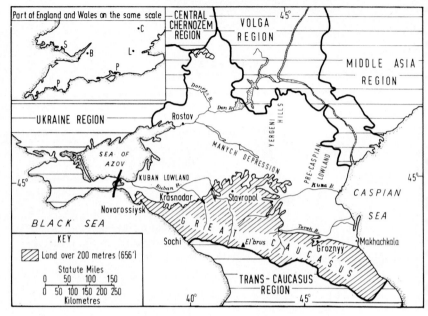

Fig. 149.—North Caucasus Region.

PHYSICAL ASPECTS

RELIEF

The most prominent physical features of the region are the northern ranges and slopes of the Great Caucasus Mountains and their northern foreland. Like the Ukrainian Carpathians and the Crimean Mountains to the west, and the Kopet-Dag and Pamirs to the east, this formidable range dates from the period of Alpine (Tertiary) folding. This area lay on the northern border of the great Alpine geosyncline. Earth movements caused by crustal pressures from north and south threw this zone into a series of anticlinal uplands and synclinal troughs. The mountains that now represent the evidence of these movements are a composite system of more or less parallel ranges with a crystalline backbone running west-northwest to east-southeast across the Caucasian isthmus and flanked by ranges running generally *en echelon*. During their relatively short history (in geological terms) they have undergone two major uplifts and suffered severe erosion, both by water and by ice. The zone of the Great Caucasus Mountains is in fact still unstable, as evidenced by the earthquakes, often locally disastrous, that disturb the area. The highest parts carry permanent mountain glaciers, the shrunken remains of Quaternary icefields and glaciers.

The Great Caucasus, extending nearly 800 miles, form an effective mountain barrier between 50 and 150 miles wide, right across the isthmus between the Black and Caspian Seas, with few readily negotiable passes. The watershed lies on the more southerly of the two principal parallel ranges; the highest peaks occur in the northerly range—Mount Elbrus, 18,481 ft (Fig. 150), Mount Koshtan-Tau, 17,096 ft, Mount Shkhara and Mount Dykh-Tau, just over 17,000 ft, and the Kasbek at about 16,550 ft.

[*Fotokhronika Tass.*

FIG. 150.—Mt Elbrus (18,481 ft) is the highest peak in the Great Caucasus.

The northern foreland, lying beyond the Caucasus foothills, has two contrasting sections separated by the dome-shaped Stavropol Plateau. In the west is a steppe plain drained by the Kuban to the Sea of Azov; in the east is a semi-desert plain drained by the Kuma–Terek Rivers to the Caspian Sea. The former is underlain by rich chernozems, the latter by sandy and salt-impregnated soils.

North of the Kuma–Manych Depression—which in late Quaternary times connected the Black and the Caspian Seas—lies the elevated, though much dissected, plain of the lower Don–Donets. This plain is separated from the Caspian desert lowland by the Yergeni Hills, a southern extension of the Volga Heights.

CLIMATE

The region as a whole is characterised by a continental climate which increases in severity towards the east. On the plains in the north the mean temperature of the warmest month (July) reaches 70°–75° F (21°–24° C) with maxima exceeding 100° F (38° C). For the coldest month (January) the temperature is about 25° F (−4° C) although cold waves accompanying northeasterly winds often cause it to drop from −10° to −15° F (−23° to −26° C). At Stavropol (1886 ft) the January and July values are 23·5° F (−5° C) and 69° F (21° C) respectively (Fig. 151), and at Ordzhonikidze (2050 ft) they are 24° F (−4° C) and 68·5° F (20° C) respectively. Annual

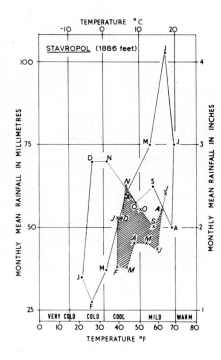

FIG. 151.—Hythergraph for Stavropol.

precipitation on the plains diminishes eastwards from 18 to 20 in. (460 to 500 mm) in the west to less than 6 in. (150 mm) in the east. Intense surface heating on the plains in summer leads to the inflow of moisture from the Black Sea and the Sea of Azov, to frequent thunderstorms, and to a summer maximum of rainfall. Annual aggregates increase from 28 to 30 in. (710 to 760 mm) in the foothills to 80–100 in. (2030–2550 mm) in the mountains, with no diminution of quantity from west to east. Above 3300 ft the mountains are permanently snow covered.

Föhn winds from the mountains in spring cause rapid snow melt and avalanches. During the summer the winds resemble the *sukhovey* and affect the sowing of crops and the harvesting of fruit.

THE ECONOMY

AGRICULTURE

The steppe-lands of the lower Don are extensively used for growing wheat, sunflowers, millet and sugar beet and for the grazing of cattle and sheep. Between Rostov and Tsimlyansk on the Don, and along the lower Donets, market gardening, dairying and fruit cultivation are carried on. The lowlands of the Kuban to the west of the foreland resemble the western Ukraine, for they have a prosperous and progressive agriculture, based on a

[*Mysl.*

Fig. 152.—Rice fields in the delta area of the River Kuban.

great variety of crops: spring and winter wheat, oil seeds (especially sunflowers), sugar beet, tobacco, maize, cotton and rice (in the swamp delta of the Kuban river) (Fig. 152). Along the shore of the Black Sea and in the shelter of the Caucasus, tobacco, tea, grapes, apricots, apples and pears are the main crops (Fig. 153).

In the dry, eastern part of the foreland, crop husbandry takes second place to cattle and sheep herding. There is some irrigation agriculture in the Kuma and Terek Valleys, and more particularly in the better-watered foothills south of the Terek where winter wheat, maize, vines, cotton, rice and fruits are grown. Within the Great Caucasus Mountains transhumance is widely practised, the stock making good use of mountain pastures during the summer.

FUELS, RAW MATERIALS AND INDUSTRY

The extreme eastern end of the Donets coalfield lies in the lower Don and Donets Valleys (i.e. in the western fringe of Oblast Rostov). Though separated from the Ukraine there are obvious links between the two areas. Anthracite coal is mined, particularly around Shakhty, Kamensk-Shakhtinskiy and Koksovyy, and there is heavy metallurgy at Krasnyy Sulin and Taganrog, and engineering at Rostov-on-Don, Novocherkassk and Taganrog.

In the northern foothills of the Great Caucasus oilfields and natural gas deposits occur. The oilfields have been known from earliest times and exploited since the latter half of the nineteenth century. By comparison with the Volga–Ural field they are small and their output, though significant, is now rivalled in importance by that of natural gas. The main oil centres are Neftegorsk, Maykop, Malgobek, Gudermes, Groznyy and Makhachkala. Refineries are located at Makhachkala, Groznyy, Krasnodar and Tuapse with pipeline links to the Black Sea, the Caspian Sea and the Donbass. A pipeline takes natural gas from Groznyy and Stavropol to the Central Industrial Region via Rostov-on-Don (Fig. 69). Another takes natural gas from Krasnodar to Novorossiysk (Fig. 154).

Non-ferrous metals such as molybdenum and tungsten (found at Tyrnyauz), zinc and lead (Sadon and Ordzhonikidze) are mined and refined, and Novorossiysk on the Black Sea has a large production of concrete. Within the Great Caucasus there is a large reserve of timber and of potential water power.

The industrial activities of the North Caucasus Region reflect the availability of coal, petroleum and gas supplies and a prosperous agricultural base. There are metallurgical and engineering industries in Oblast Rostov and oil refining, machine building (for the oil industry), flour milling, vegetable oil production, distilling, tanning, tobacco manufacture and meat packing in the Kuban Lowland and in the Caucasus foothills (Fig. 155).

The tourist industry is important and there are numerous resorts. Pyatigorsk, Yessentuki, Mineralnyye Vody and Kislovodsk have mineral springs, some radio-active, in a volcanic region along the northern foothills of the Great Caucasus. Along the Black Sea shores there is a popular holidaying area between Anapa and Sochi with numerous resorts, sanatoria and summer homes.

"Yesterday I arrived in Pyatigorsk, rented a flat on the outskirts of the town, at its highest point, at the foot of the Mashuk: during thunderstorms the clouds

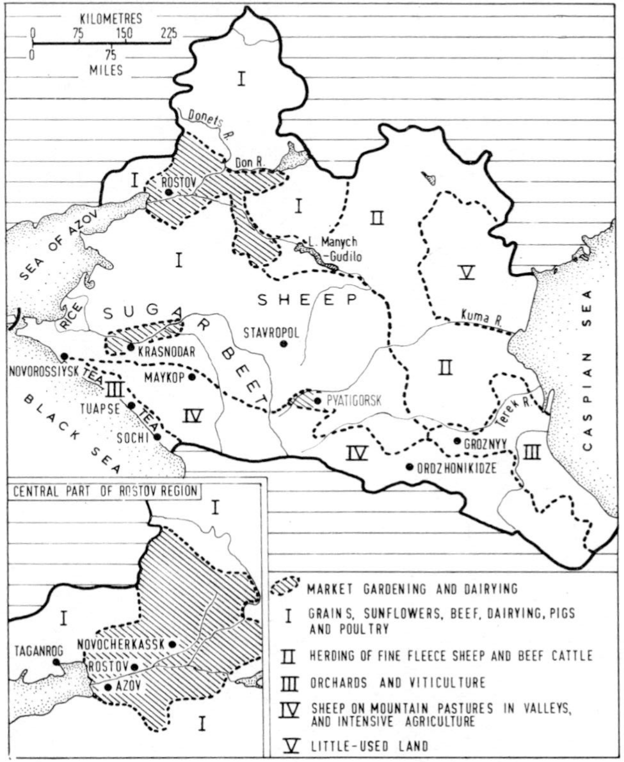

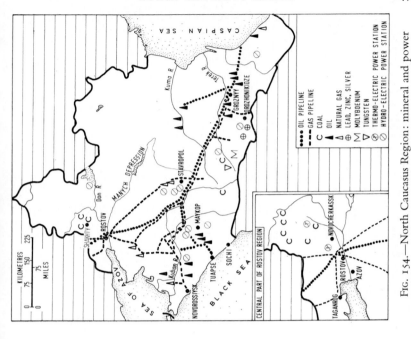

Fig. 154.—North Caucasus Region: mineral and power resources.

Fig. 153.—North Caucasus Region: agricultural land-use regions.

will be coming down to my roof. Today, at five o'clock in the morning, when I opened the window, my room was filled with the scent of flowers growing in the modest little garden at the front. The branches of the flowering cherry-trees look into my window, and sometimes the wind covers my writing desk with their white petals. I have a wonderful view on three sides. To the west the five-headed Beshtu looks blue, like 'the last cloud of a spent storm'; to the north rises Mashuk, like a shaggy Persian hat, and covers all that part of the skyline; to the east the view is gayer: below and before me glitters the clean, new little town, the healing springs roar, there is the sound of voices from the multilingual crowd, and there, further still, mountains are rising like an amphitheatre, bluer and mistier, and on the edge of the horizon stretches a silver chain of snow-clad mountain tops, beginning with Kazbek and ending with the two-headed Elbrus. It is a pleasure to live in such a land!"

M. Yu. Lermontov, from *The Hero of our Time*.

TRANSPORT AND COMMUNICATIONS

The location of the region peripheral to the remainder of the Soviet Union is expressed in several ways. With the exception of those in the somewhat anomalous Oblast Rostov most of the region's peoples are separated from the populous Ukraine and lower Volga areas by a thinly populated tract of rather poor soils and low rainfall, and from Trans-Caucasia by the high mountain barrier of the Great Caucasus. The Rostov-Makhachkala Railway was the only rail link between the south and the north of the region for over half a century up to 1890. Now it has been supplemented by railways linking Volgograd–Tikhoretsk–Krasnodar–Novorossiysk, and Astrakhan–Kizlyar–Prokhladnyy (Fig. 155). The only railways connecting the northern Caucasus with the Trans-Caucasian Republics pass along the shores of the Black and Caspian Seas at the extremities of the Great Caucasus. The former is the link between the rest of the Soviet Union and the Black Sea resorts. The only road links across the Great Caucasus are the Georgian (Ordzhonikidze–Tbilisi), Sukhumi (Cherkessk–Sukhumi) and Osetian (Alagir–Kutaisi) military roads. Mamison Pass on the Osetian road is at 9548 ft and the highest point on the Georgian road is 7813 ft. The roads are tortuous and traffic over them is light.

POPULATION AND CITIES

The distribution of population reflects economic, orographic and climatic conditions in the different parts of the region. Densities range from fewer than 6 persons per square mile in the steppe-lands of the Kalmyk A.O. immediately south of the Volga, to over 100 per sq. mile in Oblast Krasnodar and 145 per sq. mile in the Severo-Osetin A.S.S.R.; other areas of

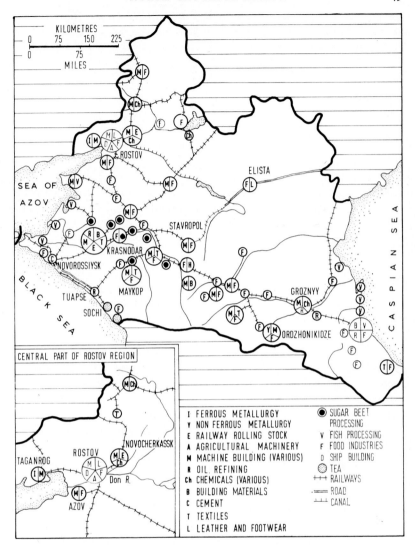

FIG. 155.—North Caucasus Region: railways and industrial structure of towns.

localised high densities are near petroleum resources. Among the high mountains, there is preserved a sparse population of perhaps the most varied collection of peoples to be found anywhere in the world. They include Osetians, Balkars and Kabardinians, some of whom have autonomous status. On the steppe-lands south of the lower Volga a Turkic (Mongol) people, the Kalmyks, settled after the thirteenth century invasions of the Golden Horde, of which they were part. Under the Soviets a Kalmyk Autonomous Oblast was set up in this area, but during the second World War, they were deported and scattered to remote parts of the Union and autonomy was suspended. It was re-established in 1958. The other inhabitants of the plains to the north of the Great Caucasus are largely the descendants of settlers many of whom were Cossacks, who were given lands here in the eighteenth century.

Rostov-on-Don (720,000) on the right bank of the River Don, 25 miles from the Sea of Azov, was founded in the eighteenth century as a frontier fortress against the Turks. It is now an important route focus, port and industrial centre. The town is also a collecting and assembly point for commodities and goods from the rich grain lands of the Kuban, the oil-producing Caucasian foreland, the Donets coalfield, and, since the opening of the Volga–Don Canal in 1952, from the Volga Basin. Rostov port, closed by ice for three months in the year, exports wheat, petroleum and manufactured goods (Fig. 155). *Azov* and *Taganrog* act as outports. Industries include engineering works (such as "Rosselmash" which specialises in tractors, combine harvesters and other agricultural machinery), aircraft, shipbuilding, footwear and the processing of tobacco and fish.

Krasnodar (385,000), on the navigable River Kuban, 140 miles from its mouth, is the chief administrative, commercial and industrial centre of the rich Kuban agricultural area. Its industries include flour milling, the manufacture and processing of butter, margarine fats and other foods, petroleum refining, and engineering (machine tools, petroleum machinery and spare parts for agricultural machinery). The town is the focus of routes from Novorossiysk, Rostov, Volgograd and Stavropol.

Groznyy (314,000) was founded in the late nineteenth century following the exploitation of nearby surface deposits of oil. Oil refinery, petro-chemical and petroleum machinery industries are located here. Pipelines link the town with Tuapse, Poli, Makhachkala and Rostov.

Taganrog (234,000), 40 miles west of Rostov on the Sea of Azov is a coal port and steel-making centre. The heavy industries include tube, pipe, and boiler making, and agricultural machinery.

Urban life is not greatly developed in this region. The only other centres of note are: *Ordzhonikidze* (208,000), associated with lead and zinc industries, based on Caucasus ores and hydro-electric power; *Shakhty* (207,000), a coal-mining centre in southeastern Donbass; *Stavropol* (165,000), with agriculture-orientated industries (renamed Togliatti in honour of the Italian Communist leader who died in 1964); *Makhachkala* (152,000) an oil transhipment port on the Caspian Sea; *Sochi* (179,000), the Black Sea resort; and the oil-refining towns of *Tuapse* and *Maykop*.

1. Suggest a division of the North Caucasus Region into geographical regions. Discuss the bearing of physical factors upon economic activities in any *two* of the regions recognised.

2. Give a geographical account of food production in the Caucasus Region.

3. Give a reasoned account of the land use of the hill country and lowland to the north of the Great Caucasus.

4. Review the main factors of the human geography of the North Caucasus Region.

5. Compare and contrast the salient features of the agricultural geography of Ukraine–Moldavia with those of the North Caucasus Region.

6. Examine the site, location and functions of the following towns: Krasnodar; Groznyy; Rostov-on-Don; Ordzhonikidze; Novorossiysk; Stravropol; Makhach-kala; Taganrog.

7. Comment on the factors influencing the distribution of the tourist industry in the North Caucasus Region.

8. Draw a sketch map to show the distribution of the main oil and natural gas deposits of the North Caucasus Region. Assess the importance of these resources to industrial economy of the North Caucasus Region and to the U.S.S.R. as a whole.

Chapter XXI

TRANS-CAUCASUS REGION

 THE Trans-Caucasus Region lies south of the main crest of the Great Caucasus Mountains. It comprises Georgia (Gruziya), Azerbaydzhan and Armeniya (Fig. 156). Trans-Caucasia is about three-quarters the size of the United Kingdom, but its population is less than a fifth of that of the United Kingdom. It is essentially a non-Russian region, with an economy based on livestock farming, food processing and oil refining.

Area . . . . 71,900 sq. miles
Population (1959) . . 9,517,000

Administrative unit	Area sq. miles	Population in thousands 1959	Density persons per sq. mile	Percentage urban
Georgian S.S.R. . . .	26,900	4,049	150	42
Azerbaydzhan S.S.R. . .	33,500	3,700	111	48
Armenian S.S.R. . . .	11,500	1,768	153	50

Towns with over 150,000 inhabitants in 1964

	Population in thousands 1959	1964	Percentage increase 1959–64
Baku	971	1,147	18·0
Tbilisi	703	812	15·5
Yerevan . . .	509	633	24·5
Kirovabad . . .	116	166	43·2
Kutaisi. . . .	128	154	20·5

PHYSICAL ASPECTS

RELIEF AND DRAINAGE

Though few parts of the Soviet Union display such variety of landscapes as occur in this region, in essence there are three main relief regions. From north to south these are the Great Caucasus, south of the main crest-line, the Rioni–Kura depression, and the Lesser Caucasus. South of the southern foothills of the Great Caucasus lies a sheltered tectonic depression which is drained to the Black Sea by the River Rioni and to the Caspian Sea by the River Kura. This depression is not a simple structural trough. Between the alluvial valleys of the Rivers Rioni and Inguri in the west and of the lower Kura and Araks in the east lies a belt of hilly, even mountainous country whose broken relief sometimes rises to over 3000 ft. This

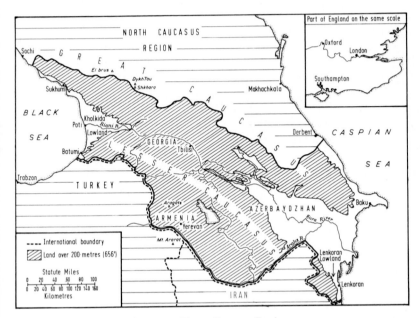

FIG. 156.—Trans-Caucasus Region.

belt is called the Suram Uplands and links the Great Caucasus with the Lesser Caucasus and the Armenian volcanic plateau. The area west of the Suram Uplands, together with the Black Sea coast south of the Great Caucasus, is the Kolkhida Lowland (*Colchis* of the ancient Greeks). East of the Suram Uplands is the larger and very flat Kura–Araks Lowland; its extension southwards along the Caspian coast to the Iranian border is the Lenkoran (Talysh) Lowland.

CLIMATE

The Great Caucasus is an important climatic divide, constituting a high barrier to atmospheric movements and sheltering the Trans-Caucasus Region from bitterly cold northern air during the winter.

The Kolkhida Lowland has a humid subtropical climate (Fig. 157).

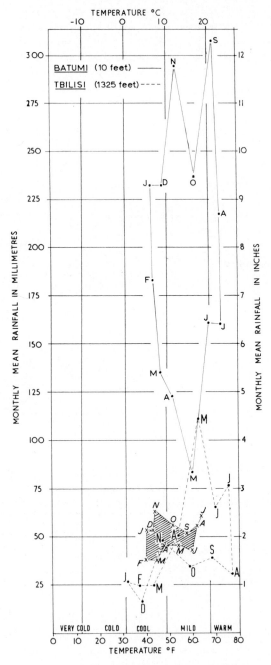

FIG. 157.—Hythergraphs for Batumi and Tbilisi.

Summers are warm (70°–75° F; 21°–24° C), winters mild (40°–45° F; 4°–7° C), and there is a very heavy rainfall by Russian standards.

The rainfall varies between 60 and 100 in. (1500 and 2540 mm) and it comes mainly in autumn and winter. This area, the south of Crimea and the extreme south of Turkmen, are the only parts of the U.S.S.R. where mean January temperatures are above freezing level. The Kura–Araks Lowland, with a steppe and semi-arid climate, is climatically an outlier of Middle Asia. Near the mouth of the River Kura the annual rainfall is no more than 10 in.

Borisov describes graphically the climate of Baku:

"Dry dusty winds are especially characteristic of the Baku district where the local 'norther' is an 'Egyptian death.' It occurs at any time of the year, but particularly in summer. The average wind velocity is fairly high—7·6 m/sec.—but individual gusts reach 20 or even 40 m/sec. The strong, dry and dusty wind blows for two or three days in succession, or at times even for 9 days or more without interruption."

The Lenkoran Lowland, facing the Caspian Sea and sheltered by the Talysh Mountains, has a subtropical climate, but is less humid (40–50 in.; 1000–1300 mm) than the Kolkhida Lowland.

[*Soviet Weekly.*

FIG. 158.—Tea picking by machine. Tea with lemon is a favourite Russian drink and both grow in Georgia.

THE ECONOMY

AGRICULTURE AND FORESTRY

The warm moist climate of Kolkhida promotes a luxuriant vegetation. Where the land is not swampy, or has been drained, conditions are ideal for oranges, lemons, grapefruit and tangerines, tea, maize and tung oil (Fig. 158). Ginger, bamboo, tobacco and mulberries (for the silk industry) are also grown. Farther east, in the warm dry valleys of eastern Georgia are

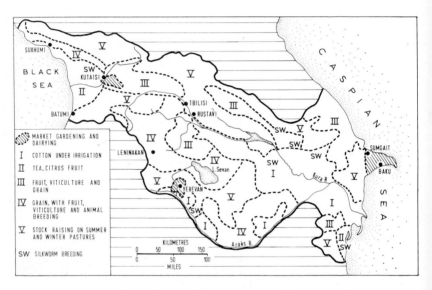

FIG. 159.—Trans-Caucasus Region: agricultural land-use regions.

some of the most important commercial vineyards of the Soviet Union and there is a flourishing wine industry. The well-drained terraces along the Iori and Alazani Valleys are particularly important for vines, tobacco and fruits (Fig. 159).

The southern slopes of the Great Caucasus west of the Suram Uplands are forested and fir, spruce, pine and beech are felled. In the east on the lower reaches of the River Kura lies an unhealthy swamp but in the irrigated areas there is large-scale growing of cotton, rice and lucerne (alfalfa). Southwards, in the Lenkoran Lowland, citrus fruits, tea, olives, wheat and barley are important.

Market gardening and dairying are common in the vicinity of Baku. Transhumance involving sheep, goats and cattle, is widely practised in the foothills of eastern Trans-Caucasia, from mountain pastures in summer to lowland pastures in winter (Fig. 160). There is a limited amount of cereal growing (winter wheat and barley) and stock raising in the Lesser Caucasus. Vines are grown around Yerevan, which is well known for its cognac, liqueurs and sherry. Lands irrigated by waters from hydro-electric schemes along the Razdan (Zanga) produce peaches, apricots and other fruit and vegetables, and alongside the Araks some cotton is grown under irrigation.

[*Fotokhronika Tass.*

FIG. 160.—Sheep breeding is widely practised in the foothills of eastern Trans-Caucasia.

RAW MATERIALS AND INDUSTRY

Citrus fruits, grapes, tea, tobacco, cotton, silk and wool provide the bases for some industries, but petroleum (with which Baku and district are virtually synonymous) is the single most important resource of Trans-Caucasia or, more specifically, of Azerbaydzhan. The oil occurs in Oligocene grits and sandstones beneath a capping of younger limestones and clays where the Kura Depression adjoins the eastern end of the folds of the Great Caucasus. Exploitation began in the 1860s and by the turn of the century the Baku field was producing half of the world's petroleum, the bulk of it

being exported abroad. Baku's position as chief oil-producing area of the
U.S.S.R. was eclipsed after World War II by the Volga–Ural field (known
as the "Second Baku"), but its production is still significant. The main
producing area, for both heavy and light oils, is within the Apsheron
Peninsula, but as the search for oil continues, more wells are being drilled
from off-shore platforms in the Caspian Sea. Some wells are 50–60 miles
from the shore and in some cases houses, flats, offices, cinemas and shops

[*United Press International (UK) Ltd.*

FIG. 161.—Neftnye Kamni ("oil stones"), near Baku. Part of the town is built
on piles over the Caspian Sea, where workers are extracting oil from beneath
the sea-bed.

have been built on the platforms which are linked to land by causeways
(Fig. 161). Smaller oilfields occur near the mouth of the Kura River. Most
of the oil is sent out of the region by rail, by tanker from the port of Baku,
or by pipeline to the refinery at Batumi on the Black Sea coast.

Manganese (at Chiatura and Kutaisi), copper (at Alaverdi, Kedabek and
Dostafyur), bauxite (at Zaglik), salt (at Beyuk Shor and Nakhichevan) and
alunite (at Alunitdag) are of more than local importance. Huge quantities
of natural gas found at Karadag, southwest of Baku, are used either within
Azerbaydzhan (e.g. to supply the Ali-Bairamly power station) or are
piped to Georgia and Armenia (Fig. 162). Hydro-electric power is being
developed; the dam and reservoir at Mingechaur on the Kura River is the

largest of the region. This is a multipurpose scheme involving hydro-electricity, irrigation, flood protection and river transportation.

Oil is not only a major source of energy but also a raw material for a whole range of petro-chemical industries. In addition, the need to provide turbo-drills, pipes, compressors, storage tanks, machinery and similar equipment for the oil industry has stimulated their manufacture within the region. Such industries and a wide range of ancillary ones are to be found in Baku. Steel, using Dashkesan iron ore, is obtained from Rustavi, near Tbilisi. Sumgait, near Baku, is another steel centre, with aluminium works and a plant for making synthetic rubber.

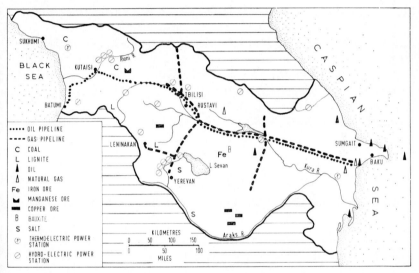

FIG. 162.—Trans-Caucasus Region: mineral and power resources.

TRANSPORT AND COMMUNICATIONS

Difficult physical conditions hinder the construction of railways in Trans-Caucasia, and it was not until the turn of the century that the local system was linked to the railways of European Russia. The Suram Uplands provided a particularly formidable obstacle to latitudinal communications along the Trans-Caucasian Lowlands and it was not until 1883 that the link between Tbilisi and Baku was achieved. The gradient on the line through the Suram Uplands is reported to be 1 in 50. No railway crosses the Great Caucasus and the classical land route, now followed by a railway, by-passes the mountains by traversing the Caspian shore via Derbent (Fig. 163). In recent years and after some difficulty, a road and railway have been built along the Black Sea shore. The narrow coastal land routes on west and east offer the simplest methods of negotiating the barrier of the Great Caucasus. A railway follows the Araks Valley through the Lesser Caucasus, along the boundary with Iran and Turkey and joins Baku with Tbilisi via Leninakan. A branch of this line to Yerevan provides a link with Tabriz and Tehran in Iran (Persia), and Erzurum in Anatolia (Turkey).

Pipelines afford valuable means of transporting oil and natural gas out of the Region (Fig. 162).

POPULATION AND CITIES

The 9½ million people who live in Trans-Caucasia are mainly non-Russian. They are of diverse ethnic origin, many with civilisations far older than that of the Russians. The three major groups—the Georgians, Armenians and Azerbaydzhanis—are numerous enough to form Union Republics. The Georgians and Armenians belong to the Caucasian ethnic group. The Georgians are Orthodox (except near Batumi), the Armenians belong to one of the oldest Christian churches, the Armenian Church, which is centred on Echmiadzin, southeast of Tbilisi. The Azerbaydzhanis, who migrated to the Caucasus from around the southern end of the Caspian Sea, belong to the Turkic ethnic group and are Moslem in religion.

The surge in development of power production, iron and steel making, metallurgy, engineering, chemicals, building materials and in food and light industries has been widespread. Consequently, new towns have been

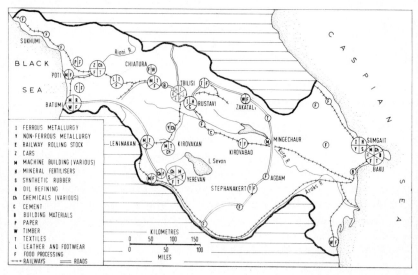

FIG. 163.—Trans-Caucasus Region: railways and industrial structure of towns.

set up in mining areas, near hydro-electric stations and around factories processing agricultural produce. Half the population of Armeniya and Azerbaydzhan now lives in towns (mainly in the Republic capitals) although there are several other localised high densities of population in all three Republics. The humid Black Sea littoral and Kolkhida Lowland support more than 150 persons per square mile, as does the thickly settled country around Baku. The drier eastern parts, notably in the steppe of the Kura Lowlands, have fewer than 25 persons per square mile, although there are some localised high densities, in areas of irrigated farming. The sparse population of the Great Caucasus is generally found in nucleated villages. The Armenian Plateau has a sparse nomadic population, but irrigated farming areas along the Rivers Razdan (near Yerevan) and Araks (Nagorno-Karabakh A.O.) are thickly settled.

Baku (1,147,000), capital of the Azerbaydzhan S.S.R., lies on the western shore of the Caspian Sea on the southern side of the Apsheron Peninsula. When the several oil towns of the Apsheron Peninsula, together with the oil settlements built on stilts in the Caspian Sea are included, Greater Baku has a population over 1 million. It is the fourth largest city of the U.S.S.R. Baku's great importance lies in its petroleum resources which have been exploited near by since 1873. Oil derricks, refineries, processing plant, pipelines and other industrial paraphernalia jostle with Moslem mosques and a Shah's palace in what was formerly a ninth-century fortress town. The port, much troubled by silting and by strong northerly winds in winter, exports petroleum across the Caspian and up the Volga. Oil is also exported by pipeline to Batumi on the Black Sea. In addition to its oil refining, it has petro-chemical, engineering, cotton textile, leather, meat packing, flour milling and timber industries (Fig. 163).

Tbilisi (Tiflis) (812,000), capital of the Georgian S.S.R. and centre of Georgian culture, is an attractive city in a fertile basin of the upper Kura River, within the lower slopes of the Suram Uplands. Its foundation dates from the fourth century, but its history has been chequered, with several plunderings at the hands of Byzantines, Arabs, Iranians, Mongols and Turks. Oriental markets, bazaars and buildings of historical and architectural interest in the old part of the town stand in stark contrast to the more modern geometrical layout of the Russian part. It is also an important rail focus and southern terminus of the Georgian military road from Ordzhonikidze via the famous Dariali Gorge. Industries in the city produce textiles (especially silk), hosiery, leather goods, tobacco, vegetable oils, wines, foods, machinery (for the tea, citrus and vine growing of Trans-Caucasia) and plastics (in association with its oil refining).

Yerevan (633,000), lying on the Armenian Plateau where historic and relatively easy passes lead to Iran and Anatolia, is capital and cultural centre of the Armenian S.S.R. It is located on the Razdan (Zanga) River, a tributary of the Araks river, over 3000 ft above sea-level and dominated by the majestic peaks of Mount Aragats (13,435 ft) in the northwest and Mount Ararat (16,916 ft) on Turkish territory in the south. The city has had a long and stormy history dating from the eighth century B.C. It was incorporated within the Russian Empire in 1828 after a war with Persia and attained capital status in 1920. In addition to its administrative functions it has several important industries. Chemicals are represented by plastics and synthetic rubber and engineering by cables, machine tools, turbines, lamps and generators. Textiles, clothing, footwear, tobacco, wines, foodstuffs, leather and woodwork are also produced. Local supplies of hydro-electricity are used in the manufacture of chloroprene rubber.

Kirovabad (166,000) in the middle Kura Valley has an important aluminium industry (using Zaglik bauxite), besides its earlier butter-making, cotton-cleaning and textile industries. *Kutaisi* (154,000), in the Kholkida Lowland, was the ancient capital of western Georgia. It is now the centre of an important fruit and vine-growing district with a variety of associated industries. Textiles (particularly silk) and motor-car assembly plants are also located here. The nearby Tkibuli bituminous coal mines supply much of the local coal requirement.

On the Black Sea *Sukhumi* and *Gagra* are popular holiday resorts and *Batumi* is an oil-refining and oil-exporting port. *Rustavi*, southeast of Tbilisi, has ferrous metallurgy and *Sumgait*, on the Caspian Sea north of the Apsheron Peninsula, is a steel and chemical centre.

STUDY QUESTIONS

1. Suggest a division of the Trans-Caucasus Region into geographical regions. Discuss the bearing of physical factors upon economic activities in any *two* of the regions recognised.

2. To what extent does the Great Caucasus form a major physical divide in the U.S.S.R.?

3. What do you understand by "vertical climates"? Illustrate your answer by reference to the Great Caucasus Mountains.

4. Write a geographical study of Trans-Caucasus routes.

5. Examine the economic development and degree of self-sufficiency achieved in Trans-Caucasia.

6. Examine the site, location and functions of the following towns: Tbilisi; Yerevan; Batumi; Baku; Sumgait; Rustavi.

7. Write an essay on the tourist industry of Trans-Caucasia.

8. Discuss the importance of viticulture in Trans-Caucasia.

9. Compare respectively the climates and ways of life in the Black Sea and Caspian Sea coastlands of Trans-Caucasia.

10. Comment on the variety of peoples, languages and religions in Trans-Caucasia.

11. Make a comparative study of the Caspian Sea ports.

Chapter XXII

MIDDLE ASIA

 MIDDLE Asia, here defined as the four republics of Turkmenistan, Tadzhikistan, Kirgiziya and Uzbekistan, together with the southern part of Kazakhstan (Fig. 164), is a vast area of deserts and high mountains, though with some densely populated oases. Southern Kazakhstan, included in this region because it is more akin to Middle Asia than to Siberia, is isolated from its northern section by an extensive area of desert and semi-desert, 250–300 miles wide. North Kazakhstan is closely related, both physically and culturally, to southwest Siberia and is considered in Chapter XXIII.

Before its annexation by Russia the whole area comprised a number of Khanates and was for long regarded by Russia as colonial territory providing a useful source of cotton and sugar. With World War II and the German occupation of the western parts of the Soviet Union there was an influx of Russians and Ukrainians into Middle Asia. At the same time the region's economy was stimulated and further developed to meet the needs arising from the loss of the food and industrial resources in enemy-occupied territories. Middle Asia is now an important region of specialised agriculture, particularly cotton cultivation, and it supplies over two-thirds of the Union's total requirement of cotton. This is supplemented by pastoral activities and diversified light industries. The irrigated oases, which have since time immemorial been the abodes of settled cultivators, include long renowned centres of Islam such as Samarkand, Tashkent and Mary which can trace their history back to the beginnings of agriculture in the first millennium. The deserts, semi-arid lands and mountains are the home of nomadic pastoralists who range over seasonal pastures on the desert fringe, or else move between mountain pastures in summer and valley pastures in winter. The differences between the settled cultivator and the nomadic pastoralist were traditional until the beginning of the Soviet era, since when they have largely disappeared, for the cattle herders have been settled in permanent communities on large stock-rearing *sovkhozy* where increasing attention is devoted to cattle breeding and the raising of good-quality stock.

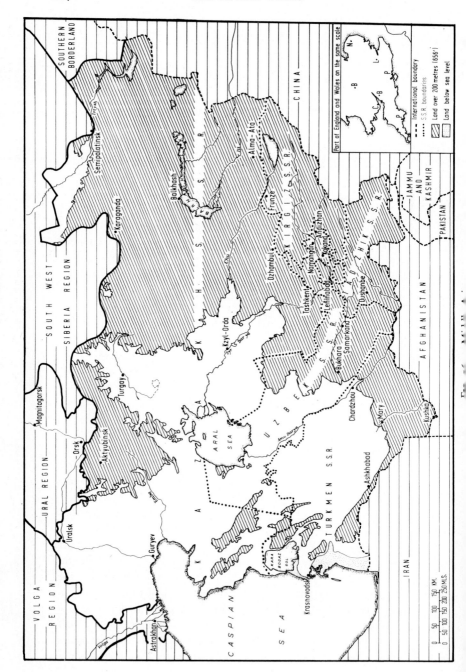

Area   .   .   .   .   1,408,000* sq. miles
Population (1959)   .   .   21,615,000

Administrative unit	Area sq. miles	Population in thousands 1959	Density persons per sq. mile	Percentage urban
Turkmen S.S.R. . . .	188,000	1,520	8	46
Uzbek S.S.R. . . .	158,000	8,113	52	34
Tadzhik S.S.R. . . .	55,000	1,982	36	33
Kirgiz S.S.R.	77,000	2,063	26	34
Kazakh S.S.R. (southern part) .	930,000*	7,937*	9*	—

*est.

Towns with over 150,000 inhabitants in 1964

	Population in thousands		Percentage increase
	1959	1964	1959–64
Tashkent . . .	912	1,106	21·2
Alma-Ata . . .	456	623	36·8
Karaganda . . .	397	482	21·4
Frunze	220	360	63·8
Dushanbe . . .	224	316	41·0
Samarkand . . .	196	233	19·0
Ashkhabad . . .	170	226	33·0
Ust-Kamenogorsk . .	150	202	34·8
Chimkent . . .	153	200	30·9
Andizhan . . .	130	159	22·4
Namangan . . .	123	150	22·0

PHYSICAL ASPECTS

RELIEF

The monotonous and arid Turanian Lowland occupies the greater part of the region. Until the end of the Tertiary period this lowland and the low-lying lands surrounding the northern part of the Caspian Sea were part of the bed of a much greater Aral Sea which extended westwards to embrace both the Black and Caspian Seas. Now the lowland is a vast basin of interior drainage, a region of dry steppe and clay and sandy (*kum*) desert. Between the Caspian and Aral Seas is the semi-arid and partially dissected Ustyurt Plateau. This is a flat, barren upland of nearly horizontal strata lying at an elevation of about 1000 ft. East of the Aral Sea, which is generally 40–60 ft deep, with a maximum depth of only 220 ft, the land rises to the Kazakh Uplands, an extensive area of separate ranges with a general elevation below 3000 ft and of subdued relief. This is the divide between drainage northwards to the Arctic and interior drainage to the Aral

Sea. Between the Mugodzhary Hills and the Kazakh Uplands is an extension of the Turanian Lowland known as the Turgay Tableland, which is, in fact, a plain dotted with residual tablelands (*turtkulei*).

In the south, between the Caspian Sea and Amu-Darya is a vast area of sand and clay depressions (*takyr*), known as Kara-Kum ("Black Sands"). Kyzyl-Kum ("Red Sands"), between the Amu-Darya and Syr-Darya is a dry alluvial plain with scattered dunes, its centre deeply buried in loose sand within which dunes (*barkhans*), varying in height up to more than 100 ft, abound (Fig. 165). This is how Vladimir Lugovskoi sees Turkestan in *A Ballad of a Desert*, of which these are a few verses:

"And so day after day barkhans were rolling,
Like silent waves of a stilled sea,
There was only the shimmer of heat left in the world,
In the yellow and blue of the glassy expanse.

No sound, no water, no people, complete isolation,
No wind, not a rustle, not a movement of air.
Bent bushes and camel's bones,
And the dull beating of heart and pulse.

The horses are swaying, the rifles, like hot coals,
The heat hands over, the knees are getting weak,
Words die unspoken, and lips have swollen.
Not a beast, not a bird, not a sound, not a shade.

Is it possible that one day the might of man,
Will rise up, conquering the solitude of the sands,
Or will the barkhan sea, the grey desert
Roll on from century to century?"

Muyun-Kum is a comparatively small desert between the Syr-Darya and River Chu. Betpak-Dala is a dry plateau rising from 450 ft in the south to 1500 ft in the north between the River Chu and the Kazakh Uplands.

Between the southern border of the Turanian Lowland and the high mountains of Middle Asia is a zone of loess-covered piedmont plains at a height of 300–900 ft. This zone includes the slopes of Kopet-Dag, the Golodnaya Steppe, the Fergana Basin, the lower slopes of the foothills of the Kirgiz Range, and of the Dzhungarskiy Ala-Tau.

A high mountain wall, extending from the east coast of the Caspian Sea to the Zaysan Depression, encloses Middle Asia on the south and east. In the south the Kopet-Dag ("Dry Mountains") and associated ranges lie mainly in Iran, where they reach heights above 9000 ft; in Turkmeniya the heights rarely exceed 3000 ft. In the southeast, wave after wave of high snow-capped mountains alternate with deep valleys. The Pamir-Alay mountains are a series of east–west orientated ranges fanning out from the Pamir massif ("Roof of the World") of Afghanistan and Pakistan. These are the highest mountains in the Soviet Union, where Mount Communism rises to 24,590 ft and Mount Lenin to 23,405 ft. Earthquakes within the Pamir often give rise to avalanches of snow and ice which dam existing streams and cause floods. The northernmost range of the Pamir-Alay Mountains is known as the Trans-Alay Range.

[*Fotokhronika Tass.*

FIG. 165.—Drifting sand dunes (*barkhans*) in the Kara-Kum desert.

The *Tyan-Shan* ("Heavenly Mountains") system is a complex of ranges, some of which are notoriously difficult to cross because of their great height (over 11,000 ft) and infrequent passes. Mount Victory (24,406 ft), near the frontier between the Kirgiz S.S.R. and China, is the second highest peak in the U.S.S.R. Individual ranges are aligned roughly west–east and enclose mountain basins. Of these, the Fergana Basin, 10–25 miles wide and 100 miles long, lying just north of Alay Range is the broadest. Others are the Issyk-Kul and the Zaysan Depression. The northernmost range of the Tyan-Shan is the Dzhungarskiy Ala-Tau which rises to 16,500 ft. Between these mountains and the Tarbagatay Range is the relatively low Dzhungarian Gate, the historic highway leading from China across Mongolia to the Kazakh Steppe and thence to the Volga.

CLIMATE

The entry of moist air masses to the region is prevented by its great distance from any oceans and the screen, on three sides, of high mountains. Precipitation over the plains is slight and unreliable. Aggregates are less than 10 in. (250 mm) per annum, but evaporation exceeds precipitation and the region is arid or semi-arid—drought is the unifying factor of Middle Asia. Only the Amu-Darya and Syr-Darya, fed in the mountains by melt-

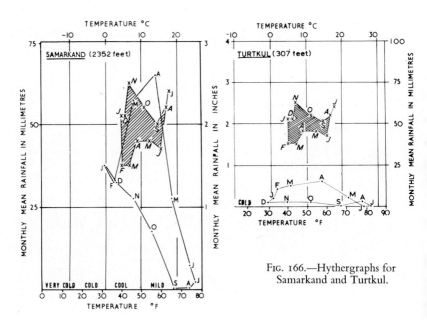

Fig. 166.—Hythergraphs for Samarkand and Turtkul.

ing snow and ice, survive the journey through the deserts to the Aral Sea. Winter temperatures are low for the latitude and, except in the extreme south, are below freezing level. Summer temperatures rise to 100° F (38° C) to make this the hottest part of the U.S.S.R. in summer. In fact, actual temperatures in summer are as high as those experienced in the Sahara or the interior of Australia. At Turtkul (formerly Petro-Alexandrovsk) in the Kyzyl-Kum (Fig. 166) the July average is 82° F (27·8° C) but maximum day temperatures may rise to between 100° F and 110° F (38° C and 43° C) and night minimum temperatures occasionally drop to 40° F (4·4° C). The air is dry and clouds are absent, but daytime conditions are turbulent and windy.

"Because of the dry air the summer heat is endured much more easily here than in the humid subtropics of Trans-Caucasia, but the midday hours are too oppressive for work in the open, even for those who live here always. The burden of the heat is increased by dry, scorching winds—the *harmsil*, which sometimes affect the harvest of cotton and grain adversely. It is interesting that temperature differences between the oases and desert are negligible in winter (0·2° C–0·4° C) but at the height of summer, the desert is three degrees warmer than its oases."[*]

Spring and autumn are fleeting seasons and pass virtually unnoticed. The climate generally is not unlike that experienced in the Great Basin of the U.S.A. or the Gobi of Mongolia. The foothill belt, along the fringe of the desert, and the valleys of the south and southeast receive rather more precipitation than the desert itself and they are also watered by the mountain-fed streams. Irrigation agriculture in these areas provides spectacular results.

Of the Pamirs, Semenov writes:

"Little snow falls (in winter) in the Pamirs, but there are hard frosts there and terrible freezing winds rage. In quiet sunny weather it often becomes so hot in the middle of the day that it is necessary to discard warm clothes but there is sometimes sufficient cloud or shade to blot out the sun's rays and chill one through with sharp cold. The side of one's face turned towards the sun is strongly heated; but the side in the shade almost freezes, and the skin sheds its outer layer several times and finally becomes dark and dry like parchment."[†]

THE ECONOMY

AGRICULTURE

In southern Turkmenistan the Kara-Kum merges into the loess-covered piedmont plain at 300–400 ft above sea-level. The rivers and small mountain streams that cross the plain have built up a series of alluvial fans along the mountain front. Only the Murgab and Tedzhen rivers succeed in flowing any distance into the desert before drying out through seepage and evaporation. The plain contains a line of wonderfully fertile oases which have attracted man since Neolithic times. The largest irrigated areas are at Ashkhabad in the west, in the Tedzhen delta and valley and in the Murgab valley (Fig. 167). The Ashkhabad area is well known for its cotton, grains and lucerne (alfalfa), the Tedzhen valley for wheat, cotton and lucerne, and the Murgab for cotton. The Kara-Kum Canal supplements local streams by conveying waters westwards from the Amu-Darya at Kelif through the oases of the Murgab and Tedzhen to Ashkhabad, a distance of 500 miles. Well over one million acres of the thirsty lands of southern

---

[*] Borisov, *Climates of the U.S.S.R.*, p. 180.
[†] O. I. Semenov–Tyan–Shanskii (eds.), *Russia*, Vol. 18, 1903.

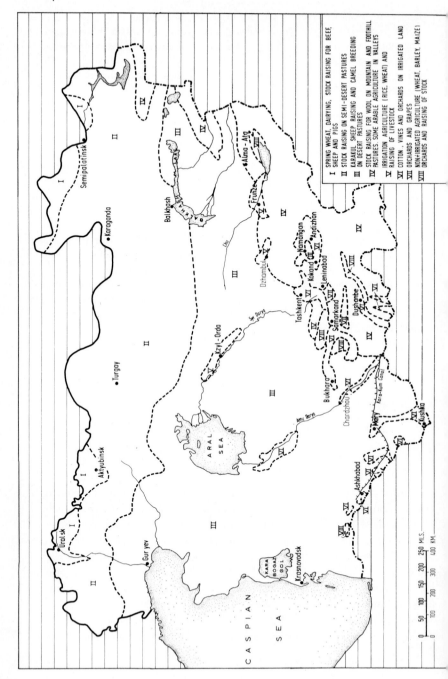

I   SPRING WHEAT, DAIRYING, STOCK RAISING FOR BEEF,
     SHEEP AND PIGS
II   STOCK RAISING ON SEMI-DESERT PASTURES
III KARAKUL SHEEP RAISING AND CAMEL BREEDING
     ON DESERT PASTURES
IV   STOCK RAISING FOR WOOL ON MOUNTAIN AND FOOTHILL
     PASTURES, SOME ARABLE AGRICULTURE IN VALLEYS
V   IRRIGATION AGRICULTURE (RICE, WHEAT) AND
     RAISING OF LIVESTOCK
VI   COTTON, VINES AND ORCHARDS ON IRRIGATED LAND
VII ORCHARDS AND GRAPES
VIII NON-IRRIGATED AGRICULTURE (WHEAT, BARLEY, MAIZE)
     ORCHARDS AND RAISING OF STOCK

Turkmenistan are irrigated thereby. There are plans to extend the Kara-Kum Canal to Krasnovodsk on the Caspian and to have a Great Turk-menian Canal skirting the Kara-Kum and linking the lower Amu-Darya with the Caspian. There has been no mention of the latter project since 1953 and it seems unlikely that construction was ever started.

[*Mysl*.

FIG. 168.—The Zeravshan River ("the river that sprinkles gold") before it debouches into the loess plains near Samarkand.

Irrigation has been practised in the basin of the Amu-Darya since ancient times. About 65% of the irrigated land is in the delta region, 15% along the west bank of the middle course (between the Soviet–Afghan frontier and the delta) and 20% in the upper basin, primarily in the valleys of the Vakhsh, Surkhan-Darya and Kafirnigan. In the upper reaches of the

Amu-Darya and its tributaries long-staple cotton and grains are the chief irrigated crops, but there are also non-irrigated crops grown by dry farming methods, such as wheat, maize and other grains. In the lower reaches, downstream from Urgench is the famous Khiva City and Oasis where the emphasis is on cotton in rotation with lucerne. The effects of World War I, the civil war and the 1917 Revolution on the delicate balance of these irrigated lands were disastrous and the Khiva Oasis was crippled. Irrigation

[*Fotokhronika Tass.*

FIG. 169.—Samarkand: harvesting cotton in the Zeravshan oasis. Uzbekistan accounts for 70% of the cotton output of the Soviet Union and an open cotton boll has become the symbol of the Republic.

works have been re-established under the Soviet administration and Khiva is once again a rich area producing cotton and lucerne, maize, onions, grapes and fruits.

Though ostensibly a tributary of the Amu-Darya the Zeravshan River dries out in the desert at Karakul (Black Lake) Oasis some 60 miles before it can reach the main stream (Fig. 168). Fed by a glacier in the Alay Mountains, it has been the source of water for scores of oases along its banks from very ancient times; in its valley there arose one of the earliest river civilisations in Central Asia. The Zeravshan now irrigates an almost unbroken belt 10–20 miles wide and 200 miles long from near the ancient city of Samarkand to just beyond Bukhara. Though devoted chiefly to irrigated cotton (Fig. 169) this area also produces wheat, rice, tobacco, grapes, fruit and vegetables. Like the Zeravshan, the Kashka-Darya peters out in the desert after having watered several oases which are given over to the cultivation of wheat, cotton, rice, tobacco and fruit.

The whole of the loess-covered piedmont zone between the Amu-Darya and the Kashka-Darya is celebrated for its fruit growing. The elaborate irrigation system was destroyed at the time of the Mongol invasions in the thirteenth century but has been completely restored and extended under the Soviet administration.

The Kara-Darya (Black River), rising in the Tyan-Shan, and the Naryn River, rising in the Alay Mountains, join to form the Syr-Darya in the basin of subsidence known as Fergana. There is no rain during the period May–September, but the Syr-Darya, tapped by the Great Fergana Canal, irrigates all but the sandy and salty central portion of the area. Hot summers with temperatures up to 95° F (35° C) and fertile soils are conducive to excellent crops of cotton which is grown in rotation with lucerne; about a quarter of the Soviet Union's cotton production comes from here. Wheat, barley, rice, fruits (especially apricots) and mulberry trees (to provide leaves for silkworms) are also cultivated and there are numerous vineyards.

The large Farkhad Dam at the western end of the Fergana Basin, besides generating hydro-electricity for local industries, provides additional irrigation water to the Pakhta Aral (Cotton Island) in the Golodnaya Steppe to the west. A long strip of irrigated land in the lower reaches of the Syr-Darya and centred on Kzyl-Orda is given over to rice growing. Tashkent, the most important cotton town in the U.S.S.R., is situated in the centre of a loess oasis, watered by the interlocking Chirchik and Keles tributaries of the Syr-Darya.

The Chu River—ostensibly a right bank tributary of the Syr-Darya, though it disappears in the sands before reaching the main stream—supports another important area of irrigation agriculture. The area centres on Frunze and is devoted to winter wheat, barley and sugar beet, the last recently introduced by Russian and Ukrainian settlers. Eastwards, along the alluvial fans which foot the Tyan-Shan, towards and around the city of Alma-Ata, there is much fruit (particularly apples) and vegetable growing under irrigation. Conditions there are too cold for cotton cultivation. Most of the irrigated land at Taldy Kurgan, south of the eastern end of Lake Balkash, is under wheat, barley and rice.

In addition to the specialised irrigation agriculture of Middle Asia there is also pastoralism. Although the natural vegetation of the desert and semi-desert is very limited, it is important for supporting migratory animal husbandry. The vegetation—ephemeral grasses, flowering herbs and some stunted trees (saxaul)—helps to fix the moving sands. Stock raising has been the traditional mainstay of agriculture in the drier lowlands with sheep, goats and camels predominating. Karakul sheep are admirably suited to desert conditions. The pelts of the new-born lambs have black curly wool and are especially valuable on the world market. In the mountain foreland areas transhumance is practised. Stock are taken to mountain pastures for summer grazing and brought down to the valley pastures for the winter. Increased attention is being directed to livestock breeding and to the use of forage and hay crops grown under irrigation in rotation with cotton and grain; consequently most nomadic herdsmen have now been resettled on permanent *sovkhozy*.

POWER AND MINERAL RESOURCES

Middle Asia is endowed with coal, petroleum, natural gas, ferrous and non-ferrous metals (Fig. 170). Karaganda coalfield in the north of the region is one of the main suppliers of coking coal to the metallurgical industries of the southern part of the Ural Region. Since the coals have a high ash content, and not all of the 30 coal seams of the field are of coking quality, Karaganda coal has to be mixed with the richer Kuznetsk coal before it can be used in blast furnaces. The coal continues to be hauled over 1000 miles from the Kuzbass to the Ural even though this is twice the distance the Karaganda coal has to travel. Coal is also worked at Eki-bastuz to the northeast of Karaganda. These coals, worked by opencast method, are more suitable for thermo-electricity generating stations (e.g. at Omsk and in the southern Ural) than for metallurgy. The minor coal reserves of the Fergana valley (Lenger, Angren, Kyzyl-Kiya) have considerable locational value.

Karaganda coal, in association with iron ore reserves from Atasuskiy 120–130 miles to the southwest, has provided the basis for a steelworks at the boom town of Temir-Tau. An iron- and steelworks at Solonichka, north of Karaganda, which started production in 1960, is said to produce some of the cheapest pig iron in the Soviet Union. Iron ore from the extensive reserves in the Turgay Tableland area of Oblast Kustanay is being sent in ever-increasing amounts to the southern Ural Region.

Oil occurs in the Emba fields (1·6 million tons in 1960) along the northern shore of the Caspian Sea, at Nebit-Dag (5 million tons in 1960), in the Cheleken Peninsula on the southeastern shores of the Caspian, and again in the Fergana Basin.

Outstandingly important are the natural gas deposits near Gazli in the Kyzyl-Kum, northwest of Bukhara, considered to be the largest single reserve of natural gas in the Soviet Union, and cheap to exploit (Fig. 170). Planned gas production in Uzbekistan for 1966 was 23·7 billion cu. m., of which 17·8 million cu. m. were to be piped to the Ural Region.

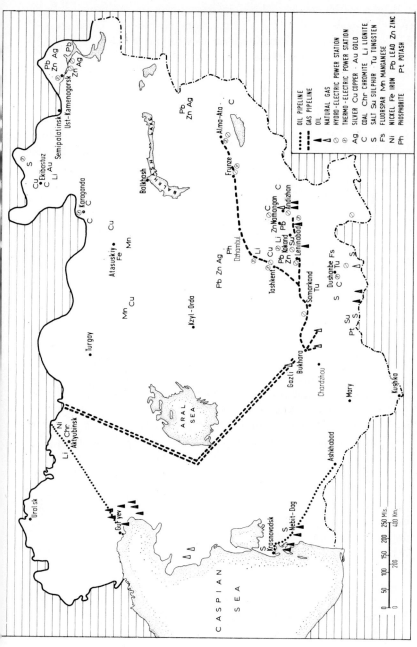

FIG. 170.—Middle Asia: mineral and power resources.

Besides the oil and natural gas, energy supplies are also provided by the rivers debouching from the Central Asian mountains. These are swift flowing and there are many suitable sites for the installation of hydro-electricity generating stations. In fact, Middle Asia is considered to have nearly a quarter of the potential hydro-electricity of the Soviet Union. Many of the installations are dual purpose in that the dams created for generating electricity also store irrigation water. This is the case at the Farkhad Dam on the Syr-Darya which supplies electricity to the Begovat steelworks, and two other stations on the Chirchik River near Tashkent which power local electro-chemical works. These are relatively small stations but that at Nurek on the Vakhsh (a tributary of the Amu-Darya) is reported to have a capacity of $2\frac{1}{2}$ million kw.

Kazakhstan is now the main Soviet supplier of copper and non-ferrous metals. The deposits of copper at Kounradskiy and Dzhezkazgan are claimed to be the second largest in the world. Lead, nickel, zinc, chromium and silver also are mined in the Kazakh Uplands. The saline waters of the natural evaporating pan of the east Caspian shore, Kara-Bogaz-Gol, provide the world's largest deposit of Glauber's salts, sodium sulphate, common salt and magnesium sulphite.

TRANSPORT AND COMMUNICATIONS

The exploitation of the natural wealth of Middle Asia has involved the laying of railway lines, and oil and gas pipelines, the digging of irrigation canals and the construction of hydro-electricity stations. The first railway, the Trans-Caspian line from Krasnovodsk on the Caspian to Tashkent via Ashkhabad, Mary, Bukhara and Samarkand, is mainly concerned with the transport of oil. The Kazalinsk line, leading directly northwest from Tash-kent across the desert to Orenburg and beyond, conveys raw cotton to the mills of Ivanovo and Moscow (Fig. 171). The Turk–Sib line provides a link around the eastern end of Lake Balkhash between the cities of Middle Asia and the Trans-Siberian Railway, and the Trans-Kazakhastan trunk line provides a direct route from the same cities northwards through the area of heavy industry around Karaganda to the new grain-growing areas of northern Kazakhstan and western Siberia (Fig. 171). The construction of these and other lines in the region has been accomplished in the face of very severe natural hazards, in particular drifting sands.

Communications of another kind are present at the Soviet "cosmo-drome" at Baykonur (near Karsakpay) in the desert of Middle Asia between Karaganda and the Aral Sea. The Baykonur site is used for the launching of sputniks and astronauts.

Mountainous areas such as the Tyan-Shan and the Pamir present serious difficulties for communications. Two motor roads have been built from

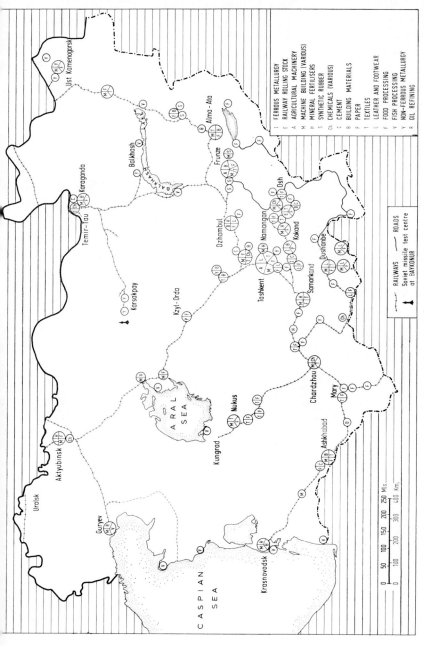

Fig. 171.—Middle Asia: railways and industrial structure of towns.

Osh in the Fergana Basin to Khorog on the frontier with Afghanistan. One follows the Afghan border (the 450-mile "Highway in the Clouds"), the other takes a more difficult and circuitous route and is probably the highest road in the world, reaching 15,000 ft.

The high-quality Emba oil is sent by pipeline to Orsk for refining and

FIG. 172.—Transporters carry huge pipes over the Kyzyl-Kum desert for the construction of the second pipeline to convey natural gas from the huge supplies at Gazli to industrial plant in the Ural.

subsequent use in the Ural Region and in Kazakhstan, or refined at Guryev on the Caspian coast and used in local petro-chemical plants. The Nebit-Dag oil is used in a refinery and petro-chemical plant at Krasnovodsk which also uses Baku oil transported across the Caspian. The oil in the Fergana Basin is refined at Fergana and used locally in industry and on the railways. The natural gas from Gazli is conveyed by pipeline through Tashkent to Alma-Ata, to the Fergana Basin, and also northwards across the desert to Chelyabinsk in the Ural Region (Fig. 172).

POPULATION AND CITIES

Practically 14 million people live in Soviet Middle Asia. The bulk are of Turkic stock, Muslim in religion (*see* Fig. 173) and Turko-Tatar in language, but there are also mixtures of indigenous and other groups, par-

[*Fotokhronika Tass.*

FIG. 173.—Bukhara: the Mausoleum of Ismail Samanid, founder of the Samanid dynasty. Bukhara is a veritable museum town which takes pride in its magnificent monuments dating from the ninth century.

ticularly Russians and Ukrainians. Settlement, generally in the form of large nucleated villages, occurs in oases, the better-watered areas, and along the railways; it is highly concentrated and localised. Population densities range from 100 to 200 persons per square mile in the oases, and in places (e.g. Fergana Basin) may even reach 2000 per square mile, in some of the richer lands, e.g. around Andizhan; the deserts are virtually uninhabited. Irrigation agriculture, the mining of mineral resources and the presence of diversified light industries account for most of the main centres of population and the rapid development of many urban areas.

Tashkent (1,106,000) is both capital of the Uzbek Republic and regional capital of Middle Asia. The old Moslem town, situated in the oasis of the

[*Fotokhronika Tass.*

FIG. 174.—Tashkent: a view of Frunze Square. Much of the old Moslem town was destroyed during an earthquake in 1966, but the town is being rapidly rebuilt on modern lines.

Chirchik tributary of the Amu-Darya, has been a centre of irrigation agriculture and the focus of caravan routes through the desert since its foundation in the seventh century A.D. The Soviet city is now the dominant settlement. It is a thriving industrial centre and rail focus in the heart of a rich and densely populated cotton-growing area. Cotton textiles, textile machinery and agricultural machinery are major industrial enterprises but there are, in addition, leather works, sawmills, food-processing plant and tobacco factories (Fig. 171). The natural gas piped from Gazli is a valuable new source of power for the city's industries.

The population of Tashkent—chiefly Uzbeks and Russians—increased by one-fifth between 1959 and 1964. There are now over a million people in the metropolitan area, and Tashkent ranks fifth in size in the Soviet Union (Fig. 174).

Alma-Ata (623,000), capital of the Kazakh Republic, differs from Tashkent in that it is an entirely Russian city and dates from the middle of the nineteenth century. It occupies an attractive site at an altitude of 2000 ft, within the foothills of the Chu-Ili Mountains. The surrounding countryside supports the fruit preserving, meat packing, leather making and wine and tobacco factories of the city, but engineering and wool textiles tend to dominate its industries (Fig. 171). Rail communications are via the Turk–Sib line which provides links with other Middle Asian cities and other parts of the Union. Russians tend to outnumber Kazakhs in the population of Alma-Ata, which rose by over a third between 1959 and 1964.

Karaganda (482,000) started in 1926 as a mining centre to supply coal to the metallurgical industries of the Ural. The functions persist and continue to expand, but with the building of giant steelworks in nearby *Temir-Tau* (142,000) and *Solonichka* and the opening of additional coal mines at *Saran* (54,000), Karanganda has become the centre of a sizeable mining-metallurgical complex with well over half a million people. In addition to its coal, iron and steel, the complex turns out constructional and mining machinery, chemicals, cement and foodstuffs. The lack of water associated with the semi-arid situation of the complex has been overcome by the construction of a canal from the Irtysh River, a distance of 300 miles.

Frunze (360,000), capital of the Kirgiz Republic, stands 2200 ft above sealevel in mountainous country near the Chu River which flows from Lake Issyk-Kul and peters out in the desert. Originally a fortress and known as Pishpek it became settled as the centre of a Russian colony in the latter part of the nineteenth century. Although it has been served by a branch of the Turk–Sib railway since 1924, which accelerated its economic development, the interests of the city remain primarily agricultural. It has one of the largest meat-processing plants of its kind in the U.S.S.R., and there are other food industries, textile and engineering (agricultural machinery, machine tools) factories. The mainly Russian population showed a remarkable increase of 64% between 1959 and 1964.

Dushanbe (316,000), capital of the Tadzhik Republic, occupies the site of an old Tadzhik village in the Gissar valley on the southern slopes of the Zeravshan Range. In 1926, when it was elevated to town status, its population was 6000. This has increased 50-fold during the last 40 years, due mainly to some thriving light industries, the presence of a large cotton textile works and the administrative functions of a capital city.

Samarkand (233,000), the ancient Maracanda, is the oldest city of Middle

Asia, dating possibly from the fourth or third millennium B.C. It lies in the fertile irrigated loess lands of the valley of the Zeravshan River, a cradle of civilisation in Middle Asia. Samarkand, in the fourteenth century A.D. was capital of the empire of Tamerlane (*Timur i Leng*, "the lame Timur") which extended over much of the Middle East. Ruins of many of its mosques (e.g. Bibi Khanum) and mausoleums remain, but several have been beautifully restored (e.g. Gur-Emir, Tamerlane's tomb). The Registan, or central square of Samarkand, has been described by Curzon as "the noblest public square in the world." But the modern Samarkand, established by the Russians in 1868 is an industrial city and has virtually engulfed the old town. Its broad tree-lined streets and Soviet-style buildings contrast markedly with the intricate labyrinth of narrow winding streets of the Moslem part. The industries include engineering (tractor parts, cinema equipment), chemicals, footwear, fruit canning, cotton processing and silk-weaving. Natural gas piped from the Gazli area, 180 miles to the west, provides a valuable new source of industrial power. The Trans-Caspian railway line links Samarkand with other parts of Middle Asia and the Russian world to the north, while the famous old Silk Road from China and India to Samarkand is now asphalted and bears heavy lorries instead of camels. The 19% increase in its Uzbek–Tadzhik–Russian population between 1959 and 1964 was the smallest growth of any of the Middle Asian cities during this period.

Ashkhabad (226,000), capital of the Turkmen Republic, is situated in the irrigated lands of the oasis of Akhal Teke, between the foothills of the Kopet-Dag and the Kara-Kum. It was founded as a fort and base for the construction of the Trans-Caspian railway between Krasnovodsk and Tashkent. A serious earth tremor in 1948 destroyed much of the town, but this has been rebuilt according to the original radial plan. It is a centre for glass, food, textiles, leather, printing, metalwork and carpets, and its importance in the film-making industry accounts for the local manufacture of cinema equipment. The Kara-Kum Canal (p. 269) provides additional water for the Ashkhabad Oasis, and a pipeline carries refined oil products from the Krasnovodsk refinery, 330 miles to the west. The city is isolated from the main concentrations of people in Middle Asia but its population, mainly Russian, has increased by 56,000 (33%) between 1959 and 1964.

Chimkent (200,000), on the Turk–Sib line 70 miles north of Tashkent, is known for its large lead smelting plant (largest in the U.S.S.R.), textiles, pharmaceuticals and food industries.

Andizhan (159,000) and *Namangan* (150,000), two of the largest towns of the Fergana Basin, process cotton and foods grown locally, although Andizhan also has engineering and chemical plant. Both towns are surrounded by areas with exceptionally high densities of population (as much as 2000 per square mile around Andizhan) and are linked with each other and with other parts of the Basin by the Fergana circular railway.

Ust-Kamenogorsk (202,000), on the Irtysh River in the extreme northeast of Kazakhstan, processes local deposits of lead, zinc, copper and silver. Power is obtained from two nearby hydro-electricity stations.

STUDY QUESTIONS

1. Suggest a division of the Middle Asia Region into geographical regions. Discuss the bearing of physical factors upon economic activities in any *two* of the regions recognised.

2. Locate the main desert areas in the U.S.S.R. and describe their utilisation by man.

3. Write a short description of the agricultural activities of the Middle Asia Region.

4. Examine the site, location and functions of the following towns: Tashkent; Alma-Ata; Ashkhabad; Dushanbe; Frunze.

5. Assess the importance of the Kara Kum Canal to agriculture in Turkmenistan.

6. Discuss the distribution of *either* cotton cultivation *or* irrigated lands in Soviet Middle Asia.

7. Examine, with particular reference to Middle Asia, the factors affecting the distribution of the textile industries of the U.S.S.R.

8. Compare the tundra and its traditional human life with the semi-arid lands of Middle Asia.

9. Critically examine the view that the economy of Soviet Middle Asia has the characteristics of a colonial country.

10. Make an assessment of the importance of the Karaganda mining and metallurgical complex to the economy of the U.S.S.R. and of the difficulties likely to be faced by further developments in this area.

11. What are your views on the feasibility and desirability of a canal link between the Irtysh River and Ekibastuz and Karaganda?

Chapter XXIII

SOUTHWEST SIBERIA REGION

 THE Southwest Siberia Region embraces the greater part of the new administrative area known as *tselinnyi kray* (the virgin land territories) formed from several oblasts in southern Siberia and northern Kazakhstan. It is the granary of the Asiatic part of the Soviet Union; animal husbandry (cattle and sheep) is also important.

Area	.	.	.	413,600* sq. miles
Population (1959)	.	.	9,202,000 (approx)

Administrative unit			Area sq. miles	Population in thousands 1959	Density persons per sq. mile	Percentage urban
Oblast Tyumen (part)	.	.	35,200*	906*	26*	—
Oblast Kurgan .	.	.	27,000	1,002	36	33
Oblast Omsk .	.	.	54,000	1,646	31	43
Oblast Novosibirsk (part) .	.	53,800*	1,100*	21*	—
Altay Kray	.	.	101,000	2,685	26	33
Oblast Tomsk (part) .	.	5,500*	390*	7*	—
Oblast Kustanay (part)	.	.	28,500*	260*	9*	—
Oblast Tselinograd (part) .	.	42,500*	390*	9*	—
Oblast Kokchetav	.	.	30,800	493	16	25
Oblast Pavlodar (part)	.	.	24,400	230	9	—
Oblast Karaganda (part)	.	.	6,200*	62*	10*	—
Oblast Semipalatinsk (part)	.	.	4,700*	38*	8*	—

* est.

Towns with over 150,000 inhabitants in 1964

				Population in thousands		Percentage increase
				1959	1964	1959–64
Omsk .	.	.	.	581	721	24·0
Barnaul	.	.	.	305	382	25·1
Tyumen	.	.	.	150	201	34·0
Kurgan	.	.	.	146	198	35·7
Semipalatinsk	.	.	156	192	23·0
Biysk .	.	.	.	146	175	20·0
Tselinograd .	.	.	102	159	56·0
Petropavlovsk	.	.	131	158	20·9

PHYSICAL ASPECTS

RELIEF AND DRAINAGE

The northern portion of the region is in an almost perfect plain in which the landscape stretches flat and unbroken to an endless horizon; there is an almost imperceptible gradient northwards. In its southern portion lie several short, low ranges which together form the Kazakh Uplands. These are fringed in the west by a lowland with isolated mesas known as the Turgay Tableland, and on the eastern boundary of the region by the Salair mountain ridge.

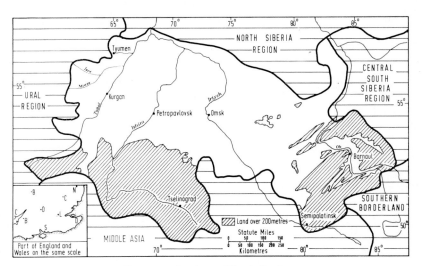

Fig. 175.—Southwest Siberia Region.

Drainage is northwards to the Arctic by means of such sluggish, branching and tortuous rivers as the Ob, Irtysh, Ishim and Tobol (Fig. 175). On the plain, the interfluves seldom rise more than 30 ft above the surrounding countryside. Widespread flooding in the middle and lower reaches of the rivers is an annual event after the spring thaw which is earlier in the upper reaches. Waterlogging of the soils is common and there are extensive areas of bog, marsh and shallow lake. The Vasyuganye Swamp between the Ob and Irtysh Rivers covers a vast area.

CLIMATE, NATURAL VEGETATION AND SOILS

Southwest Siberia has a markedly continental climate (Fig. 176). Winter is severe and lasts four to six months. It is dominated by the Siberian high pressure system; January mean temperatures range from 3° F (−16° C) in the south to −28° F (−33° C) in the north. Absolute minima of −58° F (−50° C) have been recorded. Snowfall, equivalent to 2–4 in. of rainfall, is slight, but the snow cover is of variable depth because of drifts caused by violent blizzards. It establishes itself in November and disappears usually during the last fortnight of April with the sudden arrival of spring. During the winter the ground freezes to a depth of 2–3 ft (80–100 cm).

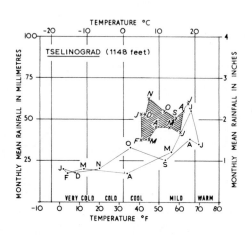

FIG. 176.—Hythergraph for Tselinograd.

Summer temperatures rise to the high sixties and may exceed 70° F (21° C) in the south. Maximum precipitation comes in spring and early summer, originating largely from evaporation of waterlogged land surfaces rather than from maritime air masses. Aggregates at this time are between 8 and 10 in. (200 and 250 mm) and there is a strong tendency for drought to occur. The scorching *sukhovey*, blowing out of the deserts of Central Asia in late spring and summer, causes the air temperature to rise to 95°–100° F (35°–38° C) and the relative humidity to drop to less than 30%. Its desiccating effect on plants injures crops and vegetation.

Pine, fir and birch forests of the southern tayga, interspersed with peat bogs and marshes, cover the north of the region. Soils are typically of the grey forest type. Southwards there is a gradation to forest steppe and brown earths which, in turn, give way in the extreme south to the steppe with chernozem and chestnut soils, and to occasional salt marshes and saline soils (*solonets*).

THE ECONOMY

AGRICULTURE

Climatic and soil conditions favour a highly developed and diversified agriculture—the most important economic factor in this part of Siberia. The area between Tyumen and Omsk has been a major dairying area since the nineteenth century and produces a surplus of butter and cheese. In 1954 the Soviets started to develop the agricultural potential of the southern

[*Fotokhronika Tass.*

FIG. 177.—Ploughing virgin soils near Tselinograd. In 1954 the Soviets started to develop the agricultural potential of Southwest Siberia. Vast acres of wild steppe were ploughed up and by 1960 over 114 million acres had been sown to grains.

part of the region under the "Virgin and Idle Lands Project," under which vast acres of wild steppe, overgrown with feather-grass and couch-grass (the virgin and fallow lands) were ploughed up (Fig. 177). By 1960 over 114 million acres, or an area almost 25% larger than that of the United Kingdom, had been sown to grains.

The Southwest Siberia Region, dominated by extensive grain farming, contains about 19% of the arable land of the Soviet Union and 37% of its wheatlands. It produces about 30% of the Union's grain and over 43% of its wheat. The grain *sovkhozy* or state farms cover several tens of thousands of acres and are fully mechanised. Spring wheat is the main crop, although oats, rye, millet, maize, rape, sunflower, linseed, sugar beet and hemp are also grown (Fig. 178).

Constant efforts are needed to avoid soil erosion and dust bowl conditions, to reduce evaporation rates, and to conserve the low moisture content of the soil. Some of the techniques adopted are the avoidance of deep ploughing, retention of stubble after harvest to retain the snow cover, and planting shelter belts to protect the exposed surfaces from *sukhovey*. Rain-

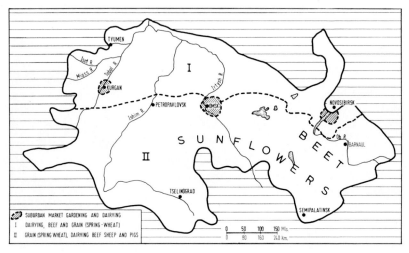

FIG. 178.—Southwest Siberia Region: agricultural land-use regions.

fall, limited in amount and irregular in occurrence and incidence, is frequently far less than the crops really need for optimum growth, and droughts are common. Despite the likelihood of only two good harvests in every five, the Soviet authorities consider the Virgin Lands enterprise to be justified, first, because it provides additional grain to help satisfy the rapidly growing food requirements of the Soviet population; secondly, it helps alleviate food shortages following harvest fluctuations elsewhere in the country; and thirdly, it enables such regions as the Ukraine and the North Caucasus to switch over to maize and other fodder crops in what is considered to be an even more urgent drive to increase meat and milk production in the country. The eventual achievements of the enterprise as yet remain to be seen.

RESOURCES AND INDUSTRY

The rich iron, gold and asbestos deposits of northwest Kazakhstan (in Oblast Kustanay) can be considered part of the Ural Region (p. 233).

Apart from these, southwest Siberia is poorly endowed with mineral resources, but some deposits of lignite (Ubagansk Basin), salt and gold do occur. Heavy industry is represented by a number of machine-building plants, catering for agricultural needs. The most common industrial enterprises are flour mills, dairies, tanneries, meat-packing factories, oil-pressing plants and canneries. Textiles are made in Omsk, Barnaul and

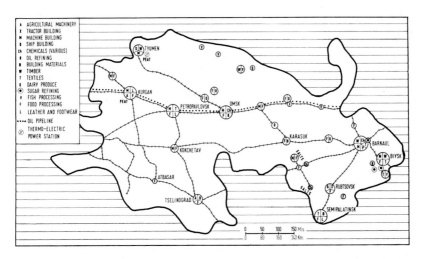

FIG. 179.—Southwest Siberia Region: railways and industrial structure of towns.

Biysk (Fig. 179). Three pipelines from the Volga–Ural oilfield converge on a large oil refinery at Omsk which satisfies the needs of the region's expanding agriculture and at the same time provides the base for an important chemical industry in the city.

TRANSPORT AND COMMUNICATIONS

Considerable progress has been made with the laying of railways in the Southwest Siberia Region. The Trans-Siberian Railway (now electrified from Moscow to Irkutsk) with an offshoot from Omsk to Sverdlovsk via Tyumen and from Kurgan to Sverdlovsk, is well used, and the section between Omsk and Novosibirsk has the highest freight flow intensity in the whole of the Soviet Union. After World War II the South-Siberian trunk line was completed. Crossing the region in the same east–west direction, but 200 miles south of the Trans-Siberian line, it connects the Kuzbass with Magnitogorsk via Barnaul, Pavlodar and Tselinograd. This line provides a valuable direct route for the transport of coking coal between the Kuzbass and the southern Ural, and is also important for the carriage of local freight. Another railway, the Middle-Siberian, has been built between Magnitogorsk and Barnaul via Kartaly, Tobol, Kustanay, Kokchetav and Karasuk. The Karaganda coalfield is linked to the Trans-Siberian line at Petropavlovsk by a branch through Tselinograd and Kokchetav. Further lines connect the Trans-, Middle- and South-Siberian lines and many feeders have been built for the transport of grain and other agricultural products from the state farms (Fig. 179). As already noted the region is crossed by oil pipelines linking the "Second Baku" with Omsk and eastwards to Novosibirsk and Irkutsk. Of goods in transit, coal, grains and timber are the most important commodities moving westwards, and oil is probably the chief east-bound item, both by rail and pipeline.

POPULATION AND CITIES

The region is almost two and a half times the size of the United Kingdom, but its predominantly rural population numbers only 9–10 million. The number of villages that have administrative functions and the low densities of population (everywhere less than 40 per square mile) reflect the rural character of the region. The indigenous scattered population of nomads has long been swamped by the influx of hundreds of thousands of Russians, Ukrainians and Belorussians and the present-day population is largely an amalgam of Slavs.

Omsk (721,000), located at the intersection of the Trans-Siberian Railway and the Irtysh River, is the largest city of the region. It grew in the first place chiefly after the Trans-Siberian line reached it in 1895, but its rapid growth in recent years (its population increased two and a half times between 1939 and 1964) is a reflection of its fast-developing hinterland. The city functions as a commercial and industrial focus and has agriculture-orientated industries, flour milling, meat packing and the making of farm machinery. Other enterprises include textiles, oil refining, petro-chemicals and railway equipment.

Barnaul (382,000) is an important railway focus. Five lines, the Turk–Sib via Semipalatinsk, the South-Siberian via Tselinograd, and the Middle-Siberian via Kokchetav, a link with the Trans-Siberian at Novosibirsk and with the Kuzbass, all meet at this point. The city, sited on the left bank of the River Ob within the rich Kulunda Steppe, is the administrative centre of the Altay Kray. Its industries comprise spinning mills and clothing factories (based on supplies of raw cotton brought along the Turk–Sib Railway from Central Asia), wood-using industries, artificial fibres, engineering (combine harvesters) and food processing (grain milling). Its population increased by 25% between 1959 and 1964.

Tyumen (201,000), on the Tura near the western head of navigation of the Ob–Irtysh system, was the first permanent Russian settlement in Siberia. It was at the eastern end of the Siberian Highway in the eighteenth century and became the terminus of the nineteenth-century Trans-Ural (Perm–Tyumen) Railway. The town has long functioned as the gateway to Siberia. It is a shipbuilding centre and a river–rail transfer point (mainly for timber and wheat). It also has wood-using industries, engineering plants and textile manufacture. Its population increased by more than one-third between 1959 and 1964.

Kurgan (198,000), like Tyumen, is a river port and an industrialised market town. It lies at the intersection of the Trans-Siberian Railway and the Tobol River, where a branch line leads to Sverdlovsk. Precision instruments and agricultural machinery are made here and there are also other agriculture-based industries. The population increased by 35% between 1959 and 1964.

Semipalatinsk (192,000) was founded in 1718 as one of a chain of forts built to secure the Russian occupation during the advance against the nomads of Central Asia. The Turk–Sib Railway now crosses the Irtysh river at this point which has become a food-processing (meat packing) and textile centre.

Biysk (175,000), terminus of the Chuya road from Mongolia, was another eighteenth-century outpost in the Altay Steppe. It processes grains, meat, wool, flax and other farm products, manufactures farm machinery and has a match combine.

Other towns are *Petropavlovsk* (158,000) where the Trans-Siberian Railway crosses the Ishim River, and *Tselinograd* (formerly Akmolinsk). Tselinograd, centre of the "Virgin Lands," has experienced a phenomenal rise in population. This was 32,000 in 1939, 102,000 in 1959 and 159,000 in 1964. It manufactures agricultural and transport equipment and processes grain.

STUDY QUESTIONS

1. Suggest a division of the Southwest Siberia Region into geographical regions. Discuss the bearing of physical factors upon economic activities in any *two* of the regions recognised.

2. Examine the economic activities of the steppes of the Asiatic part of the U.S.S.R.

3. Compare and contrast the salient features of the present geography of the Central Chernozem Region and the Southwest Siberia Region.

4. Discuss, with particular reference to the Southwest Siberia Region, the problem of soil erosion in the Soviet Union and the steps which are being taken to reduce it.

5. Discuss the climatic limitations to crop production in the U.S.S.R. with special reference to the virgin lands of Kazakhstan.

6. Examine the site location and functions of the following towns: Omsk; Barnaul; Tyumen; Kurgan; Semipalatinsk.

Chapter XXIV

CENTRAL SOUTH SIBERIA REGION

 THE Central South Siberia Region, which includes the important economic area known as the Kuzbass, comprises the eastern part of Oblast Novosibirsk, the southern part of Oblast Tomsk, the whole of Oblast Kemerovo, the southern part of Krasnoyarskiy Kray, most of the Autonomous Oblast Khakass and the southwestern part of Oblast Irkutsk. The eastern part of Oblast Novosibirsk is included because of its close functional connections with the Kuzbass (Fig. 180).

Area . . . . 254,700* sq. miles
Population (1959) . . 9,000,000 (approx.)

Administrative unit	Area sq. miles	Population in thousands 1959	Density persons per sq. mile	Percentage urban
Oblast Novosibirsk (part) . .	5,400*	1,199*	22*	—
Oblast Tomsk (part) . .	22,700*	330*	15*	—
Oblast Kemerovo . . .	37,000	2,786	76	77
Krasnoyarskiy Kray (part) . .	84,800*	2,500*	30*	—
Oblast Irkutsk (part) . . .	104,800*	1,900*	18*	—

* est.

Towns with over 150,000 inhabitants in 1964

	Population in thousands		Percentage increase
	1959	1964	1959–64
Novosibirsk . . .	886	1,029	16·0
Novokuznetsk . .	377	475	26·0
Krasnoyarsk . . .	412	541	31·0
Irkutsk. . . .	366	401	9·6
Kemerovo . . .	278	351	26·0
Tomsk. . . .	249	302	21·0
Prokopyevsk. . .	282	291	3·0
Angarsk . . .	134	176	31·0

293

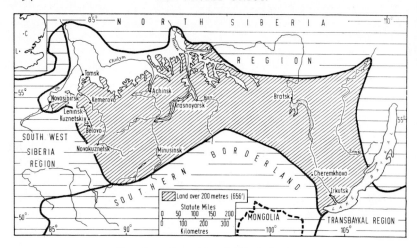

FIG. 180.—Central South Siberia Region.

PHYSICAL ASPECTS

RELIEF AND DRAINAGE

The greater part of this region comprises a complex of mountains which skirts the West Siberian Plain and the Central Siberian Plateau, separating them from the tablelands of Central (High) Asia. The mountains include the Altay, the Salair Ridge, Kuznetskiy Ala-Tau, and the Western and Eastern Sayan Ranges. The Altay Mountains in the southwest are neither as high nor as rugged as the Tyan-Shan and the Pamir, and their contemporary relief is that of an eroded plateau. Even so, they culminate at heights in excess of 14,000 ft on the Kazakh–Siberian border where they are known as the *rudny* (mining) Altay. The Salair Range and Kuznetskiy Ala-Tau, which probably represent northern continuations of the Altay, enclose the Kuznetskiy Basin (Kuzbass). Kuznetskiy Ala-Tau separates the Kuznetskiy Basin in the west from the Minusinsk Basin and the Yenisey River in the east.

The Western and Eastern Sayan Mountains lie to the east of the Altay and Kuznetskiy Ala-Tau, along the southern borders of Siberia, and enclose the Minusinsk Basin on the south and northeast respectively. Though described as of Tertiary origin it would seem that the ranges were first formed at a much earlier date. After a period of erosion which had almost reduced many of them to peneplains they were again uplifted by Tertiary earth movements. Thus the Western Sayans still show flat, eroded surfaces, even on their summit levels. The Eastern Sayans, orientated northwest–southeast between the Yenisey and Angara Rivers, reach their highest elevation at about 11,500 ft and then continue eastwards at somewhat lower altitudes to Lake Baykal.

The giant Ob–Yenisey River systems drain practically the whole of the region. The Salair Ridge in the west forms a low drainage divide between the Ob Valley and its tributary the Tom, which flows the full length of the Kuznetskiy Basin. The Yenisey drains the Minusinsk Basin and flows to within eight miles of the Chulym tributary of the Ob before flowing east and then north through Krasnoyarsk to the Arctic. In the east the Angara, also known as the Upper Tunguska, takes the overflow of Lake Baykal. This river is said to be best suited to the development of hydro-electricity. The Lena, rising near the western shore of Lake Baykal drains the extreme east of the region. Ust-Kut, the head of navigation on the Lena, has a very important rail link with the Trans-Siberian trunk line at Tayshet. This line passes through the power house of Bratsk and also through a region rich with iron ore.

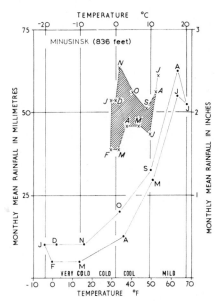

FIG. 181.—Hythergraph for Minusinsk.

CLIMATE, NATURAL VEGETATION AND SOILS

The continental climate of the region is characterised by moderately warm summers (64°–68° F; 18°–20° C) and extremely cold winters (0° to −4° F; −18° to −20° C). Annual precipitation varies appreciably. In the Novosibirsk–Kuzbass area it is about 16 in. (406 mm) and inadequate for agriculture; farther eastwards it is 16–24 in. (406–610 mm) and is barely adequate for agriculture (Fig. 181). The winter snow cover is slight and generally less than 1·5 ft deep. Calm, clear sky conditions during the winter and a comparatively thin snow cover contribute to the maintenance of permafrost which occurs as patches or islands of frozen ground throughout most of the eastern half of the region.

"As soon as the rivers freeze, the air becomes remarkably clear and transparent. The frequent calm, clear sky and bright sun are conditions well suited to the cold wintry weather. Those who are accustomed to such a winter and to the even colder one in Trans-Baykal find the winter of the European part of the country, in spite of its greater warmth, trying in consequence of the dampness, since the wind, the leaden sky and the absence of the sun sometimes continue for weeks on end." ★

There are a number of peculiarities associated with Lake Baykal—smaller daily ranges of temperature compared with the surrounding land (especially in summer), later spring, considerable summer cloudiness, and a quite intense development of local winds such as the *gorny* (or *sarma*), a northwest wind which blows from the mainland during mid-August to November. Baykal steamers have often been wrecked by the *sarma*. The lake does not freeze over until January. In spring and summer the vegetation at some distance from the lake shore is more advanced in development than the vegetation directly adjoining Baykal. It is significant that the Angara outlet from Baykal never freezes.

The middle Angara and upper Lena area in the northeast are characterised by tayga where larch and pine are the predominant species. The soil is podzol. Tayga also occurs as an altitudinal zone in the better-watered mountains of the south. Enclosed depressions are drier, and the typical vegetation is steppe or wooded steppe; enclaves of wooded steppe occur along the route of the Trans-Siberian Railway west of Lake Baykal. The soil in these depressions and enclaves is good and deep, fertile chernozém is to be found in Oblast Kemerovo, in the Minusinsk Depression and in certain parts of Oblast Irkutsk.

THE ECONOMY

AGRICULTURE

Accumulated temperatures during the summer, when the daily mean temperature remains about 50° F (10° C), amount to (1600°–2200° C), and between 6 and 16 in. of rainfall may occur. Such climatic conditions are suitable for the cultivation of wheat, rye, oats, barley, potatoes and other

★ A. I. Voeikov, edited by Academician A. A. Grigor'ev. "Selected works, Vols. I–III," *Izd. Akad. Nauk. S.S.S.R.*, 1948.

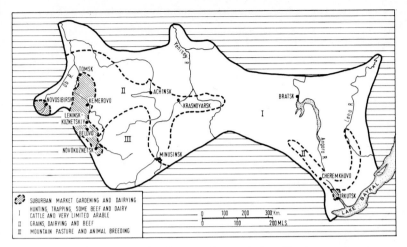

FIG. 182.—Central South Siberia Region: agricultural land-use regions.

vegetables. However, livestock farming is of greater importance. Dairy farming and "town-orientated agriculture" (fresh vegetables and pig breeding) also find adequate markets among the fast-growing urban populations (Fig. 182).

FUEL, POWER AND MINERAL RESOURCES

Agriculture could be further developed here, but at present the region is predominantly industrial. There are huge natural resources: mineral deposits, immense potential hydro-electric power and almost untouched stocks of timber. Although the existence of these riches was known in the nineteenth century they have been tapped only since industrialisation of the Soviet Union began with the first Five-Year Plan (1928–32). The resources include the Kuznetsk coal basin (Kuzbass), the Cheremkhovo coalfields (Irkutsk Basin) and the big lignite deposits of the Kansk–Achinsk Basin (Figs. 67 and 68). The Kuzbass coalfield is the second largest producer in the U.S.S.R. and is thought to have the largest reserves in the Asiatic part of the U.S.S.R. The coals include a large proportion which are of excellent coking quality. Their low sulphur and ash content and high calorific value make them eminently suitable for use in blast furnaces. The coal seams are exceptionally thick (occasionally as much as 100 ft) and lie near the surface. They thus afford excellent opportunities for mechanised working by opencast and strip methods. Production costs are half those of the Donbass. Annual output is now around 35 million tons. The metallurgical industries of the Ural Region rely heavily on Kuzbass coal (the Ural–Kuznetskiy Combine) and vast amounts of coal are transported along the

Trans-, Middle- and South-Siberian Railways. Local iron and steel plant also rely on Kuzbass coke, although more and more is being used for thermo-electric generating stations.

The massive coal deposits of the Cheremkhovo field on the Angara are not of coking quality but find increasingly important outlets in thermal power stations, on the railways and in chemical plants. Coal seams, which are as much as 25 ft thick and disposed horizontally, are worked by both opencast and deep mine methods. The Kansk–Achinsk Basin is thought to

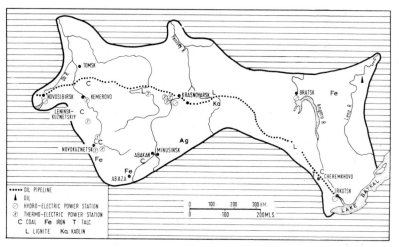

FIG. 183.—Central South Siberia Region: mineral and power resources.

contain about 40% of the lignite reserves in the Soviet Union. The lignite is readily accessible in a wide band running alongside the Trans-Siberian Railway for over 400 miles. The lignite is too brittle for long-distance transportation and is used locally for thermal power stations. The good-quality coals of the Minusinsk Basin are used for the same purpose.

The hydro-electric potential of the region is the greatest in the Soviet Union. The first rivers to be harnessed for this purpose were the Yenisey and its tributaries. The Angara tributary, fed by Lake Baykal, has a regular flow throughout the year and one station upon it, near the town of Irkutsk, with a capacity of just over ½ million kw has been in operation for several years. A somewhat similar generating station is sited on the Ob just up-stream of Novosibirsk. However, neither of these compares with the huge Bratsk station (capacity 4½ million kw) on the Angara, 350 miles down-stream from Irkutsk, or the Krasnoyarsk station (6 million kw) on the Yenisey. These two power stations have the largest capacities in the world. Plans are reported for three or four more hydro-electric stations on the same large scale, on the Angara and Yenisey Rivers. Such stations involve high capital expenditure in areas remote from the main centres of population and major technical problems related to the transmission of electricity over long distances. Now that petroleum from the Ural–Volga fields is being piped as far as Irkutsk, and natural gas has been reported in the Lena Lowland, major schemes of this kind may not be implemented.

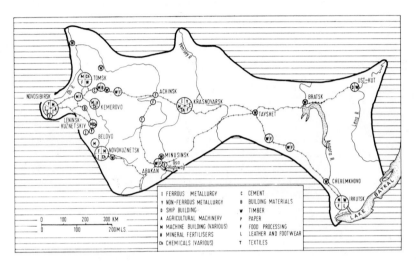

FIG. 184.—Central South Siberia Region: railways and industrial structure of towns.

INDUSTRY

Industrialisation of the region began with the construction of the first big metallurgical plant at Novokuznetsk (formerly Stalinsk) in 1929, which processed ores from the Ural and was the eastern limb of the Ural–Kuznetskiy Combine. It now works on ores from the nearby deposits of Gornaya Shoriya and from deposits at Abakan in the Autonomous Republic of Khakass. The Abakan deposits are in the Minusinsk Basin, 200 miles to the east and are linked with Novokuznetsk by the South-Siberian Railway. The same ores are sent to another steel plant at Guryevsk and to Novosibirsk. A further metallurgical plant is to be built at Tayshet to handle ores from the very large reserves of good iron ore in the region of the Ilim Valley, some 80 miles east of Bratsk. It is planned to make the Central South Siberian Region the Third Metallurgical Base of the Soviet Union after the Ukraine and the Ural Regions (Fig. 184).

No less significant is the development of non-ferrous metallurgy. The first enterprises in this field were the zinc smelter at Belovo using zinc found in the Salair Ridge, and the aluminium plant at Novokuznetsk utilising bauxite found near Angarsk and Yuzhno-Yeniseyskiy. Another aluminium plant is situated in Shelekhov, near Irkutsk, which may later be the site of other non-ferrous metallurgical enterprises. Chemical enterprises based on salt reserves near Irkutsk are for the most part concentrated in Kemerovo and Usolye-Sibirskoye and Angarsk. Other important minerals worked throughout the region are manganese, gold, graphite, mica and magnesite.

[*Fotokhronika Tass.*

Fig. 185.—Freight train on the Abakan–Tayshet Railway. This 700-mile section completes the South-Siberian rail link between Magnitogorsk in the Ural and Tayshet on the Trans-Siberian Railway.

TRANSPORT AND COMMUNICATIONS

Railways integrate the whole industrial complex of the Kuzbass and provide links with the Trans-Siberian Railway at Novosibirsk and Yurga, and with the Turk–Sib Railway at Barnaul. Another east–west connection is afforded by the South-Siberian Railway, which provides a link between the southern Ural and the Yenisey via Barnaul and Novokuznetsk. This railway has now been extended via Abakan to Tayshet (Fig. 185) on the Trans-Siberian line and provides an outlet to the east for the important minerals and the timber of the Khakass Autonomous Republic (Fig. 184).

The main traffic on the railways westwards and southwestwards is coal, wheat and timber destined for the Ural, European Russia and Central Asia. Coal and petroleum for Trans-Baykalia and beyond are the main commodities moving eastwards. The Ob, Tom and Yenisey Rivers provide a valuable means of transporting timber and other bulky goods, and Krasnoyarsk, Tomsk and Novosibirsk are important river–rail transport points. An arterial road follows the route of the Trans-Siberian Railway and there are some roads linking the railways with the north (Yartsevo, Boguchany, Dvorets) and the south (A.O. Tuva).

POPULATION AND CITIES

Although a Slavic amalgam forms the vast majority of the population of South Central Siberia, the non-Russian Khakass group was evidently large enough in numbers to be given territorial recognition through the formation of the A.O. Khakass. This native group of nomadic herdsmen and hunters is being increasingly integrated into the Soviet economy. The region as a whole provides a home for about 11 million people, three-quarters of whom live west of the Yenisey. Densities exceed 125 persons per square mile in the Kuzbass and may reach 65 per square mile in the continuously settled zone along the Trans-Siberian Railway, but elsewhere they are generally less than 25 per square mile. Changes in the rural component of the population have been slight, but the urban component has more than doubled since 1939; there are now eleven cities in the region with over 100,000 people. Increases in the urban population are similar to those which have already been noted for the Southwest Siberia Region.

Novosibirsk (1,029,000) has increased its population more than two and a half times within the last quarter of a century and is now the eighth largest city in the U.S.S.R. It is the regional capital of South Central Siberia and is fast becoming the metropolis of all Siberia. Located at the intersection of the River Ob and the Trans-Siberian trunk line (Fig. 186), Novosibirsk is a natural focus of routes and a leading transportation centre. Though not actually within the Kuzbass, its diversified industries are very important. They include steel-rolling mills (based on steel imported from both the Kuzbass and Ural), tractors and other farm machinery, motor vehicles, ships, chemicals, flour milling and other food industries, oil refining, textiles and clothes, soap, footwear and furniture.

Novosibirsk is also an important scientific centre with a scientific satellite town at *Akademgorodsk* (50,000) 15 miles away. Akademgorodsk (Fig. 187) is the focal point of a sociological experiment in that it has been designed to induce top rank scientists to leave Moscow and other cities in the western part of the Soviet Union and to work in Siberia. The town contains eleven major scientific institutes, a university, an "experiment factory," generous accommodation and a wide range of social services for the whole community. It is also the site of one of the few new and highly

L

[*Fotokhonika Tass.*

FIG. 186.—Novosibirsk. The Ob River is over three-quarters of a mile wide at
this point and the bridge one and a half miles long.

experimental boarding-schools for exceptionally gifted, scientifically
inclined children from the whole of the Asiatic part of the U.S.S.R.★

Novokuznetsk (475,000) is the centre of the Kuzbass and the site of well-
developed heavy industry. Its integrated steelworks, one of the largest in
the Soviet Union, uses local coal and iron ore from Temir-Tau, Tashtagol
and Shalym mines in the Gornaya Shoriya area, 80 miles to the south.
There are also aluminium works, locomotive works and heavy engineering
and chemical industries.

Other cities within the Kuznetskiy Basin are *Kemerovo* (351,000),
Prokopyevsk (291,000), *Leninsk-Kuznetskiy* (141,000), *Kiselevsk* (140,000),
Anzhero-Sudzhensk (119,000) and *Belovo* (114,000). These are all primarily
concerned with coal mining and associated chemical industries but also have
a variety of metal working and food industries.

Krasnoyarsk (541,000), situated at the point where the Trans-Siberian
Railway crosses the Yenisey River is regional centre for Krasnoyarskiy
Kray. It is a fast-growing city with considerable industrial potential.
Thermal electricity based on local coal and hydro-electricity from a nearby
barrage on the Yenisey is in generous supply and power-orientated in-

★ J. Watson, in *The Times*, January 17, 1966.

[Fotokhronika Tass.

FIG. 187.—Akademgorodsk. This townlet, 15 miles from Novosibirsk, is a scientific centre. It is designed to induce top-rank scientists to leave Moscow and other cities in the European part of the Soviet Union to work in Siberia.

dustries such as aluminium smelting (using nepheline from Achinsk, 90 miles to the west) are being attracted to this site. In addition there are wood-based industries, including synthetic rubber production (ethyl alcohol derived from wood cellulose), agricultural and mining machinery, railway repair works, machine tool industries, oil refining, petro-chemicals and food industries.

Of Krasnoyarsk, Chekhov wrote (taken from his letters):

". . . Siberia is a cold and long country. I am travelling and travelling and there is no end in sight. . . . I fought the overflowing rivers, the cold, impassable mud, and hunger. . . . On the whole I am pleased with my journey and am not sorry I went. . . . The mountains near Krasnoyarsk surround the town like high walls. . . . Yenisey is a wide, fast, curving river; a beauty, better than the Volga. . . . On Yenisey life began with a groan, and will end in splendour such as we never dreamed of. So at least I thought, standing on the banks of the wide Yenisey, and looking eagerly into its waters, which with frightening speed and force were rushing into the severe Arctic Ocean. . . . On this bank is Krasnoyarsk—the best and most beautiful of all the Siberian towns, and on the other—mountains, reminding me of the Caucasus, just as misty and dreamy. I stood and thought: what full, clever and fine life will light up these shores in the future."

Irkutsk (401,000), one-time fortress, trading and administrative centre of Siberia, is now developing as the centre of a rapidly growing industrial region. It is located at the confluence of the Irkut and Angara Rivers, about 30 miles from Lake Baykal; the Trans-Siberian Railway passes near by. Ample power is provided by the Cheremkhovo coalfields and hydro-electricity comes from a nearby station on the Angara River. Thus, as with Krasnoyarsk, 650 miles to the west, power-hungry industries are attracted to the site. At present chemicals (using local salt deposits and the by-products of oil refining), aluminium smelting, timber and wood-working industries, food products, general machinery (especially gold-, coal- and iron-mining machinery) and motor vehicles are the main industrial enter-prises but others are expected to be located here in the future.

It is reported that a satellite town, similar to Akademgorodsk is to be built at Irkutsk. It will house ten major research institutes, specialising mainly in organic chemistry, geology and power engineering. Six insti-tutes and houses for 36,000 scientists and their families are expected to have been completed by 1970.

Shelekhov (aluminium), *Angarsk* (chemicals) and *Cheremkhovo* (coal) are but three of the many industrial centres which have sprung up along the line of the Trans-Siberian Railway in recent years. A rapidly expanding in-dustrial area is developing to the northwest of Irkutsk which, it is suggested, may one day rival the Kuzbass. Electro-metallurgy, electro-chemistry, plastics, synthetic dyes, drugs and fibres are some of the main branches of industry planned for the area.

Tomsk (302,000), once the only Siberian city with seats of higher learning, is now an important centre of woodworking, engineering, food processing and other industries. It lies on the high right bank of the Tom tributary of the River Ob at the southern edge of the tayga and is served by a branch line from the Trans-Siberian Railway.

STUDY QUESTIONS

1. Suggest a division of the Central South Siberia Region into geographical regions. Discuss the bearing of physical factors upon economic activities in any *two* of the regions recognised.

2. Analyse the industrial development of the Kuznetsk coalfield.

3. Make a reasoned assessment of economic developments likely to take place at: (*a*) Krasnoyarsk; (*b*) Bratsk; (*c*) Irkutsk-Cheremkhovo.

4. Locate three large multi-purpose dams in the U.S.S.R. and estimate the benefits their construction is conferring upon the people of the areas in which they are located.

5. Map the developments that have taken place in the rail communications of South Central Siberia and comment upon the commodities carried.

6. Examine the site, location and functions of the following towns: Novosibirsk; Barnaul; Novo-Kuznetsk; Krasnoyarsk; Irkutsk.

7. Compare the achievements and prospects of coal with those of hydro-electric power production in Central South Siberia.

8. "The life-line of the Asiatic part of the Soviet Union." To what extent is this a fair description of the Trans-Siberian Railway?

9. Describe and offer explanations for the distribution of population in Central South Siberia.

10. "The granary of Siberia." Justify this description of the Minusinsk Basin.

Chapter XXV

SOUTHERN BORDERLAND

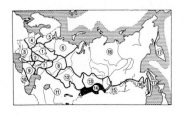 THIS region of high mountains, plateaux and intermontane basins lies between the Central South Siberian Region and the boundaries with China and Mongolia. It reaches the western end of Lake Baykal on its eastern border and includes the headwaters of the Irtysh River in the west (Fig. 188). Pastoralism and mining are the chief activities of its very sparse population.

Area . . . . 174,500* sq. miles

Population (1959) . . 400,000 (approx)

Administrative unit	Area sq. miles	Population in thousands 1959	Density persons per sq. mile	Percentage urban
Tuva A.O.	66,500	172	3	29
Kazakh S.S.R. (part) . . .	8,200*	10*	1*	—
Oblast Irkutsk (part) . . .	25,900*	5*	>1*	—
Buryatskaya A.S.S.R. (part) .	16,100*	20*	1*	—
A.O. Gorno-Altaysk . .	35,700	159	4	19
Krasnoyarskiy Kray (part) . .	22,100*	96*	17*	—

* est.

Main town: Kyzyl, population 34,000 in 1959

PHYSICAL ASPECTS

RELIEF AND DRAINAGE

The chief ranges in this mountainous region are the deeply dissected Altay and Sayan. The snow-clad and glacier-harbouring summits of the Altay are usually severely denuded, flat-topped and swampy. Altitudes range from 7500 to 10,000 ft, though occasional summits rise to over 14,000 ft. Scattered within the mountains are open grassland areas occupying flat-bottomed and broad mountain valleys. These are known locally as "steppe" and of these the Chuya, Kurai and Abai Steppes are the largest.

306

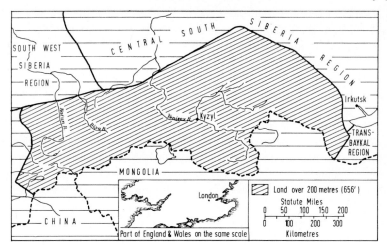

FIG. 188.—Southern Borderland.

The east–west orientated Western Sayan extending eastwards from the Altay system separates the Minusinsk Basin to the north from the A.O. Tuva to the south, a highland area, 1500–2000 ft above sea-level and enclosed by mountains rising to over 8000 ft. The longer Eastern Sayan Mountain chain aligned northwest–southeast between the Yenisey and Angara Rivers reaches heights in excess of 11,000 ft with rugged slopes and sharp peaks. While the loss of height towards the Central Siberian Plateau is gentle, towards Mongolia it is abrupt. The character of the mountains changes towards Lake Baykal, becoming a series of high plateau-blocks.

The Kemchik and Ulug-Khem Rivers collect the waters of the Tuva region and unite to form the Yenisey River which cuts through the Western Sayan almost midway along its length in a deep and narrow gorge within which navigation, even for rafts, is hazardous because of the presence of treacherous rapids (Bolshoy Porog). In the west the Biya and Katun Rivers drain the Altay and unite to form the River Ob. In the extreme west lie Lake Zaisan and the headwaters of the Irtysh.

CLIMATE AND NATURAL VEGETATION

The comparatively low latitude of the Southern Borderland and its remoteness from the sea give it a climate that is continental but also complex; in fact there is a whole series of climates, and vertical zonation is typical. In winter the dissected relief of the Altay Mountains stands out as an island of warmth amidst the cold neighbouring plains. In summer the Altay "because of the presence of cold high plateaux and alpine chains with perpetual snows and deep moist forested valleys is distinguished as a cool island amidst the strongly heated steppe" (Suslov, 1947).

Summers at lower altitudes in the Altay are warm (63°–68° F; 17°–20° C) but rather rainy (5·5–8 in.; 140–200 mm); winters are cold (0° to —7° F; —18° to —22° C) with frequent temperature inversions, and generally dry. The so-called "steppes" are exceptionally dry. The foothills carry little snow but in the west-facing highlands where annual precipitation may be 40–60 in., there is a deep snow cover.

The climate of the Sayans is somewhat similar but in the Tuva region there is a dry continental climate accompanied by strong temperature inversions. Winter temperatures may drop to —58° F (—50° C) but in summer they may attain 105° F (40·5° C). Annual precipitation is generally less than 8 in. (203 mm).

Mean monthly and annual temperatures at Kyzyl

	Jan.	Feb.	Mar.	Apr.	May	June	July	Aug.	Sept.	Oct.	Nov.	Dec.	Year
° F	—26	—23	—3	31	51	64	67	61	49	31	3	—20	24
° C	—32	—30	—19	—1	11	17	19	16	9	—1	—16	—29	—5

Mean monthly and annual rainfall at Tunka★

	Jan.	Feb.	Mar.	Apr.	May	June	July	Aug.	Sept.	Oct.	Nov.	Dec.	Year
in.	0·1	0·1	0·1	0·3	0·9	1·8	2·6	3·0	1·3	0·3	0·2	0·3	11·0
mm	2·5	2·5	2·5	7·6	22·9	45·7	66·0	76·2	33·0	7·6	5·1	7·6	279·4

The highlands and flat surfaces above 6000 ft carry a tundra-type vegetation with mosses, lichens and much peat bog. Lower than this there is mountain tayga which includes Cembra pine, larch, fir and spruce and within the depressions and intermontane basins there is steppe and semi-desert vegetation.

THE ECONOMY

There are some forest industries, reindeer herding, hunting and trapping in the mountain tayga. At lower altitudes there is a semi-nomadic pastoral economy with stock raising (mainly sheep) for meat and wool, and horse breeding (Fig. 189). It is the intention of the Soviet government to persuade the non-Russian herders of these lands to change to sedentary agriculture, devoted possibly to grains (wheat and oats) and fodder crops; as yet there appears to be little evidence that such a change has been made.

The Southern Borderland has considerable mineral wealth, which includes gold, silver, asbestos, copper and coal. Of these resources the asbestos and copper near Chadan in Tuva are best known. So far there has been little mining, possibly on account of lack of transport. There are no railways and the only roads are the Usa Highway across the Sayan Mountains

★ The mean monthly rainfall data for Kyzyl not being available, rainfall data for Tunka (51° 45′ N, 102° 34′ E, 2395 ft) are given as the nearest available for a station of similar altitude.

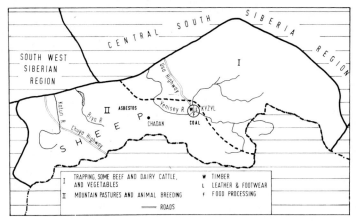

FIG. 189.—Southern Borderland: agriculture and resources.

linking Tuva (at Kyzyl) with Minusinsk, and the Chuya Highway between Biysk and Mongolia via Gorno-Altayask, the capital of A.O. Gorno-Altaysk. The Yenisey River downstream from Kyzyl is used for rafting timber.

POPULATION AND SETTLEMENT

The population is composed of Kazakhs, Altaitsy and Tuvintsy (Tuvinians) (the Tuva) but all told there are no more than 400,000. All belong to the Turkic ethnic group. The Tuvinians form a distinctive non-Russian community in an isolated homeland south of the Sayan Mountains. They were incorporated officially into the Soviet Union in 1944, but it is only a matter of time before they are fully integrated into the Soviet economy. With increased Russian settlement within the region and intermarriage, ethnographic distinctions become very blurred.

Kyzyl, the main settlement and capital of A.O. Tuva (which is directly responsible to the R.S.F.S.R.) lies at the confluence of major headstreams of the Yenisey River. It is the focus of several important routes into western Mongolia and the terminus of the Usa Highway. The town has some woodworking industries and a thermal-electric power station.

STUDY QUESTIONS

1. Describe the main features of the geography of the Southern Borderland.
2. "Tuva is unquestionably bound up geographically with the Soviet Union" (Hooson). Examine this statement in the light of Tuva's previous independent status.
3. With the aid of a sketch-map comment on the situation of Kyzyl.
4. Is "the natural frontier" a valid term? Illustrate your answer by reference to the Southern Borderland.

Chapter XXVI

TRANS-BAYKAL REGION

 TRANS-BAYKALYA lies east of Lake Bay-
kal and comprises the southern parts of
the Buryatskaya A.S.S.R. and Oblast
Chita. From an economic standpoint,
the northern parts of these administrative
units belong to the North Siberia Region
(Chapter XXIX), but in the southern
parts, traversed by the Trans-Siberian railway, the Ulan Ude–Ulan Bator–
Peking line and the Chita–Borzya–Manchouli–Harbin–Vladivostok line,
different economic conditions prevail. It is a region of mountains and
basins where mining has long been the principal industry. Agriculture is
poorly developed, but animal husbandry is widespread.

Area	. . . .	143,500 sq. miles
Population (1959)	. .	1,550,000 (approx.)

Administrative unit	Area sq. miles	Population in thousands 1959	Density persons per sq. mile	Percentage urban
Buryatskaya A.S.S.R. (part) .	34,900★	560★	16★	—
Oblast Chita (part) . . .	108,600★	990★	9★	—

★ est.

Towns with over 150,000 inhabitants in 1964

	Population in thousands 1959	1964	Percentage increase 1959–64
Ulan-Ude . . .	175	203	16·0
Chita	172	198	15·0

PHYSICAL ASPECTS

RELIEF AND DRAINAGE

Trans-Baykalya is cut into two parts by the Yablonovyy Range. These
mountains rise to 4000–5550 ft above sea-level though their broad, rounded
summits rarely rise more than 1000 ft above the floors of the intervening

valleys. Western Trans-Baykalya is a complex of mountain ranges and basins. Like the Yablonovyy Range, the mountains are flat or round-topped but exceed 6500 ft in height. They are the remnants of ancient uplifted and eroded peneplains, like the Sayan Mountains west of Lake Baykal. The Khamar–Daban Range which skirts the southeastern shores of Lake Baykal has a pronounced drop to the lake but gentle step-like slopes to the south. Eastern Trans-Baykalya comprises a series of glaciated mountains, which include the Cherskiy, Borshchovochnyy, Gazimurskiy, Nerchinskiy ranges. These ranges run northeast–southwest at 4000–6000 ft and are seamed by several deep river valleys and gorges (Fig. 190).

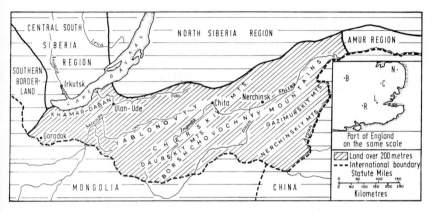

FIG. 190.—Trans-Baykal Region.

Drainage in western Trans-Baykalya is by the several tributaries of the Selenga to Lake Baykal. The lake is 400 miles long, 50 miles wide at its widest part and covers 11,780 sq. miles, equivalent to a quarter of the area of England. Its bed, formed by the collapse of adjacent troughs or rift valleys (fault graben), is at least 2000 ft deep throughout and at one point reaches a depth of 5315 ft. Baykal, the deepest fresh-water lake in the world and ninth largest in size, discharges near the southwestern end via the Angara River, a fast flowing tributary of the Yenisey. The Angara never freezes and its discharge (60,600 cusecs) is regulated by the waters of Lake Baykal. The waters of eastern Trans-Baykalya drain to the Pacific. They comprise the headstreams of the Shilka (Ingoda, Onon, etc.) and the Argun which together form the Amur.

CLIMATE

The climate of Trans-Baykalya is transitional between that of the Mongolian steppe and the Siberian tayga, complicated by the effects of appreciable variations in relief and of the water mass of Lake Baykal. Summers are dry and warm; winters are cold and snowless. Temperature inversions are frequent and there is widespread permafrost. Dry clear weather is a characteristic of all seasons, especially in winter, and there is hardly ever any really bad weather. Sixty to seventy per cent of the possible sunshine is experienced, and the cloudless air is exceptionally clear. Winter temperatures are low (mean January temperature at Chita is $-17°$ F; $-27°$ C) (Fig. 191), but with clear skies, bright sunshine and

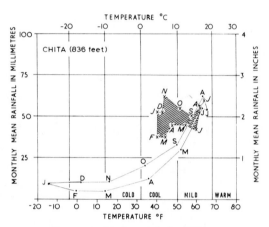

FIG. 191.—Hythergraph for Chita.

absence of winds, conditions generally are less trying than in the European part of the Soviet Union—where, though less cold, winters are damp and windy and skies overcast for long periods. Annual precipitation in Trans-Baykalya is meagre. At Chita, there is 12·2 in. (310 mm) a year, of which 8·6 in. (218 mm) or 70% comes during the summer, usually in the form of heavy downpours.

The heavy summer downpour of 1897 on the Yablonovyy Range during the construction of the railway there is well known. In the words of Imshenetskii: "a colossal wall of water about 4 m high destroyed the construction works in 24 hours and swept away hundreds of villages and tens of thousands of cattle along the Ingoda, Onon, Shilka and Amur rivers causing losses worth millions. The rivers changed their channels in places, villages had to be reconstructed and the railway was laid in a totally different location."

Baykal is a cold lake. Even in August, the temperature of the surface waters averages only 48°–50° F (9°–10° C). At depths of 800 ft and below the temperature is fairly constant at about 37·6° F (3·1° C). Freezing usually occurs in December and lasts until May. Depending on location the ice may persist on the lake for between three and a half and eight months. In the area where the Angara River flows from Baykal, neither the lake nor the river freezes. In its vicinity the lake has the effect of reducing summer temperatures, prolonging the autumn and ameliorating the winter cold, but because it is surrounded by high mountains these mollifying influences do not extend far.

". . . I sailed across Baykal and drove through Transbaykal region. Baykal is amazing, and it is not for nothing that the Siberians call it the sea and not a lake. The water is incredibly transparent, so that one can see right through it, as if through air; its colour is delicate turquoise, pleasant to the eye. The shores are mountainous, covered with forests; wilderness around is impenetrable. There is an abundance of bears, sable, wild goats and all kinds of other wild life."

Letter from Chekhov to N. A. Leiken.
June 20, 1890.

NATURAL VEGETATION

The Siberian tayga (Dahurian larch, pine, etc.) penetrates into Trans-Baykalya along the summits of the mountains. Steppe vegetation is carried northwards along the interdigitating lowlands and basins. At intermediate altitudes a woodland-type vegetation is interposed between the tayga and the steppe. Since the East Asian monsoon penetrates into eastern Trans-Baykalya, conditions are less dry and broad-leaved trees are found mixed with the conifers.

THE ECONOMY

AGRICULTURE, HUNTING AND FISHING

Crop husbandry is carried on at the intermediate altitudes where the natural cover is woodland-type vegetation, and the soils are slightly podzolised chernozems. Grains, especially wheat and rye, are the main crops but potatoes, vegetables and fodder crops are also grown (Fig. 192). On the steppe-lands stock breeding is the main occupation, carried on by both Buryats and Russians; Trans-Baykalya is one of the leading cattle-breeding regions of the Soviet Union. Sheep, goats and beef cattle are kept, and dairying is practised near the towns. Horses and some camels are kept in the semi-arid steppe of the southeast. In many instances the *yurta* (a felt-covered tent) of the semi-nomadic Buryats has been replaced by more permanent timber houses within permanent *kolkhozy*.

Hunting and fishing are pursued around Lake Baykal. The squirrel, the tarbagan (marmot) and other fur-bearing animals are hunted, and of the unique endemic fauna of Lake Baykal the omul (of the salmon family) and the carp are of major economic importance. The Baykal hair seal (*Phoca sibirica*) called the *nerpa* by the Russians, is related to similar types in the

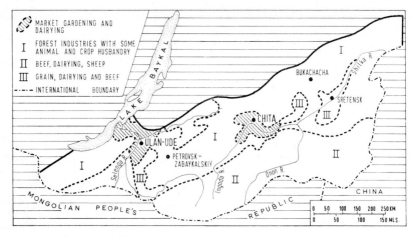

FIG. 192.—Trans-Baykal Region: agricultural land-use regions.

Arctic Ocean (*Ph. hispida*) and in the Caspian Sea (*Ph. caspia*) (Fig. 193). Fishing is organised by fishing *kolkhozy* and by the state and there are several lake-side fishing settlements engaged in the canning of fish.

[*Fotokhronika Tass.*

FIG. 193.—The seals (*Phoca sibirica*) of Lake Baykal, called *nerpa* by the Russians, are related to similar types in the Arctic Ocean and in the Caspian Sea.

MINERAL RESOURCES

Among the mineral resources of Trans-Baykalya gold (at Vershino-Darasunskiy and Baley, 45 miles northwest and 25 miles south of Nerchinsk respectively), tungsten (in southeast Trans-Baykalya), molybdenum (at Gorodok and Gutay), tin (at Shirlovaya Gora and Olovyannaya in the Onon Valley), fluorspar (at Kalangui, 150 miles southeast of Chita) and coal are the most important (Fig. 194). The town of Petrovsk-Zabaykalskiy,

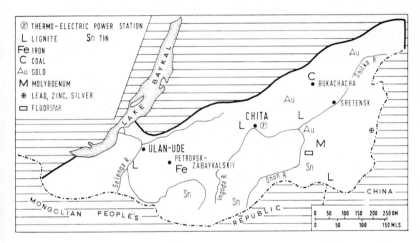

FIG. 194.—Trans-Baykal Region: mineral and power resources.

has the only major iron and steelworks in Trans-Baykalya. It receives iron ore from mines at Balagansk, 14 miles to the northwest, and coal from Tarbagatay and Khalyarta, both in the Khilok Valley. All three places lie on the Trans-Siberian Railway. There are other important iron ore deposits near Nerchinskiy Zavod (Zheleznyi Kryazh—"Iron Mountains") in eastern Trans-Baykalya.

There is no hard coal in Trans-Baykalya. What coal there is is classed as brown coal and is of Jurassic age. In addition to the Tarbagatay coal there are reserves 10 miles away at Khalyarta, at Chernovskiye Kopi, 12 miles southwest of Chita, and at Bukachacha, 200 miles east of Chita (which is linked by branch line to the Trans-Siberian Railway).

Non-ferrous metals are concentrated in southeast Trans-Baykalya within a triangle formed by the Chita–Manchouli railway, the Shilka and the Argun Rivers.

TRANSPORT AND COMMUNICATIONS

The Trans-Siberian Railway is the main artery and axis of communication of Trans-Baykalya (Fig. 195). It runs around the south of Lake Baykal to Ulan-Ude and Chita and thence to Vladivostok via the Amur and Ussuri Valleys. At Ulan-Ude a branch line leads to Naushki (158 miles) on the Mongolian border and thence via Ulan-Bator, capital of the Mongolian People's Republic, to Peking. At Karymskoye, east of Chita, another line branches off to traverse Chinese territory, eventually ter-

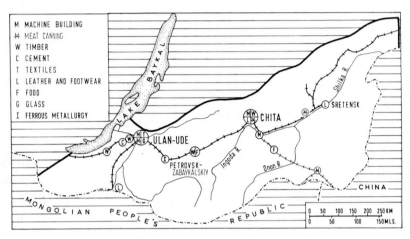

FIG. 195.—Trans-Baykal Region: railways and industrial structure of towns.

minating at Vladivostok. It leaves Soviet territory at Otpor and runs southeastwards through Harbin to link up with the Ussuri (Khabarovsk–Vladivostok) line at Grodekovo. Branches lead to mining and other centres of economic importance in the region.

Because of permanently frozen subsoil, adverse climatic conditions and a shortage of labour, the construction of the Trans-Siberian and other railways in the region was extremely difficult. Vast unpopulated stretches of countryside, unfavourable economic conditions and an insistence by the government of the day that only Russian labour and materials be employed on the construction of the railway were additional delaying factors. The Trans-Baykalyan section of the Trans-Siberian Railways was started in 1895, but floods and other hazards delayed its completion until 1900. Nevertheless it should be appreciated that considerable lengths of line were involved. For instance, the distance between Ulan-Ude and Irkutsk is 304 miles and between Ulan-Ude and Chita 344 miles. Present eastbound traffic by rail is mainly in coal and oil, and westbound in timber.

Properly constructed major roads through Trans-Baykalya are few, although there are some which are of more than local importance. Of these, that from Ulan-Ude via Kyakhta serves as a main trade route with Mongolia. A branch of this road leads to Gorodok, the centre for molybdenum extraction. Other roads from Chita lead northwards via Romanovka to the gold-producing areas of the Vitim Plateau and another southwards to the tin mines of Khapcheranga.

Water transport in the west of the region is dominated by the Selenga and in the east by Shilka and Argun tributaries of the Amur. The Selenga enters Trans-Baykalya from Mongolia near Kyakhta, and is navigable from this point to Lake Baykal, a distance of 260 miles. Traffic is mainly in rafted timber, grain, minerals, building materials and petroleum. Under favourable conditions the Shilka is navigable downstream from Chita.

POPULATION AND CITIES

Trans-Baykalya is inhabited by Russians and Buryats. The latter, the most northerly of the major Mongol peoples, are closely related to the Mongols of the Mongolian People's Republic. They make up no more than 40% of the population of Trans-Baykalya, but have been given territorial recognition through the formation of the Buryat Autonomous Republic. Traditionally they are nomadic pastoralists, but more and more they are

[*Fotokhronika Tass.*

FIG. 196.—Chita: a view of Lenin Street. The town is well known for furs and leather goods and there are mining districts in the neighbourhood.

adopting a sedentary life and forsaking their felt tents or *yurta* for the log hut or *izba*. The total population of Trans-Baykalya is little more than $1\frac{1}{2}$ million. Densities along the route of the Trans-Siberian Railway and within the broad depression of the Selenga–Uda rift valley are 25 to 65 persons per square mile but elsewhere fewer than 25 per square mile. South of the Daurskiy Range and near the Mongolian border densities are rarely more than 2 persons per square mile.

Ulan-Ude and Chita are the main urban centres. *Ulan-Ude* (203,000), capital of the Buryatskaya A.S.S.R. lies at the Uda–Selenga confluence. It was once a great centre for the Chinese tea trade but is now an administrative and industrial centre and rail junction. It has locomotive and rolling stock works, plant for the processing, preserving and packing of meat, sawmills, glass works, shipbuilding and repair yards, and plant for the treatment of furs (Fig. 195), which are obtained by hunting (chiefly squirrel and sable) or from breeding farms (silver fox and racoon). *Chita* (198,000), 350 miles east of Ulan-Ude, is capital of Oblast Chita, and has administrative and commercial functions. Locomotives and rolling stock are repaired here and there is flour milling, meat packing, sawmilling. Chita is well known for its furs and leather products (Fig. 196).

STUDY QUESTIONS

1. Describe the main features of the geography of the Trans-Baykal Region.
2. Write a geographical essay on Lake Baykal.
3. Examine the site, locations and functions of Ulan-Ude and Chita.
4. Suggest factors likely to be important in the future economic development of the Trans-Baykal Region.

Chapter XXVII

AMUR REGION

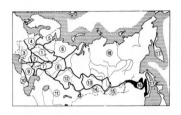

THE Amur Region, the "Granary of the Far East," embraces the continuous strip of fertile alluvial lowland that follows the Amur River, the Zeya–Bureya Plain, the Ussuri Valley and the lowlands to the south of Lake Khanka (Fig. 197). It includes parts of Oblast Amur and Kha-barovskiy Kray, the whole of the Yevreyskaya (Jewish) Autonomous Oblast and part of Primorskiy Kray. Besides its agricultural production it has important mining (coal, tin and gold) resources.

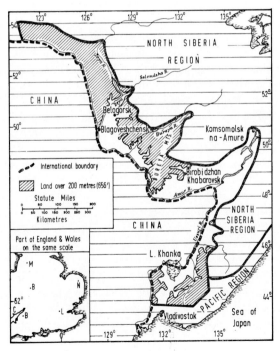

FIG. 197.—Amur Region.

319

Area   .   .   .   .   106,100* sq. miles
Population (1959)   .   .   2,215,000 (approx.)

Administrative unit	Area sq. miles	Population in thousands 1959	Density persons per sq. mile	Percentage urban
Oblast Amur (part) . . .	53,500*	660*	12*	—
A.O. Yevreyskaya (Jewish) .	14,000	163	12	72
Khabarovskiy Kray (part) . .	17,200*	942*	50*	—
Primorskiy (Maritime) Kray (part)	21,400*	450*	21*	—

* est.

Towns with over 150,000 inhabitants in 1964

	Population in thousands		Percentage increase
	1959	1964	1959–64
Khabarovsk . . .	323	408	26·2
Komsomolsk-na-Amure .	177	204	14·8
Ussuriysk . . .	104	121	16·3

PHYSICAL ASPECTS

RELIEF

In the extreme northwest the Amur Valley is restricted. It lies between the Great Khingan (Mongolia) and the Olekminskiy Stanovik Mountains. Eastwards of the latter lie the Tukuringra and Dzhagdy Mountains. The Tukuringra are breached almost on the region's boundary by the River Zeya, which thus taps the enclosed upland basin that lies to the north.

The lower Zeya River divides the wide plain of the middle Amur into two parts: the Amur–Zeya Plateau 800 ft high to the west and the alluvial Zeya–Bureya Plain to the east.

The Bureya Range separates the valley of the Bureya and the lower Amur. Below the confluence of the two rivers the Amur flows between sheer rocky banks through the mountains for a distance of 90 miles. Where breached by the Amur altitudes are only 700–1500 ft, but near the sources of the Bureya River these mountains rise northwards to 7000 ft.

The Ussuri–Khanka Plain and the part of the Amur Valley that lies downstream from Khabarovsk together form an elongated trough. It represents the subsided portions of a fault block between, on the one side, the Little Khingan and the Bureya Mountains and on the other the Sikhote-Alin Mountains. The lower Amur portion is a flat marshy plain; the Ussuri section in Soviet territory is narrow, widening only where tributary valleys meet the main valley. Conditions along the Ussuri are very boggy. Lake

Khanka is shallow, with a maximum depth of about 30 ft but covering about 2000 square miles. It is surrounded by large moors and marshes and is being rapidly silted up.

CLIMATE, NATURAL VEGETATION AND SOILS

Climatic conditions throughout the region are almost completely dependent upon seasonal changes in the major air masses. The maritime air masses from the southeast, associated with the summer monsoon, are comparatively cool and humid and accompanied by much cloud. Continental air masses from the north, associated with the winter monsoon, give very cold, dry and sunny winters. July temperatures between 68° and 70° F (20°–21° C) are not unlike those at Gorkiy or Vologda in the European part of the Soviet Union, yet the severe dry continental winter is more akin to that of Yakutsk in North Siberia (Fig. 198). January temperatures are

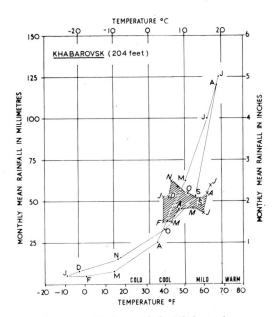

FIG. 198.—Hythergraph for Khabarovsk.

−8° to −10° F (−22° to −23° C). At Blagoveshchensk (compare the latitude of 50° N with that of the Scilly Islands off southwest England) the Amur is frozen over for about five months every year.

Annual precipitation exceeds 20 in. (500 mm) over the whole of the region but amounts diminish away from the sea. Eighty-five to ninety per cent of total precipitation is rain which falls in summer and as much as 60%

of it in the period June–August, unfortunately at a time when crops are being harvested. Thunderstorms, and fringes of typhoons which penetrate this region during summer, cause heavy downpours which lead to flooding. Winter precipitation is slight, coming in the form of snow which, though persisting for four to six months, is never more than a foot deep. The ground freezes to a great depth during winter, but permafrost is absent, except for occasional patches in the Zeya–Bureya Plain.

The climatic conditions of the region are clearly reflected in the vegetation. Oak, elm, maple, ash, lime and other broad-leaved trees that occur in the Amur Region reflect the monsoon type of climate. In the Ussuri area there is an extraordinary variety of flora, which includes characteristic southern forms such as vines, walnut, cherry and lilac.

The Zeya–Bureya Plain has fertile black soils. They lack the granular structure and accumulation of carbonates of typical chernozems, but are capable of producing excellent crops of wheat, year after year, without any manuring. Similar soils occur in the Ussuri–Khanka Plain. Between Khabarovsk and Komsomolsk-na-Amure there are thick impermeable clays, and extensive areas of boggy grasslands.

THE ECONOMY

AGRICULTURE

In the extreme northwest of the region some arable farming is carried on in the less boggy valleys between the Trans-Siberian Railway and the Amur River, but it is downstream in the Zeya–Bureya Plain (with 80% of the total arable land of the region) and in the Ussuri–Khanka Lowland that soils and climatic conditions are best suited to agriculture (Fig. 199). Dry periods in spring and early summer, and humid conditions in late summer and autumn present difficulties for growing and harvesting the wheat, oats and rye crops. Wheat is the main crop. Sunflowers, soya beans, sugar beet, rice, maize, potatoes and millet are grown and cattle, pigs and sheep raised. Practically the whole of the Soviet Union soya bean production comes from the Amur Region, which also carries 90% of the cows and 80% of the pigs of the whole of the Soviet Far East.

FUEL AND MINERAL RESOURCES

Important in the economy of the Amur Region are the lignite deposits at Raichikhinsk and Kivdinskiy, the hard coal deposits in the upper Bureya Valley and the anthracite at Bira (Fig. 200). Lignite is too friable for long-distance transport and has to be used locally, but the Bureya coals are transported as far as Khabarovsk, Komsomolsk-na-Amure and Sovetskaya Gavan (Pacific Region), to be used for power generation, and for industry

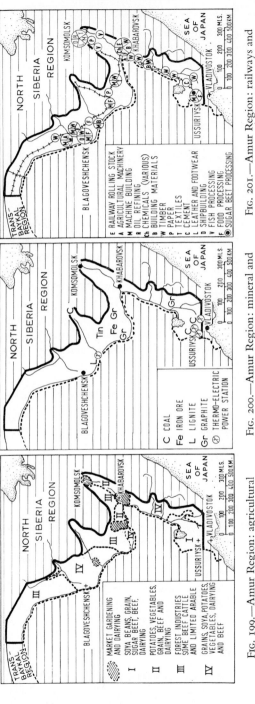

FIG. 201.—Amur Region: railways and industrial structure of towns.

Key to Fig. 201:
E RAILWAY ROLLING STOCK
A AGRICULTURAL MACHINERY
M MACHINE BUILDING
R OIL REFINING
Ch CHEMICALS (VARIOUS)
B BUILDING MATERIALS
W TIMBER
P PAPER
t TEXTILES
C CEMENT
L LEATHER AND FOOTWEAR
D SHIPBUILDING
O FISH PROCESSING
F FOOD PROCESSING
⊙ SUGAR BEET PROCESSING

FIG. 200.—Amur Region: mineral and power resources.

Key to Fig. 200:
C COAL
Fe IRON ORE
L LIGNITE
Gr GRAPHITE
⊗ THERMO-ELECTRIC POWER STATION

FIG. 199.—Amur Region: agricultural land-use regions.

Key to Fig. 199:
I MARKET GARDENING AND DAIRYING
II SOYA BEANS, GRAIN, SUGAR BEET, BEEF, DAIRYING
III POTATOES, VEGETABLES, GRAIN, BEEF AND DAIRYING
III FOREST INDUSTRIES SOME BEEF CATTLE AND LIMITED ARABLE
IV GRAINS, SOYA, POTATOES, VEGETABLES, DAIRYING AND BEEF

(e.g. the Bureya metallurgical *kombinat*). There is said to be an "Upper Amur Coal Basin" with Jurassic coals of high ash content near Chernyaevo on the Amur. Nothing is known about these reserves, but their location in an area hitherto dependent on distant coal supplies would make them of great potential importance.

There is no network for the transmission of electricity and the larger towns have their own power stations based on external supplies of coal, wood or petroleum. The generating stations at Birobidzhan are based solely on petroleum.

Apart from coal mining the most highly developed industries are the mining of tin, gold, molybdenum, antimony and iron. Tin is mined near Khingansk, where the deposits are high-quality placers from weathered igneous rocks. Gold occurs in a number of areas, such as the valley of the Sutur in A.O. Yevreyskaya (with Radostayi as its centre) and the district near Skovorodino in the extreme northwest of the region. Molybdenum and antimony extraction takes place at Umaltinskiy in the valley of the Umalta (a tributary of the upper Bureya) with a *kombinat* at Ust-Umalta. The iron-mining centre is Kimkan in A.O. Yevreyskaya. The suitability of the Amur River system for shipping and floating logs has facilitated the exploitation of the rich timber resources of the region. Khabarovsk is the main centre of the timber industry, and Komsomolsk-na-Amure has a large *kombinat* for the production of cellulose and paper.

MANUFACTURING INDUSTRY

Manufacturing industry in the Amur Region, other than that associated with timber, seems to have been determined by the application of the Soviet principle that individual regions should be self-sufficient for their principal needs. World War II also had an effect: several factories which were moved into the region at that time have remained. Shipbuilding has been developed at Komsomolsk-na-Amure which has also the famous "Amur Steel" works. These are two of the largest industrial undertakings in the eastern territories of the Soviet Union (Fig. 201).

Railway engines, coach building, motor vehicles, aircraft and engineering generally are represented at Khabarovsk, and there is a plant for the supply of agricultural machinery. Cement works (Komsomolsk-na-Amure, Khabarovsk and Londoko) and certain light industries (e.g. clothing and hosiery at Borobidzhan) are localised, but the food and provisions industries are widespread and represented by small enterprises in rural areas.

TRANSPORT AND COMMUNICATIONS

Most traffic in the Amur Region is carried by rail and the main artery is the Trans-Siberian line (Fig. 201). However, the main traffic from the

Union west of Trans-Baykalya to Vladivostok uses the line from Chita via Harbin (the route is about 600 miles shorter than by the all-Union route via Khabarovsk) and the Amur and Ussuri sections of the Trans-Siberian line tend to be of secondary and local importance. Nevertheless they are strategically safer in times of tension. The insistence on the employment of only Russian labour on the building of the track indirectly assisted the subsequent colonisation of the region.

The Trans-Siberian line passes through the more important towns and there are a number of branch lines leading to places of economic and strategic importance. Branch lines have been laid from Bureya on the main line to Raichikhinsk, centre of the largest brown coal deposits in the Amur Region (28 miles), and from Izvestkovyy across the Bureya Mountains to the upper reaches of the Tyrma and thence as far as Ust Umalta, a distance of 200 miles, thus providing access to the Bureya coal deposits. Branch lines to the Amur River include 20 miles between Arkhara and Inno-kentevka, 68 miles between Belogorsk (Kuybyshevka–Vostochnaya) and Blagoveshchensk, 30 miles between Ushumun and Chernyaevo, and 38 miles between Skovorodino and Dzhalinda.

The projected Baykal–Amur Railway (Baykal–Amur Magistrale: BAM) continues to be veiled in secrecy. It is planned to skirt the north of the Amur Region via the valley of the Gilyuy and Zeya Rivers, thence to Norsk on the Selemdzha River, and via Chekunda on the Bureya River to Komsomolsk-na-Amure. The line would tap areas rich in timber, gold and other natural resources and open up new areas for settlement.

The only important road in the region is that between Khabarovsk and Vladivostok; others are of local importance only and act as feeders for the railway. The Amur River, the Soviet–Chinese boundary for 1500 miles, is the main waterway. It is especially important because both the main stream and its numerous large tributaries are navigable for ships and suitable for timber rafts. Traffic, in bulk cargoes of timber, petroleum, grain and building materials, is limited to the summer months, since the river is frozen over for 185 days at Khabarovsk and 170 days at Blagoveshchensk.

Air transport is becoming increasingly important for passenger traffic. Khabarovsk and Magdagachi are major civil airports along the Moscow–Vladivostok route, but there are airfields at Skovorodino, Tygda, Svobodnyy and Arkhara. Khabarovsk is the usual starting-point for air routes to the north.

POPULATION AND CITIES

Population densities are no more than 30 and 60 persons per square mile in a narrow belt of settlement along the Trans-Siberian Railway. There are farming communities or lumbering towns in the Zeya–Bureya Plain, along the main railway in the Ussuri Valley, and around the fertile shores of Lake Khanka, and isolated mining communities where there are deposits of coal, gold and tin. Yet the total population for the Amur Region barely exceeds 2 millions. The Soviet government is making every effort to introduce more settlers into the region, both for strategic reasons (not least the

Fig. 202.—Khabarovsk: Komsomol Square with the Amur River in the background. The city is at the focal point of important Soviet Far Eastern rail, air and water routes.

proximity of China's 750 million people) and in order to develop its resources. Russian colonisation, attracted to the region by higher wages, tax exemptions, subsidised journeys and other benefits, or else spurred by appeals to the patriotism of young Communists, has been superimposed on the indigenous populations with the result that the population is now predominantly Russian though with a considerable Ukrainian element. West of Khabarovsk is the Yevreyskaya (Jewish) Autonomous Oblast, established in 1934, to accommodate refugees from the western part of the Soviet Union; reports suggest that 80,000 or less than half the present population, is Jewish.

Khabarovsk (408,000) is the administrative and economic centre both of the Amur Region and of the territory (*kray*) of the same name. It is located on the elevated eastern bank of the Amur River which at this point is several miles wide, 29 miles below its confluence with the Ussuri River (Fig. 202). Despite the fact that the river is frozen over from December until April, Khabarovsk is well placed on a large system of navigable

[*Fotokhronika Tass*

waterways. It is the terminus of the Ussuri section of the Trans-Siberian Railway and centre of all air traffic in the Soviet Far East. In addition it has industries which include mechanical engineering, shipbuilding, oil refining, timber manufacturing and food processing. Its population of Russians, Koreans and Chinese increased rapidly with the introduction of large industrial plant and practically doubled between 1939 and 1964.

Komsomolsk-na-Amure (204,000), was built by Komsomols (Young Communists) in 1933 as a bulwark against the Japanese. It is the most diversified industrial centre in the Soviet Far East, with metallurgical plant, shipyards, an oil refinery, pulp-paper mills and fish processing and canning plant. The rate of population increase between 1959 and 1964 was about half that of Khaborovsk.

Ussuriysk (formerly Voroshilov, 121,000), centre of the agriculturally important Khanka Plain, is important for the processing of foodstuffs, especially of soya beans and sugar beet. It is at Ussuriysk that the Ussuri section of the Trans-Siberian Railway joins the section that passes through Chinese territory.

Blagoveshchensk (114,000), founded in 1858 after the Russian occupation of the Amur Basin, lies within the Zeya–Bureya agricultural plain at the confluence of the Amur and Zeya Rivers. It is the administrative centre of Oblast Amur and has industries which include food processing, timber working, the building and repair of river craft, and the making of woollens and leather goods. A branch line links it with the Trans-Siberian Railway and it has road connections with Svobodnyy and Khabarovsk.

STUDY QUESTIONS

1. Describe the main features of the geography of the Amur region.
2. Write a short description of the agricultural activities of the Amur region.
3. In what ways does the comparative scarcity of population restrict the economic development of the Amur region of the U.S.S.R.?
4. Give a geographical account of the utilisation of the River Amur.
5. Examine the site, location and functions of the following towns: Khabarovsk; Komsomolsk; Ussuriysk; Blagoveshchensk.

Chapter XXVIII

PACIFIC REGION

THE Pacific Region (Fig. 203) includes the seaboards of Primorskiy Kray and Khabarovskiy Kray, Oblast Sakhalin and part of Oblast Kamchatka. The reason for differentiating the southern part of the Soviet Far East into the Amur Region (Chapter XXVII) and the Pacific Region is the immense importance of the latter for fishing, whaling and canning. The annual catch of fish and marine animals here represents over 30% of the Soviet Union's total catch. Its secondary industries are lumbering, woodworking and paper production.

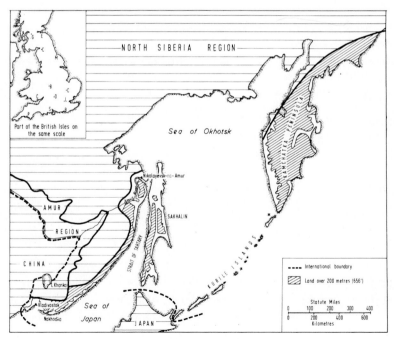

FIG. 203.—Pacific Region.

Area   .   .   .   .   194,300 sq. miles
Population (1959)   .   .   1,850,000 (approx.)

Administrative unit	Area sq. miles	Population in thousands 1959	Density persons per sq. mile	Percentage urban
Primorskiy (Maritime) Kray (part)	24,700*	930*	37	—
Khabarovskiy Kray (part) . .	15,500*	150*	10	—
Oblast Sakhalin . . .	34,000	649	19	75
Oblast Kamchatka (part) . .	120,100*	120*	10	—

* est.

Towns with over 150,000 inhabitants in 1964

	Population in thousands		Percentage increase
	1959	1964	1959–64
Vladivostok . . .	291	367	26·1

PHYSICAL ASPECTS

RELIEF AND DRAINAGE

The greater part of the region is mountainous. The seaboards of the Primorskiy and the Khabarovskiy Kray represent the submerged eastern slopes of the much eroded Sikhote-Alin Mountains. The Sikhote-Alin represent the uplifted edge of a submerged fault block, or horst, and consist of as many as eight parallel ranges between 2000 and 3000 ft high and orientated north-northeast. The coast is of the ria type in the south, but farther north it is regular and has relatively few bays.

The Amur flows through hilly and sometimes mountainous country. The course below Komsomolsk-na-Amure is about 300 miles long and expands in width to become very broad indeed, with numerous channels and islands. Only occasionally do the mountain ranges close in on the river from both sides and force it into a single undivided channel. The left bank is mainly flat and marshy, the right bank hilly and drier. Even though the lower reaches of the river are hemmed in by mountains, it is 3–6 miles wide in places. At Lake Bolshie Kizy the Amur comes within 9 miles of the sea and it is possible that its mouth may once have been located here. Its present outlet is blocked by a massive sandbank over which ocean-going vessels are unable to pass and have to be unloaded into river craft on the open ocean.

The island of Sakhalin is composed of a double range of mountains 6000 ft high, separated by a longitudinal depression extending the length of the island and drained by the Tym and Poronay rivers.

Kamchatka comprises a double line of volcanic peaks with an intervening depressions drained by Kamchatka and Elovka Rivers. Relief is everywhere accentuated. The western range reaches over 10,000 ft in the Ichinskaya Sopka (volcano) (the only active volcano in this range); the eastern range has 18 volcanoes active at the present time. Klyuchevskaya Sopka, which

[*Mysl.*

FIG. 204.—Kamchatka Peninsula. The peninsula is notable for its volcanoes, a number of which are still active.

is over 15,000 ft, is the highest and the world's most grandiose symmetrical cone (Fig. 204).

The Pacific Region was not glaciated in Quaternary times and only the northwest of Kamchatka and the lower Amur Valley have permafrost, generally in the form of isolated islands of permanently frozen ground.

CLIMATE AND NATURAL VEGETATION

The monsoon climate of the Pacific Region is characterised by cold, dry, northerly air masses from the continent in the winter and cool moist southerly air masses from the Pacific in the summer. Maritime amelioration of temperatures is slight, and winters are of the cold continental type, more severe in the north than in the south. Winter is the season of least cloud, but January temperatures are low, ranging from about 6° F (−14° C) at Vladivostok and 10° F (−12° C) at Petropavlovsk-Kamchatskiy (Fig. 205) to −12° F (−24° C) at Nikolayevsk-na-Amure. Ice covers the sea

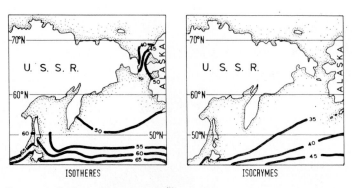

FIG. 205.—Surface sea-water temperature conditions off northeast Siberia: Calendar month isotheres and isocrymes. (See Note, Fig. 128.)

between Sakhalin and the mainland during this season (*see* Fig. 206). Winter precipitation comes as snow. Along the coastal strip from Vladivostok to the mouth of the Amur falls are slight; in Sakhalin and Kamchatka they are appreciable, and on Kamchatka, where blizzards are common, snow may reach depths of 4–6 ft.

> "Kamchatka may be called the country of blizzards. Nowhere else, save perhaps in the extreme northeast of Siberia and on the western shores of the Sea of Okhotsk, do they attain such intensity and duration, nowhere else are they observed so often."
>
> *Vlasov.*

Summers in the coastal region of Primorskiy Kray exhibit all the characteristics of a maritime climate. The cool air masses which move towards the mainland from the sea in summer are cooled still further during their passage over the Okhotsk current. July temperatures are 50° F (10° C) in coastal Kamchatka, 54°–57° F (12°–14° C) along the shores of Tatarskiy Proliv (the Strait of Tatary) but are no more than 64°–68° F (18°–20° C) at Vladivostok and near the mouth of the Amur.

While in the Amur Region precipitation is concentrated in the summer months, the coasts of the Pacific Region are affected by east Asian depressions and have precipitation spring, summer and autumn. Moist winds blow over southern Kamchatka throughout the year and at Petropavlovsk maximum precipitation occurs in the winter (Fig. 205). Thick fogs, which increase the rawness and humidity of the summer, are frequent over much of the Pacific Region.

The mountains of the mainland are covered with dense tayga. There has been some ruthless felling of trees in the peripheral areas of the Sikhote-Alin

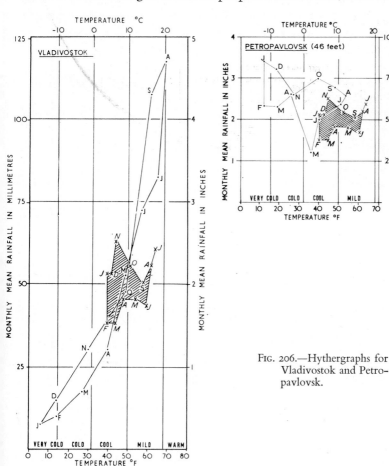

Fig. 206.—Hythergraphs for Vladivostok and Petropavlovsk.

which has resulted in serious soil erosion, but elsewhere there are rich timber reserves awaiting exploitation. Fairly good stands of forest also occur on Sakhalin although the low marshy northwest is tundra-covered. Much of Kamchatka is tundra-covered although the mountains carry scattered birch, alder and mountain ash up to 1000–1500 ft, alder, cembra pine and dwarf timber to about 2500 ft and alpine flora from about 2500 ft to about 4500 ft. Most of the volcanic peaks are snow-capped.

M

THE ECONOMY

AGRICULTURE AND FISHING

South of Lake Khanka and more particularly in the Tasuifen valley, there is fertile land where wheat, oats, barley, millet, soya beans, perilla, rice, sugar beet, potatoes, fruit and vegetables are grown. Cattle are raised and the principal livestock are cows, horses and pigs (Fig. 207). Elsewhere crop

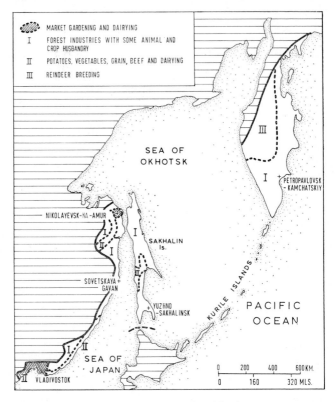

FIG. 207.—Pacific Region: agricultural land-use regions.

raising is limited and restricted to provision of food supplies for local industrial populations.

Of far greater importance than agriculture in the economy of the Pacific Region is fishing. Kamchatka is, after the Caspian Sea, the second most important fishing area of the Soviet Union. The meeting offshore of the warm waters of the Kuro Siwo current (or Kuro Shio, literally: Blue Salt) and the cold waters of the Okhotsk current provides a rich supply of plankton which assures abundant supply of many species of fish. The

waters around Kamchatka, the Kuriles and Sakhalin, in the Strait of
Tatary and in the rivers are rich in fish and marine animals. Especially
large crabs thrive on Kamchatka, and each year the rivers of the peninsula
are visited by large shoals of valuable species of salmon. The flourishing
coastal and deep-sea fishing industry now provides the mainstay of the
economy of the whole region.

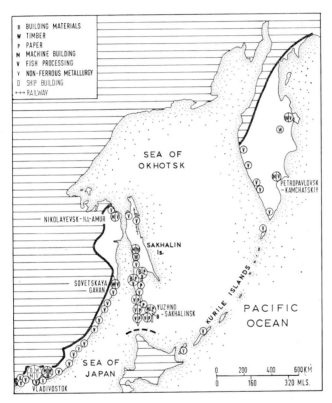

FIG. 208.—Pacific Region: railways and industrial structure of
towns.

Almost every settlement on the coast is a fishing village and the larger
ones have canneries (Fig. 208). Floating crab-tinning factories carry out
the complete process from catching to tinning. Tinned crab and salmon
from Kamchatka are exported to many countries. Herrings and sardines
are the main species caught along the coast of Primorskiy Kray. Fishing
here is done mainly in the bays, e.g. the Bay of Peter the Great south of
Vladivostok. The largest fishing fleet is based on Vladivostok where there
is a large fish-canning industry. Vladivostok is also the home port of one

of the Soviet Antarctic whaling flotillas. Nikolayevsk-na-Amure is the centre of the lower Amur fishing area where the Keta salmon, which also provides the red caviar, and the Garbusha salmon spawn. Salmon, herring, cod, tunny fish and mackerel are also caught around the Kurile Islands and along the eastern side of Sakhalin.

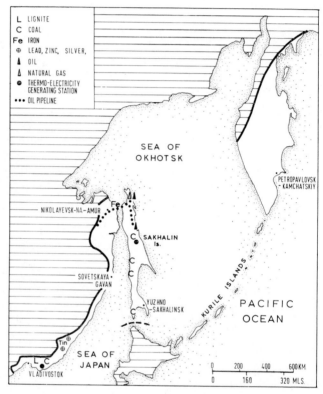

Fig. 209.—Pacific Region: mineral and power resources.

Other industries

Secondary but highly developed branches of the local economy are lumbering, woodworking and pulp production. Vladivostok and Sovet-skaya Gavan are two major centres of the timber industry. Other important towns in this sphere are Aleksandrovsk-Sakhalinskiy on Sakhalin and Petropavlovsk on Kamchatka.

There are industries devoted to the extraction of petroleum, to coal mining and to the production of tin, gold and lead. Petroleum occurs near the towns of Okha and Ekhabi in the northeast of Sakhalin and is sent by pipeline beneath the Strait of Tatary to refineries in Nikolayevsk-na-

Amure, Komsomolsk-na-Amure and Khabarovsk (Fig. 209). The oilfield provides no more than 1% (2·2 million metric tons in 1964) of the total Soviet production, but this is sufficient to supply most of the needs of the Amur and Pacific Regions. Coal is mined on Sakhalin in a narrow west coast strip near Aleksandrovsk-Sakhalinskiy and Uglegorsk, and farther south at Yuzhno-Sakhalinsk. On the mainland there is coal at Artem and Suchan near Vladivostok. The Artem coal is lignitic; the other is of a higher grade but the output is smaller. Tin, gold and lead are mined inland from Tetyukhe-Pristan in the southeastern part of the Sikhote-Alin Range.

TRANSPORT AND COMMUNICATIONS

The geographical position of the Pacific Region has favoured the development of shipping. It is estimated that it contributes a quarter of the country's annual turnover in marine transport. Vladivostok is the main seaport, but Nakhodka, 120 miles to the east, is a serious rival (Fig. 210). Sovetskaya Gavan, linked by rail with Komsomolsk-na-Amure is another important port. Korsakov and Kholmsk are the main ports on Sakhalin, and Petropavlovsk on Kamchatka. The latter is the eastern terminus of the Northern Sea Route.

[*Thompson, Topix.*

FIG. 210.—Nakhodka. A continuous range of steep volcanic hills forms a background to one of the longest and best-equipped waterfronts in the Soviet Union. Unlike Vladivostok, Nakhodka is virtually ice-free.

M 2

POPULATION AND CITIES

The whole of the Pacific Region is sparsely peopled and the total population is unlikely to be more than 2 million. The only sizable concentrations occur around Vladivostok and Nakhodka, in the coalfields of Artem and Suchan, and in the nearby agricultural area of the south Khanka Plain.

Vladivostok (367,000), was founded in 1860 and two years later made the base of the Russian Pacific Fleet. At the end of the nineteenth century the town developed as an important Pacific port. It is sited on the slope of a ridge of hills alongside a deep and well-protected bay (the "Golden Horn") at the southern end of the Muravyev Peninsula and opposite Russkiy Island. The peninsula is separated from the island by the "Eastern Bosporus." The restricted site, likened to San Francisco for its scenic beauty, has given rise to closely-packed business premises and high-density building. The side streets which run up the hill slopes are sometimes too steep for vehicular traffic. Industries in Vladivostok include fish canning, wood-using industries (sawmills, plywood factories, matchmaking plant and the prefabrication of wooden houses) and shipbuilding (Fig. 208). The port, which is kept open during the winter by ice-breakers, was a big international seaport, but in the 1940s it was made a closed city.

STUDY QUESTIONS

1. Describe the main features of the geography of the Pacific Region.
2. Assess the contribution of the Pacific Region to the fishing industry of the U.S.S.R.
3. In what ways does comparative scarcity of population and distance from other parts of the Soviet Union contribute to the difficulties of developing the Pacific Region?
4. With the aid of a large sketch-map, comment on the situation and economic importance of Vladivostok.
5. Discuss the economic and strategic value of Kamchatka to the U.S.S.R.
6. Make a comparative study of the Pacific Ocean ports of the U.S.S.R.

Chapter XXIX

NORTH SIBERIA REGION

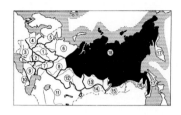

THIS vast underdeveloped region extends 4000 miles from the Ural to Bering Strait, widening from 900 miles in the west to 1400 miles in the east (Fig. 211). It is over 40 times the size of the United Kingdom, but has only about 2 million people, or 4% of the United Kingdom population. Population density is rarely greater than one person per square mile.

Bordered on the north by the Arctic Ocean, the region lies entirely within the tundra and tayga. With few exceptions average winter temperatures are below 0° F (−18° C) and permanently frozen subsoil is

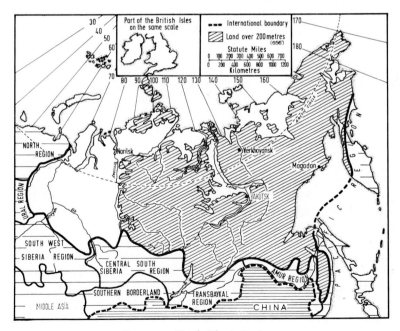

FIG. 211.—North Siberia Region.

widespread. Mining and lumbering are the most important branches of the economy.

Area   .   .   .   .   3,887,900★ sq. miles
Population (1959)   .   .   1,429,000 (approx.)

Administrative unit	Area sq. miles	Population in thousands 1959	Density persons per sq. mile	Percentage urban
Yakutskaya A.S.S.R. . .	1,210,000	488	>1	49
Oblast Magadan . . .	468,000	236	>1	81
Oblast Kamchatka (part) . .	61,900★	100★	1	—
Khabarovskiy Kray (part) . .	285,300★	80★	>1	—
Primorskiy (Maritime) Kray (part)	17,900★	1★	>1	—
Oblast Amur	87,500★	58★	>1	—
Oblast Chita	58,400★	50★	>1	—
Buryatskaya A.S.S.R. (part) .	85,000★	90★	1	—
Oblast Irkutsk (part) . . .	165,300★	71★	>1	--
Krasnoyarskiy Kray (part) . .	820,400★	19★	>1	--
Oblast Tyumen (part) . .	524,800★	186★	>1	--
Oblast Tomsk (part) . . .	94,800★	30★	>1	—
Oblast Novosibirsk (part) . .	8,700★	20★	>1	—

★ est.

Main towns

	Population in thousands		Percentage increase
	1959	1964	1959–64
Norilsk . .	109	124	14·0
Yakutsk . . .	74	89	20·0
Magadan . . .	62	79	27·0

PHYSICAL ASPECTS

RELIEF AND DRAINAGE

From the Ural to the Yenisey River stretches the almost completely flat West Siberian Plain, which embraces the basin of the Ob River. Gradients northwards are very gentle and variations in height throughout the area are insignificant. The fall of the Ob during its last 1250 miles is only 350 ft and interfluves rarely exceed 30 ft above the surrounding countryside. The wide flat plains between rivers are the most typical relief features and there are vast expanses of bog and marsh. It is assumed that the ancient Russian–Siberian Platform lies deep beneath the plain. It was once the site of a vast geosyncline in which were accumulated great thicknesses of sedimentary strata. Surface rocks are mainly of Tertiary or more recent age, but they have a veneer of moraine and other glacial deposits as far south as latitude 60° N. The Quaternary ice was thinner on the West Siberian Plain than on the Russian Lowland and in its northern part glacial deposits were either removed after a sea advance in postglacial times or else covered by marine deposits left behind after that advance.

East of the Yenisey River there is an abrupt change in the character of the landscape. Here a sharp edge rises rapidly to more than 600 ft and in one place—in the Putorana Mountains of the northwest—to over 3000 ft. Eastwards and extending as far as the middle Lena River, is an extensive dissected upland of ancient rocks known as the Central Siberian Plateau. Within this plateau the Pre-Cambrian crystalline rocks of the Siberian Platform (or Angaraland, i.e. the Asian counterpart of the Russian Platform) are exposed in worn-down mountain ranges or masked by virtually horizontal marine deposits of Palaeozoic age. The plateau has a generally mountainous character, particularly in the Putorana Mountains, but in general it is 1600–2000 ft high and surfaces are usually flat. In contrast to the Russian Lowland, which did not become dry land until Quaternary times, the Central Siberian Plateau achieved this state towards the end of Palaeozoic times. This probably accounts for the high degree of erosion in and dissection of the Siberian Plateau.

The northeast extension of the West Siberian Plain along the northern edge of the Central Siberian Plateau is known as the Taymyr (or North Siberian) Lowland. This sedimentary plain of comparatively dissected relief is practically twice the size of the United Kingdom. The Byrranga plateau north of the Taymyr Lowland is made up of two and sometimes three parallel and flat-topped ranges, 1000–1500 ft high, and separated by shallow lowlands. This plateau displays considerable evidence of glaciation.

Severnaya Zemlya (North Land) is a group of four large islands which belong to the Ural–Novaya Zemlya physiographical province. The islands are composed of Palaeozoic rocks but the northernmost, Komsomolets, shows only Pleistocene deposits and is largely ice-covered. Ice covers 40% of the total area of the islands and where glaciers reach the sea, small icebergs continually detach themselves.

The flat plains associated with the middle reaches of the Lena River and the lower reaches of the Vilyuy and Aldan Rivers are part of a large tectonic depression known as the Lena-Vilyuy Lowland. Beyond the Lena, as far as the Pacific coast, is a complex of mountains with only occasional river valleys and coastal plains. The Verkhoyansk and Kolyma Mountains form a great semicircle facing the East Siberian Sea and encircle parallel ranges such as the Cherskiy Mountains. These mountains have elevations above 10,000 ft and are heavily dissected, severely glaciated and extremely difficult of access. The Anadyr (Chukot) Mountains which run parallel to the shores of Chukchi Sea as far as the Bering Strait are over 3000 ft high. They form the watershed between the Anadyr River (flowing into the Bering Sea) and the rivers which flow to the Arctic Ocean. The Dzhugdzhur Mountains, separated from the Stanovoy Mountains by the Maya, tributary of the Uda, run along the coast of the Sea of Okhotsk.

[*Fotokhronika Tass.*]

Fig. 212.—Wrangel Island. Mosses, lichens, dwarf shrubs and bushes are among the perennial plants which appear in summer in the better-drained sites of the tundra.

Northeast of the Lena Delta are the New Siberian Islands (Novosibirskiye Ostrova) comprising four main islands and a number of islets. They are virtually uninhabited. However, the climatic amelioration in these latitudes has laid bare a great wealth of fossil mammoth remains which have proved a valuable source of ivory. Wrangel (Vrangel) Island in the Chukchi Sea is dry and barren and devoid of glaciers (Fig. 212).

CLIMATE, NATURAL VEGETATION AND SOILS

Climatic conditions in North Siberia are severe and acutely continental (Fig. 213). With few exceptions average winter temperatures are everywhere less than 0° F (−18° C) and at the "pole of cold" (Oymyakon and Verkhoyansk) the mean January temperature is −58° F (−50 °C). In summer mean July temperatures attain 40° F (4° C) along the Arctic coast and rise to 70° F (21° C) in the south of the region.

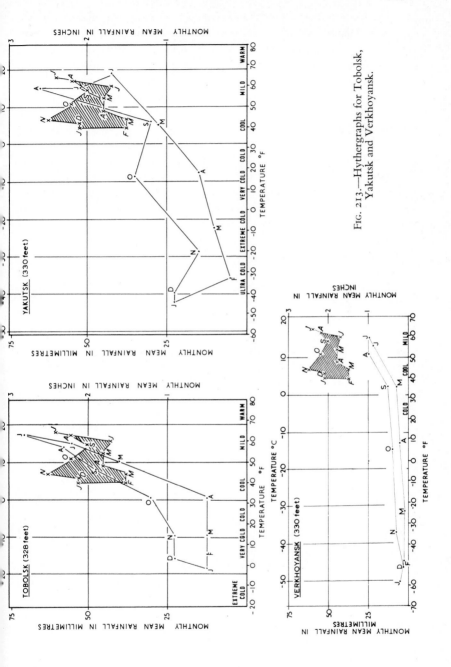

Fig. 213.—Hythergraphs for Tobolsk, Yakutsk and Verkhoyansk.

The western Siberia tundra and tayga are exposed to air masses from the remote Atlantic and from the nearer Arctic. Winters are severe, accompanied by violent gales and heavy snow storms. "The wind is so icy here that even the pine trees feel cold" (V. Inber). In eastern Siberia temperatures are lower but conditions are less disturbed; the winters are distinguished by light winds or calms and the absence of cloud and snow. Cold waves and temperature inversions are frequent and $-94°$ F ($-70°$ C) has been recorded at Oymyakon and Verkhoyansk. Rivers are frozen over for more than six months each year.

A sudden transition from the long severe winter to spring and summer conditions is characteristic. In summer the mainland is strongly heated during the day but cools quickly after sunset. Outbreaks of cold air from the Arctic Ocean are not infrequent in this season and July is the only month which is completely free from night frosts. In the high Arctic latitudes within the tundra the sun does not descend below the horizon for about three months in the warm season, and for about three months in the cold season it does not rise above it. These peculiarities of daylight introduce new concepts of such climatic phenomena as the diurnal range or the annual march of temperature (Fig. 63).

Precipitation throughout the whole of North Siberia is less than 20 in.: two-thirds comes during the summer, the remainder during the winter. Snow lies for over six months every year and attains depths of over 3 ft in the West Siberian Lowland.

The region lies within the tundra and the tayga. The soils vary from mountainous tundra soil in the northeast to turfy, marshy podzols in the western lowlands. Permafrost is widespread.

THE ECONOMY

AGRICULTURE, HUNTING, FISHING AND LUMBERING

The only region of real agricultural significance is the centre of the Yakutskaya A.S.S.R. where a quarter of a million acres of arable land are concentrated. Hardy strains of wheat, barley and rye are grown. Reindeer breeding, fur dressing, hunting and fishing are important; some 80% of all the reindeer in the Soviet Union are bred in North Siberia, especially in the Oblasts of Tyumen and Magadan and the northern part of Oblast Kamchatka (Figs. 214 and 215). Sable, ermine, squirrels and arctic fox are hunted and trapped (Fig. 216), and the lower reaches of the major rivers are fished. Whitefish and sturgeon are the main catches. Walrus and seals are present along most of the coast and there are whales in the Bering Sea. Reindeer husbandry is a non-Russian concern, carried on by people

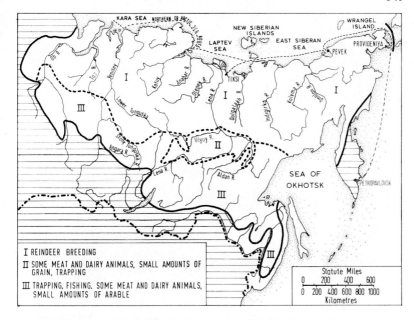

FIG. 214.—North Siberia Region: agricultural land-use regions.

[*Soviet Weekly.*

FIG. 215.—Eighty per cent of all the reindeer in the Soviet Union are bred in North Siberia, especially in the oblasts of Tyumen, Magadan and Kamchatka.

[*Fotokhronika Tass.*

Fig. 216.—For many people of North Siberia, furs constitute the main source of cash income. The Soviet Union is the world's greatest exporter of furs but excessive hunting has depleted supplies of ermine, silver fox and other valuable species. Supplies are now supplemented by fur-breeding *sovkhozy*.

such as the Nentsi and Churckchi; much the same may be said for cattle farming. The indigenous peoples also predominate in the hunting and fishing activities.

Lumbering is an important industry, but because there are more easily accessible forests elsewhere in the country, felling is restricted to river regions within the tayga. There is an important timber export trade in the Yenisey Valley where timber of good quality is found. The timber is floated to Igarka whence it is exported by way of the Northern Sea Route.

MINERAL RESOURCES

Mining is the most important industry throughout North Siberia. Some of the many mines, such as the famous Lena goldfields and the Kureyka graphite deposits were worked before the Revolution. Others have been

discovered in the last two or three decades and are important in the economy
of the Soviet Union as a whole. They contribute considerable quantities of
gold, tin, cobalt, nickel, copper, diamonds and mica (Fig. 217).

North Siberia is the major source of gold in the Soviet Union. Rich
deposits in the upper Kolyma Basin (first worked by Dal-Stroy, an organisation which was notorious as an employer of convict labour) provide
between half and three-quarters of the Soviet production; others in the

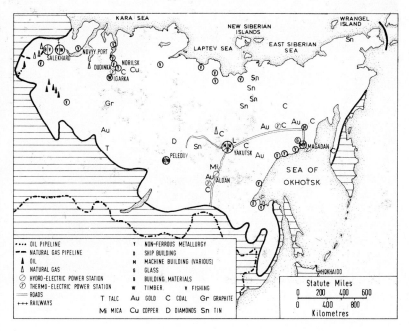

Fig. 217.—North Siberia Region: mineral and power resources and
communications.

valleys of the Aldan, Allakh-Yun and Indigirka (Yakutskaya A.S.S.R.)
contribute another fifth. Placer gold occurs in the Vitim valley (Bodaybo
area) of Oblast Irkutsk and there are further gold deposits in the upper
Yenisey valley (Verkhnyaya Tunguska) and in the Anadyr Basin (Markovo).

Native tin is in short supply, but there are two important mines at
Ege-Khaya on the Yana River and at Ryrkapya on the north coast of the
Chukchi Peninsula. The ore is concentrated at these places before being
shipped south for smelting. Nickel, cobalt, copper and platinum occur in a
large copper–nickel sulphide ore deposit at Norilsk (Fig. 218). Primary
production and smelting are carried on at Norilsk which is connected by
rail with Dudinka on the Yenisey.

FIG. 218.—Winter street scene in the copper–nickel mining and smelting town of Norilsk. The town lies well within the Arctic Circle near the mouth of the Yenisey River.

Kimberlite pipes in a tributary valley of the Vilyuy in Yakutskaya A.S.S.R. yield diamonds. Mirnyy, situated within dense tayga, was only a penal camp a decade ago, but is now the "diamond capital of Siberia" with a population of 20,000.

Natural gas which occurs at Berezovo just west of the lower Ob Valley is piped from Igrim to the north of the Ural Region. Utilisation of the oil reserves in the Ob Valley, 120–250 miles above the Ob–Irtysh confluence, is hampered by swamp and adverse climatic conditions.

TRANSPORT AND COMMUNICATIONS

Transport facilities are poor. Dirt-surfaced roads—the Aldan Highway (Amur–Yakutsk) and the Kolyma Highway (Magadan–Kolyma–Yakutsk)

[*Fotokhronika Tass.*

—link important mining centres (Fig. 217). The only railway is an 80-mile line connecting Norilsk with Dudinka. It lies within the permafrost zone (and therefore has engineering and maintenance problems) and has no connection with the national network. Other railways which will link the Ural with the Ob, and the Bodaybo goldfields with the Trans-Siberian Railway are in the planning stage. How soon they will influence the development of North Siberia remains to be seen.

The Ob, Yenisey and Lena are of limited importance for river transport because they are frozen over for long periods each year (Fig. 219). Navigation between the terminals of the Northern Sea Route (*see* Figs. 206 and 214) is limited to about two and a half months each year and requires the assistance of spotter aircraft, radar and powerful ice-breakers, such as the 25,000-ton nuclear ice-breaker *Lenin*, whose nuclear reactors are said to give enough power to grind steadily through ice which is 8 ft thick (Fig.

[*Fotokhronika Tass.*

FIG. 219.—Olekminsk, a small trading settlement on the Lena River.

220). The comparatively small amount of freight handled by ships using the Northern Sea Route includes about half a million tons of timber.

Aircraft are often the most convenient and sometimes the only way of supplying outlying settlements, although recourse is still made to the dog sledge or reindeer sledge.

POPULATION AND SETTLEMENT

The region is the most sparsely populated in the Soviet Union. Densities rarely exceed one person per square mile, except in the vicinity of the rivers in the south of the region. Only three towns, Norilsk, Yakutsk and Magadan, have populations exceeding 25,000.

Norilsk (124,000), lying 60 miles east of the Yenisey on the fringe of the tundra at latitude 69° N, is the northernmost town in the Soviet Union. It was founded in 1935 and until the mid 1950s it was one of the principal concentration camp areas for political and war prisoners. The prisoners

[*Fotokhronika Tass.*

FIG. 220.—The nuclear-powered ice-breaker *Lenin*. Technological advances which embrace well-protected and well-
equipped ships, powerful ice-breakers, radar, aircraft and
up-to-date weather reports enable the Russians to make
use of the Northern Sea Route for about 2½ months each
year during the summer.

were employed in building the town and its industries, and working in the
nickel, platinum, copper, cobalt and coal mines. Norilsk is an important
centre for the smelting of non-ferrous metals.

Yakutsk (89,000), lies within the tayga on the west bank of the Lena. It
was founded by Cossacks in 1632 during their advance through Siberia.
It is the capital of Yakutskaya A.S.S.R. It has sawmills, small engineering
works and maintenance yards for the Lena river fleet.

Magadan (79,000) on the Sea of Okhotsk is the gateway to the Kolyma
gold mining region. It has small engineering industries and a prosperous
salmon fishing industry. Year-round navigation is maintained by ice-
breakers. Magadan is notorious for its large concentration camps.

The population of all other towns and settlements in North Siberia
together totals no more than half a million. Until it has a sizeable population
and adequate up-to-date transport facilities, North Siberia will lag far

behind the fast-growing economic regions lying to the south. The Soviet Union has pursued a much more aggressive policy in the development of its northlands than has either Canada or the U.S.A., and North Siberia (together with the Northwest and North Regions) is farther ahead in numbers and size of settlements and in general exploitation of natural resources than is northern North America.

STUDY QUESTIONS

1. Map the distribution of permanently frozen ground (permafrost). Describe its physical character and its effects on agriculture, mining and transport.

2. Give a reasoned account of the geography of the basin of the Lena river.

3. Compare the North Siberia *tayga* with that of the European North Region.

4. Make a sketch-map of the Ob–Irtysh river system, and add suitable explanatory notes.

5. Examine the present day importance of the Northern Sea Route with particular reference to its economic, political and strategic effects.

6. Discuss the value of the Yenisey river system for navigation, commenting on its importance in the economic geography of the basin.

7. Outline the economic potential of the North Siberia Region and suggest ways by which it might be exploited.

8. Suggest reasons why northern agriculture is practised in the middle Lena valley.

9. Make a comparison of the exploitation of North Siberia with that of the Canadian North.

10. Compare the cool and cold deserts of the U.S.S.R. from the point of view of: (*a*) extent and shape; (*b*) their natural resources; (*c*) the modes of life of their indigenous peoples.

Part Three

THE SOVIET ECONOMY

Chapter XXX

SOVIET ECONOMIC PROGRESS[*]

In the preceding chapters reference has been made to new coal, iron and steel, petroleum, natural gas, cement, hydro-electric and other installations, and to a general expansion of heavy industry. Attention has been drawn to the mechanisation and reform of agriculture under the Soviets, to the construction and electrification of railways, the construction of waterways and irrigation canals, oil and gas pipelines, and to several other indicators of economic expansion. The expansion has taken place at a rapid pace since 1917 when the Communists secured a monopoly of power. In the half century under Communist rule the Soviet Union has been transformed from a backward agricultural country into an industrial giant capable of producing jet aircraft, hydrogen bombs, intercontinental ballistic missiles, manned space-craft, moon probes, electronic and precision instruments and consumer goods of the highest quality.

REASONS FOR ECONOMIC GROWTH

What is the explanation for this remarkable achievement in such a comparatively short space of time? How did it come about? In the first instance there are ample supplies of the basic raw materials for industry within the Union. Very often geographical locations that are inconvenient in relation to the main centres of population tend to impose a strain on the transport system but the mineral deposits that have been found are usually fairly easy to work. It would appear that the Soviet Union has unlimited quantities of coal, oil, natural gas, that iron ore is plentiful and that she is completely self-sufficient in industrial materials.

A transfer of labour from the relatively over-populated countryside to the towns has helped to swell the industrial labour force. At first, former peasants, half-trained, were poor material and were liable to produce a high proportion of spoiled work, but with the passage of time the country has acquired a fairly large and skilled labour force. There is still not enough skilled labour available in the U.S.S.R. and priority is given to supplying

---

[*] Much of this discussion derives from the works of A. Nove such as "The Pace of Soviet Economic Development" (*Lloyds Bank Review*, April 1956), *The Soviet Economy* (Allen and Unwin, 1961) and "Soviet Economic Progress" (*Lloyds Bank Review*, October 1965).

TABLE VIII

Production of selected commodities in U.S.S.R., U.S.A. and United Kingdom, 1961, 1963 and 1965

	U.S.S.R.			U.S.A.			United Kingdom		
	1961	*1963*	*1965*	*1961*	*1963*	*1965*	*1961*	*1963*	*1965*
Coal and Lignite (million tons) .	377	395	578	378	430	474	193	198	189
Petroleum (million tons) .	166	206	243	354	372	384	0·1	0·1	0·1
Natural gas (million cu. metres) . .	58·9	89·8	129	375·3	417·5	456	5·1	7·3	9·3
Electricity (million kw) .	327·6	412·4	507	881·1	1,011·4	1,157	145·9	173·6	192
Pig-iron and ferro-alloys (million tons) .	50·9	58·7	66·2	60·3	66·9	80·0	14·9	14·8	17·7
Crude steel (million tons) . .	70·7	80·2	91·0	88·9	99·1	119	22·4	22·8	27·5
Motor vehicles (thousands)									
Passenger .	149	173	202	5,544	7,632	9,100	1,044	1,608	1,922
Commercial . .	534	590	769	1,280	1,464	1,760	460	404	454
Woven cotton fabrics									

Woven woollen fabrics (million sq. metres)	454·8	450·4	465·6	262·6†	260·4†	244·8†	294·0	272·4	270·0
Woven rayon and acetate fabrics (million metres)	771·6★	921·0★	795·6★	1,344	1,584	1,632	556·8	512·4	572·0
Sulphuric acid (thousand metric tons)	5,728	6,885	8,520	16,191	18,993	24,536	2,705	2,927	3,348
Superphosphates (thousand metric tons)	6,806	7,858	12,240	11,446	11,790	12,993	665	525	445
Nitrogeneous fertilisers (thousand metric tons)	1,004·0	1,414·0	2,099·0	2,739·0	3,490·0	4,434·0	448·9	513·6	594·8
Cement (thousand metric tons)	50,864	61,018	72,396	56,718	61,609	62,448	14,377	14,059	16,968
Radio and television receivers (thousand)	6,177	7,275	8,815	23,677	25,889	33,113	4,330	4,445	3,503
Newsprint (thousand metric tons)	541	563	632·4	1,880	1,892	1,896	665	683	780

Source: U.N. Statistical Yearbook 1965 and Monthly Digest of Statistics.

★ Recorded in millions of sq. metres.   † Recorded in millions of metres.

heavy industries such as coal, engineering, ferrous and non-ferrous metal-lurgy and the oil and petro-chemical industries.

The urbanisation which accompanied the movement of people from the countryside to the towns greatly increased the consumption of industrial goods and services, which in turn led to an increase in the number of bakeries, meat-processing plant and much else besides. While not neces-sarily reflecting improved welfare for the people, urbanisation tended to expand measurable industrial growth.

Productivity per worker in many branches of industry was brought quickly to a favourable level by the borrowing of technical ideas from industrially advanced countries. In the early days of her industrialisation the Soviet Union by-passed time-consuming "trial and error processes" to which new ideas are usually subject. For instance technical assistance during the building of the huge iron and steel plant at Magnitogorsk, 1929–33, was obtained from American experts. Several foreign firms acted as consultants for the Dnieper hydro-electric station (Dneproges)—the first of the large hydro-electric stations to be built in the Soviet Union—and most of the equipment for the station was supplied by the General Electric Company (U.K.).

A further and not unimportant factor accounting for the flattering pace of Soviet industrial achievement was the low point at which the country started. For instance, Soviet output of cement in 1940 was over 300% of the 1928 figure, but the output was still only a third of the U.S.A. pro-duction in 1913. None the less, Soviet industrial growth has been more rapid than that of other countries in a comparable stage of industrialisation.

Finally, probably the most significant factor in the industrial expansion of the country has been the Soviet political system. This facilitated the concentration of resources on capital goods rather than on consumer goods in a way which would have been impossible under any democratic form of government which, to remain in office, relies on the votes of the people.

Table VIII compares the rate of progress in output in a range of products in the U.S.S.R. and includes comparable figures for the United Kingdom and the U.S.A.

THE PRESENT-DAY ECONOMY

Statistics suggest that the rapid advance has been mainly in material production rather than in any overall improvement in living standards of the population. Priority industries such as iron, steel, coal, petroleum, cement and engineering were the first to receive the largest proportion of the capital investment and they have experienced spectacular expansion.

Agriculture, in contrast, has suffered from under-investment and also a slowing down of that investment.

Here, there are material inadequacies in virtually everything from rural roads to the production of harrows. Farm workers are extremely dis-satisfied, also, with their peasant status. The effects of vagaries in the weather constitute an ever-present hazard to their conditions. Agricultural plans have hardly ever been fulfilled and growth had virtually ceased even before the disastrous drought of 1963 which resulted in a decline of some 25% in the country's wheat production. The magnitude of the subsequent

TABLE IX

Soviet Union: Changes in economic growth, 1954–64 (after Nove)

(*Per cent increase over previous year*)

	National income*	Gross industrial production	Gross agricultural production
1954	12	13	5
1955	12	12	11
1956	11	11	13·5
1957	7	10	2
1958	12	10	10·5
1959	8	11	0·5
1960	8	10	2·5
1961	7	9	2·5
1962	6	9·5	1·5
1963	4	8	−7
1964	7	7	12

* Soviet definition, i.e. material goods only; it includes construction, and also transport of and trade in goods.

Soviet wheat purchases from the U.S.A., Canada and Australia strongly suggested that the 1963 drought was merely the culminating disaster in a long succession of failures on the agricultural front. By 1964 the U.S.S.R. had contracted for the supply of over 10 million tons of Western wheat. Grain production dropped again in 1965. Because of the lag in agricultural production, food and many light industries have fallen short of their targets.

The statistics in Table IX, based on Soviet official statistics, suggest that Soviet economic growth is now showing a tendency to slow down. With the exception of the war-affected years (1939–45) the increases in industrial output in 1963 and 1964 represent the lowest officially reported growth-rates for any years since 1933. Year-by-year fluctuations in agricultural output due to the weather affect the growth in national income. The relatively high 1964 figure was due to the big increase in the harvest fol-lowing the disastrous year 1963 when large sums of gold and dollars were spent to buy foreign wheat. The downward trend, however, is unmistakeable.

Reasons suggested by foreign observers for the slowing down of Soviet economic growth are usually related to a sharp rise in military expenditure, combined with a scarcity of male labour (even though those born post-war at a time of increased birth rates are now entering employment), with a reduction in the length of the working week, and with increased purchasing power and a higher consumption of consumer goods. The changed political climate since 1964 (when Khrushchev was replaced by the Brezhnev–Kosygin leadership), a general rise in investments in industry and agriculture, and reform in the economic planning system to allow for the introduction of a profit motive into some industries (profits will belong to the state and not to the management) may result in renewed expansion of the economy.

Statistical data relating to industrial output and growth reflect material production in the Soviet Union (*see* Appendix 2), but they do not necessarily reflect any rise in the overall standard of living of the Soviet population. Living standards have not risen commensurate with the industrialisation of the country; for the bulk of the population they are still far below those of industrialised nations in the West. Some consumer goods are still in short supply in the Soviet Union and the quality of others is low. There is a shortage of adequate living accommodation in most towns and there is chronic residential overcrowding. Good roads are all too few and rural roads are in a very bad state. Farms may be cut off from their neighbours and from the outside world for months on end during the traditional Russian spring and autumn *bezdorozhye* (roadlessness). Private transport is almost non-existent. The Italian Fiat motor company and the French Renault motor company have been invited (1966) to build a plant and to reorganise antiquated car-production plant in the Soviet Union. Planned production of up to 800,000 cars a year by 1970, i.e. about four times the current output, should take the Soviet Union into the age of the private car.

The Soviet government spent more money on consumer goods and on public services than on industry during the last year of the Seven-Year Plan 1959–65. Directives for the Five-Year Plan 1966–70 envisage a 50% increase in industrial production and a 25% increase in agricultural production (30% in the case of cereals). "The absolute growth of the consumption fund, i.e. the sum-total of the material wealth going for consumption by the people, will be 70% greater in the present five-year period than in the preceding five years" (from the speech by Kosygin to the 23rd Congress of the Communist Party of the Soviet Union, Moscow, April 4, 1966). It appears that the Soviet government is now committed to a consumer-orientated economy and that the new society which has emerged in the Soviet Union—the product of Soviet technical and economic evolution —is destined to enjoy an improvement in living standards denied to the earlier generations in that country.

1. "In contrast to the rapid expansion of Soviet industry, Soviet agriculture has been relatively stagnant." Expand this statement.

2. Critically examine the degree of economic self-sufficiency possible to the U.S.S.R.

3. Compare the achievements and importance of (a) power supplies, (b) iron and steel production, (c) the motor-car industry, (d) agriculture, in the following: the U.S.S.R., the U.S.A., the E.E.C. and the United Kingdom.

4. What do you understand by Soviet planning?

5. What have been the major economic achievements of the Soviet Union in the post World War II period?

6. Compare the economic problems facing the Soviet Union with those confronting (a) the European Economic Community, (b) the U.S.A., (c) the United Kingdom.

PHYSICAL–GEOGRAPHICAL REGIONALISATION

FIGURE 221, based on Plates 248–9 of the *Physical–Geographical Atlas of the World* (Moscow, 1964), presents a synthesis of the several aspects of the physical environment of the Soviet Union (Chapters II–IV). The regions are based on "the principal patterns of distribution and development of natural complexes, as determined by their latitudinal and elevational position on the continent, and within the system of atmospheric circulation, relief and geological structure, the effect of man's activities, and other causes."

On that basis the U.S.S.R. has been divided into "natural countries" (I, II, etc.) and "provinces" (1, 2, etc.). By a natural country is meant part of a continent with a unity of geological–geomorphological structure and atmospheric circulation characteristics related to its geographical location. Major relief features and conditions of climate formation determine the composition, character and degree of distinctiveness of latitudinal natural zones in the plains, and of vertical zones in the mountains. A natural province is part of a country, and is distinguished mainly by the combination of bio-climatic characteristics and the character of the relief. Provinces are grouped in the plains according to zonal criteria, and in mountains according to the character of vertical zonality.

The regions are described as follows:

I. Fennoscandia

    1. Murman dissected coastal tundra plateau
    2. Kola north-tayga and mountain-tundra low mountains
    3. White Sea hill-and-ridge north-tayga lake lowland
    4. West Karelian north-tayga upland
    5. South Karelian middle-tayga hill-and-selga (ridge) plain

II. East European plain

    1. Arctic platform archipelago of plateau-like islands of Franz Josef Land with ice sheet and Arctic desert
    2. Timan–Kanin tundra plain with low residual mountains
    3. Northeast hilly tundra maritime plain
    4. Bolshezemelskaya moraine-hill wooded-tundra plain
    5. Dvina–Mezen north-tayga plain, dissected by broad valley-like depressions
    6. North-tayga Timan ridge
    7. Pechora north-tayga lowland with extensive swamps
    8. Onega moraine-hill middle-tayga plain with flat, swampy watersheds
    9. Dvina–Vychegda middle-tayga plain with flat swampy watersheds and broad valley-like depressions
   10. Middle-tayga Timan ridge
   11. Pechora middle-tayga upland plain
   12. Baltic moraine-hill lake plain with mixed forest

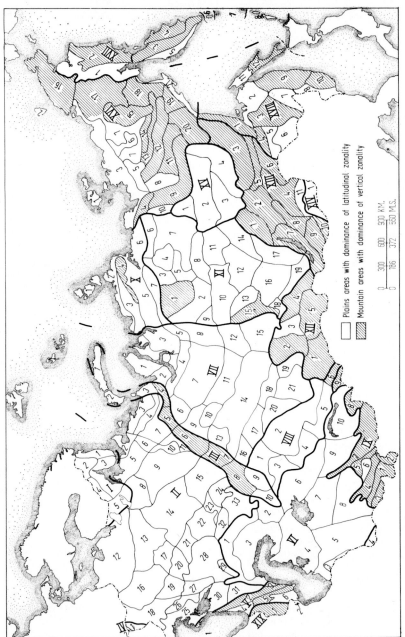

FIG. 221.—Soviet Union: physical–geographical regions. The key to the regional divisions is in Appendix 1.

13. Valday–Smolensk–Moscow upland with moraine hills and mixed forest
14. Upper Volga plain with swampy lowlands in mixed-forest zone
15. Vyatka–Kama south-tayga upland plain
16. Swampy outwash plain of the Polesye with pine-broad-leaved forest
17. North of Middle Russian upland with broad-leaved and coniferous sub-tayga forest
18. Volhynian–Podolian wooded-steppe upland with broad-leaved forest
19. Dnieper low wooded-steppe plain
20. Middle Russian wooded-steppe upland, dissected by gullying
21. Oka–Don (Tambov) wooded-steppe alluvial plain
22. Volga wooded-steppe upland, dissected by gullying
23. Trans-Volga wooded-steppe alluvial low plain
24. Trans-Volga high wooded steppe, dissected by gullying
25. Black Sea steppe low plain
26. Dnieper steppe upland
27. Donets ridge, rolling steppe plateau with islands of wooded steppe replacing eroded mountain massif
28. Don–Volga steppe elevated dissected plain
29. Yergeni dry-steppe upland
30. Kuban steppe plain
31. Stavropol steppe upland, plateau-like dome-shaped uplift, and northern foothills of Caucasus
32. Trans-Volga steppe alluvial low plain
33. Trans-Volga steppe *syrt* uplands

III. Ural–Novaya Zemlya country
1. Middle-elevation mountains of Novaya Zemlya north island with extensive ice sheets and Arctic tundra
2. Arctic-tundra low mountains and hilly plains of the south of Novaya Zemlya
3. Pay-Khoy residual hilly tundra upland
4. Polar Ural, middle-elevation mountains with alpine relief forms and denuded-summit tundra vegetation
5. Sub-polar Ural with alpine relief forms and north-tayga forest at its foot
6. Middle-elevation Northern Ural with middle-tayga forest at foot
7. Low-mountain and hill-ridge south-tayga Middle Ural
8. Wooded-steppe South Ural with mountain-tayga slopes and alpine meadows on summits
9. Trans-Ural steppe peneplaned plain
10. Mugodzhar desert-steppe residual upland

IV. Alpine–Carpathian country
1. Middle-elevation Carpaths with coniferous-broad-leaved forests on slopes and steppe summits
2. Trans-Carpathian plain with broad-leaved forests

V. Crimean–Caucasian country
1. Mountain Crimea with mountain forest on slopes and steppe summits
2. Mountain ranges of North Caucasus with steppe at foot, mixed forest on slopes, alpine meadows and glaciers
3. Dagestan mountain desert

4. West Caucasus province of humid sub-tropical forest
5. East Trans-Caucasian province of sub-tropical dry forest and steppe
6. Kura lowland with sub-tropical steppe and dry forest

VI. Caspian–Turanian country
   1. Caspian semi-desert low plain
   2. Ural–Emba semi-desert upland
   3. Caspian desert lowland
   4. Trans-Caspian desert plateau
   5. Kara-Kum sandy desert plain
   6. North Aral sand-and-clay semi-desert plain
   7. Kyzyl-Kum sandy desert plain
   8. Kyzyl-Kum residual desert plain
   9. Desert plains of Betpak-Dala and Muyunkum
  10. Balkhash sandy desert plain

VII. West Siberian country
   1. Yamal–Gydan flat tundra lake lowland
   2. Yamal–Taz rolling and hilly tundra lake plain
   3. Gydan–Yenisey hill-ridge tundra plain
   4. Ob–Taz rolling wooded-tundra plain
   5. Turukhan lake-hill moraine wooded-tundra plain
   6. Ob–Lyapin dissected elevated plain with northern-tayga forests and swamp
   7. Kazym–Pur rolling swampy north-tayga lake plain
   8. Taz–Yenisey moraine-hill elevated north-tayga plain
   9. Konda–Sosva middle-tayga elevated plain
  10. Konda swampy middle-tayga lake plain
  11. Ob middle-tayga lowland
  12. Ket–Yenisey middle-tayga elevated plain
  13. Tura swampy south-tayga plain
  14. Tobol–Vasyugan swampy south-tayga lake plain
  15. Ket–Chulym slightly swampy south-tayga elevated plain
  16. Kurgan wooded-steppe plain
  17. Ishim wooded-steppe lake plain
  18. Baraba ridge-and-vale wooded-steppe lake plain
  19. Ob ridge-and-vale wooded-steppe plain
  20. Irtysh elevated steppe plain with deep lake depressions
  21. Kulunda steppe plain with vales and basins

VIII. Kazakh hill lands
   1. Turgay steppe tabular upland
   2. Kazakh hill-land steppe
   3. Turgay semi-desert low plain
   4. Dzhezkazgan semi-desert hill upland
   5. Kazakh hill-land semi-desert
   6. Zaisan semi-desert basin

IX. Mountains of Central Asia
   1. High ranges of Tadzhikistan with vertical zonation from semi-desert to alpine meadows and eternal snows
   2. Desert highland of East Pamir

3. South Tadzhikistan desert middle mountains
4. South Tyan-Shan ranges with dominance of desert vegetation
5. West Tyan-Shan ranges with dominance of mountain steppe and islands of forest on slopes
6. Fergana desert-and-steppe basin
7. High mountains of North Tyan-Shan with flat-topped *syrt* summits, forest belts on outer (northern) slopes and steppe on inner slopes
8. Dzhungarian *syrt* highland with vertical zonation from desert to alpine meadows
9. Tarbagatay middle mountains with adjoining desert piedmont

X. Taymyr–Severnaya Zemlya country
1. Severnaya Zemlya archipelago, low-mountain Arctic-desert plateau with ice sheets
2. North Taymyr Arctic-tundra ridge plain
3. Taymyr Arctic-tundra elevated plain
4. Low-mountain, flat-topped Arctic-tundra Byrranga range
5. Pyasina–Khatanga lake-hill tundra lowland
6. Anabar–Olenek tundra ridge plain
7. Kheta lake-hill wooded-tundra plain

XI. Middle Siberian plateau
1. Middle-elevation mountain-tundra Putorana trap plateau
2. Vivi–Tutonchana open woodland tundra trap plateau with north-tayga forest in valleys
3. North Anabar mountain-tundra plateau with open north-tayga woodland on slopes
4. Anabar denuded summit, open woodland tableland
5. Moiero–Kotui lake basin
6. Anabar–Olenek residual plateau with open woodland
7. Olenek limestone plateau with open woodland
8. Olenek–Vilyuy north-tayga ridge plateau
9. Yenisey north-tayga trap plateau with denuded summits
10. Middle Tunguska middle-tayga plateau
11. Upper Vilyuy low middle-tayga plateau
12. Upper Tunguska dissected plateau with middle-tayga forest
13. Velmo–Kamo low plateau with middle-tayga larch and dark-coniferous mountain-tayga forest
14. Lena–Tunguska heavily dissected plateau with larch-pine and dark coniferous forest
15. Middle-elevation Yenisey ridge with dark-coniferous mountain-tayga forest
16. Middle Angara lightly dissected plateau with larch-pine and dark-coniferous forest
17. Upper Lena elevated plateau with south-tayga larch, larch-pine and dark-coniferous mountain-tayga forest
18. Krasnoyarsk–Kansk rolling wooded-steppe plain
19. Irkutsk–Balagansk rolling wooded-steppe plain

XII. Altay–Sayan mountains
1. Altay mountains with denuded summits, tayga and alpine meadow on slopes and steppe in depressions

2. Kuznetsk–Salair middle mountains with steppe depressions and dark-coniferous mountain-tayga forest
3. Minusinsk wooded-steppe basin
4. Sayan denuded summit and tayga highland
5. Tuva highland with denuded summits, dark-coniferous mountain-tayga and stone pine-and-larch forests on mountain ranges and steppe and semi-desert intermontane basins

XIII. Baykal country

1. Patom–North Baykal highland with mountain-larch forest on slopes and denuded summits
2. Stanovoy highland with mountain tayga and denuded summits
3. Aldan tableland with denuded summits and mountain-larch forest
4. Olekminsk highland with middle-tayga forest and open woodland below denuded summits
5. Stanovoy middle-elevation mountain-tayga range with mountain-larch forest and mountain tundra
6. Upper Zeya middle mountains with middle-tayga larch forest and *mari* (hillocky forest swamps)
7. Baykal highland with denuded summits and tayga vegetation, meadow-bog and steppe basins
8. Vitim mountain-tayga tableland with meadow-bog basins
9. Selenga middle mountains with south-tayga forest on slopes and steppe basins
10. Henteyn–Chikoy highland with South Siberian mountain larch forest
11. Chita wooded-steppe middle mountains

XIV. Daurian country

1. Daurian high steppe plain

XV. Yakutian basin

1. Lower Lena north-tayga plain
2. Lena–Vilyuy forest-meadow middle-tayga lake plain with sections of meadow steppe on permafrost
3. Middle Lena middle-tayga sloping plain
4. Aldan–Amga gently rolling middle-tayga plain with occasional meadows

XVI. Northeast Siberia

1. Archipelago of low Arctic-desert New Siberian Islands
2. Low-mountain, Arctic-tundra Wrangel Island
3. Yana–Kolyma maritime tundra lowland
4. Low-mountain tundra Chekanovskiy and Kharaulakh ranges
5. Deputatskiy chain, a system of low mountain massifs with wooded tundra open woodland
6. Alazeya rolling tableland with denuded summits and wooded tundra
7. Indigirka–Kolyma lake lowland with open larch woodland
8. Yana tundra and open woodland plateau
9. Verkhoyansk mountain system with denuded summits and open woodland slopes

10. Lower Lena lowland with floodplain meadows and open larch woodland
11. Yana–Oymyakon tundra and open woodland tableland
12. Cherskiy high-mountain system with denuded summits and open larch woodland on slopes
13. Momsk–Seimchan system of depressions separated by mountain ranges with open larch woodland
14. Momsk high-mountain ranges with denuded summits
15. Yukagir tundra-larch open woodland tableland
16. Chukchi tundra highland
17. Anadyr–Anyui mountain-tundra highland
18. Upper Kolyma tundra and open woodland highland with dwarf stone-pine growths
19. Magadan tundra and north-tayga highland with dwarf stone-pine
20. Suntar–Khayata denuded summit highland
21. Okhotsk mountain and hill-and-plains coast with open larch woodland and sections of wooded tundra

XVII. Kamchatka–Kurile country

1. Anadyr–Penzhina tundra lowland with residual mountains
2. Koryak tundra and denuded summit mountain group with dwarf alder and stone-pine
3. Kamchatka tundra-and-forest middle-elevation inner range
4. East Kamchatka volcanic province with mountain-tundra volcanic massifs and plains occupied by larch forest and Erman's birch
5. West Kamchatka meadow and forest plain with sphagnum bogs and Erman's birch growths
6. Kommandor and North Kurile volcanic islands with Erman's birch and sub-arctic grass vegetation
7. Middle Kurile volcanic islands with dwarf stone pine and heath and lichen-covered rock waste
8. South Kurile volcanic islands with vertical zonation from broad-leaved forest to lichen-covered summits

XVIII. Amur-Maritime country

1. Dzhugdzhur maritime province with mountain-tayga larch and dark-coniferous forests and denuded summits
2. Low-mountain middle-tayga ranges of the lower Amur and Amgun Rivers
3. Bureya–Khingan middle mountains with denuded summits, mountain tayga dark-coniferous and larch forests
4. Tukuringra–Dzhagdy range with south-tayga larch forest and *mari* (hillocky forest swamps), mountain larch and dark-coniferous forests
5. Amur–Zeya south-tayga plain with larch forest
6. Amur plain with grassy coniferous-broad-leaved forest and wooded steppe
7. Lower Amur swampy meadow and forest plain
8. Ussuri–Khanka plain with broad-leaved grassy forests and meadow steppe
9. Northern Sikhote-Alin with coniferous forest in lower zone
10. Southern Sikhote-Alin with coniferous-broad-leaved forest in lower zone
11. North Sakhalin middle-tayga plain with light-coniferous forest
12. Middle-mountainous South Sakhalin with coniferous forest and open woodlands of Erman's birch

XIX. West Asian highlands
    1. Armenian volcanic steppe highlands with mountain broad-leaved forests, alpine
       meadows. Xerophilic open woodlands and deserts in intermontane basins
    2. Talysh mountains with sub-tropical mountain-broad-leaved forest
    3. Kopet-Dag mountain steppe and desert middle mountains
    4. Badkhyz–Karabil desert-steppe upland

SOVIET AND WORLD PRODUCTION DATA

SOME comparisons between the Soviet Union, the United States of America, the United Kingdom and the European Economic Community (Belgium, France, Germany, Italy, Luxembourg and the Netherlands).

	U.S.S.R.	U.S.A.	U.K.	European Community
Area (thousand sq. ml.) .	8,600	3,600	94	449
Population 1965 (millions)	230·6	194·6	54·6	181·6
Active working population, 1965 (millions) .	104·0	75·6	25·7	74·7
Steel production, 1965 (millions of metric tons)	91	123	27	86
Steel consumption per head of population, 1965 (kilograms) . .	395	671	437	384
Gross energy consumption per head of population, 1965 (metric tons, coal equivalent) . . .	3·8	9·2	5·4	3·4
Grain production, average 1963–65 (millions of metric tons) . .	126·7	160·7	11·9	59·2
Meat production, average 1963–65 (millions of metric tons) . .	8·3	20·4	2·4	9·8
Milk production, average 1963–65 (millions of metric tons) . .	63·3	59·4	13·4	67·7
Motor car production, 1965 (millions) . .	0·2	9·34	1·72	5·44
Imports from rest of world, 1965 ($ millions)	8,054	21,282	16,138	28,562
Exports from rest of world, 1965 ($ millions)	8,166	27,003	13,710	27,079
Gold and dollar reserves, end-1966 ($ millions) .	2,000*	14,370	3,100	20,191

* End of 1964.

Source: European Community Information Service.

(FIGS. 222–8 adapted from *European Community—The Facts* by permission of the European Community Information Service.)

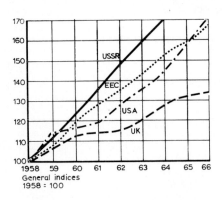

FIG. 222.—Trends in industrial production in the Soviet Union compared with those in the U.S.A., U.K. and E.E.C., 1958–66.

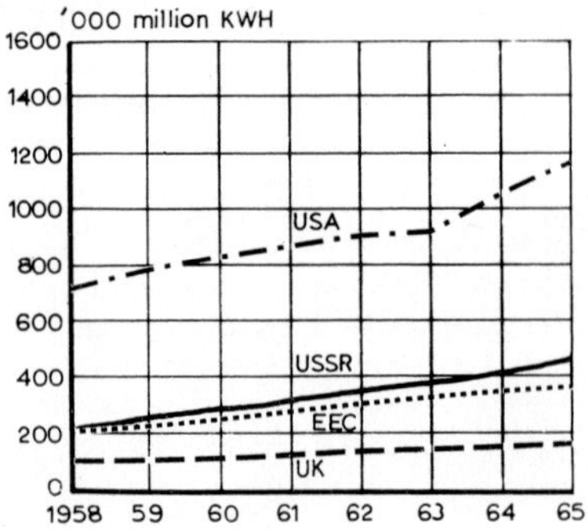

FIG. 223.—Electricity output in the Soviet Union compared with that in the U.S.A., U.K. and E.E.C., 1958–65.

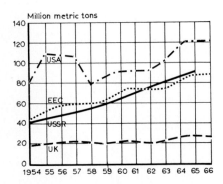

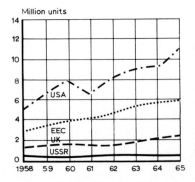

FIG. 224.—Crude steel production in the Soviet Union compared with that in the U.S.A., U.K. and E.E.C., 1954–66.

FIG. 225.—Motor vehicle production (all types, except tractors) in the Soviet Union compared with that in the U.S.A., U.K. and E.E.C., 1958–65.

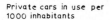
Private cars in use per 1000 inhabitants

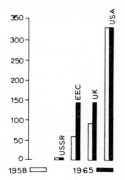

FIG. 226.—Car ownership (private cars in use per 1000 inhabitants) in the Soviet Union compared with that in the U.S.A., U.K. and E.E.C., 1958 and 1965.

FIG. 227.—Imports into the Soviet Union compared with imports into the U.S.A., U.K. and E.E.C., 1958–66.

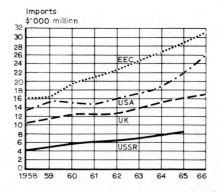

FIG. 228.—Exports from the Soviet Union compared with exports from the U.S.A., U.K. and E.E.C., 1958–66.

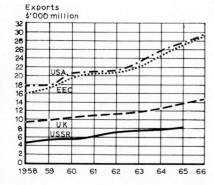

N 2

WORLD PRODUCTION DATA FOR SELECTED COMMODITIES

Unless otherwise stated all figures are in thousand metric tons for the year 1963 (1 metric ton = 0·984206 long ton)

Source: *The Geographical Digest 1966*, George Philip, London.

Coal

World	1,929,000
U.S.A. . . .	430,450
U.S.S.R. . .	395,129
China . . .	270,000
U.K. . . .	198,936
West Germany .	142,786

Crude petroleum

World	1,303,500
U.S.A. . . .	372,001
U.S.S.R. . .	206,070
Venezuela . .	169,671
Kuwait . . .	97,202
Saudi Arabia . .	81,049

Natural gas (million cu. metres)

U.S.A. . . .	417,581
U.S.S.R. . .	89,824
Canada . . .	31,581
Rumania . . .	14,548
Mexico . . .	11,371
Italy . . .	7,265

Iron ore (Fe content)

World (excl. China) . .	250,600
U.S.S.R. . .	79,460
U.S.A. . . .	41,542
China . . .	20,000
France . . .	18,812
Canada . . .	15,036

Pig iron and ferro-alloys

World . . .	281,000
U.S.A. . . .	66,998
U.S.S.R. . .	58,700
West Germany .	22,909
Japan . . .	20,434

Crude steel

World . . .	386,000
U.S.A. . . .	99,120
U.S.S.R. . .	80,198
West Germany .	31,597
Japan . . .	31,501

Bauxite

Jamaica	7,078
U.S.S.R. . .	4,300
Surinam . . .	3,508
British Guiana (now Guyana)	2,861
France . . .	2,005

Copper ore (Cu content)

U.S.A. . . .	1,100·6
Chile . . .	724·9
U.S.S.R. . .	700·0
Zambia . . .	588·1
Canada . . .	410·6

Lead ore (Pb content)

Australia .	. . .	416·9
U.S.S.R.	. . .	360·0
U.S.A. .	. .	229·9
Mexico .	. . .	190·0
Peru (1962)	. .	187·4

Zinc ore (Zn content)

U.S.A. .	. . .	480·1
Canada .	. . .	451·0
U.S.S.R.	. . .	410·0
Australia	. . .	357·1
Peru	. . .	289·1

Phosphate rock

U.S.A. .	. . .	20,153
U.S.S.R.	. . .	11,100
Morocco	. . .	8,549
Tunisia .	. . .	2,365
Nauru Is. (1962)	. .	1,566

Potash (KLO content)

U.S.A. .	. . .	2,599
West Germany	. .	2,283
France .	. . .	1,915
East Germany .	. .	1,845
U.S.S.R.	. . .	1,700

Gold (kilogrammes)

S. Africa .	. . .	853,655
U.S.S.R.	. . .	328,125
Canada .	. . .	123,534
U.S.A. .	. . .	45,683
Australia .	. . .	31,707

Salt (rock, brine, evaporated)

U.S.A. .	. . .	27,800
China .	. . .	10,500
U.S.S.R.	. . .	9,560
U.K. .	. . .	6,495
West Germany	. .	6,181

Nickel ore (Ni content)

		metric tons
Canada .	. . .	196,886
U.S.S.R.	. . .	80,000
New Caledonia	. .	45,000
Cuba .	. . .	16,700
U.S.A. .	. . .	12,792
Finland .	. . .	4,168

Manganese ore (Mn content)

U.S.S.R.	. . .	3,000·0
South Africa .	. .	567·6
Brazil (1962)	. .	515·1
India	. . .	510·0
Gabon .	. .	318·3
China .	. . .	300·0

Wheat

U.S.S.R.	. . .	70,778
China (1959)	. .	31,294
U.S.A. .	. . .	31,080
Canada .	. . .	19,689
India	. . .	10,829

Maize (corn)

U.S.A. .	. .	103,933
U.S.S.R.	. . .	23,461
China (1957)	. .	21,440
Brazil .	. . .	7,700
Mexico .	. . .	6,424

Sugar beet

U.S.S.R.	. . .	43,000
U.S.A. .	. . .	21,163
West Germany	. .	12,707
France .	. . .	12,502
Poland .	. . .	10,661

Barley

U.S.S.R.	. . .	19,500
U.S.A. .	. . .	8,831
France .	. . .	7,384
U.K. .	. . .	6,705
Canada .	. . .	4,804

Rye

U.S.S.R. (winter rye)	.	17,000
Poland .	. . .	7,124
West Germany	. .	3,239
East Germany .	. .	1,675
Turkey .	. . .	900

Potatoes

U.S.S.R.	. . .	67,499
Poland .	. . .	44,868
West Germany	. .	25,812
France .	. . .	15,974
East Germany .	. .	12,886

	Wool			*Cotton* (Lint)	
Australia	809		U.S.A.	3,339
U.S.S.R.	371		China (1959)	2,410
New Zealand	279		**U.S.S.R.**	1,756
Argentina	179		India	979
South Africa	146			

Flax (Fibre)

U.S.S.R.	432·0
France	71·7
Poland	51·7
Belgium	39·6
Netherlands	33·8

CONVERSIONS

Temperature

°F	°C	°F	°C	°F	°C	°F	°C
100	37·8	55	12·8	10	−12·2	−35	−37·2
95	35·0	50	10·0	5	−15·0	−40	−40·0
90	32·2	45	7·2	0	−17·8	−45	−42·8
85	29·4	40	4·4	−5	−20·6	−50	−45·6
80	26·7	35	1·7	−10	−23·3	−55	−48·3
75	23·9	30	−1·1	−15	−26·1	−60	−51·1
70	21·1	25	−3·9	−20	−28·9	−65	−53·9
65	18·3	20	−6·7	−25	−31·7	−70	−56·7
60	15·6	15	−9·4	−30	−34·4	−75	−59·4

Precipitation

in.	mm	in.	mm	in.	mm	in.	mm
60	1524·0	20	508·0	4	101·6	0·5	12·7
55	1397·0	15	381·0	3	76·2	0·4	10·2
50	1270·0	10	254·0	2	50·8	0·3	7·6
45	1143·0	9	228·6	1	25·4	0·2	5·1
40	1016·0	8	203·2	0·9	22·9	0·1	2·5
35	889·0	7	177·8	0·8	20·3	0·05	1·3
30	762·0	6	152·4	0·7	17·8		
25	635·0	5	127·0	0·6	15·2		

Distances

mile	km	km	mile
1	1·609	1	0·62
10	16·1	10	6·2
15	24·1	15	9·3
20	32·2	20	12·4
25	40·2	25	15·5
30	48·3	30	18·6
35	56·3	35	21·7
40	64·4	40	24·9
45	72·4	45	28·0
50	80·5	50	31·1

Areas

1 acre = 0·404 hectares
1 hectare = 2·471 acres
1 sq. mile = 2·589 sq. kms
1 sq. km = 0·386 sq. miles

GLOSSARY

Afganets	Southwest wind in Middle Asia
Barkhan	Sand dune, usually with a crescentic plan
Basseyn	Basin. Abbreviated to -*bass*, as in Donbass
Batraki	Landless workers
Biednyaki	Poor peasants
Bolsheviks (bolshinstvo)	Majority
Buran	Snowstorm
Chernozem	Fertile black soil
Comecon	The body responsible for the co-ordination of economic development in the Soviet Union and the communist block of Eastern Europe
Dolina	Valley
Gavan	Harbour
Glint	North-facing escarpment near the coast of the Gulf of Finland
Gora	Mountain
Gorny	Baykal area wind
Gorod (grad)	Town
Gryada	Ridge
Harmsil (Turk)	Hot dry wind of Middle Asia (cf. sukhovey)
Izba	Log hut
Karakul	Breed of sheep
Kazaki	Cossacks
Khata	Frame huts, adobe-filled
Khrebet	Mountain range
Kolkhoz	Collective farm
Kolkhoznik	Worker on a collective farm
Kombinat	Industrial complex
Kray	Territory; large, sparsely populated, administrative-area, usually in Siberia
Kreml (Kremlin)	Fort
Kulak	Prosperous peasant
Kum (Turk)	Sand
Loess	Fine-textured loam, greyish yellow in colour
Makhorka	Low-grade tobacco
Mensheviks (menshinstvo)	Minority
Mir	Village communes
More	Sea
Mys	Cape
Neft	Petroleum

Nizhniy	Lower
Nizmennost	Lowland
Novy (novaya)	New
Oblast	Province; large administrative area
Okrug	District: low-status administrative area
Ostrov	Island
Ottepel	Unseasonal warm spell (temporary thaw) during winter cold
Ovrag	Erosion gulley
Ozero	Lake
Podzol	Infertile acid soil, ash-grey in colour, beneath boreal forest
Polesye	Forested land (lit. "land of forest clearing"): broad marshy depression in Belorussia. In English called Pripet or Pripyat Marshes
Povolzhye	Lands along the middle and lower Volga
Prospect	Avenue
Purga	Arctic blizzard
Ravnina	Plain
Rayon	Area; lowest status administrative unit
Rasputitsa	Spring thaw (literally traffic stoppage), slush
Reka	River
Sarma	Baykal area wind (cf. gorny)
Serednyaki	Medium-placed peasants
Serozem	Grey soil of desert and semi-desert areas
Severnyy	Lower
Solonchak	Saline soil, salt marsh
Solonets	Alkali soil. Soil leached of soluble salts except sodium
Sovkhoz	State farm
Sredniy	Central
Step	Dry grassland
Sukhovey	Hot dry south or southeast wind in steppe-lands
Takyr	Clay flats
Tau (Turk)	Mountain
Tayga	Boreal forest
Travopolye	Grass-arable (ley) system of agriculture
Tundra	Treeless sub-polar vegetation zone
Ulitsa	Street
Ustye	Estuary
Velikiy	Great
Verkhniy	Upper, higher
Vechnaya merzlota	Permanently frozen ground, permafrost
Vozvyshennost	Upland
Yurta	Felt tent
Yuzhnyy	Southern
Zavolzhye	Trans-Volga lands, i.e. to the east
Zemlya	Land, earth

SHORT GUIDE TO FURTHER READING

(English references only)

BOOKS

Armstrong, T. E. *The Russians in the Arctic*. London: Methuen, 1958.
Armstrong, T. E. *The Northern Sea Route*. Cambridge: Sp. Pub. S.P.R.I., 1952.
Armstrong, T. E. *Russian Settlement in the North*. London: Cambridge U.P., 1966.
Baird, Patrick D. *The Polar World*. London: Longmans, 1964.
Balzak, S. S., Vasyutin, V. F. and Feigin, Ya. G. *Economic Geography of the U.S.S.R.* New York: Macmillan, 1949. Translated from the Russian, originally published in 1940.
Baransky, N. N. *Economic Geography of the U.S.S.R.* Moscow: Foreign Languages Publishing House, 1956.
Berg, L. S. *The Natural Regions of the U.S.S.R.* New York: Macmillan, 1950. Translated from the Russian.
Borisov, A. A. *Climates of the U.S.S.R.* Edinburgh and London: Oliver & Boyd, 1965. Translated from the second Russian edition of 1959, by R. A. Ledward and edited by Cyril A. Halstead.
Cole, J. P. and German, F. C. *A Geography of the U.S.S.R.: The Background to a Planned Economy*. London: Butterworth, 1961.
Crankshaw, Edward. *Krushchev's Russia*. London: Penguin Books (rev. edn.), 1962.
Cressey, George B. *Soviet Potentials: A Geographical Appraisal*. Syracuse U.P. N.Y.: Syracuse U.P., 1962.
East, W. Gordon. *The Soviet Union*. Searchlight Book, No. 15. Princeton, New Jersey: D. Van Nostrand, 1963.
East, W. Gordon and Moodie, Arthur E. (eds.). *The Changing World*. London: Harrap & Co., 1956. (Chapters on The U.S.S.R. by W. Gordon East and Theodore Shabad.)
East, W. Gordon, and Spate, O. H. K. (eds.). *The Changing Map of Asia: A Political Geography*. 4th edn. New York: Dutton. London: Methuen, 1961. (Chapter 6 deals with the Asiatic U.S.S.R.)
Ginsberg, N. (ed.). *The Pattern of Asia*. London: Prentice-Hall, 1958. (Chapters 38 and 39.)
Gregory, J. S., and Shave, D. W. *The U.S.S.R.: A Geographical Survey*. London: Harrap, 1945.
Gunther, J. *Inside Russia Today*. London: Hamish Hamilton, 1958.
Hodgkins, J. A. *Soviet Power: Energy Resources, Production and Potentials*. London: Prentice-Hall International, 1961.
Hoffman, George W. (ed.). *A Geography of Europe, including the Asiatic U.S.S.R.* 2nd edn. New York: Ronald Press, 1961. (Chapter 9 by Theodore Shabad, "The Soviet Union," pp. 638–728.)

Hooson, David J. M. *A New Soviet Heartland.* Searchlight Book, No. 21. Princeton, New Jersey: D. Van. Nostrand, 1964.

Hooson, David J. M. *The Soviet Union.* London: Univ. of London Press, 1966.

Jorré, Georges. *The Soviet Union: The Land and its People.* 2nd edn. London: Longmans, 1961. Translated from the French and revised by E. D. Laborde.

Lorimer, F. *The Population of the Soviet Union: History and Prospects.* Geneva: League of Nations, 1946.

Lydolph, P. E. *Geography of the U.S.S.R.* London: Wiley, 1964.

Mellor, Roy E. H. *Geography of the U.S.S.R.* London: Macmillan, 1964.

Mikhailov, N.; and Pokshishersky, V. *Soviet Russia: The Land and its Peoples.* New York: Sheridan, 1948.

Mirov, N. T. *Geography of Russia.* New York: Wiley, 1951.

Nove, A. *The Soviet Economy.* Allen & Unwin, 1961.

Shabad, Theodore. *Geography of the U.S.S.R.: A Regional Survey.* New York: Columbia U.P., 1951.

Suslov, S. P. *Physical Geography of Asiatic Russia.* San Francisco: W. H. Freeman, 1961. Translated from the Russian.

Thiel, E. *The Soviet Far East: A Survey of its Physical and Economic Geography.* London: Methuen, 1957. Translated by A. and B. M. Rookwood.

Tikhomirov, M. *The Towns of Ancient Russia.* Moscow: Foreign Languages Publishing House, 1959.

Utechin, S. V. *Everyman's Concise Guide to Russia.* London, 1961.

Van der Post, L. *Journey into Russia.* London: Hogarth Press, 1964.

ATLASES

Oxford Regional Economic Atlas: The U.S.S.R. and Eastern Europe. Oxford U.P., 1956. (Rev. edn., 1960.)

Kish, G., and Arbor, A. *Economic Atlas of the Soviet Union.* University of Michigan Press, 1960.

Taaffe, R. N., and Kingsbury, R. C. *An Atlas of Soviet Affairs.* London: Methuen, 1965.

Times Atlas of the World, Vol. 2. London: Times Publishing Co. Ltd., 1959.

ARTICLES

Armstrong, T. "The population of the north of the U.S.S.R." *Polar Record,* 1962, II, 172–8.

Cole, J. P. "Post-war work on the waterways of European Russia." *Geog. J.,* 1955, 121, 503–10.

Cole, J. P. "A new industrial area in Asiatic U.S.S.R." *Geog. J.,* 1956, 122, 354–9.

Cressey, G. B. "Changing map of the Soviet Union." *Econ. Geog.,* 1953, 29, 198–207.

Durgin, F. A. "The virgin lands programme, 1954–1960." *Soviet Studies,* 1962, 255–80.

Field, N. C. "The Amu Darya: a study in resource geography." *Geog. Rev.,* 1954, 44, 528–42.

Field, N. C. "Land hunger and the rural depopulation problem in the U.S.S.R." *Ann. Ass. Amer. Geog.,* 1963, 53, 456–78.

French, R. A. "Drainage and economic development of Poles'ye, U.S.S.R." *Econ. Geog.,* 1959, 35, 172–80.

Frolic, B. M. "The Soviet City." *Town Planning Rev.*, 1964, **34**, 285–306.

Grigoryev, A. A. "Soviet plans for irrigation and power: a geographical assessment." *Geog. J.*, 1952, **118**, 168–79.

Grigoryev, A. A. "The reclamation of the forest belt of the U.S.S.R." *Geog. J.*, 1953, **119**, 411–19.

Haden-Guest, S., Wright, J. K., and Teclaff, E. M. "A world geography of forest resources." *Amer. Geog. Soc.*, Special Publ. No. 33. New York: The Ronald Press Co., 1956.

Hooson, D. J. M. "The Middle Volga: an emerging focal region in the Soviet Union." *Geog. J.*, 1960, **126**, 180–90.

Hooson, D. J. M. "A new Soviet heartland." *Geog. J.*, 1962, **128**, 19–29.

Howe, G. Melvyn. "Geography in the Soviet Universities." *Geog. J.*, 1958, **124**, 80–4.

Jackson, W. A. D. "The Russian non-chernozem wheat base." *Ann. Ass. Amer. Geog.*, 1959, **49**, 97–109.

Jackson, W. A. D. "The virgin and idle lands programme reappraised." *Ann. Ass. Amer. Geog.*, 1962, **52**, No. 1, 69–79.

Kish, G. "Railroad passenger transport in the Soviet Union." *Geog. Rev.*, 1963, **53**, 363–76.

Letunov, P. A. *et al.* "A soils and bioclimatic regionalisation of the U.S.S.R." *Soviet Geog.*, 1960, **1**, 32–55.

Lewis, R. A. "The irrigation potential of Soviet Central Asia." *Ann. Ass. Amer. Geog.*, 1962, **52**, 99–114.

Lonsdale, R. E., and Thompson, H. "A map of the U.S.S.R.'s manufacturing." *Econ. Geog.*, 1960, **36**, 36–52.

Lydolph, P. E., and Shabad, T. "The oil and gas industries in the U.S.S.R." *Ann. Ass. Amer. Geog.*, 1960, **50**, 461–86.

Lydolph, P. E. "The Russian sukhovey." *Ann. Ass. Amer. Geog.*, 1964, 291–309.

Melezin, A. "Trends and issues in the Soviet geography of population." *Ann. Ass. Amer. Geog.*, 1963, **53**, 144–60.

Mellor, R. "Trouble with the regions: planning problems in Russia." *Scot. Geog. Mag.*, 1959, **75**, 44–8.

Mellor, R. "Some influence of physical environment upon transport problems in the Sovet Union." *Adv. Science*, 1964, **20**, 564–71.

Michel, A. A., and Klain, S. A. "Current problems of the Soviet electric power industry." *Econ. Geog.*, 1964, **40**, 206–20.

Mills, D. R. "The U.S.S.R.: a reappraisal of Mackinder's Heartland Concept." *Scot. Geog. Mag.*, 1956, **72**, 144–53.

Newth, J. A. "Some trends in the Soviet population, 1939–1956." *Soviet Studies*, 1959, 252–78.

Newth, J. A. "Soviet agriculture: the private sector, 1950–1959." *Soviet Studies*, October 1961, 160–71; October 1962, 414–32.

Nove, A. "The industrial planning system reforms in prospect." *Soviet Studies*, July 1962, 1–15.

Omarovskiy, A. G. "Changes in the geography of machine building in the U.S.S.R." *Soviet Geography*, March 1960, 42–56.

Petrov, V. P. "New railway links between China and the Soviet Union." *Geog. J.*, 1956, **122**, 471–7.

Pociuk, S. G. "The territorial pattern of industrialisation in the U.S.S.R." *Soviet Studies*, July 1961, 69–95.

Rodgers, A. "Changing locational patterns in the Soviet pulp and paper industry." *Ann. Ass. Amer. Geog.*, 1955, **45**, 85–104.

Rodgers, A. "Coking Coal Supply: its role in the expansion of the Soviet steel industry." *Econ. Geog.*, 1964, **40**, 113–50.

Roof, M. K., and Leedy, F. A. "Population redistribution in the Soviet Union." *Geog. Rev.*, 1959, **49**, 208–21.

Schlesinger, R. "The new structure of Soviet agriculture." *Soviet Studies*, January 1959, 228–51.

Shabad, T. "The Soviet concept of economic regionalisation." *Geog. Rev.*, 1953, **43**, 214–22.

Shimkin, D. B. "Economic Regionalisation in the Soviet Union." *Geog. Rev.*, 1952, **42**, 591–614.

Taskin, G. A. "The Soviet Northwest: economic regionalisation." *Geog. Rev.*, 1961, **51**, 213–35.

Taskin, G. A. "Economic Zones." *Studies on the Soviet Union* (Munich), 1962, 1, No. 4, 3–20.

Thiel, E. "The Power Industry in the Soviet Union." *Econ. Geog.*, 1951, **27**, 107–22.

Vasilyev, P. V. "Questions of the geographic study and economic use of forests." *Soviet Geography*, December 1960, 50–63.

Westwood, J. N. "John Hughes and Russian metallurgy." *Econ. His. Rev.*, April 1965, XVII, No. 3.

EXAMINATION QUESTIONS

1. Give a geographical account of *either* (*a*) the power resources of the U.S.S.R. *or* (*b*) the site and position of Leningrad, giving a sketch map. (A.E.B.)

2. With the aid of the sketch-map, delimit the major natural regions of European U.S.S.R. Describe briefly the main features of the physical geography of any *two* of these regions. (W.J.E.C.)

3. Examine the distribution of industry in European U.S.S.R. (W.J.E.C.)

4. Review the development of agriculture in the U.S.S.R. east of the Urals. (A.E.B.)

5. Relate present-day industrial development to power resources in *either* (*a*) the Ukraine *or* (*b*) the Ural Region. (A.E.B.)

6. Compare the geography (physical and human) of the Baltic and Pacific margins of the U.S.S.R. (A.E.B.)

7. From the point of view of (*a*) site, (*b*) position and (*c*) functions, compare the cities in *one* of the following pairs: Odessa and Riga; Volgograd (Stalingrad) and Leningrad; Sverdlovsk and Novosibirsk. Give sketch maps (A.E.B.)

8. Analyse the distinguishing geographical characteristics to be met with along the Trans-Siberian Railway between Moscow and Vladivostok. (A.E.B.)

9. *Either* (*a*) Account for the expansion of industry in the U.S.S.R. east of the Urals.

Or (*b*) Account for the distribution of the major natural vegetation regions in the U.S.S.R. (A.E.B.)

10. Examine the geographical bases of *one* major area of steel production within the U.S.S.R. (London)

11. What geographical facts are reflected in the following population statistics for the U.S.S.R.:

				Estimates 1962	
U.S.S.R.	.	.	.	.	219,700,000 persons
Baku .	.	.	.	.	1,067,000 persons
Gorky .	.	.	.	.	1,025,000 persons
Kiev .	.	.	.	.	1,208,000 persons
Leningrad	.	.	.	.	3,498,000 persons
Moscow	.	.	.	.	6,296,000 persons
Tashkent	.	.	.	.	1,002,000 persons

21 towns each with between 500,000 and 1 million persons.

12. Assess the importance of forests in the economic geography of Siberia. (London)

13. Compare the geography of *two* of the following capitals of Socialist Republics: Alma-Ata; Kazan; Minsk; Riga; Tallinn; Tiflis; Ulan-Ude; Vilnius (Vilna). (London)

14. Make and justify a regional division of Soviet Asia, north of Kazakhstan. (London)

15. Discuss the extent to which climate has influenced the human geography of *either* Siberia *or* Soviet Central Asia (Tadzhikistan, Kirgizia, Turkmenistan, Uzbekistan). (London)

16. Analyse the significance of oil and natural gas in the present-day economic development of the U.S.S.R. (London)

17. Locate and name on a sketch-map and describe the distribution of the textile industries of the U.S.S.R., west of the Urals. (London)

18. Compare the present-day agriculture of the Ukraine and the Baltic States (Estonia, Latvia, Lithuania). (London)

19. Examine the importance of inland waterways to the U.S.S.R. (London)

20. Evaluate the importance of the fishing industries in the economy of the U.S.S.R. (London)

21. Describe the climate, vegetation and physiographic features of the deserts of Soviet Central Asia. (Oxford)

22. Write an essay on the relief and drainage of Eastern Europe and European U.S.S.R. (Oxford)

23. Assess the importance of the Middle Volga region in the economy of the U.S.S.R. (Oxford)

24. Write an account of the location, functions and development of any *two* of the following: (*a*) Moscow; (*b*) Riga; (*c*) Kiev; (*d*) Kharkov; (*e*) Istanbul. (Oxford)

25. Describe the relief, climate and distribution of population of Soviet Central Asia. (Oxford)

26. Write an essay on the steppe-lands of Eastern Europe and the U.S.S.R. (Oxford)

27. Discuss the relationship between agriculture and physical geography in Poland and the Baltic Republics of the U.S.S.R. (Oxford)

28. Write an account of *either* (*a*) the oil industry of the U.S.S.R. *or* (*b*) the iron and steel industry of the U.S.S.R. (Oxford)

29. Examine the role of the River Volga in the economy of the Soviet Union. (Oxford)

30. Divide Siberia into physiographic regions and describe the chief elements of structure, relief and drainage in each region. (Oxford)

31. Draw a map showing the distribution of the natural vegetation zones in the U.S.S.R. *west* of the Urals (including the Caucausus). Describe briefly the vegetation of each zone and discuss the climatic factors involved. (Oxford)

32. Write an explanatory account of any *two* of the following:

(*a*) the industries of the Moscow region;
(*b*) oil in Iraq;
(*c*) iron and steel in the Ukraine;
(*d*) inland navigation in Poland and European U.S.S.R. (Oxford)

33. Describe the distribution of population in the Russian S.F.S.R. *east* of the Urals. (Oxford)

34. Divide the U.S.S.R. *west* of the Urals into climatic regions. Describe the seasonal changes in each region. (Oxford)

35. Insert on a sketch-map of the River Volga the major river ports. Discuss the trade and commerce of any *two* of these towns. (Oxford)

36. Describe the agriculture of the Ukraine. (Oxford)

37. Write an account of the coastal areas and the chief ports of the lands bordering the Baltic in Poland and the U.S.S.R. (Oxford)

38. Compare geographically the Kola and Crimean Peninsulas. (Oxford)

39. Give an account of inland navigation in Eastern Europe and the U.S.S.R. (Oxford)

40. With the help of maps describe the distribution of population in the U.S.S.R. east of the Urals. (Oxford)

41. On a sketch-map of the U.S.S.R. west of the Urals, show the major industrial regions. Write an account of the industries in any *two* of these areas. (Oxford)

42. Write an account of the physical and human geography of *either* the Caucasian Republics *or* the Baltic Republics of the U.S.S.R. (Oxford)

43. Describe the relief, climate and agriculture of the forest-steppe and true steppe of the Ukraine and Russian Republics. (Oxford)

44. Discuss the development of mining and manufacturing in recent years in those parts of the U.S.S.R. east of the Urals. (Oxford)

45. Describe the main geographical features of the larger lakes in the U.S.S.R. (Oxford)

46. Write a geographical account of the Ukrainian S.S.R. (Oxford)

47. Describe the relief and climate of the Soviet Central Asian Republics and show how recent developments have modified the traditional modes of life. (Oxford)

48. "The countries of Eastern Europe and the U.S.S.R. have no natural frontiers, only natural centres." Discuss. (Oxford)

49. Compare and contrast the climates and vegetation of the countries bordering the Black Sea with those bordering the Baltic. (Oxford)

50. "Of the 212 million people in the U.S.S.R. over half live in the Russian Republic." Discuss this statement and indicate on a map the chief areas of population in this Republic. (Oxford)

51. "Immense distances between the sources of raw materials and the manufacturing and consuming centres constitute a serious economic handicap to the U.S.S.R." Discuss this statement. (Oxford)

52. Describe the distribution of population in the U.S.S.R. *east* of the Urals and the Caspian Sea. (Oxford)

53. Write an account of the physical and human geography of the Volga Region. (Oxford)

54. Describe the physical geography of the coastal areas surrounding the Black Sea. Discuss the trade and location of the chief ports in this region. (Oxford)

55. Draw a sketch-map of the Trans-Siberian Railway. Describe the geographical regions crossed by the route, with emphasis on the relief and climate. (Oxford)

56. Give an account of the physical and economic geography of (*a*) the Lake Baikal region, (*b*) the basin of the Aral Sea. (Oxford)

57. "Temperature is the controlling factor in the human geography of the U.S.S.R." Discuss this statement with reference to the area *west* of the Urals. (Oxford)

58. Write an account on the Baltic coastal areas of the U.S.S.R. and Poland. Describe the location and trade of the ports in this area. (Oxford)

59. Show to what extent the U.S.S.R. in Asia has been developed by (*a*) the exploitation of minerals, (*b*) the production of raw materials for textiles. (Oxford)

60. Write an essay on the physical geography of the Trans-Caucasian Republics. (Oxford)

61. Write a geographical essay on *either* the value of its rivers to European U.S.S.R. *or* the rail communication of the U.S.S.R. (S.L.C.)

62. Give your reasons for the growth of population and industrial output in Asiatic U.S.S.R. (S.C.E.)

63. Select *one* of the major industrial regions of the U.S.S.R. in Europe and discuss the factors which have encouraged its growth. (S.C.E.)

64. How far have minerals been responsible for the opening up of Asiatic U.S.S.R.? (S.C.E.)

65. Make and justify a regional subdivision of the U.S.S.R. east of the Urals. (London)

66. Discuss the extent to which the geography of the Russian Soviet Republic differs from that of the rest of the U.S.S.R. (London)

67. What factors, physical and human, have influenced the present-day agriculture of *either* Kazahstan *or* Byelorussia? (London).

68. Compare the geography of the Baltic Union Republics (Esthonia, Latvia and Lithuania) with that of the Far East (the Territories of Khabarovsk and Primorye and the regions of Amur, Magadan, Kamchatka and Sakhalin). (London)

69. Discuss the geography behind the following statistics (1960).

	Byelorussia	Kirghizia
Total Area	207,600 sq. km	198,500 sq. km
	Hectares	Hectares
Total cultivated area . .	5,664,000	1,196,000
Wheat	162,000	339,000
Other grains . . .	2,500,000	319,000
Fodder crops . . .	1,603,000	374,000
Cotton	—	71,000
Flax	271,000	—
Area irrigated . . .	—	1,196,000

(London)

70. With the aid of a sketch-map, describe the distribution of population in the U.S.S.R. east of the Urals, and discuss reasons for the variations in density. (London)

71. Describe and explain the main climatic contrasts along a line from Arkhangelsk (64° 40' N, 41° 0' E) to Astrakhan (46° 25' N, 48° 5' E). (London)

72. Compare the sites, situations and functions of *one* of the following pairs of cities: (*a*) Kharkov and Rostov; (*b*) Leningrad and Moscow; (*c*) Irkutsk and Vladivostok. (London)

73. Discuss the relationship between climate and natural vegetation in the U.S.S.R. west of the Urals. (J.M.B.)

74. Assess the economic and strategic importance to the U.S.S.R. of its territories east of the River Yenisei. (J.M.B.)

75. Give a reasoned account of the distribution of sources of textile raw materials in the U.S.S.R. (J.M.B.)

76. Select any *two* major industrial areas in the U.S.S.R. and compare them. (J.M.B.)

77. Discuss the comparative importance of river and railway transport in the U.S.S.R. (J.M.B.)

78. Examine the physical and economic factors that have influenced the exploitation of forest resources in the U.S.S.R. (J.M.B.)

79. Locate the main areas for the cultivation of wheat and cotton in the U.S.S.R., and suggest reasons for their distribution. (J.M.B.)

80. Discuss the main features of the economic development of the Urals region. (J.M.B.)

81. Discuss the view that within the U.S.S.R. the area west of the Urals is always likely to remain the leading industrial area. (J.M.B.)

82. Describe the regional variations in the recent growth of population in the U.S.S.R., and discuss some of their causes. (J.M.B.)

83. Discuss the factors which have influenced the economic development of the coastlands of the U.S.S.R. (J.M.B.)

84. Contrast the distribution of petroleum production in the U.S.S.R. with that of coal mining. (J.M.B.)

85. Describe and discuss the different use of rivers in the U.S.S.R. (J.M.B.)

86. Describe and attempt to explain the differences in agricultural development between Caucasia and Southern Soviet Central Asia (the area east of the Caspian Sea and south of the Aral Sea). (J.M.B.)

87. Contrast the Moscow region with the Ukraine from the point of view of industrial development. (J.M.B.)

INDEX

References to maps and tables are distinguished by italic type. No distinction is made in the Index between administrative units and towns and cities of the same name.

Note: Rendering of Russian words in Latin characters presents some problems differently solved by various authors. No system of transliteration is fully satisfactory: when perfect, it must be rather complicated and difficult, when simple—it is not perfect. It seems, however, more important to have a transliteration system that can be consistent and generally used than a perfect one. Therefore in this Index when the geographical names used in the text are in their "traditional" form, transliteration rendered in Standard British System (BS 2979 : 1958), generally accepted also in most scientific American publications, is always added in square brackets.

This system cannot dispose of diacritical signs, which in the text are mostly omitted for technical typographic reasons. These signs mark the sound

soft *o* as ë (in text e)
hard *i* as ȳ (in text y)
hard *e* as é (in text e)
half consonant *i* as ĭ (in text y)
and the sign of palatalized consonants as ' after the corresponding letter (in text omitted).